Marriages
of
Gibson County,
Tennessee

1824-1860

Compiled by
EDYTHE RUCKER WHITLEY

With an Index by Judith McGhan

Baltimore
GENEALOGICAL PUBLISHING CO., INC.

Introduction

IBSON COUNTY, Tennessee was erected from the Western District on October 21, 1823. The Act of the Tennessee Legislature which created the county provided that, at first, the courts should hold their sessions at the house of Luke Biggs, four miles from Trenton, the county seat, which was called Gibsonport until 1825. In that year the court was held at Trenton for the first time.

The first magistrates appointed to the court were William P. Leat, Robert Edmondson, Obey Blakemore, Benjamin White, Robert Read, Mr. Rice, Abner Burgan, John D. Love, William W. Craig, W.B.C. Killingsworth, John J. Lane, and F. Davis. The first session of the court was held on January 1, 1824. William P. Leat was the chairman and Thomas Fite the clerk.

The marriage records from 1824 to 1860 are on file at the courthouse in Trenton. They are also available on microfilm at the Tennessee State Library and Archives, as provided by the 1965 Act of the Tennessee Legislature—drafted and sponsored by Edythe R. Whitley—to Preserve the County Records in the State of Tennessee.

The marriage records, abstracted herein, derive from both bonds and licenses. The first date given in each entry is the date of issue of the marriage bond. The date following (in parentheses) is the date the marriage was performed. If no date of marriage is given, then the single date provided refers merely to the date of issue of the marriage bond and does not *prove* that a marriage actually took place. The few abbreviations used in this work are universal, but the reader should note that the abbreviation *BM* signifies bondsman—one who affirms, by standing security, that there is no lawful cause to obstruct the marriage.

Edythe Rucker Whitley
Nashville, Tennessee

GIBSON COUNTY, TENNESSEE

Marriage Licenses and Bonds,

1824-1860

Elijah Davis to Jane Alexander, Nov. 29, 1824. (Nov. 29,
    1824). Watt Pistole, BM.
Gilbert Cribbs to Nancy Martin, Dec. 22, 1824. (Dec. 23,
    1824).
Johnston Cribbs to Sary Bane, Sept. 7, 1824. (Sept. 9,
    1824). Henderson Conlee, BM.
Leonard Worley to Aney Harley, Mar. 2, 1824. (Mar. 3,
    1824). David G. Hamilton, BM.
Elzey Rutledge to Judith Terrell, Apr. 6, 1824. (Apr.
    6, 1824). John H. Many and Robert Edmondson, BM.
David B. Dixon to Salley Tincle, Dec. 8, 1824. (Dec. 9,
    1824). John H. Dixon, BM.
Colbert Mathews to Jane Lovewell, Feb. 2, 1824. Edward
    Love, BM.
Joseph Curtice to Manie Mayo, June 30, 1825. By H. Y.
    Martin, J.P. Thos. Williams, BM.
Samuel S. Rust to Patsey Hurley, Dec. 22, 1825. (Dec.
    25, 1825).
William Jones to Sarah Young, Dec. 29, 1825. By H. Y.
    Martin, J.P.
John Smith to Elizabeth G. Pullen, Jan. 31, 1826. (Jan.
    31, 1826).
John H. Elder to Sally Hickey, Feb. 2, 1826. By Robt.
    Edmiston, J.P.
Stephen Roach to Elizabeth Bane, Feb. 27, 1826. By H.
    J. Martin, J.P.
William Cribbs to Jane Harbour, June 16, 1826. By Robt.
    Edmiston, J.P. George Zaricor, BM.
William J. Spencer to Elizabeth Spencer, June 27, 1826.
    (June 27, 1826).
Felix Parker to Mary O. Gibson, June 22, 1826. (June
    22, 1826). Nelson H. Hodges, BM.
James Connell to Rebecka Roach, July 25, 1826. (June
    26, 1826). Walter Thedford and John Ford, BM.
John D. Hannah to Sarah J. Blakemore, July 6, 1826.
    Thos. J. Caruthers, BM.
William Boling to Elizabeth Moss, Sept. 23, 1826. By
    Robert Edmiston, J.P.

1

GIBSON COUNTY MARRIAGES

Barnett Ferguson to Lucinda Woods, Sept. 21, 1826. (Sept. 21, 1826). John Hays, BM.

Edmond Woods to Rebecka Crockett, Nov. 22, 1826. Nathan Parker, BM.

John McIntosh to Susana Boreing, Nov. 11, 1826. Saul L. Crafton, BM.

Robert Sellers to Rebecca Fletcher, Nov. 16, 1826. James Easterwood, BM.

Daniel W. Crafton to Mary Bradford, Nov. 22, 1826. By Robt. Edmiston, J.P.

Abraham Patton to Elizabeth Woods, Nov. 6, 1826. Duke Cantrell, BM.

William Young to Leir Smith, Nov. 11, 1826. Paul S. Crafton, BM.

Robert Sellers to Rebecca Fletcher, Nov. 6, 1826. James Easterwood, BM. (See above.)

Augustus W. King to Abegail McClay, Dec. 4, 1826. (Dec. 5, 1826).

John Cole to Francis Mobley, Dec. 1, 1826. (Dec. 1, 1826).

Samuel Zericor to Nancy S. Blakemore, Jan. 4, 1827. (Jan. 7, 1827). John Parker, BM.

Salmon Sedwick to Fanny P. Fly, Jan. 22, 1827. John W. Cochran, BM.

John B. Hays to Sally M. Craig, Feb. 5, 1827. (Feb. 8, 1827). Hugh M. Bigham, BM.

William England to Polly Walker, Feb. 28, 1827. David England, BM.

Thomas Runolds to Matilda Conwell, Feb. 24, 1827. (Feb. 24, 1827).

James Kennedy to Katharine Jones, Mar. 5, 1827. (Mar. 8, 1827). Elijah Billingsly, BM.

David Gordon to Sarah Usher, Mar. 21, 1827. By Thos. Brothers, M.G. Ben Fuel, BM.

Ephraim Blair to Polly C. Miller, Apr. 12, 1827. By William P. Seat, J.P.

Ruben Pearce to Elizabeth Mobly, May 13, 1827. (May 16, 1827).

Nathan McMullen to Malinda Richardson, May 7, 1827. (May 15, 1827).

Jacob Harbour to Peggy Childress, May 8, 1827. (May 10, 1827).

Abraham McLemore to Sally Erwin, May 4, 1823. (May 8, 1827). Jno. D. Hanah, BM.

Zebulm Dill to Polly Fox, June 14, 1827. (June 25, 1827).

Benj. W. Perry to Sarah Moss, July 19, 1827. Ebenezer Donaldson, BM.

Jesse Maxwell to Martha Claiborne, July 24, 1827. By Thomas D. Stanley, M.G.

Singleton Cock to Pegy Dickson, July 11, 1827. (July 17, 1827). Jno. W. Evans, BM.

Mosses Fite to Elizabeth Lytaker, Aug. 27, 1827. (Sept. 6, 1827).

Samuel Webb to Polly Smith, Aug. 28, 1827. (Aug. 30, 1827).

GIBSON COUNTY MARRIAGES

Alexander Cooper to Rebecca Brown, Sept. 24, 1827.
(Aug. 25, 1827). Joseph J. Durley, BM.

Abner C. Roach to Sally Thedford, Oct. 24, 1827. (Oct.
24, 1827. John R. Cribs, BM.

John R. King to Docia McLeary, Oct. 4, 1827. Nelmen
I. Hess, BM. (Nelson I. Hess, BM.)

Benjamin Edwards to Elizabeth Smith, Oct. 6, 1827.
Robert Edwards, BM.

Thomas Boling to Sarah Hopkins, Nov. 21, 1827. By
Robert Edmiston, J.P. William Boling, BM.

William P. Gillum to Lucinda Owens, Nov. 2, 1827. James
Right, BM.

James Taylor to Deborah Parker, Nov. 15, 1827. (Nov.
18, 1827).

Allen White to Nancy Cribbs, Dec. 19, 1827. Jesse
Flippin, BM.

William Robertson to Jestin Rust, Dec. 9, 1827. (Dec.
9, 1827). John Davis, BM.

Francis Perry to Elizabeth Pollard, Dec. 3, 1827. (Dec.
6, 1827). Elijah Billingsley, BM.

Nathan Barksdale to Sarah S. Davis, July 25, 1827. By
David Gordon. John C. Wilson, BM.

Joseph England to Martha Walker, Jan. 21, 1828. David
England, BM.

John Roach to Nancy Morgan, Jan. 15, 1828. (Jan. 17,
1828). Solomon H. Shaw, BM.

John Cribbs to Nancy Harbor, Jan. 18, 1828. (Feb. 19,
1828). William Cribbs, BM.

Henry Colyear to Lidia Dixon, Jan. 5, 1828. (Jan. 6,
1828). John P. Hassell, BM.

William B. Moore to Piercy Bradberry, Jan. 5, 1828.
(Mar. 3, 1828). Michael Israel, BM.

Elijah Robbins to Milly Moody, Feb. 18, 1828. Benj.
White, BM.

Elijah Billingsley to Emeline Northcott, Feb. 21,
1828. (Feb. 21, 1828). Preston Conlee, BM.

Elijah Billingsley to Rebecca Pipkins, Feb. 25, 1828.
(Feb. 26, 1828). Jas. L. Totten, BM.

Stephen Pollard to Ann Stephens, Feb. 24, 1828. E.
Billingsley, BM.

David Thomas to Malinda Murphy, Feb. 25, 1828. E.
Billingsley, BM.

John H. Elder to Sally Hickey, Feb. 2, 1828. Jno. W.
Evans, BM.

Donald McIver to Matilda McClary, Mar. 14, 1828. By
Robert Edmiston. Jno. C. Gillespie, BM.

Henderson Conlee to Mary A. Tyson, Mar. 7, 1828. (Mar.
13, 1828). Preston Conlee, BM.

Richard Sharrod to Milly Hains, Mar. 4, 1828. William
Jordan, BM.

Harrison Phillips to Emily McKendrick, Mar. 4, 1828.
By Abraham B. See, J.P. Jas. L. Totten, BM.

John Charlton to Susan Adones, Mar. 12, 1828. Thos. J.
Caruthers, BM.

3

Joel Miller to Sally Baley, Mar. 26, 1828. William
Baley, BM.
William Fulghum to Elizabeth Seat, Mar. 13, 1828. By
David Gordon, M.G. Baird Hill, BM.
Alen Fox to Jane Hall, Apr. 11, 1828. Zebuln Dill, BM.
Nathaniel Sherrod to Hanah Hanes, Apr. 5, 1828. Richard
Sharrod, BM.
James Lammons to Milly Dial, Apr. 2, 1828. (Apr. 3,
1828). David Dial, BM.
Ephraim Blair to Polly C. Miller, Apr. 12, 1828. Jno.
D. Hannah, BM.
Samuel Baker to Anne Forrester, May 25, 1828. (May 29,
1828). Isham Puckett, BM.
Austin A. King to Nancy Roberts, May 12, 1828. (May 13,
1828).
Henry Brown to Sarah A. Mitchel, May 14, 1828. A.
Cooper, BM.
James P. H. Grundy to Eliza G. Hogg, May 13, 1828. By
James McKee.
Jesse Grady to Sally Elder, June 13, 1828. By B. B.
Epperson. B. G. (?) and H. B. Avery, BM.
John Mixon and Mary Mason, July 3, 1828. By Robert
Edmiston, J.P. Robert Edmiston, BM.
Hiram Davis to Sally Lowery, July 5, 1828. James Wright, BM.
John D. Scott to Susanah C. Williams, July 1, 1828.
(July 3, 1828. Robt. A. H. McCorkle, BM.
John Edwards to Mary Bayne, July 25, 1828. (July 25,
1828).
Jessee Maxwell to Martha Claiborne, July 24, 1828. Jas.
L. Totten, BM.
John Sellers to Julian Fonville, July 12, 1828. (July
17, 1828). James Turner, BM.
Robert Franklin to Elizabeth Page, Aug. 19, 1828. (Aug.
19, 1828). Jas. B. Blakemore, BM.
Thomas Geylard to Polly Seratt, Aug. 1, 1828. (Aug. 3,
1828. Jos. Seratt, BM.
Samuel Webb to Polly Smith, Aug. 25, 1828. John Witt, BM.
John W. Hutson to Polly Harrisson, Sept. 17, 1828.
(Sept. 30, 1828). Squire B. Partee, BM.
Josiah L. Thedford to Polly Kennedy, Sept. 28, 1828.
(Sept. 29, 1828). Jno. R. Thedford, BM. NOTE: On
reverse side of license Polly Campbell is shown;
also shown in M. Bond as Polly Campbell; the endorse-
ment on the Marriage License shows Polly Kennedy.
James Castles to Harriet H. Welch, Sept. 2, 1828. (Sept.
4, 1828). H. A. Welch, BM.
Silas M. McKnight to Margaret W. Craig, Sept. 21, 1828.
(Sept. 25, 1828). John H. Money, BM.
John Duncan to Leah Brummet, Oct. 2, 1828. (Oct. 2,
1828). John B. Morgan, BM.
William Thedford to Harriet Littlefield, Oct. 18, 1828.
(Oct. 19, 1828). John R. Thedford, BM.
Obadiah Lewis to Malinda Malone, Oct. 23, 1828. (Oct.
23, 1828). William Wardbanks, BM.

Daniel Tinkle to Amanda Katharine Williams, Oct. 11,
   1828. By Thos. D. Stanley. Jas. L. Totten, BM.
Benjamin Edwards to Elizabeth Smith, Oct. 6, 1828. (Oct.
   14, 1828).
Thomas Williams to Sabry Davidsson, Oct. 18, 1828.
   Johnson W. Richardson, BM.
William F. McKnight to Rebecca J. Mathews, Oct. 13,
   1828. (Nov. 13, 1828). John Overall, BM.
Jonathan Woodard to Elizabeth James, Oct. 30, 1828.
   Thos. Wiggins, BM.
Wilson Brown to Polly Glasscock, Nov. 18, 1828. (Nov.
   18, 1828). Jas. L. Totten, BM.
Benjamin Fuel to Rachel McMahon, Nov. 20, 1828. (Jan.
   9, 1829). Robt. Edmiston, BM.
Ransom H. Byrne to Dolly Cocke, Nov. 18, 1828. (Nov.
   18, 1828). John W. Evans, BM.
Edmond W. Rains to Elizabeth Lattie, Nov. 15, 1828.
   (Nov. 18, 1828). Benj. White, BM.
Robt. A. H. McCorkle to Lirzah Scott, Dec. 1, 1828.
   (Dec. 4, 1828). Lemuel Scott, BM.
Jerry McGee to Betsey Baley, Dec. 31, 1828. Joel
   Miller, BM.
James Morris to Rebecca Ford, Jan. 1, 1829. (Jan. 7,
   1829).
Mark Forest to Rebecca Pollard, Jan. 24, 1829. (Jan.
   31, 1829). A. S. Davidson, BM.
William Hall to Lidia Hall, Jan. 5, 1829. (Jan 5, 1829).
   Nathan McMullen, BM.
George Blackwell to Fanny Elder, Jan. 3, 1829. (Jan.
   8, 1829). Mathias Roberts, BM.
Joshua Wilburn to Jane Bryant, Feb. 19, 1829. Cabb
   Wilburn, BM.
Valcian C. G. Wright to Rachel Reed, Feb. 24, 1829.
   James P. Reed, BM.
James P. Alexander to Jane Patterson, Feb. 20, 1829.
   By Thos. D. Stanley. James Patterson, BM.
John D. Little to Elizabeth Bain, Feb. 5, 1829. (Feb.
   17, 1829). Stephen Williams, BM.
David Dickey to Anna Nelson, Mar. 23, 1829. (Mar. 23,
   1829). Andrew Blair, BM.
Boyd F. Bryant to Sally Little, Mar. 9, 1829. (Mar. 9,
   1829). L. B. Partee, BM.
William Elder to Eliza Harper, Mar. 4, 1829. (Mar. 7,
   1829). Henry H. Hoen, BM.
John B. Hubbard to Frances S. Dyer, Mar. 7, 1829.
   (Mar. 8, 1829). Thomas J. Caruthers, James L. Totten,
   and Milton Brown, BM.
Ebenezar Dunlap to Mary L. Harbour, Apr. 20, 1829.
   (Apr. 21, 1829). Wm. Ferguson, BM.
Edmund Britt to Betsey Sammons, May 20, 1829. (May 24,
   1829). William Butler, BM.
Boldin Finch to Lively Pitchford, May 23, 1829. (May
   23, 1829). John B. Howard, BM.
Joseph McClure to Elizabeth McBride, June 2, 1829.
   William McBride, BM.

John B. McLary to Francis H. King, June 27, 1829. Robt
Edmiston, BM.
Alfred Neding to Telitha Hodges, June 15, 1829. Michael
Edmonson, BM.
Lewis Needham to Matty Oglesby, June 6, 1829. (June 6,
1829).
Philemon Y. Bowers to Margaret McDougle, July 2, 1829.
(July 2, 1829). Young A. McLemore, BM.
Zacheriah Biggs to Sally Dunagan, July 10, 1829. (July
16, 1829). Ruben Biggs, BM.
John Gambell to Rebecka Hopkins, July 21, 1829. (July
21, 1829). Jas M. Wilson, BM.
Denis Thedford to Hester H. Gray, Aug. 4, 1829. (Aug.
5, 1829) Nicholas Gray, BM.
F. L. W. McEwen to Wineford Avery, Aug. 7, 1829. (Aug.
20, 1829). Henry H. Horn, BM.
John Pruitt to Rossan Champain, Aug. 8, 1829. (Aug. 9,
1829). Alexander G. Hamilton, BM.
Hiram Dawson to Nancy Johnston, Aug. 29, 1829. (Aug.
30, 1829). Nathan Robing, BM.
William Ferguson to Maryan Cole, Aug. 26, 1829. (Aug.
26, 1829). Abrm Betts, BM.
Joseph Fletcher to Rebecka Forrester, Sept. 8, 1829.
(Sept. 10, 1829). Thomas Fletcher, BM.
John Ford to Vilet Hall, Sept. 28, 1829. (Sept. 29,
1829). Abraham B. See, BM.
William McBride to Sarah Thomas, Sept. 23, 1829. (Sept.
24, 1829). Robert Elam, BM.
Fair M. Little to Sally Staton, Oct. 13, 1829. (Oct.
22, 1829). James Williams, BM.
Drury Martin to Elizabeth Dunnegan, Nov. 4, 1829. (Nov.
?, 1829). John Dunnegan, BM.
James Boals to Desdimony Moss, Nov. 4, 1829. (Nov. 5,
1829). Benoni Crawford, BM.
Samuel P. Rust to Ellenor Bledsoe, Nov. 10, 1829. (Nov.
12, 1829). Milton Brown, BM.
John D. Robbins to Susan Weatherspoon, Nov. 2, 1829.
(Nov. 3, 1829). Nathan Robins, BM.
William Thedford to Elizabeth Crockett, Nov. 3, 1829.
Attest by Thos. Fite. Robert Seat, BM.
Elisha Oglesby to Polly Morgan, Dec. 8, 1829. (Dec.
10, 1829). John Morgan, BM.
Thomas B. Blair to Sally Holmes, Dec. 8, 1829. By Thos.
D. Stanley. John D. Blair, BM.
Pennell Kell to Elizabeth Scallarn, Dec. 23, 1829.
(Dec. 24, 1829). John Scallarn, BM.
Arthur Williams to Mary McBride, Dec. 21, 1829. (Dec.
24, 1829). Charles Williams, BM.
John Britingham to Sally Ormes, Dec. 29, 1829. (Dec.
29, 1829).
Alen Betts to Sally Parker, Dec. 15, 1829. (Dec. 15,
1829). Luke P. See, BM.
Harrod P. Welch to Martha Pruitt, Dec. 22, 1829. (Dec.
22, 1829). Wm. R. Welch, BM.

GIBSON COUNTY MARRIAGES

Elisha Billingsly to Martha Fite, Dec. 14, 1829. (Dec. 14, 1829).

Thomas Baker to Levina Smith, Dec. 22, 1829. (Jan 26, 1830). Joseph B. Dibrell, BM.

Alexander R. McFall to Wine Bane, Jan 5, 1830. (Jan. 7, 1830). Robert Farris, BM.

James J. Bradberry to Matilda Bruff, Jan. 6, 1830. (Jan. 7, 1830). William Williams, BM.

Abraham McKirby to Sally McDaniel, Jan 11, 1830. (Jan. 19, 1830). Samuel S. Crafton, BM.

Edward Curtis to Lucinda Mahon, Jan 25, 1830. (Feb. 4, 1830). James Curtis, BM.

James Baker to Polly Mitts, Jan. 8, 1830. (Jan. 14, 1830). Solomon Seals, BM.

Henderson (Herrington) Trusty to Julian Mitchell, Jan. 16, 1830. By Robert Edmiston, J.P. John L. Davis, BM.

James Morris to Rebecca Ford, Jan. 15, 1830. Joseph Robens, BM.

James Smith to Elizabeth Reed (Reece), Jan. 26, 1830. Joseph N. Wright, BM.

John Briant to Matilda Jackson, Jan. 12, 1830. Boyd F. Briant, BM.

Stephen J. Roach to Almira Bradberry, Feb. 4, 1830. (Mar. 11, 1830). Sampson Thetford, BM.

David L. Haley to Jane Hicks, Feb. 17, 1830. (Feb. 23, 1830). Sterling B. Haley, BM.

Nelson I. Hess to Adeline Northcut, Feb. 27, 1830. (Feb. 28, 1830).

Joshua Wilburn to Jane Bryant, Feb. 19, 1829. (Feb. 20, 1829).

Hugh D. Neilson to Mrs. (?) Brassfield, Feb. 4, 1830. Solomon Shaw, BM.

Luny McDaniel to Nancy Adcock, Mar. 6, 1830. (Mar. 11, 1830). Samuel S. Crafton, BM.

Paton Fox to Catharine Murphey, Mar. 5, 1830. (Mar. 18, 1830). William Fox, BM.

William Crafton to Hester Ann Dial, Mar. 27, 1830. (Apr. 1, 1830). Jas. J. Samons, BM.

William Crockett to Clorence Boytt, Mar. 18, 1830. (Mar. 25, 1830). Michael Israel, BM.

Wile Flowers to Margaret Crockett, Mar. 22, 1830. (Mar. 25, 1830). Jesse Flowers, BM.

Ruben W. Biggs to Elizabeth Sellars, Mar. 2, 1830. (Mar. 22, 1830). Ruben Biggs, Sr., BM.

Robert Boles to Nancy Lamons, Mar. 3, 1830. James Boals, BM.

William Ridgeway to Sarey Glason, April 3, 1830. William Warren, BM.

Elijah Boyt to Susan Crane, Apr. 25, 1830. Michael Edmiston, BM.

Alexander H. Vaughn to Fanny Bradford, Apr. 7, 1830. By Robert Edmiston, J.P. Geo. C. Sanders, BM.

Thomas R. Harrisson to Darthul Lewis, Apr. 8, 1830. (Apr. 15, 1830). James L. Totten, BM.

GIBSON COUNTY MARRIAGES

Green Boland to Jane McMillin, Apr. 2, 1830. (Apr. ?, 1830). Wm. Boyles, BM.
Abraham King to Elizabeth Bloys, Apr. 17, 1830. (Apr. 18, 1830). Harry Staton, BM.
Samuel Henry to Roda Ross, Apr. 12, 1830. (Apr. 13, 1830). Sam'l. C. Webb, BM.
John Childras to Eland McMillin, May 20, 1830. (May 26, 1830). Green Boling, BM.
Stephen Rains to Clary Daugherty, May 15, 1830. (May 20, 1830). Wm. S. Dougherty, BM.
John A. Taliaferro to Caroline Harrisson, June 24, 1830. Jas. L. Totten, BM.
William Wilson to Nancy Howard, June 30, 1830. (July 1, 1830). John B. Howard, BM.
William S. Dougherty to Mary Rains, June 23, 1830. By Reuben Dougherty, M.G. Stephen Rains, BM.
William Cromes to Sally Montgomery, June 23, 1830. (June 30, 1830). Wm. L. McKinly, BM.
William Fletcher to Nancy Fisher, July 14, 1830. Reuben Biggs, BM.
David Patton to Elizabeth Cook, July 28, 1830. (July 29, 1830). Jas. Montgomery, BM.
Joseph Hamilton to Margarett McClary, Aug. 3, 1830. (Aug. 3, 1830).
David McBride to Angeline Cross, Sept. 11, 1830. (Sept. 12, 1830). John T. Cameron, BM.
William Cribbs to Elizabeth York, Oct. 1, 1830. Gilbert Cribbs, BM.
Samuel Sewell to Wynne Anders, Oct. 25, 1830. (Oct. 27, 1830). Hardy Canady, BM.
Milichi Watts to Matilda Totten, Nov. 13, 1830. William Leonard, BM.
Henry Hunter to Anna Stacup, Nov. 7, 1830. (Nov. 7, 1830).
John Dunagan to Sally Davidson, Nov. 11, 1830. (Nov. 11, 1830). Joseph Robbins, BM.
Thomas Fletcher to Sarah Lewis, Nov. 27, 1830. (Dec. 2, 1830). James Forester, BM.
Benjamin L. Rodgers to Nancy M. Fisher, Nov. 16, 1830. (Nov. 16, 1830). James Brahan, BM.
John Scallorn to Lovina Jackson, Dec. 20, 1830. Michael Higgins, BM.
Salesbury Fasthing to Martha Haley, Dec. 14, 1830. (Dec. 29, 1830). William Martin, BM.
Edwin Mathis to Patsey Sparkman, Dec. 13, 1830. (Dec. 14, 1830). John D. Carlton, BM.
William Forester to Mary Runaldo, Dec. 31, 1830. (Jan. 10, 1831). William Campbell, BM.
William Freeman to Mary Muirhead, Jan. 20, 1831. (Jan. 20, 1831). James McBride, BM.
George W. Dickey to Margarett Fulerton, Jan. 8, 1831. Lemuel Scott, BM.
Joseph Robins to Nancy Rody, Jan. 9, 1831. Edward Haskins, BM.

8

GIBSON COUNTY MARRIAGES

William Leonard to Sary Dickey, Feb. 5, 1831. (Feb. 10,
1831). Preston Conlee, BM.
Hugh M. Bigham to Rebeckha Taylor, Feb. 19, 1831. By
Mansel Babb. William Craig, BM.
Joseph Parker to Nancy Nobles, Feb. 24, 1831. (Feb. 24,
1831). Caswell Miller, BM.
George Patton to Rhoda Ann McWhorter, Feb. 26, 1831.
(Feb. 27, 1831). John W. Crockett, BM.
Lindsey K. Tinkle to Rebecka McWhorter, Feb. 23, 1831.
By Thos. D. Stanley, M.G., M.E.C. Jas. B. Blakemore, BM.
Haden McCormack to Polly Smith, Feb. 16, 1831. Wm. Breat, BM.
John A. Haley to Elizabeth Kirsey, Feb. 14, 1831. A.
P. Hughes, BM.
William Sham to Luize E. Lyon, Feb. 19, 1831. (Feb. 21,
1831).
John Kinley to Lucinda Harbour, Mar. 17, 1831. (Mar.
17, 1831). Doctor Cribbs, BM.
John G. Warren to Eliza Avery, Mar. 25, 1831. By B. B.
Epperson, J.P. James H. Warren, BM.
James P. Reed to Sarah Patterson, Mar. 7, 1831. (Mar.
?, 1831). Samuel Reed, BM.
James Babb to Elizabeth Craig, Mar. 6, 1831. By Manvil
Babb. Hugh M. Bigham, BM.
Robert Boles to Nancy Leamons, Mar. 5, 1831. By B. B.
Epperson.
Enoch Muirheid to Martha Simons, Apr. 21, 1831. (Apr.
21, 1831). William Freeman, BM.
Robert Landran to Lucresa Wilson, Apr. 28, 1831. (Apr.
28, 1831). Luke P. Seay, BM.
James B. Carnahan to Martha Bell, Apr. 1, 1831. (Apr.
2, 1831). Joseph Seratt, BM.
William Fletcher to Margaret Griffee, Apr. 28, 1831.
(May 3, 1831). John H. Griffee, BM.
Overall Sanderson to Eliza Lyon, Apr. 7, 1831. (Apr.
7, 1831). Joseph Hamilton, BM.
Elijah Boyt to Susan Crane, Apr. 25, 1831. (Apr. 25,
1831).
Dillard Forester to Malinda Cantrell, May 28, 1831. (June
17, 1831). William Forester, BM.
H. W. Wright to Mary Terrell, May 9, 1831. (May 10,
1831). Robert Terrell, BM.
Edwin Warrin to Elizabeth Hendrick, May 8, 1831. By
B. B. Epperson, J.P. Henry Warrin, BM.
William L. Goodman to Jane Coop, June 30, 1831. (June
30, 1831). William A. Varner, BM.
Thomas W. King and Martha Hector, June 25, 1831. (June
30, 1831) Jos. S. Hamilton, BM.
Josiah Moore to Lucy Smith, June 10, 1831. Edward Smith, BM.
Lewis Needham to Matty Oglesby, June 6, 1831. Benj.
White, BM.
Reuben Tyson to Exaline Boyt, July 30, 1831. (Aug. 4,
1831). Preston Conlee, BM.
Robert Seat to Martha E. Gilchrist, July 7, 1831. (July
7, 1831). H. D. Neilson, BM.

John Russell to Hester Ann Mitts, July 16, 1831. (July
17, 1831). Wm. W. B. Langley, BM.
William W. B. Langley to Merica Hawkins, July 16, 1831.
(July 17, 1831). Thomas Evans, BM.
Addison Corrington to Judia Whitley, July 10, 1831.
(Aug. 9, 1831). James Nobles, BM.
William Goodman to Ann Hardister, July 27, 1831. (July
28, 1831). William Claxton, BM.
Sampson Curtis to Charlotte Grayor, July 4, 1831. (July
5, 1835). Jordon Hassell, BM.
Watson Pridy to Sally Cook, July 5, 1831. (July 6, 1831).
Nelson Cole, BM.
Richard J. Smith to Unity Campbell, July 2, 1831. Henry
Hunt, BM.
Joshua Monan to Mary Ann Harris, July 6, 1831. William
Cribbs, BM.
Frederick Bryant to Martha Jones, July 27, 1831. David
H. Little, BM.
Alexander Cox to Elizabeth Fox, Aug. 31, 1831. (Sept.
8, 1831. Alen Fox, BM.
Dr. (?) Cribbs to Nancy Harbour, Aug. 11, 1831. (Aug.
11, 1831). John W. Crockett, BM.
Charles Parish to Francis O. L. McCullock, Aug. 29,
1831. (Aug. 29, 1831). Luke P. Seay, BM.
Joseph Suratt to Malissa Baker, Aug. 16, 1831. John
Sellars, BM.
Samuel Reed to Elizabeth Parks, Aug. 6, 1831. William
Reed, BM.
Zachariah Smith to Mary Ann White, Sept. 5, 1831. (Sept.
11, 1831). F. G. Goodman, BM.
William C. Jack to Malinda Glasscock, Sept. 24, 1831.
(Oct. 2, 1831). John N. Jack, BM.
John N. Jack to Winey Harrisson, Sept. 1, 1831. (Sept.
4, 1831). William C. Jack, BM.
Thomas Taylor to Juliana Gilchrist, Sept. 19, 1831.
(Sept. 21, 1831). H. J. Thomas, BM.
Luke P. Seay to Ann Row Hall, Sept. 22, 1831. (Sept.
22, 1831). Thos. I. Caruthers, BM.
Reuben Fletcher to Elizabeth Baysinger, Sept. 21, 1831.
(Sept. 22, 1831). Charles Forrester, BM.
Littleton Ward to Elizabeth Mitchell, Sept. 7, 1831.
(Sept. 13, 1831). Jas. F. Dougherty, BM.
John D. Shaw to Mariah Stanley, Sept. 5, 1831. By
B. B. Epperson, J.P. David Whitaker, BM.
Giles Marchbanks to Mary Lewis, Oct. 11, 1831. (Oct.
11, 1831). Williams Marchbanks, BM.
Thomas H. McAvery to Levina I. Dickson, Oct. 3, 1831.
(Oct. 4, 1831). Alford F. Cole, BM.
James A. McKnight to Louisana Hess, Oct. 31, 1831.
(Nov. 3, 1831). James A. W. Hess, BM.
William Erwin to Narcissa Wilborn, Oct. 15, 1831.
(Oct. 18, 1831). Jas. A. W. Hess, BM.
Terry Odell to Sally Davis, Oct. 25, 1831. (Oct. 25,
1831). Caswell Miller, BM.

GIBSON COUNTY MARRIAGES

William H. Bridges to Sarah B. Rust, Oct. 18, 1831.
(Oct. 20, 1831). Mosses Woodfin, BM.
John Nobles to Sally Diggins, Oct. 14, 1831. (Oct. 14,
1831). Wm. Sammons, BM.
Andrew Blair to Nancy Sellars, Oct. 8, 1831. (Oct. 9,
1831).
Nicholas L. Lankford to Sarah Willson, Nov. 29, 1831.
By William P. Seat, J.P. John Fly, BM.
John Fly to Mary F. Lile, Nov. 29, 1831. By William P.
Seat. John W. Evans, BM.
Allen Ferguson to McUla Cole, Nov. 14, 1831. (Nov. 14,
1831). Wm. Ferguson, BM.
Caswell Miller to Mary V. Stoddard, Nov. 11, 1831. (Dec.
11, 1831). Wm. C. Fite, BM.
Daniel Stephison to Martha Shane, Nov. 7, 1831. (Nov.
7, 1831). John Shane, BM.
John Jackson to Lucenda Elder, Nov. 21, 1831. Thomas
Morton, BM.
Henry H. Hunter to Anna Statcup, Nov. 7, 1831. Geo. C.
Rust, BM.
Daniel Delph to Margarett Bratton, Nov. 10, 1831. H.
A. Hardiker, BM.
William S. Runaldo to Rachel Frazer, Dec. 23, 1831.
(Dec. 29, 1831). Geo. S. Tyler, BM.
Samuel Shane to Rebecka Umstead, Dec. 5, 1831. By
William P. Seat, J.P. Thomas Walker, BM.
Louis See to Deborah Parker, Dec. 13, 1831. (Dec. 13,
1831). Nathan Parker, BM.
James A. W. Hess to Louiza Webb, Dec. 8, 1831. (Dec.
8, 1831). Nelson I. Hess, BM.
Mathew A. Glass to Nancy Putnam, Dec. 22, 1831. (Dec.
22, 1831). Thomas Ormes, BM.
James Curtis to Penelope Griffee, Dec. 27, 1831. (Dec.
27, 1831). John Nobles, BM.
Mack R. Cook to Emaline Russ, Dec. 13, 1831. By William
P. Seat, J.P. Watson Priddy, BM.
Hendleton Ingram to Charlotte Dowell, Dec. 10, 1831.
(Dec. 10, 1831). Nathan Parker, BM.
Edwin Fonville to Ann Jane Bush, Dec. 12, 1831. John
Fonville, BM.
James T. Hains to Mary C. Gentry, Dec. 14, 1831.
Richard Sharrod, BM.
Sterling B. Hogg to Elizabeth Murphy, Dec. 12, 1831.
Jas. Ricks, BM.
Isaac Parker to Susan Moore, Dec. 15, 1831. Jno. A.
Taliferro, BM.
Joseph Robbins to Nancy Rodey, Jan 9, 1832. (Jan 12,
1832).
William Baxter to Sarah Berry, Jan 7, 1832. By William
P. Seat, J.P. Green D. Stone, BM.
William Blann to Zaby McKnight, Jan. 10, 1832. (Jan.
17, 1832). Peter Ragsdale, BM.
Henry Dowland to Matilda Williams, Jan. 16, 1832. (Feb.
4, 1832). David Dowland, BM.

11

Ira Spight to Mary R. Dickson, Jan. 24, 1832. (Jan. 31, 1832). John H. Griffee, BM.

Blaney Harper to Winneford Toller, Jan 7, 1832. Eli Boytt, BM.

Charles Porter to Cary Baley, Feb. 11, 1832. (Mar. 8, 1832). Jonathan Baley, BM.

William Carradine to Emely Hall, Jan. 21, 1832. (Feb. 23, 1832. John Carradine, BM.

William E. Wade to Elizabeth C. Davis, Feb. 9, 1832. Ed Lightfoot, BM.

John Oakes to Winney Fowler, Feb. 10, 1832. Robt. Edmondson, BM.

William B. Moore to Elizabeth J. Thompson, Mar. 29, 1832. (Apr. 1, 1832). Stephen J. Roach, BM.

Spivy Fuller to Letha Dickson, Mar. 12, 1832. John Bryson, BM.

William D. McDermet to Jane Baily, Apr. 10, 1832. By Robt. Edmiston, J.P. Nathan Barksdale, BM.

William Sammons to Hinna Nobles, Apr. 10, 1832. (Apr. 10, 1832). William Butler, BM.

William Smith to Harriat Jane Bledsoe, Apr. 25, 1832. Madison Bledsoe, BM.

Stewart Flinter to Charity T. Thompson, May 31, 1832. (June 3, 1832).

Robert Sellars to Margarett Miller, May 10, 1832. (May 10, 1832). John Sellars, BM.

James Bell to Michel Bell, May 8, 1832. (May 8, 1832). William H. Bell, BM.

James Rackly to Elizabeth Cole, May 5, 1832. Aaron Jackson, BM.

Erwin Smith to Susannah Oglesby, May 19, 1832. Shnoa Smith, BM.

Abraham Kirksey to Elizabeth Boon, June 28, 1832. (June 28, 1832). Anderson Davis, BM.

Robert J. Gilchrist to Drucilla Culp, July 10, 1832. (July 10, 1832). H. J. Thomas, BM.

Gideon Tucker to Cely Johnson, July 28, 1832. Isham Johnson, BM.

Epperson W. Harper to Nancy C. Williams, Aug. 25, 1832. (Aug. 30, 1832). Humphrey Donaldson, BM.

Young Kirksey to Mary E. C. Asher, Aug. 27, 1832. (Aug. 27, 1832). Robert Seat, BM.

James Hicks to Susanah C. Sanford, Aug. 15, 1832. (Aug. 16, 1832). C. Miller, BM.

Thos. B. Murphrey to Harriett H. Carroll, Aug. 4, 1832. R. S. Slemon, BM.

Samuel Rankin to Mercilla Goodman, Sept. 18, 1832. (Sept. 18, 1832).

John Wood to Ana Bradley, Sept. 21, 1832. (Sept. 23, 1832).

Peleg Bailey to Eliza N. Bailey, Sept. 13, 1832. (Sept. 13, 1832).

James Tipton to Rachael Puckett, Sept. 20, 1832. (Sept. 20, 1832. James M. Wilson, BM.

GIBSON COUNTY MARRIAGES

William G. Moore to Nancy Smith, Sept. 3, 1832. Jas.
    W. Williamson, BM.
James C. Williams to Lorindo Roach, Sept. 26, 1832.
    (Oct. 14, 1832). James A. Connell, BM.
John Holmes to Elizabeth Singleton, Sept. 3, 1832. (Sept.
    20, 1832). Richard McKiley, BM.
Samuel B. Mixon to Harriett Joslin, Sept. 27, 1832.
    Hiram J. Thomas, BM.
John Flowers to Margaret Gregory, Sept. 1, 1832. Henry
    Flowers, BM.
Blaney Harper to Elizabeth Griffy, Sept. 3, 1832. (Sept.
    12, 1832)
Wm. C. Page to Elizabeth Welch, Oct. 8, 1832. (Oct. 9,
    1832).
Banks M. Burrow to Elizabeth Richardson, Oct. 11, 1832.
    (Oct. 12, 1832).
Calvin Jackson to Sarah Bhass, Oct. 22, 1832. (Oct. 31,
    1832). Allen Blalock, BM.
Isaac Pollard to Maniza Legate, Nov. 24, 1832. (Nov. 28,
    1832).
Johnathan Dausson to Alee Kelly, Nov. 14, 1832. (Nov.
    15, 1832). Thomas Weatherspoon, BM.
Hinton Willis to Ann Holder, Nov. 15, 1832. (Nov. 15,
    1832). James M. Wilson, BM.
John P. Steller to Julian Butler, Nov. 17, 1832. (Nov.
    18, 1832). John Harris, BM.
James Rackley to Rila McDermitt, Nov. 24, 1832. By
    Robt. Edmiston, J.P. Aaron Jackson, BM.
William G. Stephens to Jane Smith, Nov. 23, 1832. (Nov.
    24, 1832). Wm. Smith, BM.
Mark Selph to Millia Holder, Nov. 20, 1832. (Nov. 20,
    1832). Willoughby Selph, BM.
Thos. Gaskins to Delila Rains, Nov. 16, 1832. Amos
    Gaskins, BM.
Wiliam Leeton to Elizabeth Cole, Dec. 18, 1832. (Dec.
    23, 1832). John Hutson, BM.
Jefferson Wilson to Mary Mayfield, Dec. 22, 1832. By
    Robt. Edmiston, J.P. John W. Wortham and G. W.
    Gantry, BM.
Eli McMullin to Harriett Davidsson, Dec. 22, 1832. (Dec.
    27, 1832). David Miller, BM.
Thomas Hail to Elizabeth Luster, Dec. 25, 1832. (Dec.
    30, 1832). J. B. Didrell, BM.
James Scott to Vilett B. Roddy, Dec. 8, 1832. (Dec. 10,
    1832).
Sterling B. Haley to Elizabeth Massey, Dec. 25, 1832.
    (Dec. 25, 1832).
Magilba Rogers to Nancy Staton, Dec. 8, 1832. David L.
    Edwards, BM.
Joseph Pecks to Honey Thedford, Dec. 25, 1832. Sterling
    B. Haley, BM.
Robert Edmonson to Mary Clark, Jan 5, 1833. (Jan. 8,
    1833). Wm. W. Craig, BM.
Thomas Trainer to Elizabeth Ward, Jan. 3, 1833. (Jan.
    4, 1833) Wm. McGregory, BM.

Harmon Simpson to Margarett Trayner, Jan. 8, 1833. (Jan. 9, 1833). John Cummings, BM.

William J. Ferguson to Tempy Chronister, Jan. 18, 1833. (Jan. 20, 1833). Allen Ferguson, BM.

Acy Rains to Rebecca McMahan, Jan 15, 1833. Benjamin Fewel, BM.

Andrew A. Patterson to Clary Ann Richardson, Jan 5, 1833. John W. Evans, BM.

William Bowen to Easter D. Craig, Feb. 4, 1833. (Feb. 7, 1833). James M. Moore, BM.

Isham Johnson to Mary Ferguson, Feb. 6, 1833. (Feb. 7, 1833). John Harris, BM.

Benjamin M. Adair to Elizabeth Shane, Feb. 14, 1833. (Feb. 14, 1833). Alexander Campbell, BM.

Hearvy Bledsoe to Mary L. Bledsoe, Mar. 18, 1833. (Mar. 20, 1833). Richard L. Crafton, BM.

Hugh D. Neilson to Aly Jones, Mar. 7, 1833. (Mar. 7, 1833). Hiram Thomas, BM.

Thomas Bowers to Obediance Baley, Mar. 13, 1833. (Mar. 14, 1833). Humphrey Donaldson, BM.

Ruffin Yates to Nancy Crockett, Mar. 12, 1833. (Mar. 14, 1833). John Crockett, BM.

Gabriel S. Tyler to Steve Johnston, Mar. 18, 1833. (Mar. 19, 1833). Hardy Harrisson, BM.

Ezra I. Arnold to Margaret C. Patterson, Mar. 10, 1833. (Mar. 10, 1833). Robert I. Patterson, BM.

Alen King to Malinda Bratton, Mar. 4, 1833. Harry Terrell, BM.

Joseph Williams to Ann Jordan, Mar. 22, 1833. Absolom Know, BM.

John Hutchins to Caroline M. James, Apr. 7, 1833. (May 12, 1833).

Charles Yearbory to Susannah Stellar, Apr. 15, 1833. (Apr. 17, 1833).

James Bodkins to Elizabeth Speres, Apr. 23, 1833. (Apr. 24, 1833). John McAllilly, BM.

Willoughby Self to Mary Self, Apr. 2, 1833. (Apr. 2, 1833). Mark Self, BM.

Richard McAllelly to Nancy McKeown, Apr. 10, 1833. (Apr. 11, 1833). Nelson I. Hess, BM.

Absolem Knox to Sarah Ann Higgins, Apr. 13, 1833. (Apr. 14, 1833). H. J. Thomas, BM.

Luke M. Edwards to Elizabeth Parker, May 24, 1833. (May 24, 1833).

John Hutchins to Caroline M. James, May 7, 1833. Jacob Bradberry, BM.

William B. Convill to Judia Bates, May 11, 1833. Philip E. Holmes, BM.

Joseph Kelley to Lavina Thompson, June 13, 1833. (June 13, 1833). Alen Fox, BM.

Aaron Stanley to Mary Lacey, Sept. 11, 1833. (July 23, 1833). Alfred Shenill, BM.

Pleasant Hill to Martha Reynolds, June 1, 1833. (June 4, 1833). Silas M. Crafton, BM.

GIBSON COUNTY MARRIAGES

James L. Totten to Sarah Eliza Dyer, June 19, 1833.
    (June 20, 1833). Milton Brown and George W. Terrill, BM.
Nathan Parker to Huldy Durley, July 18, 1833. (July 18,
    1833). Lewis Levy, BM.
Ely Evans to Mary A. Joslin, July 17, 1833. (July 18,
    1833). Madison McLaurine, BM.
Johnson Williams to Elizabeth D. Robb, Aug. 27, 1833.
    (Aug. 27, 1833).
Preston Holt to Honey Thetford, Aug. 23, 1833. (Aug.
    25, 1833). William Goodman, BM.
Russell Conlee to Mary Ann King, Aug. 15, 1833. (Aug.
    16, 1833). Preston Conlee, BM.
John W. Crockett to Mary Mastisa, Aug. 31, 1833. John
    W. Crockett, BM.
Benjamin Roach to Polly T. Bradberry, Sept. 11, 1833.
    (Sept. 12, 1833). Stephen Roach, BM.
Alexander Black to Narcissa Bell, Sept. 25, 1833. (Sept.
    26, 1833). Pomfrett Hart, BM.
John B. Wallingford to Nancy Fowler, Sept. 16, 1833.
    (Sept. 16, 1833). Isaac Wallingford, BM.
Owen Smith to Louana Sphere, Sept. 7, 1833. (Oct. 8,
    1833. S. S. Crafton, BM.
William A. Fonville to Martha Fletcher, Sept. 7, 1833.
Edward Haley to Jans Hardister, Sept. 17, 1833. (Sept.
    19, 1833). Jobe Hicks, BM.
Benjamin May to Delitha Becton, Oct. 28, 1833. (Oct.
    29, 1833). Fred E. Becton, BM.
Joshua Bell to Louisa Bledsoe, Oct. 19, 1833. (Oct. 22,
    1833). Isaac Lawrence, BM.
Middleton McCortney to Charity Flinter, Oct. 18, 1833.
    (Oct. 20, 1833). James Kelly, BM.
Wilie Umstead to Mary P. Campbell, Oct. 3, 1833. (Oct.
    3, 1833). George Shane, BM.
James Porter to Sarah J. Craddock, Oct. 14, 1833. (Dec.
    16, 1833).
Coburn Stone to Rachael Etheredge, Oct. 5, 1833. (Oct.
    6, 1833). Jerred Etheredge, BM.
Asberry M. Webb to Eliza Jans Freeman, Oct. 5, 1833.
    (Oct. 10, 1833). George W. Bays, BM.
John Crockett to Mary Patterson, Oct. 15, 1833. (Oct.
    17, 1833). Burrel Patterson, BM.
Jesse Mydyett to Adaline T. Mitchell, Oct. 24, 1833.
    (Oct. 24, 1833). William K. Stepleton, BM.
Henry Hardester to Jane Stone, Nov. 25, 1833. (Nov. 27,
    1833). Jobe Hicks, BM.
Pleasant Fisher to Sarah Etheredge, Nov. 15, 1833. (Nov.
    16, 1833). S. J. Wilkins, BM.
Thomas Gaskins to Delila Rains, Nov. 16, 1833. (Dec.
    16, 1833).
Solomon Human to Nancy P. Porter, Dec. 17, 1833. (Dec.
    17, 1833). Charles Porter, BM.
James V. Walker to Nancy Boyls, Dec. 9, 1833. (Dec. 12,
    1833).
Jobe Hicks to Elizabeth McAlelly, Dec. 14, 1833. (Dec.
    19, 1833). Herrod Holt, BM.

William Ervin to Narcissa Wilbourne, Dec. 16, 1833.
(Dec. 17, 1833). John Dunlap, BM.
Herrod Holt to Sarah Gilland, Dec. 28, 1833. (Jan. 2,
1834). F. G. Goodman, BM.
Samuel C. Leggatte to Elizabeth Watson, Dec. 28, 1833.
By W. Lain. Frederick B. Gentry, BM.
James Carroll to Mary Singleton, Jan. 25, 1834. (Jan.
25, 1834). Wm. W. Crafton, BM.
Benjamin H. Hubbard to Mary Richardson, Jan. 30, 1834.
(Jan. 30, 1834). John D. Whitson, BM.
Saunders Utley to Nancy Robertson, Jan. 14, 1834. Edwin
G. Wood, BM.
Seth Williams to Mary Dunwoody, Feb. 15, 1834. (Feb. 20,
1834). Germon Y. Holmon, BM.
William C. Northcutt to Mahaly Billingsly, Feb. 13,
1834. (Feb. 13, 1834). James Turner, BM.
Radford McFarland to Mahaly Lowry, Feb. 3, 1834. (Feb.
4, 1834). John B. Lowry, BM.
James G. Hall to Elizabeth Thetford, Feb. 8, 1834. (Feb.
16, 1834). William N. Thetford, BM.
Stephen Fuqua to Caroline Gentry, Feb. 4, 1834. D.
Pennington, BM.
Bryant Andrews to Dorcas Jackson, Feb. 4, 1834. John F.
Linton, BM.
William Downey to Martha Colyer, Feb. 24, 1834. George
Watson, BM.
Moses A. House to Mary Ann Petis, Feb. 17, 1834.
John Cummings to Rachell Kenady, Mar. 15, 1834. (Mar.
16, 1834). William McGriegor, BM.
Finas Lytaker to Elizabeth Stanley, Mar. 3, 1834. (Mar.
6, 1834). John W. Smith, BM.
John Huckabee to Susan Boyd, Mar. 3, 1834. (Mar. 6,
1834). Elijah Boyd, BM.
George W. Durley to Eliza A. Hunt, Apr. 9, 1834. By
William Smith, M.G. Joseph J. Durley, BM.
Ephraim Burrow to Elizabeth Bobbett, Apr. 2, 1834. (Apr.
5, 1834). William Lowery, BM.
Stanley Griffin to Polly Clements, Apr. 28, 1834. (May
1, 1834). Jonathan Connell, BM.
James H. McDowell to Rutha Walker, Apr. 1, 1834. (Apr.
3, 1834). Isaac Canady, BM.
John H. Herod to Louisa Mirack, Apr. 2, 1834. (Apr. 2,
1834). Josiah Fletcher, BM.
Bird B. Stone to Mary Fly, May 21, 1834. (May 27, 1834).
Jeremiah Turner, BM.
John D. Whitson to Elizabeth G. Fields, May 14, 1834.
(May 15, 1834). Landon C. Maclin, BM.
John M. Saunders to Pripy Jackson, May 5, 1834. (May
8, 1834). H. Donaldson, BM.
Thomas S. Stone to Matilda J. Fielding, May 17, 1834.
(May 18, 1834). Henry G. Covington, BM.
Robert Pope to Elizabeth Smith, May 16, 1834. Wilborn
W. Smith, BM.
Thomas Spight to Catharine Evans, June 5, 1834. (June
6, 1834). Simon R. Spight, BM.

GIBSON COUNTY MARRIAGES

Daniel M. Wallice to Bitha Lavina Northcutt, June 14, 1834. By William Smith, M.G. Thos R. Hall, BM.

Kinchin Freeman to Rutha Murchean, June 11, '34. (June 11, '34). Robert Landrum, BM.

Abner D. Thomas to Nancy Taner, June 19, 1834. (June 19, 1834). S. Y. Thomas, BM.

Gideon Tucker to Ann Bradberry, June 11, 1834. Green McCaslin, BM.

James T. Hunt to Matilda W. Gant, July 8, 1834. By William Smith, M.G. Alfred Gay, BM.

William Elder to Sarah F. Ramsey, July 23, 1834. (July 23, 1834). Lewis Levy, BM.

John W. Bratton to Mary Ward, July 3, 1834. (July 3, 1834). George S. Bratton, BM.

James A. Harwood to Virlinda C. Beazly, July 22, 1834. (July 22, 1834). H. R. Buchanan, BM.

Henry Fletcher to Mary Wilkins, July 17, 1834. (July 17, 1834). Josiah Fletcher, BM.

Alex Foren to Sarah Stiller, July 5, 1834. William Butler, BM.

David Watson to Catharine Stiller, July 5, 1834. William Butler, BM.

James Trosper to Rachael Glasscock, July 12, 1834. John W. Crockett, BM.

Melvin Ross to Rebecca Smith, Aug. 23, 1834. (Aug. 25, 1834). Richard Smith, BM.

Milton H. Johnson to America J. Thomas, Aug. 30, 1834. (Sept. 2, 1834). James M. Dyson, BM.

Alexander McDougald to Elanor Wade, Aug. 8, 1834. Daniel McDougald, BM.

James H. Dyson to Angeline J. L. Seat, Sept. 29, 1834. (Oct. 10, 1834). G. Waddell and Seth Z. Waddiee, BM.

Joshua Little to Jane Jackson, Sept. 15, 1834. (Sept. 18, 1834). Richard Sherrod, BM.

Hearvy Nettles to Nancy Welch, Sept. 9, 1834. (Sept. 10, 1834).

Thomas Word to Rosonna Crider, Sept. 25, 1834. (Sept. 25, 1834). Aaron Word, BM.

Abner C. Beacham to Lean G. Dibrill, Sept. 4, 1834. (Sept. 4, 1834). Lewis Levy, BM.

Jackson Mathis to Mary Crockett, Oct. 15, 1834. (Oct. 16, 1834). James Mathis, BM.

William Connell to Polly Sandford, Oct. 16, 1834. (Oct. 23, 1834). James Connell, BM.

Harvey M. Latta to Charlott H. Alsabrooks, Oct. 16, 1834. (Oct. 16, 1834). Landon C. Maclin, BM.

Nicholas C. Stone to Martha T. Fly, Oct. 18, 1834. (Oct. 26, 1834). Stephen Pollard, BM.

Green Jacobs to Mary Ann H. Wallingsford, Oct. 21, 1834. (Oct. 23, 1834). Isaac Wellingsford, BM.

Wesley Myrick to Dorcas Myrick, Oct. 7, 1834. (Oct. 7, 1834). Micajah Mackleroy, BM.

Micajah Mackleroy to Elvira Myrick, Oct. 7, 1834. (Oct. 7, 1834). Weasly Myrick, BM.

17

Walter Thetford to Barbary Holt, Oct. 4, 1834. (Oct. 9, 1834). James Connell, BM.

Samuel McLary to Jane Isabella McKnight, Nov. 18, 1834. (Nov. 20, 1834).

Richard H. Berge to Jane G. Hall, Nov. 27, 1834. (Nov. 27, 1834). Stephen Luster, BM.

Adam Trout to Francis Gilliland, Nov. 23, 1834. Herrod Holt, BM.

William A. Bridgemon to Elvira L. Roundtree, Nov. 18, 1834. (Nov. 18, 1834). Robert F. Finley, BM.

George W. Mitchell to Martha Carrahan, Nov. 22, 1834. (Nov. 23, 1834). James P. Carrahan, BM.

Thomas B. Lourence to Sarah H. Medeoris, Nov. 15, 1834. (Nov. 16, 1834). Crawford Prewit, BM.

Watson Forest to Sarah Crafton, Nov. ?, 1834. William Cantrell, BM.

Mark Gosey to Nancy Diggins, Dec. 28, 1834. (Dec. 30, 1834). Person C. Vaughan, BM.

William Banister to Elizabeth Conell, Dec. 18, 1834. (Dec. 23, 1834). John Thedford, BM.

Barnett Smith to Mary Bell, Dec. 20, 1834. William Smith, BM.

Josiah Baker to Mary Forester, Dec. 2, 1834. (Dec. 2, 1834). Geo. W. Cantrell, BM.

Absolom Smith to Mahaly Conlee, Dec. 22, 1834. (Dec. 25, 1834). James Turner, BM.

Enoch Walker to Elizabeth Walker, Dec. 23, 1834. (Dec. 23, 1834). Baily Madison, BM.

William T. Blakemore to Mary J. H. Rolls, Dec. 13, 1834. (Dec. 13, 1834). Lewis Levy, BM.

Johnson Isbell to Elizabeth H. Sloan, Dec. 24, 1834. (Dec. 26, 1834). Riley Staton, BM.

Richard Heath to Elizabeth Cole, Dec. 20, 1834. John L. Davis, BM.

Edwind York to Caroline Spears, Dec. 5, 1834. Sherrod Smith, BM.

Robert H. Goodlow to Nancy Baldridge, Dec. 9, 1834. Elihu G. Walker, BM.

William Dowell to Malinda Lowry, Dec. 30, 1834. (Jan. 1, 1835). John Heathcock, BM.

Moses B. Wallingsford to Martha Fowler, Jan. 15, 1835. (Jan. 20, 1835). Green Jacobs, BM.

Purcell C. Vaughn to Sarah Nobles, Jan. 10, 1835. (Jan. 13, 1835). Williamson P. Vaughn, BM.

John Heathcock to Harriet Donel, Jan. 14, 1835. (Jan. 15, 1835). Wm. Doonel, BM.

William P. Wilson to Nancy Clemons, Jan. 26, 1835. (Feb. 9, 1835). Wm. D. Fly, BM.

Samuel Glidwell to Nancy Dill, Feb. 6, 1835. (Feb. 8, 1835). Zebolum Dill, BM.

William Goodman, Jr. to Martha A. McMinn, Feb. 17, 1835. (Feb. 19, 1835). Preston Holt, BM.

John B. Lowry to Mary Tidwell, Feb. 21, 1835. (Apr. 27, 1835). James Brown, BM.

18

GIBSON COUNTY MARRIAGES

Samuel J. Crider to Mary Yates, Feb. 28, 1835. (Feb. 29, 1835). David Crider, BM.

John J. Fielder to Rebecca J. Mays, Feb. 12, 1835. (Feb. 19, 1835). Joseph Nicholson, BM.

William Hobbs to Sally H. Knight, Feb. 2, 1835. Hardy Kennedy, BM.

Owen Tombs to Lucenda Glasscock, Feb. 28, 1835. John D. Agee, BM.

Thomas Fletcher to Lucratis Whitley, Mar. 19, 1835. (Mar. 19, 1835). Josiah Fletcher, BM.

John D. Cabler to Julia L. Davidson, Mar. 15, 1835. (Mar. 17, 1835). W. H. Davidson, BM.

Edward Jeffreys to Penelope Simmons, Apr. 8, 1835. (Apr. 13, 1835). William McCaslin, BM.

Hillorry Flowers to Nancy Thetford, Apr. 4, 1835. (Apr. 5, 1835). William Thetford, BM.

John Morgan to Susana A. Bysinger, Apr. 23, 1835. William A. Bysinger, BM.

Francis Edney to Nancy Bowling, Apr. 23, 1835. Burges Bowling, BM.

David F. Matthews to Caroline Howard, May 27, 1835. (May 28, 1835). Humphrey Donaldson, BM.

Joseph E. Matthews to Nancy McCaslin, May 15, 1835. (May 19, 1835). Green McCaslin, BM.

Abraham S. Dial to Anna Beaver, May 2, 1835. William Butler, BM.

Thomas M. Watson to Kisiah Sellars, June 29, 1835. (July 2, 1835). Wm. Rabey, BM.

John Steuart to Elizabeth W. Taliaferro, June 16, 1835. (June 16, 1835). James Browne, BM.

William D. Scott to Amanda G. Gilchrist, June 9, 1835. (June 9, 1835). H. R. Buchanan, BM.

Thos. C. D. Howell to Sarah Stewart, June 15, 1835. Baptist Boyt, BM.

Wilban Webb to Nancy Crockett, June 11, 1835. (June 11, 1835). James Vickers, BM.

Joseph D. Rentfro to Sarah Dial, June 24, 1835. Paul C. Crafton, BM.

Jesse Turner to Elizabeth Alford, June 15, 1835. (June 16, 1835). Thomas G. Turner, BM.

Moses B. Hawkins to Nancy Lattie, July 29, 1835. (Aug. 2, 1835). Peter Sinclair, BM.

Lewis Levy to Phebe Fite, July 15, 1835. (July 15, 1835). L. Winchester, BM.

William Maxley to Sarah Watson, July 13, 1835. (Aug. 6, 1835). Jefferson Conlee, BM.

Daniel McDougald to Susan N. Morton, Aug. 13, 1835. By A. G. McNutt. John M. Moore, BM.

Benjamin W. Murphy to Martha M. Crafton, Aug. 25, 1835. (Aug. 27, 1835). Thos. B. Murphy, BM.

Jesse D. Partee to Ann E. Higgins, Aug. 15, 1835. (Aug. 16, 1835). James Brown, BM.

George W. Bledsoe to Sarah Lynch, Aug. 4, 1835. (Aug. 4, 1835). Humphrey Donaldson, BM.

GIBSON COUNTY MARRIAGES

Archells Thompson to Unica McGeehe, Aug. 6, 1835. (Aug. 6, 1835). John D. Hannah, BM.

James Forester to Mary A. McKinney, Aug. 5, 1835. (Aug. 15, 1835). David D. Blair, BM.

Jerome Griffin to Caroline Thomas, Aug. 22, 1835. (Aug. 23, 1835). John W. Crockett, BM.

Henry Kenneday to Susannah Mainor, Aug. 12, 1835. Josiah Whitley, BM.

John C. Bates to Mary Bowers, Aug. 25, 1835. Joshua Donaldson, BM.

Cincematus Roach to Lethia Bruff, Aug. 25, 1835. Jas. J. Bradberry, BM.

James Welch to Francis Fields, Sept. 29, 1835. (Sept. 30, 1835). Henry Welch, BM.

Steel Bodkin to Nancy Meurhead, Sept. 16, 1835. (Sept. 16, 1835). Kinchen Freeman, BM.

Thos. Ross to Rachael Smith, Sept. 12, 1835. (Sept. 20, 1835). Melvan Ross, BM.

John D. Wright to Rebecca W. Pettus, Sept. 9, 1835. (Sept. 22, 1835). Moses A. House, BM.

John D. Davidson to Zella Mainor, Sept. 20, 1835. Benj. Smith, BM.

John W. Flowers to Elizabeth Flowers, Sept. 29, 1835. By Benj. White, J.P. Asher Flowers, BM.

Jeremiah McWhorter to Martha Boon, Oct. 1, 1835. (Oct. 1, 1835). George W. Gentry, BM.

James M. Brewer to Rebecca G. Richardson, Oct. 3, 1835. (Oct. 7, 1835). James M. Sharp, BM.

Andrew Blair to Nancy Sellars, Oct. 8, 1835. Robert Holmes, BM.

Jeremiah Wright to Francis Jeffers, Oct. 2, 1835. Green McCaslin, BM.

John W. Moore to Sobina Yates, Oct. 29, 1835. (Oct. 29, 1835). J. W. D. Mays, BM.

Robert F. Finley to Nancy Aiken, Nov. 16, 1835. (Nov. 18, 1835). Thos. M. Wetherspoon, BM.

Thomas Fletcher to Elizabeth Miller, Nov. 17, 1835. (Nov. 18, 1835). Charles Forester, BM.

Thomas Edwards to Mary Robertson, Nov. 26, 1835. (Nov. 26, 1835). Spill C. Haskins, BM.

Green McCaslin to Mary Holmes, Nov. 6, 1835. Felix E. Holmes, BM.

Jeremiah Cherry to Sarah G. Bunting, Nov. 6, 1835. By A. L. Davidson, J.P. John W. Crockett, BM.

William Hendrick to Rachael Coope, Nov. 7, 1835. (Nov. 12, 1835). John W. Crockett, BM.

Peter S. Reeves to Nancy Rooker, Nov. 12, 1835. James T. Hunt, BM.

Humphrey Donaldson to Judith J. Davidson, Nov. 5, 1835. By A. L. Davidson, J.P. W. C. Fite, BM.

Nathan Carry to Ann Carry, Nov. 26, 1835. John Mays, BM.

Smith H. Gee to Sarah Beckham, Dec. 12, 1835. (Dec. 12, 1835). Hiram J. Thomas, BM.

Charles W. Williams to Clarissa Young, Dec. 16, 1835. (Dec. 17, 1835).

GIBSON COUNTY MARRIAGES

Richard B. Hutcherson to Mira Jourden, Dec. 21, 1835.
(Dec. 22, 1835). Charles C. Phillips, BM.
H. B. Hoover to Anna H. Newhouse, Dec. 22, 1835. (Dec.
29, 1835). Daniel W. Crafton, BM.
Samuel Malone to Elizabeth Philips, Dec. 12, 1835. (Dec.
17, 1835). Caleb R. Clement, BM.
Richard Ellington to Ruthy Watson, Dec. 19, 1835. (Dec.
22, 1835). William Smith, BM.
Reuben Whichard to Lucrecca Nobls, Dec. 13, 1835. Jolee
Harris, BM.
James M. Walker to Nancy Boyles, Dec. 9, 1835. Wm.
Walker, BM.
Nathan Barron to Elizabeth Sherron, Dec. 17, 1835. (Dec.
17, 1835).
John W. H. Mays to Julia A. Fields, Jan. 30, 1836. (Jan.
31, 1836). Watson P. Mays, BM.
John M. Thompson to Sarah Barnes, Jan 19, 1836. (Jan.
20, 1836). Edmond Ford, BM.
Martin Briant to Dicy Smith, Jan 28, 1836. (Feb. 5,
1836). David Little, BM.
David Little to Sarah McGarett, Jan. 28, 1836. (Feb. 2,
1836). Martin Bryant, BM.
Thomas Staton to Lavina Spellings, Jan. 21, 1836. (Jan.
22, 1836). Benj. Spellings, BM.
William Gentry to Lavina Scallion, Jan. 9, 1836. (Jan.
10, 1836). David Little, BM.
William C. Webb to Hester Crockett, Jan 7, 1836. (Jan.
7, 1836). James Vickers, BM.
William S. Williams to Malissa Waldrip, Jan. 18, 1836.
(Jan 19, 1836). Charles Williams, BM.
Stephen Snowden to Nancy Fletcher, Jan. 25, 1836. (Jan.
?, 1836). Henry Fletcher, BM.
Robert R. Sloan to Frances Sloan, Jan 5, 1836. (Jan. 6,
1836). Thomas Sloan, BM.
John D. Davidson to Narcissa Gailard, Jan. 30, 1836.
Wilson L. Davidson, BM.
Elijah Spencer to Hannah Jackson, Feb. 27, 1836. (Feb.
28, 1836). Solomon Hines, BM.
Henry Welch to Caroline Smith, Feb. 15, 1836. (Feb. 18,
1836). John Parker, BM.
Eli Dickason to Margaret Basinger, Feb. 4, 1836. (Feb.
4, 1836). Malichi Watts, BM.
Thomas J. Hines to Mary Hignight, Feb. 29, 1836. Thos.
Williams, BM.
John Robertson to Mary R. Mayfield, Feb. 5, 1836. Isaac
N. Mayfield, BM.
Thomas Smith to Mary Ann Ross, Mar. 2, 1836. (Mar. 3,
1836). Thomas Ross, BM.
James McDummet to Charity Webb, Mar. 16, 1836. (Mar.
16, 1836). Francis Bledsoe, BM.
Thompson Bruff to Sarah Smith, Mar. 12, 1836. James D.
Rollings, BM.
Henry Gately to Martha B. Wallingsford, Mar. 7, 1836.
Moses B. Wallingsford, BM.

GIBSON COUNTY MARRIAGES

Johnathan Henry to July Strother, Apr. 15, 1836. (Apr. 17, 1836). Bryant Flowers, BM.
Jerry Traynor to Harriet Forran, Apr. 23, 1836. (Apr. 29, 1836). John P. Hassell, BM.
James Arnold to Mary Thedford, Apr. 6, 1836. (Apr. 6, 1836). David McCollum, BM.
William K. Love to Louisiana L. Jones, Apr. 21, 1836. (Apr. 21, 1836). James W. Moore and A. W. O. Totten, BM.
Aaron Word to Precilla H. Freeman, Apr. 15, 1836. (Apr. 21, 1836). Isaac Word, BM.
John M. White to Nancy Handcock, May 26, 1836. (May 27, 1836). Jesse Flippin, BM.
William Foren to Arreana Griffin, May 9, 1836. (May 10, 1836). Thomas Yarbery, BM.
Richard Freeman to Margaret Nevils, May 6, 1836. (May 6, 1836). James Odel, BM.
Jonathan B. Dryden to Nancy F. Allison, May 12, 1836. (May 13, 1836). Henry Allison, BM.
Jacob Flowers to Margaret Thedford, May 21, 1836. (May ?, 1836). William Baker, BM.
Ben Littlefield to Miss B. M. McGarrity, June 11, 1836. (June ?, 1836). Perry H. L. Littlefield, BM.
James M. Woods to Sarah S. White, June 18, 1836. (June 19, 1836). Geo. R. Mosely, BM.
Wm. R. Sawyers to Sarah H. Gibson, June 22, 1836. (June 23, 1836). William Gibson, BM.
John S. Mayfield to Martha Laughter, June 16, 1836. (June 16, 1836). A. B. P. Mayfield, BM.
Joseph Pate to Nancy Glasscock, June 22, 1836. Robt. P. Crockett, BM.
Milton T. Tarvin to Mary L. McClary, July 8, 1836. (July 14, 1836). Joshua Donaldson, BM.
Solomon Hines to Malinda White, July 23, 1836. (July 28, 1836). Garrat Tarvin, BM.
Jas. M. Lassiter to Catherine Jones, July ?, 1836. (July 28, 1836). J. W. Herndon, BM.
William Counts to Elizabeth Ann Davidson, July 12, 1836. (July 13, 1836). Allen Read, BM.
John Dill to Eda Smith, July 5, 1836. (July 7, 1836). James G. Riddle, BM.
Burrell Patterson to Pricilla Boun, July 9, 1836. James P. Alexander, BM.
Macca Write to Martha Bone, July 23, 1836. (July 24, 1836). James M. Boyd, BM.
James Carter to Jane Hart, July 6, 1836. Jas. R. Weatherspoon, BM.
Thomas J. Walton to M. A. E. Mitchell, July 2, 1836. James W. Wright, BM.
John H. Reed to Louisa Kevit, July 26, 1836. Hugh Reed, BM.
A. B. Mayfield to Martha Ervin, Aug. 20, 1836. (Aug. 20, 1836). Robert Ervin, BM.
Rigdon Grady to Nancy Gleason, Aug. 1, 1836. (Aug. 19, 1836). Bryant M. Branch, BM.
Briant Flowers to Susan Strauther, Aug. 4, 1836. (Aug. 14, 1836). Jesse Flowers, BM.

William Nedry to Nancy Boyt, Aug. 23, 1836. (Aug. 25, 1836). Caleb Howell, BM.

David Todd to Amey P. Mayfield, Aug. 19, 1836. (Aug. 20, 1836). Robert Ervin and Thos. Edwards, J.E.G.C., BM.

James H. Martin to Violet L. Carr, Sept. 11, 1836. (Sept. 13, 1836). Silas L. Clark, BM.

William Mathis to Martha Ann Harber, Sept. 16, 1836. (Sept. 18, 1836). Geo. W. Harley, BM.

Noah Curtis to Mary Bran, Sept. 28, 1836. (Sept. 29, 1836). Benjamin Nobles, BM.

John Phaling to Izabellar Alexander, Sept. 20, 1836. (Sept. ?, 1836). James Hays, BM.

Jerramiah P. Woodard to Elizabeth Thompson, Sept. 29, 1836. (Oct. 2, 1836). James Holly, BM.

William D. Chamberling to Polly Lane, Sept. 5, 1836. (Sept. 8, 1836). Thos. Chamberling, BM.

Henry Flowers to Mary T. Halliburton, Sept. 20, 1836. By. Saml. Halliburton. Martin Halliburton, BM.

John F. Rogers to Elizabeth E. Mosely, Sept. 26, 1836. G. B. Mosely, BM.

Washington Scallion to Margarett Toten, Oct. 12, 1836. (Oct. 13, 1836). Wm. B. Connell, BM.

Phillips Holcomb to Sarah B. Harlean, Oct. 27, 1836. (Nov. 25, 1836). L. L. Holcomb, BM.

Jessee J. McCloud to Abigal Davis, Oct. 15, 1836. (?, 1836). John W. Flowers, BM.

Crawford Prewitt to Margrat G. Griffin, Oct. 25, 1836. (Oct. 27, 1836). H. C. Lawrance, BM.

R. T. S. Avery to Polly Babb, Oct. 13, 1836. Alex Avery, BM.

John Smith to Mary A. Martin, Dec. 1, 1836. (Dec. 8, 1836). A. H. White, BM.

Jno. Baysinger to Mary Ann Morgan, Nov. 10, 1836. (Nov. 10, 1836). Reuben Fletcher, BM.

Wesley Ely to Elizabeth Anderson, Nov. 1, 1836. (Nov. 2, 1836). William McLand, BM.

Benjamin Bean to Eliza Bass, Nov. 21, 1836. (Nov. 22, 1836). H. Parkin, BM.

Wm. T. Huckby to Sarah Glasscock, Nov. 22, 1836. (Nov. 23, 1836). Allen Read, BM.

Dickson Jackson to Tibatha Rasberry, Nov. 5, 1836. (Nov. 5, 1836). Henry Cassels, BM.

John Laymon to Elizabeth Stuart, Nov. 24, 1836. James Laymon, BM.

Thos. McKneely to Leathen Fuller, Nov. 21, 1836. (Dec. 1, 1836). Allen Edmundson, BM.

Isack Word to Rachael Freeman, Dec. 5, 1836. (Dec. 8, 1836). Franklin Barrot, BM.

F. G. Goodman to Dilila P. Woodson, Dec. 15, 1836. (Dec. 28, 1836). Saml. Aslin, BM.

Thos. Bell to Elizabeth Goodman, Dec. 17, 1836. (Dec. 22, 1836). Jacob T. Smith, BM.

E. H. Crocker to Susan Walker, Dec. 26, 1836. (Jan. 5, 1837). Burrell Gossett, BM.

GIBSON COUNTY MARRIAGES

Absolum A. White to Nancy Harley, Dec. 1, 1836. (Dec. 1, 1836). John Smith, BM.

James Montgomery to Mahaly McKezick, Dec. 17, 1836. James Pircey, BM.

Charles W. Williams to Clarissa Young, Dec. 16, 1836. John D. Agee, BM.

Arthur Fuller to Levina Moore, Dec. 5, 1836. (Dec. 6, 1836). William Talley, BM.

John W. Webb to Martha W. Ragan, Dec. 21, 1836. Joseph Hollaman, BM.

Thomas W. Goff to Vilott Amanda Henderson, Dec. 26, 1836. (Dec. 29, 1836). H. Sherron, BM.

Henry Shearer to Pennlope June Berry, Jan. 16, 1837. (Jan. 19, 1837). Andrew Berry, BM.

Obed Nicholasson to Elizabeth A. Donaldson, Jan. 26, 1837. (Jan. ?, 1837). W. D. Bethell, BM.

Samuel Blackley to Mulinda Treumen, Jan. 28, 1837. (Feb. 2, 1837). James Waldress, BM.

John B. Stuart to Mahaly Allen, Jan. 2, 1837. (Jan. 5, 1837). Young W. Allen, BM.

William Jackson to Polly A. Lacy, Jan. 6, 1837. (Jan. 10, 1837). Wiley Bishop, BM.

Jno. M. Northern to Mahetable Ballintine, Jan. 9, 1837. (Jan. 17, 1837). John Wert, BM.

Robert Jackson to Catherine Tincle, Jan. 14, 1837. (Jan. 15, 1837). F. J. Terrell, BM.

Andrew Porter to Polly Howell, Jan 2 , 1837. (Jan. 17, 1837). Caleb Howell, BM.

N. B. Jones to Sarah Farris, Jan. 5, 1837. (Jan. 5, 1837). Joshua Donaldson, BM.

S. C. Harpoll to Elizabeth McMahon, Jan. 6, 1837. (Mar. 1, 1837).

John J. McKnight to Ellendor L. Thomas, Feb. 21, 1837. (Feb. 21, 1837). James M. Sharp, BM.

Hiram H. Banks to Martha Ann Bean, Feb. 15, 1837. (Feb. 23, 1837). George Locke, BM.

P. E. Holmes to Martha Pound, Feb. 6, 1837. (Feb. 9, 1837). Pleasant R. Page, BM.

Christopher Hite to Mary Care, Feb. 21, 1837. James M. Watson, BM.

F. K. Peary to Miss H. H. Hopkins, Feb. 22, 1837. Moses E. Cole, BM.

John D. Stone to Nancy E. McKnight, Feb. 6, 1837. (Feb. 7, 1837). Wm. J. Becton, BM.

William W. Gooden to Rebecca C. Humphris, Mar. 8, 1837. (Mar. 12, 1837). Wm. H. Burton, BM.

Hugh A. Fullerton to Elizabeth H. Reed, Mar. 13, 1837. (Mar. 16, 1837). Benjamin Holmes, BM.

Laurel Bryant to Elizabeth McGarrity, Mar. 18, 1837. (Mar. 20, 1837). Boyd F. Bryant, BM.

James Hays to Mary Ann Finey, Apr. 13, 1837. (Apr. 15, 1837). David C. McCutchan, BM.

Thos. Canady to Elizabeth Canadey, Apr. 6, 1837. (Apr. 6, 1837). John (?), BM.

GIBSON COUNTY MARRIAGES

S. Shaw to Miss M. A. Clay, Apr. 28, 1837. (May 2,
1837). C. D. Simmons, BM.
John W. Pope to Haskey Dennis, Apr. 30, 1837. John
Tate, BM.
John Connell to Mary Bates, May 29, 1837. Samuel Reed,
BM. (Returned, not executed, July 3, 1837)
Carroll Holt to Mary Connell, May 13, 1837. (May 25,
1837). Johnathan Dawson, BM.
Daniel W. Word to Lucinda Hawkins, May 16, 1837. (May
?, 1837). Jno. J. Edwards, BM.
Simpson Shaw to Elizabeth D. Jones, May 30, 1837. (June
?, 1837). M. B. Hawkins, BM.
Wm. N. Jones to Sarah Speer, May 29, 1837. (May 30,
1837). Kindred Spears, BM.
Edward Fox to Mary Morris, May 2, 1837. (June 8, 1837).
Allen Fox, BM.
O. Conlee to Juley A. Richardson, May 29, 1837. (June
1, 1837).
Joseph Bellue to Mary McCleur, May 29, 1837. Thos. A.
Patton, BM.
John H. Terry to Frances A. White, May 29, 1837. Saml.
Booth, BM.
Green B. Chambers to Margaret Edwards, May 26, 1837.
Jesse Cassels, BM.
Freeman Cross to Nancy Patterson, June 19, 1837. (June
20, 1837). John Udaley, BM.
Elijah Quick to Sarah Moss, June 17, 1837. (June ?, 1837).
Julus Clark, BM.
Wm. M. Irwin to Ruth Jones, June 24, 1837. (June 26,
1837). Wm. L. Neilson, BM.
Isah Webb to Mary Moore, June 21, 1837. (June 22, 1837).
Isral Moore, BM.
James M. Balleu to Mary McClure, June 5, 1837. (June 5,
1837). Wilson Baird, BM.
Alex C. Ridgway to Elizabeth Serratt, June 17, 1837.
(June 18, 1837).
Hudson W. Moss to Cary H. Massee, June 22, 1837.
Thos. Smith, BM.
Berry Patterson to Lucenda Gibson, June 13, 1837.
M. F. Garrison, BM.
John Ashlin to Margaret L. B. McDowell, July 25, 1837.
Jessee R. Irwin, BM.
Francis A. Bledsoe to Martha Ann Bledsoe, July 31,
1837. John Lynch, BM.
Philip B. Carter to Susana E. Mathis, July 26, 1837.
(July 27, 1837). Jacob Mathis, BM.
Hugh D. Hays to Ann M. Hawkins, July 17, 1837. (July
18, 1837). J. M. McDowell, BM.
Herbert A. Ragsdale to Nancy Arnold, July 29, 1837.
(Aug. 1, 1837). Titus Caudell, BM.
George P. Muyrhead to Elizabeth Vaughn, July 12, 1837.
(July 12, 1837). Richard B. Jones, BM.
James W. Carten to Jane Harts, July 6, 1837. By Jabez
Hickman, M.G.

William H. Ivy to Ann D. Moore, July 22, 1837. By (?).
Jonas Brown to Mary Carroll, July 17, 1837. Green
Chambers, BM.
William N. Dillard to Martha Ann Walker, Aug. 22, 1837.
(Aug. 24, 1837). Henry A. Welch, BM.
John Campbell to Aley A. H. Welch, Aug. 24, 1837. (Aug.
24, 1837). Pyton Woods, BM.
Nathanial Dickson to Martha A. Kirksey, Aug. 24, 1837.
(Aug. 24, 1837). A. H. McNeely, BM.
John Stewart to Roseana M. Bates, Aug. 23, 1837. (Aug.
24, 1837). P. P. Elliott, BM.
Joseph J. Etheridge to Centha Vickers, Aug. 24, 1837.
(Aug. 24, 1837). Robert Crockett, BM.
Gideon W. Mainard to Dovey Smith, Aug. 21, 1837. (Aug.
31, 1837). Everitt Smith, BM.
Abron Kenaday to Lucy Hall, Aug. 28, 1837. (Sept. 21,
1837). Thos. Kenaday, BM.
Frances M. Crocker to Liddy Gilliland, Aug. 9, 1837.
(Aug. 13, 1837). Herrod Holt, BM.
John Kimbro to Sarah P. Bellew, Aug. 12, 1837. Richard
Blair, BM.
Andrew Littlefield to Elizabeth Bellew, Aug. 17, 1837.
(Aug. 20, 1837). W. Thedford, BM.
Andrew J. Ross to Leer Smith, Sept. 14, 1837. (Sept.
21, 1837). R. L. Smith, BM.
James P. Stewart to Jane Cross, Sept. 7, 1837. (Sept.
8, 1837). John R. Patterson, BM.
Mark Bullington to Nancy Browning, Sept. 26, 1837.
P. P. Elliott, BM.
Joseph Y. Diskill to Elizabeth Williamson, Sept. 28,
1837. William Durley, BM.
Zachariah Bowen to Hanah Holaway, Sept. 21, 1837.
(Sept. 28, 1837). D. C. McCutcheon, BM.
Minor C. Cole to Winiford Fly, Sept. 15, 1837. (Sept.
15, 1837). Julas Hall, BM.
Everett Smith to Margrett Newell, Sept. 17, 1837.
Elum Newell, BM.
Allen Griffin to Miss E. J. Care, Oct. 31, 1837. (Nov.
2, 1837). Andrew A. Care, BM.
James A. Richardson to Evelina L. Clay, Oct. 9, 1837.
(Oct. 19, 1837). James Scott, BM.
David B. Mason to Martha Ann Hickman, Oct. 6, 1837.
(Oct. 10, 1837). Samuel Y. Thomas, BM.
Thos. L. Boswell to Charlete Jones, Oct. 6, 1837.
(Oct. 6, 1837). James L. Bledsoe, BM.
William Thedford to Polly Williams, Oct. 13, 1837.
(Oct. 15, 1837). James A. Conal, BM.
Wilson L. Davidson to Nancy Barton, Oct. 18, 1837.
(Oct. 19, 1837). Henry Bobbitt, BM.
Wm. D. Bethell to Julia Donaldson, Oct. 30, 1837.
(Oct. 30, 1837). Wm. L. Ester, BM.
Jas. M. Halford to Eliza A. H. Burton, Oct. 30, 1837.
(Oct. 31, 1837). T. M. Johnson, BM.
Cooper B. Jones to Eliza A. Harpoll, Oct. 7, 1837.
(Oct. 10, 1837). George R. Snell, BM.

Robt. A. Rankin to Tabitha A. Legat, Oct. 10, 1837.
A. L. Burrow, BM.
Jas. W. Glasgow to Mary Jane Fisher, Oct. 25, 1837.
(Oct. 26, 1837). J. P. Hapell, BM.
John Keith to Polly Robertson, Nov. 11, 1837. Jessee
Allen, BM.
James Runolds to Nancy Jenkins, Nov. 2, 1837. (Dec. 7,
1837). William Pritchett, BM.
Munroe B. Elder to Lucy A. Baber, Nov. 2, 1837. (Nov.
2, 1837). James M. Moon, BM.
James Gibson to Elizabeth Battle, Nov. 22, 1837. (Nov.
23, 1837). Henry Battle, BM.
Zachariah Biggs to Martha A. Penney, Nov. 23, 1837.
(Nov. 23, 1837). Rubin Biggs, BM.
James Cunningham to Catharine Robertson, Nov. 29, 1837.
(Nov. 30, 1837). James M. Walker, BM.
J. M. White to Carroline Bryant, Nov. 6, 1837. Z. Smith, BM.
Wm. H. Clemmont to Mary A. Hail, Dec. 26, 1837. (Jan.
17, 1838). Archd. C. Levy, BM.
Elisha Easterwood to Nancy Sellers, Dec. 27, 1837.
(Dec. 27, 1837). A. L. Davidson, BM.
John C. Porter to Susan Ellen, Dec. 6, 1837. (Dec. 6,
1837). James Porter, BM.
John W. James to Lucenda D. McWherter, Dec. 6, 1837.
(Dec. 6, 1837). James Morton, BM.
George M. Fisher to Martha E. Thomas, Dec. 14, 1837.
(Dec. 14, 1837). N. J. Hess, BM.
Wm. Bowman to Eliza G. Crisp, Dec. 21, 1837. (Dec. 21,
1837). Wm Serape, BM.
Major Bledsoe to Centha Shaw, Dec. 22, 1837. (Dec. 22,
1837). A. Davis, BM.
Wm. N. Mitchell to Margarett Tyson, Dec. 5, 1837.
(Dec. 7, 1837). W. J. Walton, BM.
Bryant Ringgold to Mary A. Nobles, Dec. 28, 1837. (Dec.
28, 1837). Rubin Whitchard, BM.
Julus Clarke to Jane Calhoun, Dec. 30, 1837. (Dec. 31,
1838). Elijah Quick, BM.
Thomas G. Jones to Sophia W. Woods, Jan. 15, 1838.
(Jan. 18, 1838). John B. Jones, BM.
John Keath to Hannah R. Hollan, Jan. 29, 1838. (Jan.
31, 1838). Wiley Melton, BM.
James Doxey to Ellenander Etherage, Jan. 11, 1838.
(Jan. 21, 1838. John Wert, BM.
Philip R. K. Claiborne to Mary Billingsley, Jan. 18,
1837. (Jan. 18, 1837). W. C. Fite, BM.
Henry Head to Elizabeth S. Beazley, Jan. 13, 1838.
(Jan. 24, 1838). Thos. S. Scott, BM.
Jackson Dunning to Nancy Williams, Jan. 11, 1838.
(Jan. 18, 1838). James Woods, BM.
Jno. M. Carroll to Nancy Smith, Jan. 1, 1838. (Jan. 2,
1838).
Solomon C. Harpole to Elizabeth McMahon, Jan. 6, 1838.
E. W. Rains, BM.
Thos. M. Witherspoon to Roenna McCalvy, Jan. 23, 1838.
Jas. R. Witherspoon, BM.

James McClary to Emley James, Feb. 3, 1838. (Feb. 8, 1838). John S. Curry, BM.

Simeon Butram to Elizabeth Fletcher, Feb. 5, 1838. (Feb. 14, 1838). George W. Watson, BM.

Lions C. Scott to Martha Chafero, Feb. 22, 1838. (Feb. 22, 1838). Thomas Mathews, BM.

Nathan Ray to Emaline Bledsoe, Feb. 6, 1838. B. G. Holder, BM. (Returned Mar. 22, 1838, no endorsement)

Eli Jackson to Margarett James, Feb. 22, 1838. (Feb. 27, 1838). Joshua Donaldson, BM.

Andrew P. Foster to Sibly Johnston, Feb. 17, 1838. (Feb. 21, 1838). Joseph Holaman, BM.

Henry Patison to Lavina Oneal, Feb. 24, 1838. (Mar. 1, 1838). Joseph Garwood, BM.

Benjamin F. Spellings to Louisa Genest, Feb. 20, 1838. Wm. C. Hicks, BM.

F. E. Becton to Pressilla Harper, Feb. 17, 1838. (Feb. 18, 1838). N. D. Sandeford, BM.

Jno. L. Flippin to Sarah A. Bryant, Feb. 3, 1838. Allen S. White, BM.

Henry Lowary to Julia Ann Dowell, Mar. 5, 1838. Mar. 8, 1838). Johnathan Dawson, BM.

Julius M. Hall to Mulindy Cole, Mar. 28, 1838. (Mar. 28, 1838). S. S. Paul, BM.

John Ronalds to Patsey Smith, Mar. 17, 1838. (Mar. 20, 1838). Charles W. Smith, BM.

Marcus Holeman to Peletha Curtis, Mar. 30, 1838. Edward Curtis, BM.

Bennet Ragan to Susan Yancy, Apr. 17, 1838. (Apr. 19, 1838). Joseph Holoman, BM.

Wellington H. Bledsoe to Centhy Bledsoe, Apr. 1, 1838. (Apr. 4, 1838). John Lynch, BM.

Thomas Hamack to Margratt Warren, Apr. 26, 1838. (Apr. 28, 1838). Thos. T. Rodgers, BM.

Elgin C. White to Mary C. Page, Apr. 21, 1838. (Apr. 22, 1838). James P. Hunt, BM.

Jesse Carray to Elizabeth Keathly, Apr. 16, 1838. (Apr. 17, 1838). James Carraway, BM.

John Flowers to Parzada Borrin, May 24, 1838. (May 24, 1838). Burrell Patterson, BM.

Daniel B. Crider to Eliza H. Rigsby, May 26, 1838. (May 27, 1838). T. B. Crider, BM.

Jacob F. Penn to Margrett Odle, May 21, 1838. (May 21, 1838). Henry Meek, BM.

Duncan Massey to Mary Olsabrooks, May 12, 1838. (May 17, 1838). Wilson Barret, BM.

Arther Smith to Martha Warrin, May 7, 1838. (May 8, 1838). Derham Boyett, BM.

Wm. Smith to Elizabeth Gilliland, May 8, 1838. (May 12, 1838). Jno. R. Cribbs, BM.

A. S. Davidson to Meriah E. Landin, May 5, 1838. (May 5, 1838). A. C. Nimmo, BM.

Benjamin Boon to Unicy T. Hunt, May 16, 1838. (May 17, 1838). Cyrus Sharp, BM.

William Murphy to Rebecca Adams, May 9, 1838. Wm. Craig, BM.
James Scott to Mary Landers, June 14, 1838. (June 14, 1838). B. Crawford, BM.
T. R. Turner to Martha Howell, June 20, 1838. (June 24, 1838). B. Pope, BM.
David D. Blair to Lucy R. Smith, June 18, 1838. (June 21, 1838). David Tanner, BM.
Woodson Rountree to Rosannah L. Biard, June 18, 1838. (June 18, 1838). William Long, BM.
Sherod S. Paul to Mary Miller, June 19, 1838. (June 21, 1838). John Finley, BM.
Wm. Pritchett to Lucinda Traynor, June 7, 1838. (June 7, 1838). John Cummings, BM.
John S. Fullerton to Rachal L. Thomas, July 24, 1838. (July 26, 1838). Hugh Y. Bone, BM.
Wiley Taylor to Nany Dozer, July 7, 1838. (July 8, 1838). Washington Terrall, BM.
William Dozer to Edney Ann Simmons, July 3, 1838. (July 12, 1838). S. Oneal, BM.
Walter E. Daniel to Sarah Atkenson, July 6, 1838. (July 6, 1838). R. P. Raney, BM.
William Sain to Frances Lathain, July 10, 1838. July 12, 1838). Wm. B. Conwill, BM.
Walter M. Thedford to Rutha Canaday, July 3, 1838. (July 8, 1838). Wm. L. Pritchett, BM.
William Reason to Levina Tatom, July 7, 1838. (July 9, 1838).
Wm. C. Love to Catharine Smith, July 3, 1838. (July 3, 1838). L. J. Wilkins, BM.
Henson Howard to Eliza E. Walker, July 30, 1838. (July 30, 1838). E. H. Crocker, BM.
Solomon Pinion to Anny Brunson, July 21, 1838. (July 21, 1838). Peter Trosper, BM.
John Edmundson to Mulindy Trosper, Aug. 25, 1838. (Aug. 30, 1838). John R. Halford, BM.
D. G. Boyett to Chrrinda Crews, Aug. 17, 1838. (Aug. 20, 1838). Geo. W. Watson, BM.
James R. Witherspoon to America Barnes. By N. J. Hess, M.G. Thos. M. Witherspoon, BM.
John Crews to Sarrah Edmundston, Aug. 14, 1838. (Aug. 14, 1838). Jas. Maynor, BM.
Garland Adams to Elizabeth Cook, Aug. 11, 1838. (Aug. 16, 1838). Wm. McFarlen, BM.
Wm. J. Davidson to Dorraty Bobbitt, Aug. 30, 1838. (Aug. 30, 1838). H. M. L. Barton, BM.
Samuel Houghs to Nancy Gleason, Aug. 19, 1838. (Aug. 19, 1838). Charles Crue, BM.
Nicholas W. Cabler to Tibetha C. Harper, Aug. 22, 1838. Joel G. Lemmons, BM.
Edmund V. Tucker to Elizabeth A. Horskins, Aug. 20, 1838. Alex Baber, BM.
Isral C. Moore to Nancy A. Burkhart, Aug. 1, 1838. Wm. Gee, BM.
Allen L. Woods to Polly Adair, Aug. 8, 1838. J. W. C. Mitchell, BM.

29

GIBSON COUNTY MARRIAGES

Thos. J. Baysinger to Merris Horn, Sept. 8, 1838.
(Sept. 9, 1838). Wm. A. Baysinger, BM.
H. L. M. Barton to Susan Bobbett, Sept. 15, 1838.
(Sept. 16, 1838). Silas H. McKay, BM.
Scarlet M. Glascock to Jane Trosper, Sept. 15, 1838.
(Sept. 16, 1838). Jno. Edmundson, BM.
James Sexton to Tennessee Mathews, Sept. 4, 1838.
(Sept. 4, 1838). Linsfield Sexton, BM.
Henry Long to Martha Pate, Sept. 8, 1838. (Sept. 11,
1838). B. A. Pate, BM.
Isaack Alexander to Sarah Word, Sept. 11, 1838. (Sept.
11, 1838). Dr. (?) Alexander, BM.
Wm. P. S. Fielder to Miss L. B. Williams, Sept. 13,
1838. (Sept. 13, 1838). David R. Mays, BM.
J. J. Fielder to Caron Ann Turpin, Sept. 1, 1838.
(Sept. 4, 1838). D. R. Mays, BM.
Andrew A. Carr to Everlina Rony, Sept. 12, 1838.
(Sept. 14, 1838). John N. Kerr, BM.
Edmund Holland to Hawkins Hall, Sept. 17, 1838. Wm.
Mobly, BM.
William McFarland to Lucinda Jacobs, Sept. 18, 1838.
Thornton McFarland, BM.
Wm. D. Fly to Sarah L. Lite, Oct. 30, 1838. (Nov. 1,
1838). Green Williams, BM.
Merradett Alvis to Mary Bradford, Oct. 1, 1838. (Oct.
3, 1838). Thos. S. Alvis, BM.
Preston Holland to Sarah H. Cole, Oct. 1, 1838. (Oct.
2, 1838). John Lynch, BM.
Numan Haynes to Susanah Jones, Oct. 10, 1838. (Oct.
10, 1838).
Wm. E. Tinkle to Willie S. Harvy, Oct. 1, 1838. (Oct.
2, 1838). James P. Grier, BM.
Franklin Wood to Mary Ann McKee, Oct. 10, 1838. (Oct.
15, 1838).
William Gibson to Sarah Edmundson, Oct. 20, 1838.
(Oct. 21, 1838). Arthur Smith, BM.
Jeremiah Webb to Peggy Stafford, Oct. 31, 1838. (Nov.
3, 1838). Josh Harris, BM.
John W. Davidson to Frances Montgomery, Oct. 18, 1838.
(Oct. 18, 1838). L. J. Wilkins, BM.
Jackson Fox to Dilly Morris, Oct. 27, 1838. Allen
Fox, BM.
Richard Robertson to Sarah Griffin, Nov. 24, 1838.
(Nov. 25, 1838). V. N. Allen, BM.
Daniel H. Barns to Louisa J. Akins, Nov. 29, 1838.
(Dec. 6, 1838). Jas. McKelvy, BM.
Leroy H. Bell to Martha Glascock, Nov. 12, 1838. (Nov.
12, 1838). S. M. Glascock, BM.
Willis Joslin to Mary Dorset, Nov. 8, 1838. (Nov. 8,
1838). Daniel Conlee, BM.
Wilson D. Hunt to Jamima E. Durley, Nov. 14, 1838.
(Nov. 16, 1838). Alexander Lyons, BM.
Wm. C. Robertson to Eliza J. Montgomery, Nov. 28, 1838.
S. D. Givens, BM.

GIBSON COUNTY MARRIAGES

Joshua Donaldson to Emela Jackson, Dec. 19, 1838. (Dec. 20, 1838). Saml. Shepard and John Overall, BM.

Eli Howard to Centha Ann Melton, Dec. 14, 1838. (Dec. 20, 1838).

Aaron Sherron to Elizabeth Hailey, Dec. 3, 1838. (Dec. 4, 1838). I. Thomas, BM.

Aaron Branch to Catherine Harrison, Dec. 5, 1838. (Dec. 6, 1838). Joseph Massay, BM.

Ephram Thompson to Elizabeth Brown, Dec. 4, 1838. (Dec. 4, 1838). Daniel Gouger, BM.

Parson M. Sherman to Rebecca J. Alsabrooks, Dec. 18, 1838. (Dec. 18, 1838). W. H. Serape, BM.

Samuel Hodge to Margaret J. Allison, Dec. 18, 1838. (Dec. 18, 1838). M. Woodfin, BM.

Jas. H. Sheron to Emely Webb, Dec. 7, 1838. (Dec. 11, 1838). Samuel Goodman, BM.

William Price to Maria Hess, Dec. 31, 1838. (Jan. 2, 1839). John C. Gillespie, BM.

Wm. A. Lemmons to Juliana Craige, Dec. 24, 1838. James A. Moore, BM.

Arther Barns to Frances Shern, Dec. 18, 1838. (Dec. 20, 1838). James Wilson, BM.

Humphrey Curtis to Elizabeth Grice, Dec. 26, 1838. (Dec. 26, 1838).

Robert B. Davidson to Mary Hendricks, Dec. 24, 1838. Henderson Montgomery, BM.

Green Williams to Nancy A. Philips, Jan 1, 1839. (Jan. 3, 1839). W. P. Williams, BM.

Robert Edmundson to Nancy Edmundson, Jan. 11, 1839. (Jan. 14, 1839). John Edmundson, BM.

V. H. Bell to Fanny Carter, Jan. 23, 1839. (Jan. 24, 1839). Volentine Bell, BM.

William A. Estes to Cintha W. Bridges, Jan. 23, 1839. (Jan. 24, 1839). Jno. W. Meek, BM.

Vinson R. Allen to Nancy R. Robertson, Jan. 29, 1839. (Jan. 31, 1839). Josiah Allen, BM.

Andrew J. Hodges to Martha Morphus, Jan. 23, 1839. (Jan. 23, 1839). James Cunningham, BM.

John Rackley to Elizabeth Guess, Jan. 3, 1839. (Jan. 3, 1839). Wm. Rains, BM.

Robert P. Edmundston to Delila Short, Jan. 7, 1839. (Jan 13, 1839). R. Edmondston, BM.

John W. Avery to Margaret Hicks, Jan. 8, 1839. John Babb, BM.

James G. Carter to Hulda E. Mayfield, Jan. 12, 1839. (Jan. 15, 1839). John L. Davis, BM.

George Himbrough to Rebecka E. Crockett, Feb. 25, 1839. (Feb. 26, 1839). N. J. Hess, BM.

Samuel Craige to Carroline Alvis, Feb. 16, 1839. (Feb. 16, 1839). John Lynch, BM.

Ruffin Yates to Harriett Word, Feb. 27, 1839. (Feb. 28, 1839). Thos. Traynor, BM.

John Smith to Sarah Bartlett, Mar. 20, 1839. (Mar. 20, 1839). Henry Kinsey, BM.

GIBSON COUNTY MARRIAGES

Daniel R. Hendrick to Sarah Fields, Mar. 29, 1839.
(Apr. 2, 1839).
Joseph Sharp to Jurasha Taylor, Mar. 6, 1839. (Mar.
7, 1839). John Claybrook, BM.
John B. Hogg to Berlinda Turner, Mar. 28, 1839. (Mar.
28, 1839). Henry C. Levy, BM.
William Patterson to Mary Sexton, Mar. 13, 1839. (Mar.
14, 1839). Hosa Parker, BM.
Gilbert Boon to Nancy L. Hatchett, Mar. 29, 1839.
(Apr. 4, 1839). A. Lyons, BM.
Hardy Fowler to Sarah Dockings, Mar. 15, 1839. (Mar.
20, 1839). Noel E. West, BM.
James Thompson to Letha Campbell, Mar. 22, 1839. (Mar.
22, 1839). Robt. Warran, BM.
Daniel R. Hendrick to Sarah Fields, Mar. 29, 1839. Wm.
R. Hendrick, BM.
Thos. Johnston to Martha Pope, Apr. 9, 1839. (Apr. 11,
1839). Caleb Howell, BM.
Rubin Pirce to Susan Volentine, Apr. 15, 1839. (Apr.
17, 1839). Zachariah Mobley, BM.
George W. Crockett to Elizabeth Wilks, Apr. 15, 1839.
(Apr. 16, 1839). E. W. Cross, BM.
Ezechal Armstrong to Margarett Armfield, Apr. 19, 1839.
(Apr. 21, 1839). John Ford, BM.
Hugh Y. Bone to Martha Jane Robb, Apr. 25, 1839. B. E.
Holms, BM.
James B. Blakemore to Catharine Rucker, May 30, 1839.
(May 30, 1839). Hosa Parker, BM.
William Warran to Elizabeth C. Keathley, May 11, 1839.
(May 15, 1839). Robt. Warran, BM.
Jackson Brown to Lyda Ann Bunnell, May 20, 1839. Benj.
Myers, BM.
Orvill Conlee to July A. Richardson, May 29, 1839.
Surgner Atchison, BM.
Albert G. Love to Mira Jordan, June 24, 1839. (July 3,
1839). T. W. Jordan, BM.
Caleb Howell to Ann M. Hobbs, June 24, 1839. (June 27,
1839). Sidney J. Porter, BM.
William Bailey to Hollan Patrick, June 3, 1839. (June
13, 1839). Thos. N. Bowers, BM.
James E. Vickers to Sarah Carroll, June 10, 1839.
(June 10, 1839). Joel Morris, BM.
Milton Ray to Pheby Furgarson, July 26, 1839. (June
26, 1839). Josiah T. Morton, BM.
Alex C. Ridgway to Elizabeth Serratt, June 17, 1839.
Washington Serratt, BM.
P. P. Patterson to Hannah M. Britenham, July 30, 1839.
(July 30, 1839). P. P. Eliott, BM.
William Harron (Herron, Horron) to Sarah C. Hubbard,
July 24, 1839. (July 24, 1839). Hiram Partee, BM.
Eli Tilghman to Nancy Crain, July 20, 1839. (July 23,
1839). Allfred Warrin, BM.
John B. Crafton to Elizabeth Haguewood, July 23, 1839.
(July 25, 1839). Hardy Harrison, BM.

H. T. Burnam to Rebecca A. Page, July 22, 1839. (July 25, 1839).

Alvadas Hill to Mary Bowlen, Aug. 13, 1839. (Aug 13, 1839). W. Dickins, BM.

Isah Holland to Eliza Flowers, Aug. 27, 1839. (Aug. 27, 1839). Wiley Melton, BM.

James N. Higgins to Emeline Wilkins, Aug. 2, 1839. (Aug. 4, 1839). M. M. Higgins, BM.

William H. Rains to Elizabeth Bledsoe, Aug. 20, 1839. (Aug. 22, 1839). Archd. C. Levy, BM.

Wm. Jones to Manurva Roberts, Aug. 13, 1839. (Aug. 22, 1839). E. Easterwood, BM.

Allen Reed to Frances M. Crider, Aug. 8, 1839. (Aug. 8, 1839). J. D. Rentfro, BM.

Allen L. Wood to Polly Adair, Aug. 8, 1839. (Aug. 8, 1839).

John McLeod to Ann McDougold, Aug. 20, 1839. G. W. Miller, BM.

Harvy Belew to Rachal Holcomb, Aug. 14, 1839. Geo. M. Whitlow, BM.

Charles H. Ross to Patience White, Aug. 11, 1839. Joseph McWhite, BM.

Robert Warrin to Sina Keathley, Sept. 11, 1839. (Sept. 12, 1839). William Warrin, BM.

Saml. D. Spate to Rebecca Richardson, Sept. 26, 1839. (Sept. 26, 1839). Drury Mays, BM.

Edmond W. Goodrich to Susan E. Harcey, Sept. 3, 1839. (Sept. 3, 1839). Jesse Lassiter, BM.

Wm. C. McClour to Sarah Ing, Sept. 15, 1839. (Sept. 19, 1839). Jas. M. Belleu, BM.

Wm. G. Bledsoe to Emeline Merritt, Sept. 18, 1839. (Sept. 18, 1839). Calvin A. Stanfield, BM.

George W. Terrill to Ann Bell, Sept. 5, 1839. (Sept. 5, 1839). James M. Terrill, BM.

Peter Sexton to Martha Woods, Sept. 12, 1839. (Sept. 12, 1839). W. D. Fields, BM.

Benjamin F. Terrell to Mary J. Davis, Oct. 31, 1839. (Oct. 31, 1839). D. I. Rogers, BM.

George O. Richmon to Martha H. Morton, Oct. 28, 1839. (Oct. 29, 1839). Jordan Jackson, BM.

Franklin Barrott to Sarah Massee, Oct. 3, 1839. (Oct. 3, 1839). A. C. Nimmo, BM.

John Wolard to Peney Pope, Oct. 30, 1839. (Oct. 31, 1839). Whery Wolard, BM.

Thomas C. Jordian to Martha Ann Williams, Oct. 16, 1839. (Oct. 17, 1839). A. J. Williams, BM.

Henry Duffy to Margaret Latty, Oct. 22, 1839. (Oct. 24, 1839). A. A. P. Grigsby, BM.

Charles Forrester to Kizza Sellers, Oct. 23, 1839. (Oct. 23, 1839). John Sellers, BM.

Alfred Stewart to Join Goff, Oct. 7, 1839. L. P. Seay, BM.

John Richardson to Sarah Mathews, Nov. 21, 1839. (Nov. 21, 1839). James McBride, BM.

E. W. Hale to Martha Jordian, Nov. 23, 1839. (Nov. 28, 1839). Wm. P. Kelton, BM.

Samuel Oneal to Mary Greggory, Nov. 4, 1839. (Jan. 1, 1840). J. W. Northern, BM.

Jessee Flowers to Dibby E. Robertson, Nov. 19, 1839. (Nov. 29, 1839). Martin Halliburton, BM.

Turner R. Gibbs to Nancy Borran, Nov. 30, 1839. (Dec. 1, 1839). B. Baker, BM.

Michal McNutty to Angaline E. Davis, Dec. 23, 1839. (Dec. 24, 1839). S. S. Paul, BM.

John Knox to Ellen Bell, Dec. 4, 1839. (Dec. 5, 1839). Absolem Knox, BM.

Calvin C. Clemment to Mary E. Hamilton, Dec. 9, 1839. (Dec. 10, 1839). Thos. J. Fite, BM.

Elleson Howard to Jane Hawkins, Dec. 25, 1839. (Dec. 25, 1839). Stephen P. Childress, BM.

Tucker Hutchens to Sarah Stan, Dec. 12, 1839. (Dec. 22, 1839). Wilson Jarvis, BM.

Wm. B. Howard to America Hayns, Dec. 27, 1839. (Dec. 29, 1839). L. P. Seay, BM.

Needham Holland to Ann E. Donaldson, Dec. 7, 1839. (Dec. 19, 1839). M. T. McCulloch, BM.

Samuel Aslin to Mary A. Barham, Dec. 19, 1839. (Dec. 19, 1839). F. G. Goodman, BM.

Madison Conlee to Sarah Rigsly, Dec. 9, 1839. (Dec. 11, 1839). Jas. Rigsley, BM.

Hugh S. Stone to Mary Ann Nuckles, ? 14, 1839. Miles T. McCulloch, BM.

Robert W. Barton to Harratt E. Davidson, Dec. 5, 1839. M. T. McCulloch, BM.

George D. Stone to Anney Jones, Jan. 6, 1840. (Jan. 8, 1840). L. D. Mathews, BM.

Stephen P. Childress to Mary J. Howard, Jan. 8, 1840. (Jan. 9, 1840). Jas. P. Duggan, BM.

Zachariah Bryant to Elizabeth A. Floyd, Jan. 8, 1840. (Jan. 9, 1840). Marmaduke Gammon, BM.

Archibald C. Levey to Christina Jane Overall, Jan. 9, 1840. (Jan. 9, 1840). A. W. Totten and Wm. C. Fite, BM.

Wm. R. Wallis to Penny E. Wollard, Jan. 17, 1840. (Jan. 17, 1840). Ruffin Yates, BM.

Willis Spear to Sarah McMinn, Jan. 18, 1840. (Apr. 30, 1840). Wm. H. Jones, BM.

John Smith to Awella D. Hill, Jan. 22, 1840. (Jan. 23, 1840). Allen Hill, BM.

Burrell Gossett to Evalina M. Roundtree, Jan. 28, 1840. Wm. T. Roundtree, BM.

Miles L. Davidson to Dicy Pate, Jan. 30, 1840. Alfred F. Davidson, BM.

Samuel L. Lorance to Mary M. C. Reed, Jan. 30, 1840. (Feb. 2, 1840). Chas. S. McLain, BM.

Wm. R. Sawyer to Mary Gibson, Jan. 27, 1840. M. H. Sawyer, BM.

William P. Tate to Sophia Kelly, Feb. 7, 1840. (July 30, 1840). B. F. Meddleton, BM.

Francis L. Conner to Hannah M. Martin, Feb. 10, 1840. (Feb. 13, 1840). N. J. Hess, BM.

GIBSON COUNTY MARRIAGES

Lemuel Love to Mary A. Thomas, Feb. 26, 1840. (Feb. 27, 1840). S. R. Tucker, BM.
Moses E. Senter to Margaret J. Elam, Feb. 10, 1840. Jno. G. Atchison, BM.
James McCollum to Charlott Brooton, Feb. 11, 1840. Wilson Worthy, BM.
Isaac Fowler to Sabra Cooper, Mar. 17, 1840. (Mar. 17, 1840). Jas. D. Harrison, BM.
George W. Tinkle to Elizabeth Ann Hall, Mar. 18, 1840. (Mar. 19, 1840). Robert Terrell, BM.
David Gardner to Martha A. Thomason, Apr. 8, 1840. (Apr. 8, 1840). Thos. J. Fite, BM.
Charles W. Smith to Mary Kenady, Apr. 10, 1840. (Apr. 12, 1840). Jno. Ronalds, BM.
Abner D. Thomas to Nancy Bean, Apr. 15, 1840. (Apr. 16, 1840). Benj. J. Holmes, BM.
Samuel Kellough to Elizabeth P. Allison, Apr. 16, 1840. (Apr. 16, 1840). Andrew Allison, BM.
Semion E. Buford to Mary Ann Fields, Apr. 20, 1840. (Apr. 22, 1840). Saml. D. Givens, BM.
Wesley B. Davis to Louisa Frost, Apr. 30, 1840. Calvin Webb, BM.
Burwell Warmack to Avy Cook, May 9, 1840. (May 12, 1840). E. G. B. Cook, BM.
Edwin Warren to Mary Blankenship, May 9, 1840. (May 14, 1840). Carroll Duncan, BM.
John N. Bell to Elizabeth M. Serratt, May 14, 1840. (May 14, 1840). Wesley Bell, BM.
William P. Jacob to Margrett D. Little, May 27, 1840. (June 25, 1840). William Cole, BM.
Archalus Keathly to Sarrah Branch, May 28, 1840. (May 31, 1840). Jessee Caraway, BM.
Wilson Barrett to Susan Robertson, June 4, 1840. (June 4, 1840). M. T. McCulloch, BM.
Beverly Cannon to Nancy Pendergrass, June 22, 1840. (June 23, 1840). Green Chandler, BM.
Nasibet Petit to Sarah Jones, June 27, 1840. (June 28, 1840). Isaac Ward, BM.
Irvin Gibson to Martha Lewis, June 17, 1840. Pete M. White, BM.
Michael H. Hicks to Elizabeth J. Fields, June 16, 1840. (June 16, 1841). Wm. C. Hicks, BM.
Eno Real Madaras to Elizabeth Goodman, July 2, 1840. (July 2, 1840). S. S. Paul, BM.
Neilson J. Hess to Catharine H. Hill, July 2, 1840. (July 2, 1840). James M. Moore, BM.
John Williamson to Mary Morris, July 20, 1840. (July 23, 1840). Wm. C. Hicks, BM.
William H. Rogers to Mary A. Wilson, July 25, 1840. (July 30, 1840). Benj. E. Holmes, BM.
Robert Melton to Penelope Pate, July 30, 1840. (Aug. 30, 1840). Spencer G. Barton, BM.
William Freeman to Sarah Word, July 30, 1840. (July 30, 1840). Timothy H. Word, BM.

GIBSON COUNTY MARRIAGES

Philip Flinn to Cloa Hillard, July 30, 1840. (July
    30, 1840). Jas. Penny, BM.
Jno. H. Dinwiddy to Francis M. Bobbett, July 1, 1840.
    Henry Bobbett, BM.
William H. Morris to Mary Baird, Aug. 6, 1840. (Aug.
    13, 1840). John W. Elder, BM.
Jethro Howell to Elizabeth Needham, Aug. 17, 1840.
    (Aug. 18, 1840). Michael Flowers, BM.
G. D. Stone to Mary Bratton, Sept. 23, 1840. (Sept.
    24, 1840). George Shane, BM.
Rhodham Martin to Jane Hix, Sept. 28, 1840. (Sept.
    30, 1840). S. S. Paul, BM. (Note: R. Martin will
    be 80 years old in May, 1841; his wife, 41.)
A. J. Williams to Mary Jane Seat, Sept. 29, 1840.
    (Oct. 1, 1840). Henry D. Harper, BM.
Wm. C. Robertson to Martha A. Cooper, Oct. 28, 1840.
    (Oct. 29, 1840). Benj. E. Holmes, BM.
Andrew Grave to Nancy Duffee, Oct. 30, 1940. (Nov.
    5, 1840). P. M. Duffee, BM.
Green Hall (Hill) to Eliza Jane Blankenship, Oct. 30,
    1840. (Nov. 4, 1840). Jas. Blankenship, BM.
David S. Phelan to Selay A. Hart, Oct. 5, 1840. (Oct.
    5, 1840). J. Harte, BM.
Zachariah Biggs to Elizabeth Perteat, Oct. 31, 1840.
    (Nov. 1, 1840). David Simons, BM.
Benjamin Holmes to Margaret E. Bone, Nov. 4, 1840.
    (Nov. 5, 1840). James P. Grier, BM.
Howell Little to Mary E. Butler, Nov. 12, 1840. (Nov.
    12, 1840). Wm. Butler, BM.
J. B. Hinsen to Lucretia A. Webb. (Nov. 17, 1840).
    Wm. Fite, BM.
Cornelas Woolard to Sarah Bradley, Nov. 19, 1840.
    (Nov. 22, 1840). Riley Wallice, BM.
William Mobley to Hawkins Bledsoe, Nov. 12, 1840.
    Wm. Furgarson, BM.
Larkin L. Moore to Charlott Palmore, Nov. 17, 1840.
    Jas. Rochelle and Jas A. Rochelle, BM.
Allen Parr to Martha Jones, Dec. 8, 1840. (Dec. 8, 1840).
    Henry A. Wood, BM.
Joseph W. Halford to Elizabeth M. Smally, Dec. 19,
    1840. (Dec. 23, 1840). Allen Edmondson, BM.
Thos. A. Flippin to Hanah Belew, Dec. 20, 1840. (Dec.
    20, 1840). J. T. Flippin, BM.
Zachariah Shaw to Cassandra Bowman, Dec. 21, 1840.
    (Dec. 22, 1840). A. Davis, BM.
William Lane to Isabella Baley, Dec. 21, 1840. (Dec.
    22, 1840). Richard Dickins, BM.
James Cannon to Mary Taylor, Dec. 22, 1840. (Dec. 22,
    1840). Henry Parker, BM.
Charles P. McLean to Mariah J. Mathis, Dec. 24, 1840.
    (Dec. 24, 1840). Sion Boon, BM.
Alexander Cook to Eliza Ann Witt, Dec. 24, 1840. (Dec.
    26, 1840). Richard Dickins, BM.
John Curtis to Mary J. Howard, Dec. 24, 1840. (Dec.
    24, 1840). Edward Curtis, BM.

GIBSON COUNTY MARRIAGES

James T. Wade to Frances A. Wade, Dec. 24, 1840. (Dec. 24, 1840). I. B. Gilchrist, BM.
Jefferson Robertson to Elizabeth Trout, Dec. 28, 1840. (Dec. 31, 1841). J. M. Terrill, BM.
William Fuqua to Martha E. Dean, Dec. 29, 1840. (Dec. 31, 1840). Clement F. Fuqua, BM.
Hugh Vanhog to Elvy Fletcher, Dec. 31, 1840. (Dec. 31, 1840). Jonah Fletcher, BM.
Robert Clark to Jane Crockett, Dec. 26, 1840. (Dec. 29, 1840). S. S. Paul.
Mathew Quinn to Martha York, Jan. 2, 1841. E. C. Dougherty, BM.
Samuel Neely to Mary E. J. White, Jan. 2, 1841. (Jan. 7. 1841). Edw. H. White, BM.
William B. Harpole to Mary Ann Lindsly, Jan. 2, 1841. (Jan. 7, 1841). Cooper B. Jones, BM.
John C. Simms to Matilda Montgomery, Jan. 4, 1841. Erastus White, BM.
James B. Worden to Jamima Nobles, Jan. 4, 1841. (Jan. 7, 1841). David Simmons, BM.
Lemual W. Hollan to Carroline Pettus, Jan 11, 1841. (Jan. 14, 1841). James P. Grier, BM. (at the home of Sam K. Pettus)
John M. Reeves to Charlott Ballance, Jan. 15, 1841. (Jan. 17, 1841). F. H. Emerson, BM.
John F. Sinclear to Isabella R. Dunwoody, Jan. 21, 1841. (Jan. 21, 1841). Wm. J. Donaldson, BM.
George W. Wallingsford to Elizabeth H. Stone, Jan. 23, 1841. (Jan. 24, 1841). Green Jacobs, BM.
Dr. U. Alexander to Elizabeth J. Lavis, Jan. 27, 1841. (Jan. 27, 1841). Abner Ewing, BM.
John H. Fisher to May Grigory, Jan. 27, 1841. Thos. H. Fisher, BM.
James W. Gardner to Jane Holt, Feb. 2, 1841. (Mar. 1, 1841). Alvin Senter, BM.
John Hail to Emeline J. Hail, Feb. 4, 1841. (Feb. 7, 1841). Asher Flowers, BM.
Felise G. Whetty to Carline M. Goff, Feb. 6, 1841. (Feb. 10, 1841). G. B. Boling, BM.
Elisha Bilch to Mary A. E. Word, Feb. 9, 1841. (Feb. 9, 1841). Isaac Word, BM.
Henderson Baker to Willey Jones, Feb. 15, 1841. (Feb. 18, 1841). E. G. Wood, BM.
Ferney G. Driskell to Ann E. Mayfield, Feb. 16, 1841. (Mar. 1, 1841). A. B. Mayfield, BM.
Joshua Bledsoe to Eliza Craige, Feb. 24, 1841. A. Butram, BM.
Thos. C. Taylor to Celina Phillips, Feb. 25, 1841. (Feb. 25, 1841). Wm. C. Hicks, BM.
Martin B. Jones to Kissiah C. Sloan, Feb. 25, 1841. (Feb. 26, 1841). Wm. B. Jones, BM.
Jerrimiah H. Dill to Anney Roach, Feb. 28, 1841. (Feb. 28, 1841). Z. N. Dill, BM.
John E. Halford to Rebecca M. Rigsby, Mar. 1, 1841. (Mar. 9, 1841). Martin Halliburton, BM.

Aaron Belew to Jane Belew, Mar. 6, 1841. (Mar. 9, 1841). James M. Belew, BM.

Thos. W. Jordian to Idortha S. A. Seat, Mar. 8, 1841. (Mar. 11, 1841). A. J. Williams, BM.

John C. Shavour to Sabra Madison, Mar. 17, 1841. (Mar. 17, 1841). Joel Morris, BM.

Berry Cantrel to Mahaly Runalds, Mar. 20, 1841. (Mar. 28, 1841).

Vollentine Bell to Matilda T. McCall, Mar. 20, 1841. (Mar. 21, 1841). Wesley Bell, BM.

G. B. Mosely to Sarah J. Flowers, Mar. 21, 1841. (Mar. 28, 1841). J. E. Mosely, BM.

James A. Carroll to Nancy Kensey, Mar. 21, 1841. (Mar. 21, 1841). R. L. Smith, BM.

Joseph Mathis to Ellender Fowler, Mar. 22, 1841. (Mar. 30, 1841). D. Mathis, BM.

Isaac Rogers to Elsey Cook, Mary 22, 1841. Wm. Atchison, BM.

Philip Dozer to Lener Doxey, Mar. 31, 1841. (Apr. 1, 1841). A. Pursell, BM.

Thos. Coley to Ann M. Stokes, Mar. 31, 1841. (Apr. 1, 1841). H. D. Harper, BM.

Ivy S. Alfin to Eliza Kenady, Apr. 1, 1841. (Apr. 8, 1841). Thos. C. D. Howell, BM.

John Evans to Rebecca Puckett, Apr. 1, 1841. (Apr. 1, 1841). Dr. V. Alexander, BM.

John A. Rigsly to Lee Ann Webb, Apr. 2, 1841. (Apr. 6, 1841). John Hayes, BM.

James N. Watt to Elizabeth Lyon, Apr. 3, 1841. (Apr. 4, 1841). N. T. Neavill, BM.

Lebanon D. Mathis to Margarette Scott, Apr. 18, 1841. (Apr. 18, 1841). Wm. Bell, BM.

Robert Howell to Tempy Flowers, Apr. 21, 1841. (May 13, 1841). Sidney J. Porter, BM.

Thos. Yarbery to Elizabeth Rentfro, Apr. 22, 1841. (Apr. 22, 1841). Jas. D. Rentfro, BM.

William Williams to Nancy Joiner, May 5, 1841. (May 6, 1841). Richard Joiner, BM.

John Etheridge to Mary West, June 1, 1841. (June 3, 1841). Jesse Jolliff, BM.

Henry T. Burnam to Ann H. Turner, June 3, 1841. (June 9, 1841). R. P. Rains, BM.

Peter Claybrooks to Mrs. Rebecca Estes, June 7, 1841. (June 10, 1841). John Claybrooks, BM.

Alfred Ray to Adaline Armstrong, June 9, 1841. W. H. Serape, BM.

John A. Harpole to Elviry Jackson, June 23, 1841. (June 29, 1841). B. G. Holder, BM.

Andrew J. Klyce to Mary E. Hammon, June 24, 1841. (June 24, 1841). Thos. W. Jones, BM.

Willis H. Lane to Susan Thomas, June 29, 1841. (June 29, 1841). Martin Halliburton, BM.

James J. Logan to Nancy P. Bell, July 3, 1841. (July 3, 1841). John H. Pole, BM.

Benj. C. Fewell to Thvizah Merritt, July 12, 1841. (July 13, 1841). N. J. Hockaday, BM.

R. W. Mitchell to Nancy Jane Grier, July 22, 1841.
(July 29, 1841). Wm. S. Wyatt, BM.
Daniel E. Jetton to Jestina Yates, July 22, 1841.
(July 22, 1841). M. T. McCullough, BM.
William Haily to Mahaley Rushin, July 26, 1841. (July
29, 1841). Bennet Gooch, BM.
A. C. Penn to Lavina Kelton. M. T. McCulloch, BM.
Anderson Gibson to Elizabeth Rodgers, July 30, 1841.
(Aug. 3, 1841). Carson Patterson, BM.
Bennet Gooch to Polley Ann Brogden, Aug. 5, 1841.
(Aug. 5, 1841). W. H. Hailey, BM.
Solomon Walls to Eliza J. Barns, Aug. 5, 1841. (Aug.
6, 1841). T. B. Crider, BM.
William Lane to Cyntha P. Sales, Aug. 13, 1841. (Aug.
26, 1841). S. J. Porter, BM.
Robert Atchison to Moley J. Higgins, Aug. 18, 1841.
John G. Atchison, BM.
Robert Trosper to Elizabeth Short, Aug. 19, 1841. (Aug.
22, 1841). Wm. Edmondson, BM.
Wm. Tinsley to Sarah P. Harpole, Aug. 21, 1841. (Aug.
30, 1841). Jesse L. Branch, BM.
Freeman Cross to Martha Baley, Aug. 24, 1841. (Aug. 24,
1841). Elisha Rogers, BM.
James Lewis to Edney Reasons, Aug. 31, 1841. Alfred
Connley, BM.
Gray Barker to Celey Barker, Sept. 1, 1841. (Sept. 2,
1841). Jordian Jackson, BM.
Hosey Holcomb to Mary Brooten, Sept. 4, 1841. Caleb
Walker, BM.
Barnet Furgarson to Mariah Orms, Sept. 12, 1841.
(Sept. 13, 1841). John Randle, BM.
William H. Holmes to Mary Jane Thomas, Sept. 14, 1841.
(Sept. 14, 1841). T. Cooper, BM.
David Arnold to Siney Walker, Aug. 10, 1841. (Aug. 10,
1841). James Arnold, BM.
A. J. Roycroft to Margaret Reed, Sept. 21, 1841. (Sept.
21, 1841). P. A. Doolin, BM.
Isaac Spencer to Mrs. Susan Flowers, Sept. 21, 1841.
(Sept. 26, 1841). M. L. Davidson, BM.
H. H. Word to Anne M. Rains, Sept. 23, 1841. (Sept.
23, 1841). R. H. Harvy, BM.
Alfred A. Thomas to Manervia S. Murphy, Sept. 29, 1841.
(Sept. 29, 1841). Charles W. Murphy, BM.
Richard Madison to Sarah Chavers, Sept. 30, 1841.
(Sept. 30, 1841). S. P. Dill, BM.
Robert L. Smith to Elizabeth Carroll, Sept. 4, 1841.
(Sept. 4, 1841). T. W. Smith, BM.
Joseph Elam to Catherine Jones, Oct. 6, 1841. Joseph
H. Jones, BM.
Owen West to Jane McClur, Oct. 12, 1841. Ollin West, BM.
William C. Fite to Sarah A. F. Hogg, Oct. 14, 1841.
(Oct. 14, 1841). Henry C. Levy, BM.
William Riley to Mary Orms, Oct. 14, 1841. (Oct. 14,
1841). John D. Agee, BM.

Robert P. Crockett to Matilda Porter, Oct. 16, 1841.
(Oct. 21, 1841). Benjamin F. Burgan, BM.
Rubin Fuel to Martha Johnston, Oct. 20, 1841. (Oct.
20, 1841). Drury Price, BM.
Richard Hall to Rutha Hopkins, Oct. 21, 1841. (Oct.
21, 1841). Wyatt Bass, BM.
Martin Halliburton to Edney Flowers, Oct. 23, 1841.
(Oct. 26, 1841). Michael Flowers, BM.
Smith Park to Juliza F. A. Miller, Oct. 26, 1841.
(Oct. 26, 1841). J. A. Miller, BM.
Saml. D. Speake to Lucy D. Richardson, Oct. 27, 1841.
(Oct. 27, 1841). J. W. N. Mays, BM.
James W. Tucker to Sarah S. McCallester, Nov. 1, 1841.
Patrick Waister, BM.
Solomon Reed to Delila F. English, Nov. 10, 1841.
(Nov. 10, 1841). T. B. Crider, BM.
John Williams to Parmela Armstrong, Nov. 10, 1841.
(Nov. 11, 1841). Hiram Hall, BM.
George Shane to Martha A. T. Arnold, Nov. 16, 1841.
(Dec. 6, 1841). James Lyon, BM.
Wm. Thedford to Nany Fox, Nov. 16, 1841. John Carroll, BM.
Massalon Whitten to Mary Ann E. M. Miller, Nov. 11,
1841. (Nov. 11, 1841). Jno. A. Miller, BM.
John W. Foster to Matilda Fletcher, Nov. 22, 1841.
(Nov. 23, 1841). Thos. H. Foster, BM.
James M. Terry to Mary A. R. Stone, Nov. 26, 1841.
(Dec. 7, 1841). Wm. Johnson, BM.
Thomas Flowers to Catherine Graddy, Nov. 29, 1841.
(Nov. 30, 1841). Michael Flowers, BM.
James A. Thomas to Malinda Porter, Nov. 29, 1841.
(Nov. 30, 1841). Michael Flowers, BM.
Joseph Jones to Jamima Beard, Dec. 6, 1841. Granville
Haynes, BM.
Samuel R. Fuquea to Mary Lemmons, Dec. 6, 1841. (Dec.
9, 1841). Isaac Lemmons, BM.
Robert Madison to Elizabeth Holder, Dec. 10, 1841.
(Dec. 16, 1841). Hinton Miles, BM.
Mark Selph to Ann M. Hays, Dec. 16, 1841. (Dec. 16,
1841). A. W. Bledsoe, BM.
James O. Phillips to Allee M. Edmundson, Dec. 20, 1841.
(Dec. 21, 1841). B. F. Burgan, J. P., BM.
Daniel Sepune to Nancy M. Vaughn, Dec. 20, 1841. S. C.
Hughs, BM.
William S. Wyatt to Lucy Hale, Dec. 22, 1841. (Dec. 23,
1841). Thos. H. Fisher, BM.
Jessee Tyner to Frances Watson, Dec. 22, 1841. (Dec.
23, 1841). Wm. O. Davidson, BM.
Green R. Manley to Nancy S. Crafford, Dec. 23, 1841.
(Dec. 23, 1841).
M. T. McCulloch to Sarah C. Carthal, Dec. 23, 1841.
(Dec. 23, 1841). John L. Davis, BM.
Andrew Udaley to Jane Rogers, Dec. 23, 1841. (Dec.
23, 1841). Wm. B. Davis.
Spencer G. Barton to Mildred Ward, Dec. 23, 1841.
(Dec. 23, 1841). J. H. Benett, BM.

GIBSON COUNTY MARRIAGES

Michael Flowers to Zady M. Mitchel, Dec. 27, 1841.
(Dec. 28, 1841). L. P. Seay, BM.
Thomas Corley to Mary Flowers, Dec. 27, 1841. (Jan.
4, 1842). Leoma Flowers, Jr., BM.
John Dill to Carroline Malone, Dec. 28, 1841. (Dec.
29, 1841). Larry Dill, BM.
James E. McGehee to Martha Kelly, Dec. 29, 1841. By
M. Wallis, J. P. Watson Pridy, BM.
William A. Basinger to Nancy J. Fields, Jan. 3, 1842.
(Jan. 7, 1842).
Joel G. Lemmons to Margaret M. Adams, Jan. 5, 1842.
(Jan. 5, 1842). Wm. H. Craig, BM.
Thomas C. Mitchell to Rebecca Killingsworth, Jan. 11,
1842. (Jan. 11, 1842).
Aaron Jackson to Emeline Motley, Jan. 13, 1842. (Jan.
13, 1842). Levi R. Bradford, BM.
John P. Anderson to Jane Gregory, Jan. 13, 1842. (Jan.
15, 1842). Wm. H. Witt, BM.
Archabald Canady to Eliza Pope, Jan. 14, 1842. (Jan.
20, 1842). George Canady, BM.
John H. Poll to Margaret Hassell, Jan. 18, 1842.
(Jan. 18, 1842). L. B. Gilchrist, BM.
William Fortune to Elizabeth A. F. Gill, Jan. 25, 1842.
Wm. Edmundson, BM.
Jacob T. Grier to Elizabeth H. Wyatt, Jan. 26, 1842.
(Jan. 27, 1842). James Bobbett, BM.
James Vincent to Gletha Smith, Jan. 27, 1842. (Jan.
28, 1842).
Milford Gage to Martha Cooper, Jan. 27, 1842. (Jan.
27, 1842). John Wallis, BM.
Henry J. Simons to Margaret W. Bradley, Feb. 5, 1842.
(Feb. 23, 1842). W. B. Womack, BM.
Nathanial Williams to Hannah Robertson, Feb. 8, 1842.
(Feb. 10, 1842).
Peter Glascock to Carroline Butler, Feb. 12, 1842.
(Feb. 15, 1842). J. A. Hayes, BM.
Joseph T. Flippin to Elizabeth Hancock, Feb. 12, 1842.
(Feb. 17, 1842). Jno. W. White, BM.
Spincer Bradford to Eliza Summons, Feb. 14, 1842.
Henry King, BM.
John B. Patton to Levinia E. Thompson, Feb. 22, 1842.
(Feb. 23, 1842). James Patton, BM.
James U. Hobbs to Utha Overman, Feb. 26, 1842. (Feb.
28, 1842). Caleb Howell, BM.
John H. Miller to Jane Phillips, Feb. 26, 1842. (Mar.
1, 1842). R. B. Love, BM.
William Walker to Martha Belew, Feb. 28, 1842. Mark
Jackson, BM.
Spencer M. A. G. W. Harris to Sarah M. Thedford, Feb.
28, 1842. Mar. 28, 1842). Francis Elliott, BM.
Lewis Smith to Portia H. Jones, Mar. 3, 1842. (Mar. 3,
1842). A. A. P. Grigsby, BM.
Scarlet M. Glascock to Nancy Long, Mar. 7, 1842.
(Mar. 10, 1842).

McKelva Bean to Martha A. T. Thompson, Mar. 14, 1842.
H. C. Trout, BM.
John A. Hays to Julian Miller, Mar. 16, 1842. (Mar.
17, 1842). Harrison Conlee, BM.
Henry King to Sarah W. Crafton, Mar. 19, 1842. (Mar.
24, 1842). Wm. W. Newhouse, BM.
William H. Gant to Keziah A. Durley, Mar. 22, 1842.
(Mar. 22, 1842). Leonard Taylor, BM.
Allen Edmundson to Sarah L. Halford, Apr. 4, 1842.
(Apr. 6, 1842).
Matt W. Flowers to Lucinda Young, Apr. 16, 1842. (Apr.
17, 1842). James A. Smith, BM.
William H. Woodson to Julia Bullington, Apr. 9, 1842.
Wm. Bullington, BM.
Algermon S. Currey to Martha A. Nimmo, Apr. 20, 1842.
(Apr. 21, 1842). A. W. Hunt, BM.
Samuel D. Givens to Susan A. Morton, May 5, 1842. (May
5, 1842).
Joshua Gaza to Elendar A. Phelan, May 5, 1842. (May
5, 1842). Harrison Conlee, BM.
John P. Henry to Mary Sharp, May 10, 1842. (May 11,
1842). L. B. Gilchrist, BM.
Thomas W. Smith to Sarah A. Borran, May 14, 1842. (May
15, 1842). R. L. Smith, BM.
David Simons to Mary Crockett, May 24, 1842. (May 24,
1842). Luke P. Seay, BM.
Benjamin F. Taylor to Margaret E. Frierson, June 8,
1842. (June 8, 1842). A. W. Hunt, BM.
Thomas C. Morgan to Love Oneal, June 11, 1842. H. F.
Reed, BM.
James Penney to Pheby Hailey, July 2, 1842. (July 3,
1842). Caleb Penny, BM.
Nehemiah Biggs to Gemima Ringold, July 8, 1842. (July
8, 1842). John Ringold, BM.
Pinkny Baker to Nancy McDurmit, July 12, 1842. (July
13, 1842). Jesse Cassell, BM.
Robert M. Strain to Mary A. Foster, July 13, 1842.
(July 14, 1842). John C. Foster, BM.
Turner Woodall to Rebecca Mathis, July 13, 1842.
(July 13, 1842). Richard Dickens, BM.
Henry Battle to Martha Dunlap, July 14, 1842. (July
14, 1842). Harmon Battle, BM.
Harrison Holt to Elizabeth A. Waltrop, July 14, 1842.
(July 17, 1842).
Hazekiah J. Davis to Rebecca J. Boyt, July 16, 1842.
(July 20, 1842).
John P. Tucker to Martha Boytt, July 19, 1842. (July
20, 1842).
Frances Perry to Nany Glidewell, July 23, 1842.
(July 26, 1842). Zebelum N. Dill, BM.
L. F. Bonfels to Mariah D. Whitlocke, July 26, 1842.
(July 27, 1842). Ro. E. Whitlocke, BM.
William Harrison to Elizabeth R. Pounds, Aug. 1, 1842.
(Aug. 3, 1842). James T. Elliott, BM.

GIBSON COUNTY MARRIAGES

John A. McKentosh to Nancy A. McKentosh, Aug. 6, 1842.
(Aug. 7, 1842). John Flowers, BM.
William F. Carr to Rebecca Olaver, Aug. 9, 1842.
John Reasons, BM.
John Reason to Mary Solles, Aug. 10, 1842. (Aug. 11,
1842). W. F. Cabb, BM.
Richard A. Edwards to Susan Wildar, Aug. 11, 1842. W.
H. Serape, BM.
William Donaldson to Hellena Jenings, Aug. 17, 1842.
John T. Fields, BM.
William Edmundson, Jr. to Elizabeth J. Burgan, Aug. 20,
1842. (Aug. 21, 1842). William M. Halford, BM.
Calvin J. Curtis to Anjanet Jackson, Aug. 20, 1842.
(Aug. 21, 1842).
Sterling Strother to Mary Daughtry, Aug. 30, 1842.
(Sept. 1, 1842). James Crews, BM.
Wiley B. Dowell to Harett J. Heath, Sept. 7, 1842.
(Sept. 7, 1842). Henry Parker, BM.
Perrey Holt to Mildred A. Jones, Sept. 12, 1842. (Sept.
13, 1842). Harrison Holt, BM.
John F. Tuter to Elizabeth Kinsey, Sept. 13, 1842.
(Sept. 15, 1842). J. H. Carroll, BM.
Samuel Lepperd to Susan Joinor, Sept. 15, 1842. (Sept.
15, 1842). B. Baker, BM.
John Kirkpatrick to Rebecca J. Denwiddie, Sept. 17, 1842.
(Sept. 21, 1842). David C. Robertson, BM.
William M. Halford to Francis M. Wilks, Oct. 1, 1842.
(Oct. 2, 1842). Edmund Flowers, BM.
Leoma Flowers to Mary A. E. Wright, Oct. 5, 1842.
(Oct. 6, 1842). Wm. Thompson, BM.
James G. Phalen to Amanda M. Spencer, Oct. 7, 1842.
(Oct. 7, 1842). Harrison Conlee, BM.
Lemuel Nance to Mary Runalds, Oct. 7, 1845. (Oct. 11,
1845). Thos. Reynolds, BM.
James Ringgold to Elizabeth Easterwood, Oct. 11, 1842.
(Oct. 14, 1842). Barnet Brand, BM.
James S. Hayns to Ann Holder, Oct. 22, 1842. (Oct. 25,
1842). A. J. Simmons, BM.
William K. Thweatt to Mary Wildur, Oct. 25, 1842.
(Oct. 27, 1842). A. C. Nimmo, BM.
William R. Driskill to Sopha W. Laughter, Oct. 24,
1842. (Dec. 15, 1842). A. B. P. Mayfield, BM.
Absolum Carns to Elizabeth Gunter, Oct. 27, 1842. (Dec.
5, 1842). Andrew T. Fields, BM.
Anderson Dickey to Joana Hale, Oct. 29, 1842. L. J.
Wilkins, BM.
James H. Fields to Nancy J. Trout, Oct. 31, 1842.
(Oct. 31, 1842). William Parks, BM.
George M. Harder to Mildred Hoskins. N. S. Sandeford, BM.
Josiah Allen to Lucy J. Roberson, Nov. 3, 1842. Alfred
Ferrell, BM.
Charles J. Lawrance to Charlott Cantrol, Nov. 3, 1842.
(Nov. 3, 1842). James Bobbett, BM.
William B. Jones to Mary C. Jones, Nov. 3, 1842. (Nov.
10, 1842). Jno. G. Atchison, BM.

GIBSON COUNTY MARRIAGES

Wm. D. Fields to Elizabeth Hail, Nov. 7, 1842. (Nov.
8, 1842). Wm. C. Hicks, BM.
William G. Adams to Elvira Craig, Nov. 7, 1842. (Nov.
7, 1842). Wm. H. Craig, BM.
Willis Ballard to Frances Nichols, Nov. 7, 1842. (Nov.
8, 1842). B. Ragan, BM.
James T. Swindle to Isabella E. McCalister, Nov. 8,
1842. (Nov. 10, 1842). E. H. Crocker, BM.
William P. Steuart to Susan E. Adams, Nov. 9, 1842.
(Nov. 9, 1842). Jas. T. Steuart, BM.
David Jackson to Rachal Paine, Nov. 15, 1842. (Nov. 17,
1842). John Jackson, BM.
John Word to Drucilla M. Conel, Nov. 16, 1842. (Nov.
16, 1842). Timothy P. Word, BM.
Kentiance G. Tally to Clemsa Watts, Nov. 18, 1842.
William Lester, BM.
John C. Sale to Elizabeth N. Milton, Nov. 22, 1842.
(Nov. 22, 1842). Ezekiel Sale, BM.
Isaac Laymon to Mahalia Webb, Nov. 22, 1842. James
Emison, BM.
John H. Carroll to Susan M. Bruce, Nov. 27, 1842. (Nov.
27, 1842). John H. Bruce, BM.
Henry Babb to Sarah A. E. Avery, Nov. 28, 1842. Henry
P. C. Avery, BM.
Henry D. Harper to Eliza J. Underwood, Nov. 28, 1842.
L. B. Gilchrist, BM.
Joseph W. Cooper to Elizabeth J. Moore, Dec. 1, 1842.
(Dec. 1, 1842). Joseph W. Moore, BM.
Edwin H. Crocker to Centha Riley, Dec. 5, 1842. (Dec.
6, 1842). Jno. R. McCalister, BM.
James Turner to Mary Patterson, Dec. 5, 1842. (Dec. 8,
1842). Francis Eddlemon, BM.
William Thompson to Elizabeth A. Crenshaw, Dec. 6, 1842.
(Dec. 8, 1842). James P. Grier, BM.
Alexander Turner to Martha Scipper, Dec. 9, 1842. (Dec.
10, 1842). R. P. Rains, BM.
William C. McKilvy to Manerva Tate, Dec. 10, 1842.
(Jan. 22, 1842). John Lite, BM.
Jacob S. Shipman to Martha Benson, Dec. 13, 1842. Joel
F. Furgarson, BM.
Thos. W. Williams to Hester R. McBride, Dec. 16, 1842.
(Dec. 21, 1842). John L. Davis, BM.
Clinton Galey to Lucinda Cunningham, Dec. 19, 1842.
John W. Baley to Nancy P. Shipman, Dec. 20, 1842.
(Dec. 20, 1842). Wm. T. Dickson, BM.
Thomas Watt to Mary Fowler, Dec. 21, 1842. N. O. K.
Cole, BM.
William Loving to Amanda M. Zerrico, Dec. 27, 1842.
(Dec. 28, 1842). L. B. Gilchrist, BM.
Benjamin Trafton to Elizabeth Flowers, Dec. 28, 1842.
(Dec. 29, 1842). Peter Sawyers, BM.
Francis Elliott to Sarah M. Alexander, Jan. 2, 1843.
(Jan. 5, 1843). Jas. S. Alexander, BM.
John C. Carroll to Sarah Howard, Jan. 2, 1843. (Jan.
5, 1843). B. E. Holmes, BM.

GIBSON COUNTY MARRIAGES

William G. James to Barbary J. Harpoll, Jan. 4, 1843.
(Jan. 5, 1843). Luke P. Seay, BM.
Alfred Ferrell to Susan A. Richardson, Jan. 5, 1843.
Josiah Allen, BM.
Thomas Gregory to Winney Gooch, Jan. 11, 1843. James
M. Terrell, BM.
Edward Robins to Lotta Ray, Jan. 16, 1843. (Jan. 16,
1843). David B. Ray, BM.
John Watson to Martha Hazelwood, Jan. 16, 1843. J.
Pennington, BM.
Bryant Carnigay to Hester Grady, Jan. 16, 1843. Abram
Glisson, BM.
Wellington H. Bledsoe to Ellender Rust, Jan. 19, 1843.
(Jan. 19, 1843). H. N. Bledsoe, BM.
Thos. B. Crider to Nancy Word, Jan. 19, 1843. (Jan. 19,
1843). T. H. Word, BM.
Jordan Jackson to Ann Brown, Jan. 21, 1843. Jeptha
T. Bailey, BM.
Samuel McMinn to Elizabeth Lyon, Jan. 23, 1843. (Jan.
25, 1843). Benj. M. Adair, BM.
Major Ferrell to Mary J. Turner, Jan. 24, 1843. (Jan.
24, 1843). James P. Alexander, BM.
John S. Hill to Mariah E. Davidson, Jan. 26, 1843.
(Jan. 26, 1843). John L. Davis, BM.
John P. B. Fuell to Mary Nunn, Jan. 30, 1843. (Feb. 2,
1843). Benj. Fewel, BM.
Thomas N. Paine to Marzell Welch, Feb. 1, 1843. (Feb.
1, 1843). William F. Nash, BM.
George W. Moore to Christian S. Jones, Feb. 2, 1843.
(Feb. 2, 1843). L. B. Gilchrist, BM.
Watkins Moore to Linington Jones, Feb. 2, 1843. L. B.
Gilchrist, BM.
Asa Perry to Lyda Smith, Feb. 2, 1843. (Feb. 4, 1843).
S. S. Paul, BM.
Bryant Word to Banna E. Wilson, Feb. 3, 1843. (Feb. 5,
1843). L. P. Seay, BM.
Adam Sollis to Sina Sollis, Feb. 3, 1843. (Feb. 4,
1843). John Reasons, BM.
Sandford Thedford to Manerva Gilliland, Feb. 6, 1843.
(Feb. 9, 1843). Thos. S. S. Young, BM.
James Pate to Unia Avery, Feb. 13, 1843. Henry D. Avery, BM.
David W. Powers to Nany Howell, Feb. 16, 1843. (Feb.
20, 1843). B. Boyett, BM.
Lewis Perry to Jane Newell, Feb. 18, 1843. (Feb. 23,
1843). Elum Newell, BM.
William B. Binyon to Lydia J. Turner, Feb. 21, 1843.
(Feb. 21, 1843). James Morton, BM.
Joseph R. Taylor to Mary Claiborne, Feb. 27, 1843.
(Feb. 27, 1843). John C. Claiborne, BM.
Abraham Karnes to Martha McKelvy, Feb. 27, 1843. (Feb.
28, 1843). Jos. Weatherspoon, BM.
Carroll S. Parker to Elizabeth A. L. McWhirter, Mar.
2, 1843. (Mar. 2, 1843). Saml. W. Hatchett, BM.
Sidney J. Porter to Malinda Fletcher, Mar. 2, 1843.
(Mar. 9, 1843). Myranda McWhirter, BM.

John Carey to Eliza Nobles, Mar. 6, 1843. (Mar. 7, 1843). William Carey, BM.

Alexander Terry to Emeline R. Bell, Mar. 6, 1843. (Mar. 6, 1843). James F. Smith, BM.

Thomas Barnes to Nancy Jones, Mar. 9, 1843. (Apr. 1, 1843). Thomas Akin, BM.

William Reed to Kesia Thomas, Mar. 15, 1843. (Mar. 16, 1843). A. C. Nimmo, BM.

Wilson Cooper to Magdalana Handcock, Mar. 16, 1843. (Mar. 16, 1843). I. Harrison, BM.

Peter Sexton to Francis May, Mar. 20, 1843. (Apr. 1, 1843). Wm. T. Dickens, BM.

Hugh Cooper to Penelope Word, Mar. 22, 1843. (Mar. 23, 1843). Joel W. Harrison, BM.

Walker Taliaferro to Sarah A. Yancy, Mar. 28, 1843. E. T. Taliaferro, BM.

William C. Edwards to Jane Karns, Apr. 3, 1843. (May 3, 1843). Thomas Aken, BM.

Joel W. Harrison to Elviry A. Hutchens, Apr. 4, 1843. (Apr. 13, 1843). I. Harrison, BM.

Alfred Gage to Elizabeth Doland, Apr. 5, 1843. (Apr. 9, 1843). Johiathan Wallace, BM.

Daniel Gauger to Sarah E. Lyon, Apr. 11, 1843. (Apr. 11, 1843). Jos. T. Rentfro, BM.

John H. Yancey to Nancy M. Jackson, Apr. 23, 1843. Henry Jackson, BM.

William C. Warrin to Nancy L. Driskell, Dec. 25, 1843. (Dec. 25, 1843). J. B. Landis, BM.

John R. Bledsoe to Sarah McDougald, Apr. 27, 1843. (Apr. 27, 1843). Thos. H. Ethridge, BM.

John Darnald to Mris Milley Sammons, Apr. 29, 1843. (May 1, 1843). Washington Riley, BM.

William Bell to Mary E. Whitlow, Apr. 8, 1843. (May 11, 1843). Alderson Davis, BM.

Joseph J. Bass to Elizabeth S. Hunt, May 9, 1843. (May 9, 1843). S. W. Hatchett, BM.

Daniel Holder to Mrs. Martha Simpson, May 9, 1843. (May 9, 1843). Willoughby Salph, BM.

Johnston Fox to Nany Ingram, June 13, 1843. Harmon Reed, BM.

David Flowers to Nancy Keathly, June 15, 1843. (June 18, 1843). Booker Arnold, BM.

James McAlexander to Winerford Johnson, Aug. 21, 1843. (Aug. 21, 1843).

Richard Welch to July Wade, June 17, 1843. (June 18, 1843). A. C. Nimmo, BM.

Benjamin W. Clement to Elizabeth W. Lock, June 21, 1843. (June 22, 1843). Wesley F. Jones, BM.

Jerman W. Lea to Mary Cooper, June 29, 1843. (July 4, 1843). Elisha Belch, BM.

Richardson Arnold to Polly Dickey, July 3, 1843. (July 27, 1843). J. M. Halford, BM.

Thomas James to Margaret R. Dunlap, July 11, 1843. (July 13, 1843). H. R. Hall, BM.

William Sexton to Zuby Boyd, July 17, 1843. (July 18, 1843). Linsfield Sexton, BM.

James Bullard to Maranda Ferrell, July 27, 1843. (July 28, 1843). Thos. T. Turner, BM.

Needham Moore to Sapponia Cox, July 29, 1843. (July 31, 1843). Stephen Moore, BM.

Samuel J. Wilkins to Miranda Webb, Aug. 3, 1843. (Aug. 3, 1843). Thos. B. Cousins, BM.

Leroy R. Dill to Rurey Mynor, Aug. 4, 1843. (Aug. 4, 1843). Z. N. Dill, BM.

Henry Fletcher to Caroline Piolate, Aug. 8, 1843. (Aug. 8, 1843). J. W. Glasgow, BM.

David Haist to Rebecca Varner, Aug. 10, 1843. (Aug. 10, 1843). Harrison Conlee, BM.

John McFarlen to Polly Welch, Aug. 18, 1843. (Aug. 18, 1843). Z. L. Bobbitt, BM.

James McAlexander to Winerford Johnson, Aug. 21, 1843. (Aug. 21, 1843).

John C. Foster to Martha A. Cole, Aug. 30, 1843. (Aug. 31, 1843). A. B. Harris, BM.

Patrick Glesson to Sarah Brown, Sept. 6, 1843. H. H. Davis, BM.

John F. Sinclear to Nancy Joyce, Sept. 11, 1843. (Sept. 13, 1843).

John F. Walker to Sarah A. Barten, Sept. 13, 1843. (Sept. 14, 1843). J. H. Burton, BM.

Solsly Farthing to Elizabeth Ross, Sept. 25, 1843. (Sept. 26, 1843). Robert Clark, BM.

Constant Thedford to Lucretia Sherron, Oct. 2, 1843. (Oct. 12, 1843). Sanford Thetford, BM.

John W. Sile to Mary Jane Wit, Oct. 14, 1843. (Oct. 19, 1843). Gabriel Brown, BM.

A. B. Orr to Nancy Lovett, Oct. 14, 1843. (Oct. 15, 1843). John F. Thomas, BM.

George A. Akins to Angeline Rutlidge, Oct. 19, 1843. (Oct. 19, 1843). Adam Carnes, BM.

Isaac Fowler to Rebecca Cooper, Oct. 21, 1843. (Oct. 24, 1843). Hugh Cooper, BM.

Bryant C. Carraway to Sidney Hall, Oct. 28, 1843. (Oct. 29, 1843). John F. Thomas, BM.

John Busby to Patiance C. Mainor, Oct. 31, 1843. (Oct. 31, 1843). J. N. Dill, BM.

Albert W. Bledsoe to Martha S. Vaden, Oct. 31, 1843. (Oct. 31, 1843). H. H. Bledsoe, BM.

Britten H. Holland to Martha J. Gant, Oct. 2, 1843. (Dec. 7, 1843). L. B. Gilchrist, BM.

Joseph Barrott to Sarah J. McBride, Nov. 8, 1843. (Nov. 8, 1843). P. D. McRee, BM.

William Forren to Elizabeth Vaughn, Nov. 16, 1843. (Nov. 16, 1843). Alex Forren, BM.

William H. Holaman to Sarah J. Wright, Nov. 20, 1843. (Nov. 26, 1843).

Jessee Blancett to Elizabeth F. Baker, Nov. 21, 1843. (Nov. 21, 1843). L. B. Gilchrist, BM.

John M. Alexander to Lenory Dyal, Nov. 23, 1843.
(Nov. 23, 1843). Jas. S. Alexander, BM.
William Costler to Jane M. Wilson, Nov. 26, 1843.
(Dec. 3, 1843). Jobe Beantrell, BM.
Thomas Akins to Nancy Edwards, Nov. 25, 1843. (Nov.
26, 1843). D. H. Barns, BM.
Nathaniel Taylor to Elizabeth Richardson, Nov. 27, 1843.
(Nov. 30, 1843). Lemuel Taylor, BM.
Elijah Wilbourn to Nancy Stuard, Nov. 29, 1843. (Nov.
30, 1843). Moddica Baily, BM.
William Grice to Elizabeth Ringgold, Nov. 30, 1843.
(Nov. 30, 1843). Henry Meek, BM.
John Ringgold to Mary Harrison, Nov. 30, 1843. (Dec.
12, 1843). Henry Meek, BM.
Alexander Smith to Catharine Arbuckle, Nov. 9, 1843.
S. S. Paul, BM.
William O. Davidson to Elizabeth J. Rankins, Nov. 9,
1843. (Nov. 9, 1843). Alfred Davidson, BM.
Thos. Waller to Eliza Johnston, Nov. 15, 1843. John
Johnston, BM.
Charles G. Baird to Nancy Hayns, Nov. 20, 1843.
Benjamin F. Jones, BM.
William H. Holamon to Sarah J. Wright, Nov. 20, 1843.
Bethel Reeves, BM.
George Smith to Prissa Coley, Dec. 2, 1843. (Dec. 4,
1843). S. S. Paul, BM.
James D. Harrison to Margarett Cooper, Dec. 5, 1843.
(Dec. 12, 1843). Isaac Fowler, BM.
Alfred B. Harris to Nancy Thedford, Dec. 6, 1843.
(Dec. 7, 1843). Wiley A. Waldrop, BM.
William Gant to Mrs. Nancy Holland, Dec. 7, 1843.
(Dec. 7, 1843). Leonard Taylor, BM.
Reddiee Berry to Catherine Allen, Dec. 12, 1843. (Dec.
13, 1843). J. A. Bradshaw, BM.
Edmond Sanders to Nancy Lyons, Dec. 13, 1843. (Dec.
14, 1843). A. S. Currey, BM.
A. S. Underwood to Sarah J. Nuckles, Dec. 13, 1843.
(Dec. 14, 1843). Thos. H. Fisher, BM.
Joseph Weatherspoon to Emaly Rentfro, Dec. 16, 1843.
(Dec. 21, 1843). Harvey T. Jackson, BM.
William McLinn to Rebecca McDougold, Dec. 18, 1843.
(Dec. 21, 1843). Isaac Hopkins, BM.
William Sales to Rebecca Howard, Dec. 18, 1843. (Dec.
20, 1843). H. F. Reed, BM.
Henry Parker to Matilda McCalop, Dec. 20, 1843. By
L. Taylor, M.G. Samuel R. Tucker, BM.
William H. Bailey to Martha A. Biggs, Dec. 20, 1843.
(Dec. 20, 1843). P. W. Powell, BM.
William J. C. Spellings to Harriott Wilkerson, Dec.
20, 1843. (Dec. 20, 1843). Wm. C. Hicks, BM.
James S. Alexander to Elizabeth Elliott, Dec. 20, 1843.
(Dec. 21, 1843). Wm. A. Alexander, BM.
Edwin H. Hintom to Sarah A. Alsabrooks, Dec. 20, 1843.
James B. Duggan, BM.

Timothy H. Word to Mary E. Abbott, Dec. 21, 1843.
(Dec. 21, 1843). John Word, BM.
Aqula J. Goodloe to Margarett A. Jones, Dec. 23, 1843.
(Dec. 27, 1843). David E. Thomas, BM.
James Crews to Harrett Flowers, Dec. 23, 1843. (Dec.
26, 1843). D. G. Boyett, BM.
William Bain to Polly Knott, Dec. 25, 1843. (Dec. 28,
1843). Geo. P. McAlilly, BM.
William W. Connell to Elizabeth R. Thedford, Dec. 27,
1843. (Dec. 28, 1843). Joshua Harris, BM.
Elum F. Newell to Rutha Palmer, Dec. 29, 1843. Lewis
Perry, BM.
Elisha Mandenall to Mary A. Donaldson, Jan. 2, 1844.
(Jan. 2, 1844). J. T. Fields, BM.
Watkins H. Dodson to Sarah T. Morten, Jan. 6, 1844.
(Jan. 9, 1844). Samuel H. Stout, BM.
David P. Jenkins to Mildred A. Elum, Jan. 9, 1844.
(Jan. 11, 1844). Surgener Atchison, BM.
Thomas Thorn to Judy Hast, Jan. 11, 1844. (Jan. 11,
1844). Joel Mayo, BM.
William Smith to Kesiah Kannaday, Jan. 12, 1844. (Feb.
17, 1844). Philip Smith, BM.
Jessee L. Branch to Sarah J. Gillespie, Jan. 16, 1844.
(Jan. 18, 1844). J. W. Hockaday, BM.
Elisha Belch to Mulinda Walls, Jan. 6, 1844. (Feb. 3,
1844). W. C. Crawford, BM.
Daniel Barns to Catharine Parker, Jan. 22, 1844. (Jan.
25, 1844). Adam Carnes, BM.
John K. Pearce to Jane E. Nesbitt, Jan. 22, 1844. (Jan.
23, 1844). R. B. Love, BM.
George M. D. Lawrance to Rebecca Smith, Jan. 23, 1844.
(Jan. 23, 1844). C. W. Smith, BM.
Jones Glascock to Sarah Phelan, Jan. 24, 1844. (Jan.
24, 1844). John D. Agee, BM.
Charles L. Thompson to Nancy Mayfield, Jan. 27, 1844.
(Jan. 30, 1844). John L. Davis, BM.
John D. Crank to Elenor M. Runalds, Feb. 3, 1844.
(Feb. 7, 1844). D. A. McDaniel, BM.
Harbert Edwards to Martha Carns, Feb. 5, 1844. (Feb.
13, 1844). Robt. Anderson, BM.
Harvey Jackson to Cornelia Bryant, Feb. 6, 1844.
Henry M. Gault, BM.
John Donaldson to Mary Vaughn, Feb. 7, 1844. (Feb.
8, 1844). James A. Harwood, BM.
George C. Harley to Martha J. Blair, Feb. 8, 1844.
(Feb. 8, 1844). Jas. M. Armstrong, BM.
Phillip Holland to Mrs. Anney Casey, Feb. 8, 1844.
(Feb. 13, 1844). Jefferson Holland, BM.
David Bowers to Polly Mayfield, Feb. 10, 1844. (Feb.
13, 1844). T. Billingsley, BM.
Bevely Cannon to Mary Gunter, Feb. 10, 1844. (Feb.
15, 1844). Robt. E. Bogle, BM.
Nathaniel K. Sherron to Elizabeth Wilson, Feb. 13,
1844. (Feb. 13, 1844). Arthur Barron, BM.

Thomas Walker to Fanny Green, Feb. 13, 1844. (Feb. 13, 1844). Samuel Booth, BM.

William C. Stuart to Elizabeth Fuqua, Feb. 13, 1844. (Feb. 14, 1844). Miles L. Allen, BM.

James H. Gibson to Alley Edmondson, Feb. 17, 1844. (Feb. 18, 1844). A. C. Ridgeway, BM.

Parnemus Fifer to Jane Walker, Feb. 20, 1844. (Feb. 21, 1844). Daniel West, BM.

Robert Bogle to Mary F. Tucker, Feb. 21, 1844. (Feb. 22, 1844). A. Parker, BM.

Julis Hall to Parthena Holland, Feb. 23, 1844. (Feb. 23, 1844). John Reason, BM.

William B. Conwell to Ann Dicky, Feb. 26, 1844. L. B. Gilchrist, BM.

C. F. Hames to Martha E. Bryant, Feb. 27, 1844. Henry M. Gault, BM.

James H. Hays to Amanda E. Penn, Feb. 27, 1844. (Feb. 27, 1844). Caswell E. George, BM.

James E. Weathers to Mary J. Crisp, Feb. 28, 1844. (Feb. 28, 1844). R. J. Vanhock, BM.

John Blanchet to Anney Baker, Feb. 28, 1844. (Feb. 28, 1844). H. Parker, BM.

William McMinn to Matilda Wallingford, Feb. 29, 1844. (Feb. 29, 1844). William B. Wallace, BM.

Alfred Stuart to Amanda J. Allen, Mar. 12, 1844. Elijah Kilzer, BM.

James P. Grier to Parmelia A. Moore, Mar. 19, 1844. (Mar. 19, 1844). S. A. Grier, BM.

Marcus Barrott to Martha A. Thomas, Mar. 19, 1844. (Mar. 19, 1844). R. D. McKee, BM. (Note: At the house of James S. Thomas.)

Turner R. Gibbs to Monan Milton, Mar. 20, 1844. (Apr. 3, 1844). Archd. C. Levy, BM.

Benjamin F. Harris to Sarah E. Penn, Mar. 20, 1844. (Mar. 20, 1844). A. H. Smiley, BM. (Note: At the house of Mr. Penn.)

Clement Eudaly to Harrit Eudaly, Apr. 1, 1844. (Apr. 2, 1844). Wm. H. Craig, BM.

William J. Newbern to Mrs. Polly Underwood, Sr., May 2, 1844. (May 2, 1844). Leonard Taylor, BM.

Ratliff Boon to Lucrety C. Hopkins, May 6, 1844. Henry G. Hunt, BM.

Bryant T. Dawtry to Catherine Morgan, May 22, 1844. (May 22, 1844). John Basinger, BM.

William Gardner to Jane F. Welch, May 23, 1844. (May 23, 1844). Lewis Levy, BM.

Daniel West to Martha A. Lea, May 28, 1844. (June 15, 1844). William A. Ross, BM.

Duke Klyce to Mary E. Epperson, June 8, 1844. (June 12, 1844). J. H. Brooks, BM.

James Ward to Martha A. Cooper, June 15, 1844. (June 18, 1844). Abner Evins, BM.

George W. Gill to Lucy D. Pruitt, June 17, 1844. (June 17, 1844). David W. Hamilton, BM.

Alfred F. Davidson to Mary J. Moore, June 20, 1844.
(June 20, 1844). R. W. Barton, BM.
David W. Jarvis to Alley M. Edmundson, July 2, 1844.
(July 4, 1844). A. R. Brickhouse, BM.
Robert Rankin to Mary Cedona Terril, July 3, 1844.
(July 3, 1844). Paul Fletcher, BM.
William M. McWhirter to Martha A. V. Parker, July 17,
1844. (July 18, 1844). Sion Boon, BM.
William C. Barton to Roeana P. Abbott, July 18, 1844.
(July 18, 1844). James T. Abbott, BM.
John Evins to Mary Tally, July 27, 1844. (July 29,
1844). Andrew Lassiter, BM. (Note: At the house
of Mrs. Nancy Tally.)
James Pettit to Levina Scott, Aug. 15, 1844. (Aug. 15,
1844). N. Pettit, BM.
Thomas J. Thedford to Mrs. Margarett W. McKnight, Aug.
15, 1844. (Aug. 15, 1844). Wm. H. Craig, BM.
Enoch G. Ivey to Elizabeth O. Wade, Aug. 15, 1844.
(Aug. 15, 1844). Geo. C. Ferris, BM.
Daniel W. Word to Louisa Simpson, Aug. 22, 1844. (Aug.
22, 1844). W. H. Hawkins, BM.
James M. Baysinger to Martha Dickerson, Aug. 24, 1844.
(Aug. 25, 1844). John B. Forester, BM.
John L. Jordian to Martha N. Harlan, Aug. 8, 1843.
(Sept. 12, 1844). S. Craven, BM.
David Hisaw to Sentha J. Pope, Sept. 2, 1844. E.
Billingsley, BM.
Jessee Price to Sarah J. West, Sept. 9, 1844. (Sept.
12, 1844). William A. Ross, BM.
William C. Cunningham to Rutha C. Wright, Sept. 12,
1844. John Young, BM.
Vinson M. L. Taylor to Margaret Patterson, Sept. 17,
1844. (Sept. 19, 1844). Thos. Carlton, BM.
William A. Ross to Mary J. Bratton, Sept. 21, 1844.
(Sept. 25, 1844). William C. Roe, BM.
Benjamin Fuell to Mahala Merritt, Oct. 2, 1844. (Oct.
2, 1844). James C. Bradford, BM.
James Walker to Jane Walker, Oct. 2, 1844. (Oct. 15,
1844). Elias H. Crocker, BM.
Spenson Glascock to Nany Glascock, Oct. 14, 1844. (Oct.
14, 1844). Jones Glascock, BM.
Moses B. Hawkins to A. U. M. S. Word, Oct. 16, 1844.
A. C. Nimmo, BM.
John T. Armour to Jacksy Baley, Oct. 16, 1844. (Oct.
17, 1844). Peleg Bailey, BM.
George C. Ferris to Abagal A. Bowman, Oct. 24, 1844.
(Oct. 24, 1844). Willis I. Ingram, BM.
William C. Scrape to Frances Wysong, Oct. 24, 1844.
E. L. Taliafero, BM.
Benjamin A. Bailey to Mary Sain, Oct. 26, 1844. (Oct.
29, 1844). D. B. Dickson, BM.
Elijah Kilzar to Mary Pruitt, Oct. 31, 1841. Levi R.
Bradford, BM. (Note: Not executed.)
George W. Hadin to Rebecca Gee, Nov. 6, 1844. (Nov.
6, 1844). Wm. T. Webb, BM.

Willis J. Ingram to Elenor E. Bourman, Nov. 7, 1844.
(Nov. 12, 1844). Thomas W. Jones, BM.
George Canada to Sarah Mitchell, Nov. 9, 1844. (Nov.
20, 1844). H. F. Reed, BM.
Joel W. Harrison to Elizabeth J. McWherter, Nov. 12,
1844. (Nov. 12, 1844). A. Cooper, BM.
James T. Wood to Elizabeth J. Cartwright, Nov. 12, 1844.
(Nov. 14, 1844). Jno. B. Edmundson, BM.
Samul. Cunningham to Julia A. Driskell, Nov. 19, 1844.
(Nov. 20, 1844). J. S. Driskell, BM.
Burton Hall to Jane Cherry, Nov. 30, 1844. J. Hall, BM.
Alston Bailey to Martha Motly, Dec. 2, 1844. (Dec. 26,
1844). Aaron Jackson, BM.
William M. Dunlap to Rebecca E. Allison, Dec. 2, 1844.
(Dec. 3, 1844). Wm. A. Allison, BM.
Tilghman Milton to Harrett Moore, Dec. 2, 1844. (Dec.
3, 1844). A. Mifflin, BM.
John Lynch to Mary N. Bledsoe, Dec. 3, 1844. (Dec. 4,
1844). John L. Davis, BM.
Moses F. Whitehurst to Elizabeth J. Crockett, Dec. 7,
1844. (Dec. 8, 1845). James Turner, BM.
James C. Bradford to Mary Williams, Dec. 9, 1844.
Levi R. Bradford, BM.
Levi Webb to Elizabeth Dement, Dec. 9, 1844. (Dec. 10,
1844). Jas. H. Sherron, BM.
George Badget to Fanny Hall, Dec. 9, 1844. (Dec. 9,
1844). Nathan Reed, BM.
Edward R. Jones to Martha A. Montgomery, Dec. 11, 1844.
(Dec. 11, 1844). Samuel Cherry, BM.
John H. Bledsoe to Nancy E. McCutcheon, Dec. 11, 1844.
(Dec. 11, 1844). Madison Bledsoe, BM.
John Cock to Sirena Moore, Dec. 18, 1844. (Dec. 19,
1844). T. H. Bryett, BM.
David Gage to Martha A. Pinion, Dec. 24, 1844. (Dec.
24, 1844). M. Bohanan, BM.
John Polk to June Hisaw, Dec. 24, 1844. (Dec. 25,
1844). Thos. B. Murphy, BM.
John H. Lasly to Isabella N. Baldridge, Dec. 30, 1844.
(Jan. 1, 1845). John A. Wilkins, BM.
Robert S. Kirkman to Lemiza Shaw, Dec. 30, 1844. (Jan.
2, 1845). John Green, BM.
George W. Grisham to Mrs. Teletha Furgarson, Dec. 31,
1844. (Jan. 1, 1845). Wm. C. Crawford, BM.
Joel Furgarson to Sarah Peal, Jan. 1, 1845. (Jan. 2,
1845). Thos. Furgarson, BM.
Benj. F. Trusty to Ellender McCarey, Jan. 1, 1845.
(Jan. 2, 1845). P. P. Baker, BM.
William Blackburn to Nancy M. Ward, Jan. 2, 1845.
(Jan. 2, 1845). Harrison Conlee, BM.
William J. Featherston to Willy Corley, Jan. 8, 1845.
(Jan. 9, 1845). Thomas H. Akin, BM.
Stephen J. Bobbett to Lucy Holt, Jan. 13, 1845. (Jan.
16, 1845). Gaston Rollins, BM.
Richardson P. White to Malinda Gilliland, Jan. 13, 1845.
(Jan. 16, 1845). James A. Flippin, BM.

Benjamin C. Branch to Sarah Pettyjohn, Jan. 18, 1845.
  (Jan. 18, 1845). Stephen O'Daniel, BM.
Bennett G. Hall to Mary E. Randolph, Jan. 20, 1845.
  (Jan. 21, 1845). Thos. J. Thedford, BM.
William C. Hunt to Heneretta T. Hopkins, Jan. 21, 1845.
  (Jan. 23, 1845).
James H. Bass to Sarah A. Benthel, Jan. 28, 1845.
  (Jan. 28, 1845). C. E. George, BM.
Jas. M. Williamson to Rachal Bulleton, Jan. 29, 1845.
  (Jan. 30, 1845). John Swindle, BM.
Claiborn A. Freeman to Mary Phillips, Feb. 3, 1845.
  (Apr. 2, 1845).
Johnathan Baley to Mary Thompson, Feb. 5, 1845.
  (Feb. 5, 1845). Archuelas Thompson, BM.
Archibald C. McDougald to Sarah E. Avery, Feb. 5, 1845.
  Marion J. Clay, BM.
William Cannon to Elizabeth Jonigan, Feb. 7, 1845.
  (May 14, 1845). Peter Raney, BM. (Note: New
  license issued May 14, 1845 to Mary P. A. Blankenship.)
William Pettus to Martha A. McDaniel, Feb. 7, 1845.
  (Feb. 13, 1845). S. W. Holland, BM.
William J. Jennings to Sarah J. Donaldson, Feb. 9,
  1845. (Feb. 9, 1845). William Humphry, BM.
John Young to Polly Wallace, Feb. 8, 1845. (Feb. 9,
  1845). W. Cook, BM.
James Step to Mrs. Priscilla Conway, Feb. 10, 1845.
  (Feb. 10, 1845). Wm. C. Crawford, BM.
William Bishop to Mary A. Bryant, Feb. 12, 1845. (Feb.
  13, 1845). Wm. T. Rountree, BM.
William Walston to Mary E. Pennington, Feb. 12, 1845.
  Green B. Babb, BM.
James T. George to Mahala A. Baker, Feb. 12, 1845. By
  James S. Armstrong, J.P. Jesse Cassels, BM.
John H. Carroll to Martha Bruce, Feb. 12, 1845. (Feb.
  18, 1845). Robt. L. Smith, BM.
Elijah Kilzoe to Margaret King, Feb. 20, 1845. (Feb.
  23, 1845). Levi R. Bradford, BM.
James Thompson to Sarah Yates, Feb. 22, 1845. (Feb.
  23, 1845). Carson Patterson, BM.
William T. Dickins to Martha B. Wallace, Feb. 26, 1845.
  (Feb. 27, 1845). D. J. Bobbett, BM.
Benjamin Yarbrough to Mary J. McAllila, Mar. 5, 1845.
  (Mar. 6, 1845). Geo. P. Yarbrough, BM.
Jesse M. Allen to Delphi Williams, Mar. 5, 1845. (Mar.
  12, 1845). Nathan Reed, BM.
William A. Allison to Sarah C. Dunlap, Mar. 6, 1845.
  (Mar. 6, 1845). N. H. Dunlap, BM.
William Henderson to Elizabeth West, Mar. 6, 1845.
  George C. Medlin, BM.
David Hurt to Louisa E. Jordian, Mar. 6, 1845. John
  R. Hall, BM.
James E. Boon to Sarah B. Atkins, Mar. 11, 1845. (Mar.
  11, 1845). C. E. George, BM.
William R. Edmundson to Sentha L. N. McWhirter, Mar.
  11, 1845. Michael Edmundson, BM.

James F. Smith to Mary M. Bell, Mar. 19, 1845. (Mar. 20, 1845). J. T. Coleman, BM.

Peter M. Connel to Nancy Williams, Mar. 19, 1845. (Mar. 25, 1845). Thos. Jas. Nicholas King and Hiram Thetford, BM.

James S. Baker to Hursay Wortham, Mar. 26, 1845. (Apr. 1, 1845). Levi R. Bradford, BM.

Daniel McLane to Mary N. W. Avery, Apr. 1, 1845. (Apr. 3, 1845). James Porter, BM.

Modnca Wilks to Mary Flowers, Apr. 7, 1845. (Apr. 10, 1845). Henry Thomas, BM.

James T. Jackson to Elizabeth Gather, Apr. 18, 1845. (Apr. 18, 1845). William Grady, BM.

John Baxter to Mary W. Powell, May 1, 1845. (May 1, 1845). G. M. Sharp, BM.

Harris Bradford to Elizabeth James, May 12, 1845. (May 15, 1845). John Cooper, BM.

William Cannon to Pemilia A. Blankenship, May 14, 1845. (May 15, 1845). Vinson Garrott, BM. (Note: See entry on page 53.)

James Blackburn to Martha J. Ward, May 15, 1845. (May 15, 1845). Horatio Durley, BM.

Andrew J. Spruwell to Martha Millone, May 17, 1845. (May 23, 1845). Edwin T. Taliaferro, BM.

Calvin Flowers to Susan C. Crews, May 17, 1845. (May 22, 1845). John Crews, BM.

Edwin T. Taliaferro to Jane B. Pope, May 27, 1845. (May 27, 1845). M. B. King, BM.

Elijah R. Bower to Jane N. Keating, May 28, 1845. (June 12, 1845). Blanchett (?), BM.

Joseph Liggett to Elizabeth Cannon, June 2, 1845. (June 4, 1845). Hugh Cassels, BM.

Martin B. Arnold to Elizabeth Knott, June 12, 1845. (June 12, 1845). John Martin, BM.

Michel Keenan to Pemela S. H. Hamilton, June 18, 1845. (June 19, 1845). David W. Hamilton, BM.

Silas Avery to Lucinda Pentegrass, June 18, 1845. (June 23, 1845). A. S. Camy, BM.

Levi G. Danner to Charlotte C. Harlan, June 23, 1845. W. T. Rountree, BM.

Henry Thomas to Susan Haliburton, July 1, 1845. (July 2, 1845). Barnabas Flowers, BM.

William H. Witt to Mary N. Arnold, July 2, 1845. (July 2, 1845). John W. Lile, BM.

John W. Ballentine to Rebecca Barker, July 3, 1845. (July 3, 1845). J. B. Humble, BM.

David Dair to Nany E. Estas, July 7, 1845. July 17, 1845). Henry Estes, BM.

Daniel Irvin to Martha N. McGhee, July 7, 1845. (July 7, 1845). A. B. Mayfield, BM.

Enoch Fox to Darcus Fox, July 15, 1845. (July 15, 1845). John Martin, BM.

Hiram C. Trout to Frances C. Clements, July 15, 1845. (July 15, 1845). William May, BM.

James T. Woods to Eudora M. Booth, July 19, 1845.
(July 29, 1845). John W. Hockaday, BM.
Harris B. Pruitt to Elizabeth Motly, July 30, 1845.
(July 31, 1845). Levi R. Bradford, BM.
Wiley S. Carter to Levina Statum, Aug. 4, 1845. (Aug.
5, 1845). Wm. T. Dickson, BM.
Charles B. Jester to Mariah P. Sanders, Aug. 5, 1845.
Cyrus E. Mathis, BM.
W. H. Stillwell to Mary A. Hockaday, Aug. 8, 1845.
(Aug. 11, 1845). Wilson Williams, BM.
James Humble to Mary K. Balentine, Aug. 8, 1845. (Aug.
9, 1845). S. S. Paul, BM.
Henderson Bailey to Eliza Jackson, Aug. 14, 1845. (Aug.
22, 1845). Peleg Bailey, BM.
Levi Stone to Eliza Ann Price, Aug. 16, 1845. (Aug.
17, 1845). Jno. J. McAlexander, BM.
John C. Blankinship to Margaret Cannon, Aug. 21, 1845.
(Aug. 26, 1845). Elijah Sanders, BM.
David B. Dickson to Mrs. Margaret Taylor, Aug. 25,
1845. (Aug. 26, 1845). Smith Parks, BM.
Samuel Hollaway to Mariah Harris, Aug. 25, 1845. Jas.
W. Nuckolds, BM.
William Mosley to Mary S. Salemon, Aug. 26, 1845.
(Sept. 11, 1845). Pernu Giles, BM.
Lewis Dickerson to Zelpha Howell, Aug. 26, 1845. Lamb
Taylor, BM.
Jessee Ballentine to Elizabeth B. Bledsoe, Aug. 26,
1845. (Aug. 27, 1845). Wm. N. Bledsoe, BM.
Armstrong Mifflin to Louisa Blunt, Aug. 30, 1845.
Archd. C. Levy, BM.
Benj. Hue to Margrett Betts, Sept. 8, 1845. (Sept. 10,
1845). Henry Sain, BM.
John F. Phillips to Elizabeth Sinclear, Sept. 9, 1845.
(Sept. 9, 1845). Isaac N. Frost, BM.
Lewis S. Hutcherson to Camantha J. Harber, Sept. 16,
1845. (Sept. 16, 1845). David McKnight, BM.
Jessee Flowers to Sarah Halford, Sept. 18, 1845.
(Sept. 18, 1845). S. S. Paul, BM.
Edmund Green to Lemory Word, Sept. 25, 1845. (Sept.
25, 1845). Thos. N. Bowers, BM.
Jessee J. Hays to Epsey M. Butler, Sept. 25, 1845.
(Sept. 25, 1845). J. M. Hays, BM.
John M. Wells to Sarah Patterson, Sept. 27, 1845.
(Sept. 28, 1845). Alfred Flowers, BM.
Peter G. Fields to Emely V. Jetton, Sept. 30, 1845.
(Sept. 30, 1845). Thos. W. Jones, BM.
Ichabud Moore to Mary E. Cooper, Oct. 1, 1845. (Oct.
1, 1845). John Harrison, BM.
Joseph Harrison to Martha Peal, Oct. 1, 1845. (Oct.
2, 1845). J. T. Thetford, BM.
Hugh M. McBride to Marcila A. Bunnell, Oct. 6, 1845.
(Oct. 9, 1845). J. F. McBride, BM.
Saml. J. Andrews to Nany Kelzoe, Oct. 18, 1845.
Wm. Andrews, BM.

A. J. Tilghman to Mahala Tyson, Oct. 21, 1845. (Oct.
    29, 1845). Smith Parks, BM.
John R. Waldrop to Susan Harris, Oct. 22, 1845. (Oct.
    23, 1845). John C. Davis, BM.
Robert H. Carr to Margaret A. Ellison, Oct. 27, 1845.
    (Oct. 28, 1845). Andrew A. Carr, BM.
John A. Cunningham to Mary Hampton, Oct. 27, 1845.
    (Dec. 28, 1845). James B. Phipps, BM.
Walter Thedford to Elizabeth Runalds, Nov. 3, 1845.
    (Nov. 6, 1845). James Arnold, BM.
William R. Tyson to Ann E. Rutledge, Nov. 13, 1845.
    (Nov. 16, 1845). T. D. Tyson, BM.
Thomas Furgarson to Winaford Peal, Nov. 17, 1845.
    (Nov. 20, 1845). Allen Fergarson, BM.
Green B. Y. McEwen to Sarah A. Arbuckle, Nov. 25, 1845.
    (Nov. 25, 1845). George P. McAliley, BM.
Wright H. Rutherford to Artina Billingsley, Nov. 25,
    1845. (Nov. 25, 1845). W. Billingsley, BM.
John H. Jones to Frances C. Moudy, Dec. 2, 1845.
    (Dec. 7, 1845). Wm. Atchison, BM.
James S. Witt to Juda Dickens, Dec. 2, 1845. A. M.
    Shane, BM.
William Davidson to Emely Ballance, Dec. 3, 1845. John
    Davidson, BM.
George C. Harley to Martha C. Stone, Dec. 8, 1845.
    (Dec. 8, 1845). Eli W. Ing, BM.
Joshua Swindle to Prissilla Hancock, Dec. 9, 1845.
    (Dec. 17, 1845). Henry Williamson, BM.
Benj. F. Tally to Elizabeth N. Bowers, Dec. 11, 1845.
    (Dec. 11, 1845). Wm. B. Jeffous, BM.
Leander D. Lawrence to Sarah Wallace, Dec. 13, 1845.
    (Dec. 15, 1845). Thos. Wallace, BM.
Richard S. Vaden to Cyntha I. Boon, Dec. 16, 1845.
    (Dec. 16, 1845). Henry G. Hunt, BM.
Jas. S. McWherter to Mary Patterson, Dec. 20, 1845.
    (Dec. 21, 1845).
Alfred James Thomas to Polly S. Childress, Dec. 23,
    1845. (Dec. 23, 1845). Henry Long, BM.
John Y. Harrison to Judy F. Gibbs, Dec. 23, 1845.
    (Dec. 25, 1845). H. Harrison, BM.
Otha C. Pollard to Nancy Rowntree, Dec. 24, 1845.
    (Dec. 25, 1845). Jno. C. McCollum, BM.
Alfred Flowers to Martha Patterson, Dec. 26, 1845.
    (Dec. 28, 1845). Barnabas Flowers, BM.
Gabriel Barnes to Phebi Jane Goodrich, Dec. 28,
    1845. (Dec. 28, 1845). Jas. McElvy, BM.
James T. Richardson to Mary L. Brightwell, Dec. 29,
    1845. (Jan. 1, 1846). L. L. Brightwell, BM.
Thomas J. Alford to Frances Richardson, Dec. 29, 1845.
    (Dec. 30, 1845). Jas. W. Alford, BM.
William Patterson to Mary Patterson, Dec. 29, 1845.
    (Jan. 7, 1846). James Patterson, BM.
William Williams to Clementine Taylor, Dec. 30, 1845.
    (Dec. 31, 1845). Richard C. Penn, BM.

Dr. J. Bobbett to Elizabeth J. Wallace, Dec. 31, 1845.
(Jan. 1, 1846). James S. May, BM.
Jessie J. Wills to Sarah M. Grayer, Jan. 1, 1846.
(Jan. 1, 1846). A. N. Smiley, BM.
Woodson J. Sanders to Mary B. Sartor, Jan. 2, 1846.
(Jan. 5, 1846).
Sion Boon to Mary A. Hatchett, June 6, 1846. By L. L.
Shipman, M.G. John V. Morton, BM.
Wiley A. Waldrop to Julia Pounds, Jan. 3, 1846. (Jan.
8, 1846). J. M. Pounds, BM.
Howel Vick to Martha A. Pinington, Jan. 6, 1846. J. A.
Bradlow, BM.
John B. Hay to Margaret E. Coop, Jan. 7, 1846. Jerimiah
Hay, BM.
John McSharp to Elizabeth Trout, Jan. 9, 1846. (Jan.
12, 1846). Thos. F. Fields, BM.
John A. Roe to Nancy Newhouse, Jan. 10, 1846. (Jan.
15, 1846). Robert Philips, BM.
Redden C. Thomas to Martha E. Hobbs, Jan. 12, 1846.
(Jan. 15, 1846). James Witson, BM.
Timothy Dowlen to Sarah Mitts, Jan. 13, 1846. (Jan.
13, 1846). William Fox, BM.
Elias Miller to Helana S. Frayer, Jan. 22, 1846. (Jan.
22, 1846).
Gedion Goodrich to Rebecca Vier, Jan. 24, 1846. (Jan.
27, 1846). Thos. G. Taylor, BM.
William R. Gammon to Sandal Bryant, Jan. 27, 1846.
(Jan. 28, 1846). Thos. H. Jackson, BM.
William C. Hicks to Margarett McAlelly, Jan. 29, 1846.
(Jan. 29, 1846). Bradford Edwards, BM.
David Flowers to Charrity Keathly, Jan. 31, 1846.
(Feb. 1, 1846). Elisha Keathly, BM.
John T. Coleman to Elizabeth Merritt, Feb. 2, 1846.
(Feb. 3, 1846). T. A. Sharp, BM.
James M. Pounds to Nancy Sherron, Feb. 2, 1846. (Feb.
4, 1846). Preston Waldrop, BM.
Alexander McAnelly to Martha Flowers, Feb. 10, 1846.
Barnabas Flowers, BM.
Moses Hurley to Martha Burrow, Feb. 10, 1846. (Feb.
12, 1846). Chesterfield Tigret, BM.
Thos. J. N. K. H. Thedford to Elvira Thedford, Feb.
10, 1846. (Feb. 12, 1846). Jas. A. Connall, BM.
George S. Brassfield to Sarah Nunn, Feb. 11, 1846.
(Feb. 12, 1846). Marion I. Clay, BM.
Henry Cooper to Catharine Moore, Feb. 11, 1846. (Feb,
12, 1846). Nathan Daly, BM.
Cullen J. Boyett to Delilah Watts, Feb. 12, 1846.
Thomas Boyett, BM.
Joseph Newell to Maria Davis, Feb. 12, 1846. Uriah
Newell, BM.
John Bradbury to Martha Combs, Feb. 19, 1846. (Feb.
19, 1846). Jacob Flowers, BM.
Richard McGee to Eliza E. Scrape, Feb. 19, 1846. (Feb.
19, 1846). M. B. King, BM.

GIBSON COUNTY MARRIAGES

James Perminter to Nany Smith, Feb. 19, 1846. Jessee Graddy, BM.
Peleg Bailey to Margarett J. Donaldson, Feb. 23, 1846. (Feb. 26, 1846). James Donaldson, BM.
Jessee Sandford to Manirva Karnes, Feb. 24, 1846. (Feb. 25, 1846). B. F. Arnold, BM.
Nathan Nicholls to Cass Ann Cayton, Feb. 25, 1846. (Feb. 26, 1846). Smith Parks, BM.
Caswell J. Moore to Levy White, Mar. 2, 1846. (Mar. 8, 1846). Isiah Webb, BM.
William Taylor to Mary Patterson, Mar. 7, 1846. (Mar. 11, 1846). Abram Taylor, BM.
William R. White to Julia A. Armstrong, Mar. 11, 1846. (Mar. 12, 1846). J. M. Armstrong, BM.
James T. Smith to Jane C. Grady, Mar. 12, 1846. (Mar. 12, 1846). John W. Lyon, BM.
Martin L. Baley to Dizey Bledsoe, Mar. 13, 1846. (Mar. 15, 1846). Peleg Bailey, BM.
William R. Edmondson to Amanda F. Isrial, Mar. 14, 1846. (Mar. 17, 1846). Thompson Edmonson, BM.
Minor M. Winn to Nancy Yarbory, Mar. 15, 1846. (Mar. 15, 1846). J. C. Foster, BM.
Thomas J. West to Eliza J. Lea, Mar. 16, 1846. (Mar. 19, 1846). George W. Lea, BM.
William P. Sanders to Martha J. Webb, Mar. 16, 1846. (Mar. 17, 1846). Robert C. Harrisson, BM.
Lunsford M. R. Wallis to Ann E. Boon, Mar. 17, 1846. (Mar. 17, 1846). C. E. George, BM.
Phillip King to Emaly Furgarson, Mar. 18, 1846. (Mar. 18, 1846). Eli W. Ing, BM.
Hugh Webb to Mrs. Racal Copeland, Mar. 19, 1846. (Mar. 19, 1846). Wm. Sanders, BM.
John Bradberry to Martha Gardner, Mar. 21, 1846. (Mar. 25, 1846). John Umsted, BM.
Laban Benthel to Mrs. Teracey Acock, Mar. 31, 1846. (Mar. 31, 1846). H. Barker, BM.
Thomas Skipper to Martha A. Quinn, Apr. 1, 1846. (Apr. 2, 1846). Wm. S. C. Gaynin, BM.
Thomas H. Parker to Catharine P. Elliott, Apr. 2, 1846. (Apr. 2, 1846). Isham J. Parker, BM.
Jessee Tharp to Catharine Dalton, Apr. 2, 1846. (Apr. 2, 1846. (Apr. 2, 1846). Isaac Burns, BM.
Mortica Bailey to Elizabeth McDurmit, Apr. 7, 1846. (Apr. 8, 1846). Joiner Bailey, BM.
James T. Abbott to Rebecca E. Barton, Apr. 8, 1846. (Apr. 10, 1846). L. P. Seay, BM.
David Holt to Nancy Shane, Apr. 13, 1846. (Apr. 16, 1846). Alvin Senter, BM.
William M. Jones to Harrett Brickhouse, Apr. 16, 1846. (Apr. 26, 1846). Isham Boyce, BM.
William Williams to Susan Thedford, Apr. 28, 1846. (May 29, 1846). E. P. Waldrop, BM.
James H. Bratton to Mary P. Fifer, Apr. 29, 1846. Jno. E. Cash, BM.

GIBSON COUNTY MARRIAGES

Griffin Wright to Vilett C. Jetton, May 7, 1846. (May
7, 1846). J. J. Smith, BM.
James Harrison to Alleline Adams, May 7, 1846. (May
10, 1846). Leon Adams, BM.
Robert J. Dodson to Emely J. Nobles, May 9, 1846. (May
14, 1846). M. F. Bayn, BM.
Mastin F. Bayn to Lucy Ann Owen, May 9, 1846. (May 14,
1846). R. J. Dodson, BM.
William C. Guinn to Harrett Skipper, May 16, 1846.
(May 17, 1846). Thomas Ferrill, BM.
Richard C. Sellars to Mariah Hampton, May 18, 1846.
(May 18, 1846). Thos. Hampton, BM.
John L. H. Tomlin to Amanda C. Elder, May 19, 1846.
(May 19, 1846). B. F. O. Stillwell, BM.
Leon Adams to Alta Counsal, May 21, 1846. (June 1,
1846). Daniel W. Norman, BM.
George W. Lee to Lucinda Umstead, June 1, 1846. (June
3, 1846). W. C. Lyon, BM.
Leroy D. Webb to Euvilinah M. Carroll, June 13, 1846.
(July 14, 1846). Wm. J. Sherman, BM.
E. H. Hancock to Irena M. Crocker, June 27, 1846.
July 2, 1846). R. C. Crocker, BM.
Elijah Sanders to Mary J. Winn, June 30, 1846. (July
1, 1846). Pleasant Sanders, BM.
James H. Lynch to Martha M. Evans, July 2, 1846. (July
2, 1846). James Motley, BM.
John W. Gately to Nancy McCleur, July 3, 1846. (July
7, 1846). J. M. Gately, BM.
Samuel D. Spake to Susan Mays, July 7, 1846. (July 9,
1846). L. L. Brightwell, BM.
Benj. F. Scallion to Matilda C. Berry, July 10, 1846.
Jessee Cassels, BM.
Enoch D. Waldrop to Martha A. Waldrop, July 12, 1846.
John C. Davis, BM.
Jessee Cassells to Jane Craige, July 13, 1846. (July
15, 1846). Jas. McDermitt, BM.
William B. Craige to Amanda Berry, July 13, 1846. (July
15, 1846). James McDermitt, BM.
Solomon Dinny to Nancy Howell, July 15, 1846. (July
16, 1846). Jethro Howell, BM.
Calvin M. Harrison to Mary A. E. Rentfro, July 15, 1846.
(July 16, 1846). Jno. V. Morton, BM.
William Edwards to Martha C. Wynn, July 21, 1846. (July
23, 1846). Jas. H. Nunn, BM.
Wesley R. Gossett to Candis Brown, July 22, 1846. (July
23, 1846). Young W. Allen, BM.
John J. J. Lee to Marting S. Dement, Aug. 3, 1846.
(Aug. 3, 1846). M. T. Barlow, BM.
William P. Maclin to Jane C. Donaldson, Aug. 5, 1846.
(Aug. 6, 1846). R. W. Hawkins, BM.
Arthur A. Williams to Margaret Conell, Aug. 8, 1846.
W. W. Conell, BM.
Jonah Y. Dodson to Ann Bayn, Aug. 11, 1846. (Aug. 13,
1846). William May, BM.

James W. Gardner to Maranda J. Shaw, Aug. 12, 1846.
(Aug. 12, 1846). William Gardner, BM.
William E. Jackson to Mary A. Umstard, Aug. 12, 1846.
(Aug. 12, 1846). Wm. J. Walker, BM.
Abraham E. Norrid to Mary Ann West, Aug. 18, 1846.
(Aug. 25, 1846). Abner N. Reed, BM.
John H. Butram to Sarah Dunlap, Aug. 20, 1846. (Aug.
20, 1846). Samuel Dunlap, BM.
William R. Carroll to Rebecca C. Moudy, Aug. 25, 1846.
(Aug. 27, 1846). M. L. Richardson, BM.
Caswell E. George to Mary T. Bass, Aug. 25, 1846.
(Aug. 26, 1846). Henry G. Hunt, BM.
Henry G. Hunt to Jane W. Allen, Aug. 24, 1846. (Aug.
25, 1846). Caswell E. George, BM.
Franklin Hayns to Elizabeth Bryant, Sept. 1, 1846.
(Aug. 29, 1846). Micajah House, BM.
James H. May to Eva J. Lane, Sept. 3, 1846. (Sept.
3, 1846). Joel Lane, BM.
Benjamin Warmack to Frances C. Arnold, Sept. 4, 1846.
(Sept. 6, 1846). T. C. Bueff, BM.
Jessee J. Smith to Katharine J. Massey, Sept. 7, 1846.
(Sept. 6, 1846). Algernon S. Currey, BM.
William Staton to Elizabeth Little, Sept. 10, 1846.
Dawson Hancock, BM.
Micajah Fly to Frances Senter, Sept. 15, 1846. (Sept.
17, 1846). William Boon, BM.
Robert Dickins to Mary Dickey, Sept. 16, 1846. (Oct.
10, 1846). Wm. B. Wallace, BM.
Willis L. Reeves to Mary Robinson, Sept. 19, 1846.
(Sept. 24, 1846). D. Harpole, BM.
James B. Jones to Rachal A. Tate, Sept. 22, 1846.
(Oct. 10, 1846). James M. Senter, BM.
William Scott to Biddy King, Sept. 24, 1846. (Sept.
26, ?). Jas Weatherspoon, BM.
William J. Walker to Jane A. R. Jackson, Oct. 3, 1846.
(Oct. 6, 1846). John Green, BM.
Levi Wright to Mary A. M. Clements, Oct. 5, 1846.
(Oct. 5, 1846). A. F. Clements, BM.
Alfred Pruett to Sarah Canada, Oct. 5, 1846. (Oct. 7,
1846). David P. Hamilton, BM.
John S. Baldridge to Martha Moore, Oct. 5, 1846. (Oct.
6, 1846). John A. Wilkins, BM.
Nathaniel Nobles to Margaret E. Griffy, Oct. 5, 1846.
(Oct. 6, 1846).
Hugh S. McCaleb to Nancy Duberry, Oct. 7, 1846. (Oct.
10, 1846). James Ross, BM.
Franklin Needham to Mirna Tilghman, Oct. 13, 1846.
(Oct. 5, 1846). Jethro Howell, BM.
Ratliff Booth to Elizabeth Adkins, Oct. 13, 1846.
Isaac Ham, BM.
Leander Pearce to Laretha Rogers, Oct. 14, 1846. (Oct.
14, 1846). James B. Humble, BM.
Nathan Daley to Elizabeth Swindle, Oct. 15, 1846. (Oct.
15, 1846). D. W. Swindle, BM.

GIBSON COUNTY MARRIAGES

Leander M. Richardson to Mary B. Rader, Oct. 17, 1846.
W. R. Carroll, BM.
James R. Keath to Luisa C. Ward, Oct. 17, 1846. (Sept.
18, 1846). John Smith, BM.
Richard D. Harris to Narcissa Bowman, Oct. 20, 1846.
(Oct. 20, 1846). M. B. Elder, BM.
Dority Turner to Susan M. Lewis, Oct. 23, 1846. (Oct.
27, 1846). Ansell Quick, BM.
James A. Flippin to Manirva White, Oct. 24, 1846.
(Oct. 28, 1846). A. R. Flippin, BM.
Johnathan Mobley to Mary A. Robinson, Oct. 26, 1846.
(Oct. 28, 1846). Wm. Mobley, BM.
Thomas Beard to Mary Easterwood, Oct. 27, 1846. (Oct.
27, 1846). Westly Easterwood, BM.
Nathaniel H. Corley to Nancy S. Cooper, Oct. 27, 1846.
(Nov. 28, 1846). T. A. Wilkins, BM.
Wm. M. Stone to Sarah J. Cribbs, Oct. 31, 1846. Wm.
T. C. Cribbs, BM.
Thomas Woodson to Jane Edwards, Oct. 31, 1846. (Nov.
1, 1846). Emry Williams, BM.
Henry McGee to Margaret M. C. Martin, Nov. 21, 1846.
(Nov. 3, 1846). H. H. Walker, BM.
James M. Dodd to Precilla L. Wade, Nov. 5, 1846. (Nov.
5, 1846). Wm. J. Yeates, BM.
Phillip E. Waddell to Sarah E. Moore, Nov. 5, 1846.
(Nov. 5, 1846). Granville H. Marlin, BM.
William N. McCain to Tibitha Armstrong, Nov. 9, 1846.
(Nov. 11, 1846). J. R. Mason, BM.
James Caton to Marinda Shipman, Nov. 10, 1846. (Nov.
10, 1846). Peter L. Dozier, BM.
William J. N. Wilbourn to Rebecca J. McLamore, Nov.
17, 1846. (Nov. 17, 1846). J. A. W. Hess, BM.
Daniel W. Norman to Mary A. Dorset, Nov. 17, 1846.
(Nov. 17, 1846). Hosa Parker, BM.
Joel B. Lewis to Martha M. Davidson, Nov. 19, 1846.
(Nov. 19, 1846). Charles Griffey, BM.
Josiah M. Alexander to Amanda McCalab, Nov. 23, 1846.
(Nov. 23, 1846). B. Crawford, BM.
William J. Taylor to Catharine Goodrich, Dec. 2, 1846.
(Dec. 9, 1846). Wilson Barrett, BM.
George Akers to Mary J. E. Hening, Dec. 2, 1846. (Dec.
3, 1846). J. W. Williams, BM.
Absolum W. Nobles to Nancy Vanog, Dec. 2, 1846. Felix
Parker, BM.
Andrew Patrick to Susannah B. Harpole, Dec. 7, 1846.
(Dec. 7, 1846). James Grissom, BM.
James Latta to Martha J. Harrison, Dec. 7, 1846. (Dec.
8, 1846). E. W. Rains, BM.
James Cannon to Mary Pate, Dec. 12, 1846. (Dec. 13,
1846). M. L. Davidson, BM.
Isaac Bobbett to Hasty Dickens, Dec. 14, 1846. (Dec.
17, 1846). James M. Senter, BM.
David W. Hamilton to Prudance Newhouse, Dec. 14, 1846.
(Dec. 15, 1846). Thos. D. Newhouse, BM.

William Fox to Susan Ann Morris, Dec. 15, 1846. (Dec. 20, 1846). Joel Arnold, BM.

William G. Crank to Zada P. Wright, Dec. 17, 1846. (Dec. 19, 1846). Wm. T. Wilkins, BM.

James E. Cole to Rebecca Dean, Dec. 17, 1846. (Dec. 18, 1846). Jno. W. Elder, BM.

Josiah S. Ford to Huldy Jones, Dec. 18, 1846. (Dec. 20, 1846). Saml. R. Tucker, BM.

Henry F. Reed to Sarah A. Trout, Dec. 19, 1846. (Jan. 6, 1847). Hugh R. Reed, BM.

Joshua Sanders to Charrity Cooper, Dec. 28, 1846. (Dec. 31, 1846). R. C. Harrison, BM.

William H. Baldridge to Elizabeth Nuckles, Dec. 28, 1846. (Dec. 29, 1846). Robt. J. Corley, BM.

William K. Dial to Rachal Mobley, Dec. 30, 1846. John C. Porter, BM.

William D. Umstard to Martha W. Shelton, Jan. 4, 1847. Samuel Shane, BM.

Isaac C. Mitchell to Mary A. Reed, Jan. 5, 1847. (Jan. 7, 1847). George Canada, BM.

Richard Thompson to Mariah Lyons, Jan. 7, 1847. (Jan. 7, 1847). Hosa Parker, BM.

Richard Wormack to Mary L. Billingsley, Jan. 9, 1847. (Jan. 12, 1847). Benj. Wormack, BM.

Washington Needham to Elizabeth E. Tilghman, Jan. 14, 1847. (Jan. 14, 1847). Franklin Needham, BM.

John M. Barton to Sarah J. Barrott, Jan. 13, 1847. (Jan. 15, 1847). H. M. L. Barton, BM.

Samuel Sainford to Jane Strain, Jan. 19, 1847. (Jan. 20, 1847).

Caswell Miflin to Tabitha Ray, Jan. 21, 1847. (Jan. 21, 1847). H. Parker, BM.

William L. Bodkin to Fany C. Alexander, Jan. 21, 1847. Samuel D. Alexander, BM.

James M. Holt to Mary A. Martin, Jan. 25, 1847. (Jan. 28, 1847). John Martin, BM.

Jefferson Holland to Nancy Rose, Jan. 26, 1847. (Jan. 27, 1847). Julias Hall, BM.

John C. Davis to Martha A. Roach, Jan. 27, 1847. (Jan. 28, 1847). Jas Connell, BM.

Andrew J. Elliott to Mary Clark, Jan. 30, 1847. (Feb. 3, 1847).

Henry W. Hefley to Eliza James, Feb. 5, 1847. James M. Dunlap, BM.

John R. Runalds to Selina A. Hague, Feb. 6, 1847. D. A. Williams, BM.

Irwin Parker to Catharine Howell, Feb. 8, 1847. Richard Tidwell, BM.

Dr. W. Taylor to Emaline M. McFarlen, Feb. 9, 1847. (Feb. 11, 1847). Jno. W. Gatley, BM.

James M. Halford to Rebecca E. Kimbro, Feb. 9, 1847. Wm. M. Halford, BM.

Wiley B. Massey to Isabella R. Montgomery, Feb. 10, 1847. Thos. W. Kelton, BM.

James M. Dial to Hanabell M. Alexander. (No dates.)

GIBSON COUNTY MARRIAGES

Thomas Ray to Mary Morgan, Feb. 13, 1847. (Feb. 14,
    1847). Wm. A. White, BM.
Jeremiah G. Weddle to Jane Ann Gardner, Feb. 15, 1847.
    (Feb. 15, 1847).
William Hampton to Sarah Knott, Feb. 15, 1847. (Feb.
    16, 1847).
Henry Walker to Hannah Shaw, Feb. 16, 1847. (Mar. 14,
    1847). Jas. H. Richardson, BM.
Isaac Tharp to Sopha Mayfield, Feb. 18, 1847. (Feb.
    18, 1847). Thos. Tharp, BM.
Frederick Becton to Pherraby Hillard, Feb. 18, 1847.
    David Manring, BM.
Edwin Crossland to Mary Adaline Hess, March 2, 1847.
    By S. Y. Thomas, M.G.
Geo. W. Blankenship to Martha A. Jackson, Mar. 15, 1847.
    (Mar. 16, 1847).
Benjamin J. Williams to Mrs. Martha J. Sanders, Mar.
    17, 1847. (Mar. 17, 1847). William A. King, BM.
Alex M. Beadles to Mary Fite, Mar. 17, 1847. B.
    Billingsley, BM.
Bevely Price to Mary Hailey, Mar. 29, 1847. (Apr. 7,
    1847).
George W. Simpson to Mary Nail, Apr. 8, 1847. (Apr. 9,
    1847).
William Husbands to Susannah M. Thompson, Apr. 16,
    1847. (Apr. 22, 1847).
William H. Hall to Virginia A. Joleff, Apr. 16, 1847.
    Davis Ballentine, BM.
William Runalds to Kissiah Smith, Apr. 21, 1847. (Apr.
    22, 1847).
Thomas D. Thomas to Susan M. Hamilton, May 4, 1847.
    (May 4, 1847). Luther M. Caldwell, BM.
Thomas J. Wrenn to Martha A. Temple, May 10, 1847.
    (May 13, 1847). Robert M. Lett, BM.
Grant Z. Harrison to Angaline Riley, May 13, 1847.
    (May 13, 1847). D. S. Riley, BM.
Allen Dunagan to Rebecca Twigg, May 15, 1847. (May
    16, 1847). W. J. McKenny, BM.
Cooper B. Jones to Emay K. Reddin, May 27, 1847. Thos.
    D. Reddin, BM.
Benjamin F. Cowen to Nancy N. Hutchions, May 26, 1847.
    (May 26, 1847). H. Barker, BM.
Johnithan Dawson to Tennessee Sexton, June 10, 1847.
    (June 15, 1847). H. Parker, BM.
Wadkins D. Dodson to Jarusa A. Blakemore, June 15,
    1847. (June 17, 1847).
Jimion S. Clements to Martha J. Locke, June 22, 1847.
    (June 22, 1847). Wilson Williams, BM.
Henry W. Estes to Rosa Ann Duet, July 6, 1847. (July
    6, 1847). S. S. Estes, BM.
Daniel J. Riley to Milly Benson, July 10, 1847. (July
    11, 1847). Washington Riley, BM.
Alex M. Denwiddie to Nancy F. Chrisp, July 17, 1847.
    (July 20, 1847). M. B. Elder, BM.

63

GIBSON COUNTY MARRIAGES

Robert H. Taylor to Mary A. Jackson, July 20, 1847.
(July 21, 1847). Milton Pollard, BM.

Bartlett Gooden to Jamima Spencer, July 20, 1847.
(July 27, 1847). David Flowers, BM.

Henry F. Cowen to Margarett Wrenn, July 21, 1847. (July
22, 1847).

Daniel England to Louisa Ann James, Aug. 2, 1847.
(Aug. 3, 1847). Levi G. Danner, BM.

Joel B. Sigmon to Barbary R. Martin, Aug. 2, 1847.
(Aug. 2, 1847). W. H. Tuggle, BM.

Wiley W. West to Elizabeth McMinn, Aug. 9, 1847. J. L.
Penyman, BM.

William H. Simms to Sarah A. McCracken, Aug. 10, 1847.
(Aug. 11, 1847). Smith Parks, BM.

Edward Bass to Nancy Hall, Aug. 10, 1847. (Aug. 12,
1847). Charles Robinson, BM.

William B. Dyall to Hannah H. Darnald, Aug. 12, 1847.
(Aug. 12, 1847). John M. Alexander, BM.

William H. Abbott to Mary J. Baker, Aug. 16, 1847.
J. W. Williams, BM.

Robert Spellings to Lucy Browning, Aug. 17, 1847.
(Aug. 18, 1847).

William Gibson to Nancy Gwinn, Aug. 17, 1847. (Aug.
17, 1847).

Major Bledsoe to Mary Welch, Aug. 26, 1847. (Aug. 26,
1847).

William R. Sparkman to Ann M. Selph, Aug. 30, 1847.
(Sept. 1, 1847). J. W. Carter, BM.

William H. Webb to Martha Jane Crockett, Sept. 6, 1847.
Benj. P. Williams, BM.

W. B. Dowell to Nancy Lowry, Sept. 6, 1847. G. G.
McIlwain, BM.

Hosia Parker to Elizabeth Strong, Sept. 7, 1847. (Sept.
7, 1847).

Nathaniel J. Hockaday to Pricella J. Sanderford, Sept.
7, 1847. (Sept. 7, 1847).

M. D. Holder to Polly Ray, Sept. 11, 1847. (Sept. 14,
1847). John A. Jackson, BM.

Josiah L. Horn to Sarah M. Baisinger, Sept. 15, 1847.
T. J. Baisinger, BM.

William Rogers to Jane Dolan, Sept. 21, 1847. (Sept.
23, 1847).

James N. Martin to Morning P. Evans, Sept. 23, 1847.
(Sept. 23, 1847). Nathan Reed, BM.

Joseph H. Harrison to C. A. Short, Sept. 23, 1847.
W. H. Wrenn, BM.

John E. Alexander to Mary Ann Nobles, Sept. 23, 1847.
Hosia Parker, BM.

John L. Fly to Mary J. McDaniel, Sept. 25, 1847. (Dec.
3, 1847).

Allen Brogdon to Sidney Phillips, Sept. 29, 1847.
(Sept. 29, 1847). Young W. Allen, BM.

Jerrod J. Ethridge to Mary A. Smith, Oct. 1, 1847.
(Oct. 3, 1847).

GIBSON COUNTY MARRIAGES

William Mainor to Martha A. Edwards, Oct. 8, 1847.
Daniel E. McAllister, BM.
John N. Bush to Rachal Glisson, Oct. 12, 1847. (Oct.
12, 1847). W. Arhart, BM.
Benassa King to Sarah A. Flowers, Oct. 12, 1847. (Oct.
12, 1847). Wiley O. Mobley, BM.
Allen Rasberry to Elizabeth Weatherford, Oct. 18, 1847.
(Oct. 19, 1847). Wills Rasberry, BM.
Allen Taylor to Susan B. Johnson, Oct. 20, 1847. (Oct.
21, 1847). John L. Poston, BM.
Albert J. Webb to Virginia F. Sanderford, Oct. 21, 1847.
(Dec. 3, 1847). W. B. Seat, BM.
Daniel E. McAlester to Margarett A. E. Johnson, Oct.
25, 1847. (Oct. 28, 1847). Samuel L. Pittman, BM.
J. J. G. Cutler to Eliza J. McDaniel, Oct. 26, 1847.
(Nov. 9, 1847).
John S. McCulloch to Sarah L. Wilkins, Oct. 28, 1847.
(Oct. 28, 1847). Robt. B. Foster, BM.
Wesley F. Jones to Mary A. Wilkins, Oct. 28, 1847.
(Oct. 28, 1847). T. W. Jones, BM.
Alpia G. Ray to Catharine Carter, Nov. 4, 1847. (Dec.
1, 1847). John A. Jackson, BM.
Edmund A. Freeman to Nancy E. Hamilton, Nov. 4, 1847.
(Dec. 3, 1847).
William Ingram to Jane Hays, Nov. 8, 1847. (Nov. 11,
1847). Jno. F. Hays, BM.
Rubin Wichard to Eliza J. Brent, Nov. 12, 1847. (Nov.
14, 1847).
L. G. H. Pittman to Leuvenia M. Pittman, Nov. 16, 1847.
(Nov. 18, 1847). Smith Parks, BM.
William M. McBryde to Sarah Grigsby, Nov. 16, 1847.
(Nov. 16, 1847).
James Thomason to Sarah Jane Rogers, Nov. 17, 1847.
(Nov. 17, 1847). George T. White, BM.
Milton R. Morgan to Mary Jane Johnson, Nov. 17, 1847.
(Nov. 18, 1847). Wm. H. Holloman, BM.
John Martin to Elizabeth Holt, Nov. 19, 1847. (Nov.
21, 1847). Joel Arnold, BM.
John Crage to Carline Cassells, Nov. 20, 1847. (Nov.
21, 1847). G. W. Cress, BM.
Sterling B. Scott to Mary E. Biggs, Nov. 23, 1847.
(Nov. 23, 1847). Robt. B. Foster, BM.
James C. Mathis to Lucy J. Olaver, Nov. 29, 1847.
(Dec. 2, 1847).
William Haislip to Mary A. Malone, Dec. 10, 1847.
(Dec. 14, 1847). Johnathan J. Haislip, BM.
James Biggs to Elizabeth C. Thomasson, Dec. 16, 1847.
(Dec. 16, 1847).
Wilson Doxey to Martha Biggs, Dec. 17, 1847.
Peter Ballentine to Elizabeth C. Bunnell, Dec. 17, 1847.
(Dec. 22, 1847). D. Ballentine, BM.
William J. Jernagun to Eliza Clark, Dec. 20, 1847.
(Dec. 20, 1847). Andrew J. Elliott, BM.
Isaac Canaday to Mahala Yates, Dec. 22, 1847. (Dec.
23, 1847). P. M. Connell, BM.

John F. Hays to Sarah E. Ingram, Dec. 22, 1847. (Dec. 23, 1847). Wm. Ingram, BM.

James Gibson to Martha A. Richardson, Dec. 22, 1847. (Dec. 23, 1847). Daniel Richardson, BM.

George W. Moore to Eliza J. Hoozer, Dec. 23, 1847. (Dec. 30, 1847). Tillman Melton, BM.

James R. Burrow to Mary A. King, Dec. 23, 1847. (Dec. 23, 1847). Wm. Durley, BM.

Hamilton Foster to Nancy Chandler, Dec. 27, 1847. (Dec. 28, 1847). C. R. Parhan, BM.

Jacob W. Arnold to Angaline K. Hamilton, Dec. 27, 1847. (Jan. 25, 1848).

William G. Baker to Nancy J. Weatherford, Dec. 27, 1847. (Dec. 28, 1847). P. P. Baker, BM.

Samuel Lowry to Rebecca J. James, Dec. 27, 1847. Sterling B. Ford, BM.

Person K. Dorsett to Nancy J. Lowry, Dec. 28, 1847. (Dec. 28, 1847). Nathan J. Norman, BM.

Arthur Moore to Mildred E. Farmer, Dec. 28, 1847. Johnathan B. Agee, BM.

Lafayett Morris to Lucinda Holt, Dec. 30, 1847. (Dec. 31, 1847). B. F. Arnold, BM.

Phillip West to Deby D. Butler, Jan. 3, 1849. E. C. Butler, BM.

Samuel C. Liggett to Levina Bird, Jan. 8, 1849. James Turner, BM.

Herbert Edwards to Sarah Love, Jan. 12, 1848. (Jan. 13, 1848). Jas. Edwards, BM.

James M. Patterson to Dionico M. Oneal, Jan. 15, 1848. (Jan. 18, 1848). Jos. Tucker, BM.

Francis Perry to Rebecca Reed, Jan. 24, 1848. (Jan. 25, 1848). J. N. Diel, BM.

Jerman Tucker to Emaly V. Patton, Jan. 23, 1848. (Jan. 27, 1848). R. E. Boyle, BM.

Lucion B. Gilchrist to Valiria M. Wright, Jan. 26, 1848. (Jan. 26, 1848). Luther M. Caldwell, BM.

Richard Chandler to Lucy McMullen, Jan. 31, 1848. (Feb. 1, 1848). C. D. McMullen, BM.

James C. Davidson to Barbary Fletcher, Feb. 2, 1848. (Feb. 2, 1848). Samuel D. Woods, BM.

Calvin B. Reasons to Lavina Reasons, Feb. 2, 1848. (Feb. 2, 1848). Alfred Combs, BM.

Robert Ervin to Mary A. E. Price, Feb. 5, 1848. (Feb. 10, 1848). Geo. H. Price, BM.

Edmund K. Flowers to Susan Lyons, Feb. 7, 1848. Barnabus Flowers, BM.

Joseph A. W. Mathis to Eliza E. Rone, Feb. 14, 1848. S. Williams, BM.

Allen F. Cunningham to Nancy Cox, Feb. 14, 1848. Wm. T. Cox, BM.

Abner A. Evins to Hester A. Patterson, Feb. 15, 1848. Jas. P. Alexander, BM.

William Durley to Sarah A. Hall, Feb. 15, 1848. (Feb. 15, 1848). S. Williams, BM.

GIBSON COUNTY MARRIAGES

Jordian W. Sadberry to Clayrindy May, Feb. 16, 1848.
(Feb. 16, 1848). William May, BM.
Howell Adams to Darcus E. Allen, Feb. 19, 1848. J.
E. Allen, BM.
William M. Darnold to Delila Waldrop, Feb. 19, 1848.
(Feb. 21, 1848). J. T. Rentfro, BM.
Samuel H. Reed to Ellen C. Bell, Feb. 22, 1848. (Feb.
24, 1848). Saml. C. Fullerton, BM.
John F. McCalab to Elizabeth C. Shipman, Feb. 24, 1848.
(Feb. 24, 1848). F. R. McRee, BM.
John Kimbro to Elizabeth Page, Feb. 28, 1848. Smith
Parks, BM.
Jessee Blackburn to Flora Gunter, Feb. 29, 1848. (Mar.
2, 1848). Jas. W. Edwards, BM.
Thomas L. Pounds to Eliza J. Connell, Feb. 29, 1848.
(Feb. 29, 1848). Edwards Thetford, BM.
Daniel L. Williams to Lucinda C. English, Feb. 29,
1848. (Feb. 30, 1848). Joel Arnold, BM.
John N. Cooper to Eliza Davis, Mar. 3, 1848. (Mar. 5,
1848). Milford Gage, BM.
James F. Randolph to Melinda Doud, Mar. 10, 1848. By
J. T. Asbray, J.P. Johnston Williams, BM.
Rufus Crocker to Martha Walker, Mar. 11, 1848. (Mar.
16, 1848). Miles H. Travis, BM.
Milton Thomas to Lyda Dolan, Mar. 11, 1848. (Mar. 12,
1848). George W. Wood, BM.
William S. Oakford to Mary E. McLaurine, Mar. 15, 1848.
(Mar. 15, 1848).
Jeremiah Hay to Ibby M. J. Harbour, Mar. 20, 1848.
James Pyland, BM.
Moladeous B. Carroll to Cornelia F. Henry, Mar. 20,
1848. (Mar. 22, 1848).
Francis M. Livingston to Dorithey Sale, Mar. 20, 1848.
(Mar. ?, 1848). Jas. M. Livingston, BM.
Thomas Hampton to Dolly Wilson, Mar. 29, 1848. (Mar.
31, 1848).
Benj. F. Arnold to Louisa Waldrop, Mar. 30, 1848.
(Mar. 30, 1848). J. W. Gilliland, BM.
J. D. Mitchell to Martha Ann Grier, Apr. 5, 1848.
(Apr. 6, 1848). R. W. Mitchell, BM.
James L. Benthel to Martha E. Bass, Apr. 6, 1848.
(Apr. 6, 1848). N. J. Akins, BM.
William Fifer to Carissa R. Edwards, Apr. 7, 1848.
E. A. Butler, BM.
Sidney H. Tomlinson to Martha T. Phillips, Apr. 8, 1848.
(Apr. 15, 1848). Jas. R. S. Walker, BM.
Joshua Nobles to Sarah J. Dickson, Apr. 10, 1848.
Nathaniel Nobles, BM.
William E. Barker to Mary E. Lea, Apr. 10, 1848. (Apr.
17, 1848). J. J. J. A. Lea, BM.
William M. Bratton to Winaford Umstard, May 6, 1848.
(May 9, 1848). Alexander Bass, BM.
William C. Livingston to Eliza J. Johnson, May 8, 1848.
(May 9, 1848).

Charles C. Stell to Mary C. Hague, May 13, 1848. (May 17, 1848).

Absolum B. Laymon to Mary R. Crossby, May 27, 1848. (May 31, 1848). Franklin Laymon, BM.

Samuel R. Tucker to Marilda M. Dale, June 7, 1848. (June 7, 1848). J. V. Morton, BM.

William A. Ross to Clarrissa E. Price, July 19, 1848. (July 23, 1848). John B. Overall, BM.

James Price to Nancy Campbell, June 26, 1848. Edwin A. Spears, BM.

Newton C. Patton to Martha C. Yancey, June 23, 1848. Wm. T. Wilkins, BM.

William Farris to Elizabeth Crawford, July 3, 1848. Jas. M. Griffin, BM.

William T. Mathis to Elizabeth A. Scott, July 12, 1848. (July 16, 1848). P. P. Elliott, BM.

Thomas W. Jones to Elizabeth E. Mitchell, July 12, 1848. (July 13, 1848). S. W. Hatchett, BM.

William M. Coates to Elizabeth Sharp, July 24, 1848. Wm. W. Lowry, BM.

John A. Rentfro to S. E. McCaleb, July 25, 1848. Thos. N. Yarbrough, BM.

Levi Brown to Martha H. Ferril, July 26, 1848. (July 27, 1848). J. D. McDowell, BM.

Neil Alexander Holt to Sabrina E. Adams, Aug. 8, 1848. (Aug. 10, 1848). James S. Shane, BM.

Nathan Meadows to Lucy Carroll, Aug. 8, 1848. (Aug. 10, 1848). Jas. Mojles, BM.

Allen Leroy Dunlap to Nancy Butram, Aug. 16, 1848. (Aug. 17, 1848).

Quincy M. Grier to M. J. Bobbett, Aug. 26, 1848. B. Y. Youngs, BM.

Henry Edwards to Mary Ann Goodman, Aug. 28, 1848. William B. Goodman, BM.

William L. Crocker to Patience W. Hancock, Aug. 31, 1848. G. B. Tinsley, BM.

Gilbert A. West to Martha E. Sexton, Sept. 2, 1848. (Sept. 10, 1848). E. A. Butler, BM.

John M. Watt to Catharine Ann McClure, Sept. 8, 1848. Arthur Cash, BM.

William R. Hazlewood to Susan M. Cassels, Sept. 13, 1848. (Sept. 14, 1848). Jas. L. Cassels, BM.

James L. Cassels to Lucinda E. Fuqua, Sept. 13, 1848. (Sept. 19, 1848).

Samuel Dunlap to Matilda Cela Ann Sellars, Sept. 14, 1848. (Sept. 14, 1848).

Thomas B. Davidson to Katharine Emery, Sept. 14, 1848. Samuel D. Woods, BM.

E. C. Butler to Sarah Ann Sexton, Sept. 14, 1848. E. N. Butler, BM.

Joseph Holloman to Mary Underwood, Sept. 14, 1848. (Sept. 14, 1848). Benj. Landis, BM.

John P. Gill to Elizabeth W. Pruitt, Sept. 15, 1848. (Sept. 15, 1848).

GIBSON COUNTY MARRIAGES

William G. Skiles to Mary W. Brown, Sept. 26, 1848.
(Sept. 27, 1848). Daniel D. Hassell, BM.
William G. Butler to Ann S. Skyles, Sept. 27, 1848.
(Sept. 28, 1848). Julius T. Thompson, BM.
J. T. J. Avery to Harriett A. T. Avery, Oct. 2, 1848.
Miles S. Allen to Elizabeth Berry, Oct. 7, 1848.
(Oct. 11, 1848). Young W. Allen, BM.
William Atchison, Jr. to Sarah B. Knox, Oct. 11, 1848.
L. B. Gilchrist, BM.
John W. Young to Emeline Dunigan, Oct. 11, 1848. B. F.
Young, BM.
James E. Langford to Mary Elizabeth Rust, Oct. 11,
1848. (Oct. 18, 1848). N. S. Langford, BM.
Frunler Parker to Nancy Ann Semons, Oct. 14, 1848.
(Oct. 15, 1848).
William Cannon to Eliza Ann Durley, Oct. 18, 1848.
Joseph Hail, BM.
Daniel Fox to Matilda Ingram, Oct. 18, 1848. (Oct.
19, 1848).
Lewis Robinson to Mary Ward, Oct. 21, 1848. Smith
Parks, BM.
Robert L. P. Oliver to Sarah Ann Brunson, Oct. 25,
1848. Jas. M. Collingsworth, BM.
John M. Holt to Partenia J. Umstead, Nov. 1, 1848.
(Nov. 2, 1848). James M. Senter, BM.
Jordan Knox to Sarah Grist, Nov. 4, 1848. (Nov. 5,
1848).
Robert M. Webb to Martha Cooper, Nov. 7, 1848. (Nov.
9, 1848). R. F. King, BM.
Isaac S. Oliver to Martha Jane Brunson, Nov. 8, 1848.
J. M. Collingsworth, BM.
Thomas Vinson to Elizabeth Johnson, Nov. 13, 1848.
(Nov. 14, 1848).
Robert H. Reed to Eliza Bell, Nov. 14, 1848. S. C.
Fullerton, BM.
Stephen King to Mary Eliza Dickson, Nov. 14, 1848.
V. C. Wright, BM.
Isham F. Davis to Sarah Jane Gordon, Nov. 15, 1848.
Jas. Donaldson, BM.
Willis F. McCasling to Mary S. Campbell, Nov. 15,
1848. (Nov. 16, 1848). Wm. O. Fisher, BM.
John N. Cannon to Sarah A. Clark, Nov. 15, 1848. Marcus
L. Grady, BM.
I. H. D. Webb to Mary Cooper, Nov. 15, 1848. Wm. H.
Webb, BM.
John R. Walker to Sarah Linton, Nov. 17, 1848. James
Martin, BM.
Whitson Pool to Caroline Phillips, Nov. 21, 1848.
C. R. Groom, BM.
Allen Fox to Mary Ann Reed, Nov. 23, 1848. (Nov. 23,
1848). Wm. Fox, BM.
Emanuel Davis to Elizabeth Price, Nov. 23, 1848. John
Price, BM.
Samuel Kincey to Adaline Billingsley, Nov. 27, 1848.
L. D. Webb, BM.

GIBSON COUNTY MARRIAGES

Isaac F. Cowan to Mary Branch, Nov. 29, 1848. B. S.
   Cowan, BM.
Jessee Childers to Harrett Bledsoe, Dec. 1, 1848.
   (Dec. 3, 1848). Henderson Kirby, BM.
John A. Argo to Sonya Billingsly, Dec. 2, 1848.
   Shelton G. Ham, BM.
John W. Pierce to Susan J. Conley, Dec. 5, 1848. Wm.
   E. Crenshaw, BM.
James W. Scott to Emeline Harris, Dec. 6, 1848. Daml.
   W. Harchett, BM.
John Etheridge to Rachael Ann Hall, Dec. 11, 1848. Wm.
   H. Hale, BM.
George L. Pratt to Margaret R. McCallister, Dec. 11,
   1848. (Dec. 14, 1848). Wellington D. W. Johnson, BM.
Absolum H. O.Neal to Rebecca Jane Dickey, Dec. 12,
   1848. J. M. Patterson, BM.
Hardy W. Shelton to Martha T. Green, Dec. 12, 1848.
   (Dec. 14, 1848). Jos. J. J. Hale, BM.
William J. Flippin to Elizabeth Palmore, Dec. 13,
   1848. (Dec. 21, 1848). Jas. A. Flippin, BM.
Theodrick Minton to Mary Reed, Dec. 16, 1848. D. C.
   Dickey, BM.
Peyton J. Smith to Teressa H. Dickins, Dec. 16, 1848.
   (Dec. 17, 1848). P. H. Simmons, BM.
Arthur Turner to Nancy Ferril, Dec. 25, 1848. William
   Hunt, BM.
John A. Argo to Soniza Bullington, Dec. 26, 1848.
   (Dec. 27, 1848). Leonard Taylor, BM.
Joel Arnold to Sarah Paris, Dec. 28, 1848. (Dec. 28,
   1848). Wm. Williams, BM.
Richard L. Shephard to Eliza Jane Holmes, Jan. 1, 1849.
   (Jan. 2, 1849).
Samuel Kinsey to Sarah Bruce, Jan. 1, 1849. (Jan. 2,
   1849).
William H. Bells to Sarah J. Sexton, Jan. 3, 1849.
   (Jan. 4, 1849).
John Cole to Sarah Ann James, Jan. 3, 1849. (Jan. 4,
   1849).
Benj. N. D. Harper to Hardinia J. Hatchett, Jan. 8,
   1849. (Jan. 9, 1849).
James Canada to Partilla Yates, Jan. 10, 1849. (Jan.
   11, 1849).
Simeon Cudd to Sarah Ann Pollard, Jan. 11, 1849. (Jan.
   11, 1849).
George Perry to Spnzy Jane Randolph, Jan. 15, 1849.
   (Jan. 15, 1849).
Alexander Ross to Mary W. Stone, Jan. 16, 1849. (Jan.
   18, 1849).
Hansford A. Fields to Lavinia Susan Roachell, Jan. 17,
   1849. (Jan. 24, 1849).
Rowland Greer to Susan Anthony, Jan. 19, 1849. (Feb.
   6, 1849).
Hillory W. Moseley to Martha Flowers, Jan. 20, 1849.
   (Jan. 24, 1849).

GIBSON COUNTY MARRIAGES

Samuel Taylor to Fanny M. Watts, Jan. 22, 1849. (Jan. 25, 1849).
William H. Terrell to Rachael M. Thomas, Jan. 29, 1849. (Jan. ?, 1849).
Alexander Mobley to Dorithy Frances Vaden, Feb. 1, 1849. (Feb. 1, 1849).
Henry Knott to Camilla Martin, Feb. 6, 1849. (Feb. 7, 1849).
David H. James to Margaret H. Cox, Feb. 12, 1849. (Feb. 13, 1849).
James S. Wood to Elizabeth W. Yancy, Feb. 12, 1849. (Feb. 13, 1849).
Caswell P. Hall to Tennessee Thompson, Feb. 17, 1849. (Feb. 22, 1849).
Martin Y. Taylor to Susan Whitley, Feb. 21, 1849. (Feb. 22, 1849).
Braton Permenter to Elizabeth Jernigan, Feb. 21, 1849. (Feb. 22, 1849).
George W. Moore to Ann Louiza J. Gardner, Feb. 22, 1849. (Feb. 22, 1849).
William B. Foster to Susan G. Donaldson, Mar. 5, 1849. (Mar. 5, 1849).
Pleasant H. Simmons to Emely K. Dickens, Mar. 5, 1849. (Mar. 7, 1849).
John B. Simons to Mary Jane Duncan, Mar. 5, 1849. (Mar. 6, 1849).
Timothy Gleason to Martha B. Sanders, Mar. 5, 1849. (Mar. 13, 1849).
John Sale to Louiza Chadwick, Mar. 9, 1849. (Mar. 11, 1849).
William McGehe to Rutha Hall, Mar. 13, 1849. (Mar. 13, 1849).
William T. Cox to Eliza J. Redick, Mar. 13, 1849. (Mar. 13, 1849).
James M. Armstrong to Rebecca A. Yarbrough, Mar. 15, 1849. (Mar. 15, 1849).
Stephen McPherson to Frances C. Belew, Mar. 17, 1849. (Mar. 16, 1849).
James S. Blakemore to Sarah King, Mar. 22, 1849. (Mar. 22, 1849).
William B. Fields to Mary M. Fields, Mar. 26, 1849. (Mar. 27, 1849).
Sterling B. Ford to Martha W. Parker, Mar. 29, 1849. (Mar. 29, 1849).
James Hutchins to Iredell Jones, Apr. 2, 1849. (Apr. 2, 1849).
S. B. Miller to Eliza Phaland, Apr. 4, 1849. (Apr. 4, 1849).
Herrod C. Anderson to Almira A. Cherry, Apr. 11, 1849. (Apr. 24, 1849).
Edward Fair to Mary Jane Fair, Apr. 16, 1849. (Apr. 17, 1849).
James T. Hall to Rhoda Ethridge, Apr. 18, 1849. (Apr. 19, 1849).

71

William A. Varner to Frances Martin, Apr. 19, 1849.
(Apr. 19, 1849).
Miles H. Travis to Martha Jane Woodson, Apr. 28, 1849.
(Apr. 29, 1849).
William D. Scott to Sutelda E. Webb, Apr. 30, 1849.
(Apr. 1, 1849).
Ephraim Cooper to Eliza Davis, May 3, 1849. (May 4,
1849).
John Cokeley to Delila S. Field, May 5, 1849. (May
10, 1849).
John S. Toler to Mary Ann Dickey, May 5, 1849. (May 7,
1849).
Jessee A. Sonthers to Christina M. Jones, May 9, 1849.
(May 9, 1849).
Ren Pruit to Eathea M. B. Summers, May 17, 1849. (May
17, 1849).
John W. Bell to Sarah Bell, June 2, 1849. (June 5,
1849).
Joseph F. Hazelwood to Malinda Raines, June 6, 1849.
(June 7, 1849).
Josiah L. Claybrook to Elizabeth Jane McCollister,
June 26, 1849. (June 27, 1849).
Joseph P. Boyett to Manerva M. West, June 30, 1849.
(July 12, 1849).
Green B. Goodwin to Elizabeth P. Eliott, July 7,
1849. (July 8, 1849).
William B. Peace to Lydia A. Hail, July 11, 1849.
(July 11, 1849).
E. D. Y. Hundley to Sealia Ann Hudson, July 16, 1849.
(July 17, 1849).
Prier W. Nobles to Mary Craddock, July 18, 1849. (July
18, 1849).
James H. King to Rebecca J. Walker, July 21, 1849.
(July 25, 1849).
Duncan H. Black to Harrett Hopkins, July 23, 1849.
(July 25, 1849).
Matthew M. Garrison to Ann Eveline Van Atty, July 24,
1849. (July 26, 1849).
James W. Edwards to Jane Cole, Aug. 9, 1849. (Aug. 9,
1849).
Joseph J. J. Hale to Manerva J. Walker, Aug. 15, 1849.
(Aug. 16, 1849).
Daniel Womack to Soniza C. Fawbess, Aug. 20, 1849.
(Aug. 27, 1849).
Greenwood Booth to Julia Ann Jane Shane, Aug. 29, 1849.
(Aug. 30, 1849).
Wilson Williams to Sarah Ann Sanderford, Sept. 4, 1849.
(Sept. 5, 1849).
William H. Rust to Martha Jane Senter, Sept. 6, 1849.
(Sept. 6, 1849).
Benj. F. Young to Harriet Young, Sept. 13, 1849.
(Sept. 12, 1849).
Caleb A. Robertson to Martha McCutchan, Sept. 17,
1849. (Sept. 19, 1849).

GIBSON COUNTY MARRIAGES

S. C. Bivens to Sarah A. Griffy, Sept. 19, 1849. (Sept.
19, 1849).
Calvin M. Reese to Mary M. Fields, Sept. 22, 1849.
(Oct. 3, 1849).
William C. Roberts to Emely J. Rutledge, Sept. 29, 1849.
(Oct. 4, 1849).
William Bradford to Harriet E. Moore, Oct. 2, 1849.
(Oct. 2, 1849).
James Carr to Eliza Ann M. Carr, Oct. 3, 1849. (Oct.
4, 1849).
James P. Foster to Margaret A. Hailey, Oct. 4, 1849.
(Oct. 4, 1849).
Reuben Lidrow to Margaret A. Nobles, Oct. 4, 1849.
(Oct. 4, 1849).
Charles Griffey to Heneretta C. Wilks, Oct. 10, 1849.
(Oct. 10, 1849).
Richard B. Lyon to Virginia F. Phillips, Oct. 10, 1849.
(Oct. 11, 1849).
William S. Brooks to Mary Ann E. Glaason, Oct. 15, 1849.
(Oct. 18, 1849).
William S. Brambalow to Milly A. Self, Oct. 18, 1849.
(Oct. 18, 1849).
Henry Cook to Elizabeth Yates, Oct. 19, 1849. (Nov.
8, 1849).
Clinton D. Portis to Sarah A. Portis, Oct. 20, 1849.
(Oct. 20, 1849).
Martin F. Cashar to Mary E. Duberry, Oct. 21, 1849.
(Oct. 21, 1849).
Zachariah Bledsoe to Phebe Turner Allen, Oct. 22, 1849.
(Oct. 21, 1849).
Richard I. Benson to Narcisas Smith, Oct. 23, 1849.
(Oct. 23, 1849).
Charles Morris to Martha Ann Mathis, Oct. 26, 1849.
(Oct. 28, 1849).
Horace R. Barksdale to Cenith C. Glason, Oct. 27, 1849.
(Oct. 28, 1849).
Andrew P. B. R. Butram to Sarah M. Smith, Oct. 27, 1849.
(Oct. 27, 1849).
John S. Wood to Sidy Burr, Oct. 30, 1849. (Oct. 30,
1849).
Alfred Ross to Margarett Ann Bratton, Oct. 31, 1849.
(Nov. 1, 1849).
John B. Arnold to Mary A. Johnson, Oct. 31, 1849.
(Nov. 1, 1849).
William Gague to Jane Mariah White, Nov. 3, 1849.
(Nov. 4, 1849).
Wilie Markham to Martha McCoy, Nov. 5, 1849. (Nov. 8,
1849).
James Crews to Mary Pope, Nov. 5, 1849. (Nov. 8, 1849).
Richard Chradick to Margarett S. Nobles, Nov. 8, 1849.
(Nov. 11, 1849).
William J. Billips to Elizabeth Strain, Nov. 10, 1849.
(Nov. 15, 1849).
Hezekiah Womack to Caroline N. Hutchens, Nov. 18, 1849.
(Nov. 13, 1849).

GIBSON COUNTY MARRIAGES

Hiram R. A. McCorkle to Margarett A. Cowan, Nov. 14,
1849. (Nov. ?, 1849).
Wiley Taylor to Mariah S. Watt, Nov. 15, 1849. (Nov.
18, 1849).
Pleasant A. Vencir to Mary Hobbs, Nov. 19, 1849. (Nov.
20, 1849).
William H. Harvey to Mary R. Penn, Nov. 15, 1849. (Nov.
15, 1849).
Sean Dawtry to Elizabeth S. Crockett, Nov. 20, 1849.
(Nov. 20, 1849).
A. J. Murdock to Mary Moore, Nov. 20, 1849. (Nov. 20,
1849).
Martin Benson to Martha J. Furgenson, Dec. 3, 1849.
(Dec. 4, 1849).
William G. Ward to Jane W. Brown, Dec. 5, 1849. (Dec.
6, 1849).
Isham I. Parker to Mary Ann Ford, Dec. 6, 1849. (Dec.
6, 1849).
H. I. Easterwood to Mary Ann F. Rodgers, Dec. 6, 1849.
(Dec. 6, 1849).
E. R. Bower to Mary Ann Heath, Dec. 6, 1849. (Dec. 6,
1849).
Abner J. Fletcher to Mary J. Wilkes, Dec. 10, 1849.
(Dec. 12, 1849).
Dr. F. Lucas to Martha T. Huce, Dec. 12, 1849. (Dec.
12, 1849).
Robert J. Norman to Mary Elizabeth Self, Dec. 12, 1849.
By T. D. Shipman, M.G.
Thos. L. Woodson to Luzuna M. Fields, Dec. 14, 1849.
(?, 1849).
George W. Price to Gatson Ann S. Anderson, Dec. 17,
1849. (Dec. 20, 1849).
John W. Langford to Sarah R. Tate, Dec. 17, 1849. (Dec.
18, 1849).
John R. Thadwick to Martha Tyler, Dec. 23, 1849. (Dec.
23, 1849).
John Stricklin to Jane Clark, Dec. 24, 1849. (Dec. 24,
1849).
John W. Allison to Elizabeth W. Harrington, Dec. 21,
1849. (Dec. 27, 1849).
Richard L. West to Mary E. Blair, Dec. 21, 1849. (Dec.
23, 1849).
John H. Robinson to Elizabeth Traftor, Dec. 25, 1849.
(Dec. 27, 1849).
Leoma Flowers to Nanny Hobbs, Dec. 27, 1849. (Dec.
27, 1849).
John Cherry to Jane Roberts, Dec. 17, 1849. (Jan. 8,
1849).
Saml. D. Woods to Mary C. Keas, Jan. 2, 1850. (Jan. 2,
1850). Jasper N. Beaty, BM.
D. I. Asler to Ann Barham, Jan. 3, 1850. (Jan. ?, 1850).
Elias Miller, BM.
William White to Amanda Hyett, Jan. 5, 1850. (Jan. 4,
1850). Thos. Greer, BM.

74

GIBSON COUNTY MARRIAGES

John Hobbs to Susan Spencer, Jan. 9, 1850. (Jan. 10, 1850).
William H. Smith to Mahala Simpson, Jan. 12, 1850. (Jan. 14, 1850).
Benjamin Boon to Mary E. Little, Jan. 15, 1850. (Jan. 15, 1850).
Samuel Blackley to Winney Jack, Jan. 16, 1850. (Jan. 17, 1850).
G. S. Allen to Susan S. Clement, Jan. 16, 1850. (Jan. 17, 1850).
Jessee B. Morgan to Eliza Waller, Jan. 17, 1850. (Jan. 17, 1850).
James S. Reed to Sarah Jane Smith, Jan. 21, 1850.
John W. Nichols to Margaret E. Cook, Jan. 22, 1850. (Jan. 23, 1850). Arthur Cash, BM.
A. L. Lett to E. C. Abbott, Jan. 28, 1850. (Jan. 31, 1850). Thos. G. Barton, BM.
John L. Thedford to Margaret Jane Cribbs, Jan. 30, 1850. (Jan. 30, 1850). Jacob Flowers, BM.
James Alford to Jane Arnol, Jan. 30, 1850. (Feb. 5, 1850). Admira Turner, BM.
Young W. Allen to Mary Hammond, Feb. 1, 1850. (?) Blancett, BM.
George W. Foren to Elizabeth Webb, Feb. 9, 1850. (Feb. 13, 1850).
James G. English to Margaret J. Cowan, Feb. 11, 1850. (Feb. 12, 1850).
Felix G. Kinsey to Mary J. Jones, Feb. 11, 1850. (Feb. 15, 1850).
T. S. Feeman to Susan Thomas, Feb. 12, 1850. (Feb. 12, 1850).
John W. Baker to Mary C. Blain, Feb. 13, 1850. (Feb. 14. 1850).
Ruben S. Ingram to Julia A. Mays, Feb. 19, 1850. (Feb. 19, 1850). Jno. W. Elder, BM.
Wilson P. Harpole to Milly B. Fowler, Feb. 23, 1850. (Feb. 26, 1850).
Henry Valentine to Sarah E. Dibrell, Mar. 4, 1850. (Mar. 6, 1850).
Beverly B. Watson to Nancy E. Page, Mar. 4, 1850. (Mar. 4, 1850).
Thomas Ferrel to Susan Bullard, Mar. 6, 1850. (Mar. 6, 1850).
Andrew Sexton to Martha Butler, Mar. 7, 1850. (Mar. 8, 1850).
William Laymon to Mary Ann Mathis, Mar. 9, 1850. (Mar. 10, 1850). Valentine Mathis, BM.
Green Reynold to Sarah Wallace, Mar. 13, 1850. (Mar. 13, 1850). Wm. R. Wallace, BM.
Benjamin Landis to Jane N. Nimmo, Mar. 13, 1850. (Mar. 13, 1850). S. W. Hatchett, BM.
Peter H. Kinsey to Mary E. Peel, Mar. 19, 1850. (Mar. 27, 1850). Dempsey Connel, BM.
Joseph Witherspoon to Susan Y. Bledsoe, Mar. 22, 1850. By J. W. Jones, L.E. W. S. Jones, BM.

GIBSON COUNTY MARRIAGES

Jacob M. Twigg to Minerva Meritt, Mar. 23, 1850. (Mar. 26, 1850). Joel Nunn, BM.
William Hunt to Martha Turner, Mar. 26, 1850. (Mar. 28, 1850). P. Ford, BM.
Christopher S. Cooper to Susan M. Porter, Mar. 30, 1850. (Mar. 31, 1850). E. M. Cashion, BM.
Archelus B. Branch to Martha E. Pate, Apr. 17, 1850. (Apr. 21, 1850). John R. Pate, BM.
Coleman Roberson to Sarah Ann Stray, Apr. 20, 1850. (Apr. 21, 1850). Wm. B. Billingsly, BM.
Joseph P. Hale to Susan Chandler, Apr. 24, 1850. (Apr. 24, 1850). Rufus K. Hatchett, BM.
John O. Fox to Alsey M. Beck, May 6, 1850. (May 8, 1850). Wm. T. Fox, BM.
William Hickman to Sarah Robertson, May 14, 1850. (May 14, 1850). Henderson Baker, BM.
Franklin J. Terrill to Sarah A. Roberson, May 16, 1850. (May 16, 1850). Hugh W. Reed, BM.
Isaac W. Bass to Sarah Hunt, May 20, 1850. (May 28, 1850). William Hunt, BM.
Noah C. Smith to Sarah P. Sandford, May 20, 1850. (May 21, 1850).
Branch Keathly to Manirva Burnes, May 27, 1850. Murtial B. Keathly, BM.
Samuel H. Sloan to Mary E. McKnight, May 28, 1850. (May 28, 1850). David M. McKnight, BM.
Daniel Feeley to Rutha Caton, May 28, 1850. (May 28, 1850).
John O. Henderson to Elizabeth Pearce, June 30, 1850. (June 6, 1850).
James R. Jones to Louiza C. Tate, July 1, 1850. (July 4, 1850).
William S. Fowler to Martha Ann McCaslin, July 15, 1850. (July 17, 1850).
James H. Gibson to Ann F. Wright, July 15, 1850. (July 23, 1850).
John Trout to Sarah J. Gibson, July 15, 1850. (July 16, 1850).
James S. Reed to Sarah Jane Smith, July 16, 1850. (July 16, 1850).
William Wormack to Adaline E. Billingsley, July 18, 1850. (July 23, 1850).
Abner S. Thomas to Chana Lovett, July 18, 1850. (Aug. 8, 1850).
Thos. Cunningham to Lucy Crafton, July 24, 1850. (July 25, 1850).
James M. Cunningham to Meniza Joyce, July 24, 1850. (July 24, 1850).
James Burris to Eliza A. Easterwood, July 27, 1850. (July 29, 1850).
Allen C. James to Nancy Rains, July 29, 1850. (Aug. 1, 1850).
Thomas Bradford to Mariah W. Gillespie, July 30, 1850. (July 30, 1850).

GIBSON COUNTY MARRIAGES

Nathaniel Creel to Mary Flowers, Aug. 7, 1850. (Aug.
8, 1850).
Jasper W. Craig to Lucretia C. Tatum, Aug. 8, 1850.
(Aug. 8, 1850).
George L. Ousler to Thena Jane Cox, Aug. 13, 1850.
(Aug. 14, 1850).
Seth T. Moore to Elizabeth Freeman, Aug. 19, 1850.
(Aug. 21, 1850).
Benj. A. Cooper to Elvira Crockett, Aug. 20, 1850.
(Aug. 22, 1850).
Micajah W. Warmath to Martha Eudaley, Aug. 23, 1850.
(Aug. 27, 1850). J. A. Jennings, BM.
James Cash to J. Emly Watt, Aug. 24, 1850.
William H. Baldridge to Lucy E. H. Nichold, Aug. 26,
1850. (Aug. 26, 1850).
G. W. Tatum to Elizabeth C. Sims, Aug. 31, 1850. (Sept.
3, 1850). James Porter, J.P.
David C. Galard to Sarah Ann Warren, Sept. 4, 1850.
(Sept. 5, 1850).
S. B. Nance to Nancy J. Harrison, Sept. 5, 1850.
(Sept. 5, 1850).
John A. Hurt to Julia A. Clark, Sept. 12, 1850. (Sept.
12, 1850).
Isaac B. Wallingford to Mary S. McMinn, Sept. 12, 1850.
(Sept. 13, 1850).
William Johnson to Martha A. Brown, Sept. 14, 1850.
(Sept. 18, 1850).
Fonzey Jones to Elizabeth Walls, Sept. 16, 1850. (Sept.
17, 1850).
James Cannon to Sarah Cook, Sept. 17, 1850. (Sept.
18, 1850). Jno. Cannon, BM.
Elam Goodwin to Elizabeth A. House, Sept. 18, 1850.
John R. Pate to Clarissa Glisson, Sept. 19, 1850.
(Sept. 22, 1850). Saml. Glisson, BM.
Jefferson Marcum to Surmanthilus E. Ward, Sept. 21,
1850. (Sept. 22, 1850).
Alexander Clark to Jane T. Mayfield, Sept. 24, 1850.
(Sept. 25, 1850).
John Hix to Susan Parrish, Sept. 25, 1850. (Sept. 25,
1850).
James Bell to Susan J. Willis, Sept. 26, 1850. (Sept.
26, 1850).
Travis E. Hall to Elenor M. Turner, Sept. 27, 1850.
(Sept. 27, 1850).
A. B. Blair to Harriet A. Dunlap, Sept. 28, 1850.
(Oct. 10, 1850).
S. K. Duncan to S. P. Lenord, Oct. 7, 1850. (Oct. 15,
1850).
H. L. Cannon to Mary Jane Taylor, Oct. 8, 1850. (Oct.
8, 1850).
James Turner to Julia A. West, Oct. 9, 1850. (Oct. 9,
1850).
Thomas Stockard to Nancy Edward, Oct. 10, 1850. (Oct.
10, 1850).

Jonas S. Pipkin to Susan C. Dockins, Oct. 10, 1850.
(Oct. 13, 1850).
E. A. Butler to Martha E. Sexton, Oct. 12, 1850.
(Oct. 13, 1850).
Joseph G. Mayfield to Rebecca M. Bowman, Oct. 12, 1850.
(Oct. 13, 1850).
Valentine Bell to Precilla Holder, Oct. 12, 1850.
(Oct. 13, 1850).
Bryant Andrews to Penina Wollard, Oct. 15, 1850.
(Oct. 15, 1850).
George W. Dickson to Alley E. Holford, Oct. 15, 1850.
(Oct. 17, 1850).
Wm. H. Phelan to Mary Spencer, Oct. 16, 1850. (Oct. 16,
1850). John Phelan, BM.
Calaway Mathews to Sarah A. Phelan, Oct. 21, 1850.
(Oct. ?, 1850).
Joseph D. Hardin to Nancy Israel, Oct. 22, 1850. (Oct.
23, 1850).
Crawford Jones to Tempa F. Jones, Oct. 23, 1850. (Oct.
24, 1850).
Paul S. Proctor to Nancy Marcum, Oct. 23, 1850. (Nov.
26, 1850). Wm. C. Penn, BM.
David C. Evans to Lucanda E. Tatum, Oct. 27, 1850.
(Oct. 31, 1850).
J. W. Sharp to E. V. C. Hockaday, Oct. 28, 1850. (Oct.
28, 1850). T. A. Sharp, BM.
George C. Hellard to Lucendia Arnold, Nov. 4, 1850.
(Nov. 4, 1850).
Edward Thedford to Louiza Peel, Nov. 4, 1850. (Nov. 6,
1850). James Connell, BM.
O. B. Caldwell to Mary E. Houston, Nov. 6, 1850. (Nov.
6, 1850).
Josiah F. Penn to Mrs. Frances A. Wade, Nov. 7, 1850.
(Nov. 7, 1850).
Simon Doxey to Jane Bittney, Nov. 9, 1850. (Nov. 10,
1850).
William McCasling to Flora Holt, Nov. 16, 1850. (Nov.
13, 1850).
Joshua L. Pemberter to Sarah M. Irvin, Nov. 12, 1850.
(Nov. 13, 1850).
William M. Zearicor to Mary N. Baldridge, Nov. 18, 1850.
(Nov. 18, 1850).
Henry Roane to Mrs. L. E. A. Parker, Nov. 12, 1850.
Nov. 16, 1850). S. W. Hatchett, BM.
Governor Belew to Elizabeth Scott, Nov. 13, 1850.
(Nov. 14, 1850).
Chesley L. Burnwant to Elizabeth A. Bird, Nov. 16,
1850. (Nov. 21, 1850).
George W. Brewer to Rebecca Hall, Nov. 16, 1850. (Nov.
17, 1850).
Geo. B. Tinsley to Margaret C. White, Nov. 17, 1850.
(Nov. 20, 1850). J. V. Morton, BM.
William D. Childress to Sarah L. Taylor, Nov. 22, 1850.
Dec. 2, 1850). Wm. D. Childress, BM.

GIBSON COUNTY MARRIAGES

William R. Nail to Sarah R. Coop, Nov. 25, 1850. (Dec.
4, 1850). Jno. Schrborough, BM.
William J. Yeates to Jane E. Ray, Nov. 27, 1850. (Nov.
28, 1850). Wm. S. Buchanan, BM.
Elijah Rains to Martha Armstrong, Nov. 30, 1850. (Dec.
3, 1850). Jno. W. Baker, BM.
B. G. Smith to Malvinia Medlin, Dec. 2, 1850. (Dec. 1,
1850). John C. Lee, BM.
James J. Giles to Margaret E. Edward, Dec. 2, 1850.
(Dec. 2, 1850). Saml. S. Pittman, BM.
William H. Stilwell to Mary Ann Gillespie, Nov. 26, 1850.
(Nov. 28, 1850). W. W. Yandell, BM.
Robert N. James to Martha A. M. James, Dec. 9, 1850.
W. H. Tuggle, BM.
Thos. D. Baird to Nancy A. M. Bryant, Dec. 9, 1850.
(Dec. 8, 1850). Abner G. Lain, BM.
James H. Boon to Caroline C. Thomas, Dec. 11, 1850.
(Dec. 12, 1850). Thos. King, BM.
Jas. A. Cox to Margaret W. Collingsworth, Dec. 16,
1850. (Dec. 19, 1850). Wm. M. Craddock, BM.
Caleb H. Covington to Nancy E. Shane, Dec. 16, 1850.
(Dec. 17, 1850). Alfred Stone, BM.
William H. Holmes to Canzey Burgan, Dec. 17, 1850. (Dec.
17, 1850). Jno. A. Wilkins, BM.
John H. Glass to Virginia C. Taliaferro, Dec. 18, 1850.
(Dec. 18, 1850).
Jonathan B. Agee to Sarah E. Burrow, Dec. 18, 1850.
(Dec. 18, 1850). Harmon Battle, BM.
Alexander M. Jones to Matilda W. Bass, Dec. 18, 1850.
(Dec. 18, 1850). Wm. Benthall, BM.
John A. King to Mary Hale, Dec. 19, 1850. (Dec. 19,
1850). John A. Hart, BM.
John W. Williams to Mary O. Elum, Dec. 21, 1850. (Dec.
24, 1850). Jas. B. W. Jordan, BM.
Robert F. Lea to Sarah Ann White, Dec. 24, 1850. (Dec.
24, 1850). John Belew, BM.
Robert E. Burgess to Mary Arnold, Dec. 25, 1850. (Dec.
31, 1850). Jas. L. Bethshares, BM.
James W. Thompson to Elizabeth M. J. Yarbrough, Dec. 28,
1850. (Jan. 2, 1851). Z. P. McAttiby, BM.
John W. Blankinship to Sarah G. Reeves, Dec. 30, 1850.
(Jan. 1, 1851). J. C. Haynes, BM.
Howel H. Mahon to Matilda C. Holder, Dec. 30, 1850.
(Dec. 31, 1850). Bentley Mahon, BM.
Willis C. Ward to Lucy A. Gillespie, Jan. 1, 1851.
(Jan. 1, 1851). James Connell, BM.
Andrew J. Webber to Susan M. Patterson, Jan. 1, 1851.
Robert Alexander, BM.
Josiah Vick to Ester E. Waldrope, Jan. 3, 1851. (Jan.
9, 1851).
Gray B. Barker to Nancy Taylor, Jan. 7, 1851. (Jan. 8,
1851). E. G. Wood, BM.
John Dugan to Sarah M. Johnson, Jan. 9, 1851. (Jan.
14, 1851).

Bryant Carraway to Isabella King, Jan. 9, 1851. (Jan. 9, 1851). John D. Taylor, BM.

Young J. Hammons to Susan E. McCaslin, Jan. 15, 1851. (Jan. 16, 1851). J. W. McKelvy, BM.

James A. Connell to Emly A. Baker, Jan. 22, 1851. (Jan. 23, 1851). Dempsy Connell, BM.

Henry D. Harper to Ruth Irwin, Jan. 22, 1851. (Jan. 22, 1851). T. J. Carthel, BM.

John E. Smith to Hannah Fowler, Jan. 23, 1851. (Jan. 28, 1851).

John Berry to Betheny Hill, Jan. 25, 1851. (Jan. 26, 1851). John H. Hill, BM.

Christopher C. Strother to Susan C. Dawtry, Jan. 27, 1851. (Jan. 28, 1851). Wm. S. Crews, BM.

Alvin Senter to Nancy Elum, Jan. 27, 1851. (Feb. 7, 1851).

Sterling Haley to Nancy Foster, Jan. 27, 1851. (Jan. 30, 1851). J. B. Asler, BM.

James A. Crank to Sarah Howard, Jan. 28, 1851. (Jan. 28, 1851). Valsain C. Wright, BM.

John B. Williams to Martha C. Bobbett, Jan. 29, 1851. (Jan. 31, 1851). M. G. Bobbett, BM.

John G. Keathley to Elizabeth Bowder, Feb. 1, 1851. Branch Keathley, BM.

James M. Price to Atlanta E. Coats, Feb. 3, 1851. (Feb. 2, 1851).

James Wilson to Matilda Tyson, Feb. 6, 1851. (Feb. 9, 1851).

James W. Edward to Sarah J. Cashar, Feb. 6, 1851. (Feb. 6, 1851).

Robert Bell to Ruth A. New, Feb. 15, 1851. John James, BM.

Jas. M. Blankenship to Mary Irvin, Feb. 17, 1851. (Feb. 15, 1851).

James Mathis to Catharine J. Warren, Feb. 17, 1851. (Feb. 22, 1851).

Daniel Glisson to Docia M. Sims, Feb. 18, 1851. (Feb. 20, 1851).

Henry V. C. Wynne to Adaline S. Walker, Feb. 27, 1851. (Feb. 27, 1851).

Thomas Palmore to Jane Kelly, Mar. 5, 1851. (Mar. 6, 1851).

Hooper J. Powden to Lydia A. F. Messick, Mar. 6, 1851. (Mar. 5, 1851). Thos. J. Kennedy, BM.

Christopher C. Butler to Eliza Jane Sexton, Mar. 8, 1851. (Mar. 8, 1851).

Calvin Flowers to Lucenda Boyett, Mar. 11, 1851. (Mar. 14, 1851).

William Ward to Jane Arbrough, Mar. 11, 1851. (Mar. 13, 1851).

John R. Thedford to Sarah Pounds, Mar. 12, 1851. (Mar. 12, 1851).

Rayland R. Walls to Gabrella Waldrop, Mar. 13, 1851. (Mar. 13, 1851). Iehabud Moore, BM.

Abram Hancock to Leander Caroline Jones, Mar. 19, 1851. (Mar. 20, 1851).

J. J. A. Lee to Martha E. Dement, Mar. 20, 1851. (Mar. 20, 1851). Wm. H. Wren, BM.
Richard H. Ridgeway to Malissa Wilson, Mar. 28, 1851. (Apr. 1, 1851).
William H. Mann to Saphona Vinney, Apr. 10, 1851. (Apr. 11, 1851). M. R. Caldwell, BM.
James H. Weaks to Ann E. Tyler, Apr. 11, 1851. (Apr. 11, 1851).
Henry Howell to Elizabeth Tatum, Apr. 21, 1851. (May 1, 1851).
William H. West to Sarah Jane Foutch, Apr. 23, 1851. (May 1, 1851). John McMin, BM.
Alexander S. Wallace to Adaline Laurance, Apr. 26, 1851. (Apr. 26, 1851).
George A. Harbour to Eliza Dean, Apr. 28, 1851. (Apr. 29, 1851). Henry C. Brown, BM.
T. W. Yeates to R. F. Freeman, May 3, 1851. (May 7, 1851). D. N. Ingram, BM.
Henry Nichold to Mary Ann Parrish, May 7, 1851. (May 8, 1851).
Robert P. Caldwell to Harrett J. Wilkins, May 15, 1851. (May 19, 1851).
Wm. B. Billingsly to Eliza P. Wilson, May 19, 1851. (May 19, 1851). J. Conle, BM.
Joseph J. Kinsey to Lura A. McDaniel, May 26, 1851. (May 27, 1851). G. T. White, BM.
James Tucker to Martha F. Morgan, June 4, 1851. (June 4, 1851). Alfred Tucker, BM.
Thos. A. J. Cassels to Amanda Sanders, June 7, 1851. Jos. Ballentine, BM.
Andrew J. Griffin to Mary E. Furgarson, June 7, 1851. (July 8, 1851). Anderson Rose, BM.
Charles H. Tidrow to Nancy E. Sellers, June 10, 1851. (June 11, 1851).
John P. Tatum to Sarah Hopper, June 12, 1851. (June 12, 1851).
James Coker to Sarah Bradberry, June 20, 1851. (June 20, 1851). J. B. Dibrell, BM.
Henry Hatcher to Lucy Fletcher, June 26, 1851. (June 20, 1851). Calvin S. Ezell, BM.
John F. Burney to Nancy Ann M. Parks, July 9, 1851. (July 13, 1851). Smith Parks, BM.
John D. Davis to Charlotta Canaday, July 9, 1851. (July 10, 1851). Frances M. Taylor, BM.
James W. Robinson to Mary C. A. Canaday, July 17, 1851. (July 17, 1851).
John Karnes to Cynthia Sainford, July 21, 1851. (July 23, 1851).
James B. Bird to Jonnah Payne, July 24, 1851. (July 24, 1851). Z. C. Ewing, BM.
Jeremiah A. Tilman to Mary A. Rutledge, July 24, 1851. (July 24, 1851). P. B. Albed, BM.
Marion M. Dyer to Elizabeth E. Hosley, July 26, 1851. (July 26, 1851). Thos. J. Fite, BM.

Eleazer P. Orr to Jane Lovett, Aug. 6, 1851. (Aug. 6, 1851). Jas. H. Orr, BM.

George D. McDonald to Sarah Ann Weseney, Aug. 11, 1851. John St. John, BM.

James Rutledge to Mary Ann Taylor, Aug. 11, 1851. (Aug. 13, 1851). Geo. W. Akin, BM.

Robert Norman to Louiza C. Davis, Aug. 20, 1851. (Aug. 21, 1851). Phillip G. Terry, BM.

William J. Gowan to Dicey McFarland, Aug. 21, 1851. Richard M. Gowan, BM.

George W. Akin to Sinah M. Mullins, Aug. 21, 1851. (Aug. 22, 1851).

William Motley to Missouri F. Lynch, Aug. 30, 1851. (Sept. 7, 1851). Alfred Combs, BM.

William S. Cherry to Elizabeth B. Reasons, Aug. 30, 1851. (Aug. 31, 1851). Alfred Combs, BM.

Pinkney R. Penn to Frances O. Alexander, Aug. 30, 1851. (Aug. 29, 1851). Wm. T. Agee, BM.

John M. Watt to Trifena Jester, Sept. 1, 1851. (Sept. 2, 1851).

James R. Porter to Catharina Gregory, Sept. 4, 1851. (Sept. 4, 1851). Allen Flowers, BM.

Joyner W. Bady to Lucenda J. Cassell, Sept. 8, 1851. (Sept. 10, 1851).

Jacob S. Shipman to Susan A. Darnell, Sept. 9, 1851. (Sept. 9, 1851).

Jason Greer to Eliza Jane Patrick, Sept. 12, 1851. (Sept. 14, 1851). Jno. W. Gilliland, BM.

Andrew J. Jester to Elizabeth M. Madison, Sept. 16, 1851. (Sept. 17, 1851). Jno. E. Cash, BM.

Andrew J. Bowling to Eliza Smith, Sept. 17, 1851. (Sept. 18, 1851).

Samuel Ferrell to Mary E. Wyatt, Sept. 17, 1851. (Sept. 17, 1851).

John D. Pepkins to Louisa Dickins, Sept. 23, 1851. (Sept. 23, 1851).

Robert P. McCraken to Eliza Jane Miller, Sept. 24, 1851. (Sept. 24, 1851).

George W. Burress to Nancy O. Greer, Sept. 29, 1851. (Sept. 29, 1851).

William W. Roberts to Sibby Hamilton, Oct. 2, 1851. Zachariah Wainwright, BM.

Benjamin Walker to Mary Nevils, Oct. 15, 1851. (Oct. 17, 1851). Ira T. Little, BM.

Joshua D. Young to Sarah Cunningham, Oct. 16, 1851. (Oct. 16, 1851). Z. Biggs, BM.

James Ham to Mary Crafton, Oct. 18, 1851. (Oct. 21, 1851).

James H. Pearce to Mary E. Hail, Oct. 21, 1851. (Oct. 22, 1851). Jas. S. Hinson, BM.

Henry T. Wetherington to Sophonia E. Keathley, Oct. 21, 1851. (Oct. 29, 1851). Absolum Witherington, BM.

George H. Price to Mary E. Mathis, Oct. 22, 1851. (Oct. 22, 1851). Thos. P. Mathis, BM.

Robert B. Trimble to Lucinda J. Nance, Oct. 27, 1851.
David B. Hall, BM.
Robert C. Tilghman to Lydia Tyson, Oct. 31, 1851.
W. Needham, BM.
Calvin Ashley to Jemmina A. Gardner, Nov. 4, 1851.
(Nov. 6, 1851). Smith Parks, BM.
Sampson Blaloch to Sarah E. White, Nov. 10, 1851. Jas.
Gilbrath, BM.
Joshua J. Griffin to Sarah S. Wilkins, Nov. 13, 1851.
(Nov. 13, 1851). Humphrey P. (?), BM.
Thomas W. Freeman to Cynthia W. Freeman, Nov. 18, 1851.
T. J. Carthel, BM.
Buckner S. Sollis to Martha Boon, Nov. 21, 1851. (Nov.
21, 1851). H. R. Halls, BM.
Wm. C. Brewer to Absgllah H. Ragder, Nov. 24, 1851.
N. F. Barksdale, BM.
Absolum Witherington to Harrett Glisson, Nov. 26, 1851.
J. R. Pate, BM.
James H. Crissman to Elizabeth A. Harder, Nov. 26, 1851.
(Nov. 27, 1851). W. H. Bills, BM.
J. G. Keathley to Hepsey Ann Branch, Dec. 1, 1851.
Jesse Caraway, BM.
Julias M. Tucker to Clarissa Ann Ammons, Dec. 8, 1851.
W. Taylor, BM.
Henry M. Pierce to Elizabeth Pettus, Dec. 12, 1851.
(Dec. 16, 1851).
Wesley G. Barker to Nancy W. Wortham, Dec. 13, 1851.
(Dec. 14, 1851).
James Dowell to Martha Boyett, Dec. 15, 1851. (Dec. 18,
1851).
John A. Carr to Nancy A. Sigmor, Dec. 17, 1851. (Dec.
18, 1851).
David Cyrus to Mary McLour, Dec. 17, 1851. (Dec. 19,
1851).
John W. McKelvey to Polly J. Coats, Dec. 20, 1851.
(Dec. 22, 1851).
Zachariah Greer to Abigale E. Wren, Dec. 20, 1851.
(Dec. 23, 1851).
Nathaniel P. Norman to Sarah C. Alleson, Dec. 22, 1851.
Jas. A. McGee, BM.
William E. Elder to Almira Carthel, Dec. 24, 1851.
Wm. E. Penn, BM.
David N. Rutledge to Martha Jane Taylor, Dec. 26, 1851.
(Dec. 26, 1851).
William Mobley to Dorethy Harrisson, Dec. 29, 1851.
By J. W. Jones, M.G.
Thomas W. McCollam to Susan Pollard, Dec. 29, 1851.
(Jan. 8, 1852). Wm. L. Hill, BM.
William O. Fisher to Eliza Jane Jones, Dec. 30, 1851.
By S. E. Gardiner, M.G. W. R. Hall, BM.
Zachariah Wainright to Esper Ann Clement, Jan. 3, 1852.
(July 8, 1852). Wm. Roberts, BM.
Wm. N. Hammond to Nancy K. McKelva, Jan. 5, 1852. (Jan.
8, 1852). J. E. Merrick, BM.

GIBSON COUNTY MARRIAGES

Thos. R. Blankenship to Martha A. Farris, Jan. 5, 1852.
  (Jan. 6, 1852). Thos. H. Farris, BM.
David Jones to Tibitha Martin, Jan. 5, 1852. (Jan. 5,
  1852). Jos. W. Jones, BM.
James P. Arnold to Mary E. Shane, Jan. 5, 1852. (Jan.
  6, 1852). W. H. Witt, BM.
Jessee A. Patrick to Nancy J. Pounds, Jan. 8, 1852. Jno.
  W. Gilliland, BM.
George W. Glisson to Harrett Flowers, Jan. 10, 1852.
  W. H. Glisson, BM.
Wm. J. Carroll to Terza Jane Ellington, Jan. 10, 1852.
  J. R. Carroll, BM.
Rufus F. King to Mary W. Harrison, Jan. 12, 1852. L.
  B. Gilchrist, BM.
Columbus W. Caleb to Elizabeth A. Patterson, Jan. 12,
  1852. V. N. S. Taylor, BM.
David Jordan to Elizabeth M. Hight, Jan. 14, 1852.
  R. A. Hight, BM.
Marian Moore to Margaret McMullen, Jan. 22, 1852. (Jan.
  22, 1852). Archer T. Grey, BM.
Robert Taylor to Nancy S. Hoover, Jan. 23, 1852. A. H.
  McNeely, BM.
Wallace Bills to Louiza J. Hardin, Jan. 23, 1852.
  (Jan. 27, 1852). W. H. Bills, BM.
William P. Scott to Elizabeth A. Little, Jan. 24, 1852.
  Larcus Covington, BM.
Newton Mayfield to Margaret Patterson, Jan. 24, 1852.
  Jas. M. Kennady, BM.
George W. Hardin to Eliza J. Bells, Jan. 26, 1852.
  (Jan. 29, 1852). William Bells, BM.
Tandy M. Branson to Amedia A. Sigman, Feb. 3, 1852.
  (Feb. 3, 1852). J. L. Graves, BM.
James P. Thompson to Nancy Brightwell, Feb. 2, 1852.
  (Feb. 5, 1852). Jno. C. Thompson, BM.
Jacob C. Flowers to Elizabeth A. House, Feb. 3, 1852.
  (Feb. 5, 1852). Wiley O. Mobley, BM.
Stephen Jones to Barbery Glisson, Feb. 6, 1852. W. H.
  Glisson, BM.
Isaac Solomon to Avira R. Bryant, Feb. 10, 1852. (Feb.
  12, 1852). Jas. W. Alexander, BM.
James Davis to Rebecca A. Yarbrough, Feb. 11, 1852.
  (Feb. 11, 1852). Newton R. Yarbrough, BM.
A. M. Grier to Frances E. Becton, Feb. 11, 1852. (Feb.
  12, 1852). James Davis, BM.
Robert Boyd to Elizabeth Cassles, Feb. 11, 1852. David
  Cassles and Johnston Williams, BM.
William V. Foutch to Martha Attman, Feb. 12, 1852. Jno.
  W. McMinn, BM.
Thos. J. Craddock to Susan T. Collinsworth, Feb. 14,
  1852. (Feb. 17, 1852). Wm. M. Craddock, BM.
Robert Counts to Susan C. Greer, Feb. 16, 1852. (Feb.
  16, 1852). James Greer, BM.
James G. Bell to Ann M. Carney, Feb. 17, 1852. (Feb.
  19, 1852). R. G. Bell, BM.

84

GIBSON COUNTY MARRIAGES

Leander Latham to Mary Hill, Feb. 18, 1852. (Feb. 19,
  1852). Wm. L. Hill, BM.
William Henderson to Nancy J. Arnold, Feb. 25, 1852.
  T. G. Arnold, BM.
W. Wilson Yandell to Martha Sanderford, Feb. 25, 1852.
  (Feb. 26, 1852). Jesse I. Wills, BM.
Elijah B. Russell to Mary M. Barron, Feb. 26, 1852.
  (Feb. 26, 1852). Harmon Battle, BM.
Joseph B. Stanley to Frances S. Terrill, Feb. 26, 1852.
  (Mar. 9, 1852). Jno. W. Northern, BM.
Philemon Hurt to Mary J. Cunningham, Mar. 8, 1852.
  (Mar. 10, 1852). Bradford Edwards, BM.
Israel M. L. Barker to Mary H. Hassell, Mar. 8, 1852.
  (Mar. 9, 1852). J. L. Gibbs, BM.
Littleberry B. Arnold to Sarah A. Lewis, Mary 9, 1852.
  (Mar. 9, 1852). E. M. Witt, BM.
John W. Varner to Deborah J. Battle, Mar. 11, 1852.
  (Mar. 11, 1852).
William C. Turner to Martha A. Nisbitt, Mar. 13, 1852.
  (Mar. 15, 1852).
James T. Dement to Gingeanna Alford, Mar. 17, 1852.
  (Mar. 17, 1852).
Reuben C. Dickins to Elizabeth Price, Mar. 20, 1852.
  (Mar. 25, 1852). T. D. Atchison, BM.
George Haley to Purnetta A. Berry, Mar. 20, 1852. (Mar.
  25, 1852).
Joseph S. Graves to Ann Brown, Mar. 29, 1852. (Mar.
  29, 1852).
R. H. Alexander to Ann E. Wicks, Mar. 29, 1852. (Mar.
  30, 1852). G. M. Lovett, BM.
Isaac J. Biggs to Julia Ann Greer, Apr. 1, 1852. (Apr.
  1, 1852). Jas. W. Landrum, BM.
Samuel G. Talkington to Frances Goodman, Apr. 3, 1852.
  Thos. Greer, BM.
Thomas Spencer to Harrett A. Miller, Apr. 8, 1852.
  (Apr. 8, 1852). S. R. Tucker, BM.
John McFarland to Cassandra Berry, Apr. 17, 1852. (Apr.
  21, 1852). Jas. H. Grist, BM.
Benjamin D. Caple to Nancy H. Johnston, Apr. 20, 1852.
  F. W. Murray, BM.
George Cleaves to Elizabeth Dolan, Apr. 28, 1852. By
  Wm. Sugg, J.P. Jno. T. Dowland, BM.
Benjamin F. Everett to Mary J. Jetton, May 5, 1852.
  (May 6, 1852). H. R. Buchanan, BM.
Andrew Mayo to Martha A. Hix, May 10, 1852. (May ?,
  1852). Redin Hix, BM.
William Easterwood to Nancy Keas, May 13, 1852. (May
  17, 1852). Benj. F. Woods, BM.
Nathaniel F. Barksdale to Sarah C. Jones, May 20, 1852.
  (May 20, 1852). Robt. N. Davis, BM.
William McCartney to Nancy Irvin, May 24, 1852. (May
  27, 1852).
John M. Lovell to Rebecca Watt, May 26, 1852. (May 26,
  1852). J. M. Gateley, BM.

85

GIBSON COUNTY MARRIAGES

John R. Reynolds to Martha E. England, May 26, 1852.
William Reynolds, BM.
John H. Ragsdale to Mary F. Jones, July 28, 1852.
(May 30, 1852). W. T. Ownsby, BM.
Shadrack Wilson to Margaret A. McWherter, June 8, 1852.
(June 8, 1852). L. B. Gilchrist, BM.
John L. Ogles to Malinda R. I. Smith, June 19, 1852.
(June 20, 1852). Irvin Smith, BM.
James M. Baird to Sarah J. Baird, June 21, 1852. Thos.
D. Baird, BM.
George Vail to Mary Lions, June 22, 1852. (June 24,
1852). G. M. Sharp, BM.
Stephen H. Glisson to Nancy Hall, June 22, 1852. W. H.
Glisson, BM.
Thomas Curtis to Mary E. Caple, June 24, 1852. (June
24, 1852). Jno. C. W. Nunn, BM.
Erasmus A. Fleming to Jemima J. Hopper, June 24, 1852.
(June 24, 1852). Gillum W. Hopper, BM.
William H. Partiel to Nancy Biggs, June 29, 1852.
(June 30, 1852). W. R. Cox, BM.
William Carr to Harriet M. Berry, June 29, 1852. Frances
M. Allen, BM.
William T. Moseley to Nancy Flowers, July 1, 1852.
(July 6, 1852). Jno. W. Brickhouse, BM.
Hezekiah C. Thompson to Susan Parker, July 3, 1852.
(July 8, 1852). D. E. A. Reese, BM.
Hugh Shaw to Aberville Jane Ince, July 6, 1852. (July
6, 1852). Wm. Shaw, BM.
Jacob T. Mathis to Sarah C. Oliver, July 10, 1852.
(July 12, 1852). James Ham, BM.
Elisha Scott to Elizabeth G. J. Scott, July 12, 1852.
(July 29, 1852). B. J. Cooper, BM.
Solomon Cooper to Elizabeth Ball, July 13, 1852. Isaac
Fowler, BM.
Moody Young to Sarah Reasons, July 22, 1852. (July 23,
1852). Jas. D. Smith, BM.
Mathew Yeates to Barbary Ann Bell, July 24, 1852.
(July 25, 1852). R. Bridges, BM.
George W. Lawrence to Martha Griffin, July 27, 1852.
(July 27, 1852). Saml. C. Lane, BM.
Thomas J. Freeman to Martha L. Raines, July 28, 1852.
(July 28, 1852). John Hassell, BM.
Alexander M. Robertson to Meedy Goodwin, July 29, 1852.
Wm. J. Nonan, BM.
Allen C. Williams to Harriet M. Alexander, Aug. 4, 1852.
(Aug. 5, 1852). Wm. R. Hodge, BM.
R. W. Peacock to Mary J. Woodson, Aug. 4, 1852. Isaac
C. Haynes, BM.
Wiley F. Sammons to Sarah Ann Bane, Aug. 5, 1852. Garret
G. Mitchell, BM.
William Hoskins to Mary Moore, Aug. 5, 1852. (Aug. 5,
1852). Wm. Y. Butler, BM.
James G. Tinsley to Frances M. Yeates, Aug. 7, 1852.
(Aug. 12, 1852). Jno. A. Barker, BM.

86

GIBSON COUNTY MARRIAGES

Robert W. Jones to Mary Ann Fletcher, Aug. 9, 1852.
(Aug. 10, 1852). Adam Landrum, BM.
James A. Williamson to Mary Jane Cleaver, Aug. 11, 1852.
(Aug. 11, 1852). Jas. J. Giles, BM.
James W. Ray to Sintha Morrow, Aug. 16, 1852. (Aug. 17,
1852).
Thomas H. Meek to Mary E. Davidson, Aug. 19, 1852. Harmon
Battle, BM.
James E. Wood to Mary D. Moody, Aug. 21, 1852. (Aug.
22, 1852). W. H. Wood, BM.
William W. Duncan to Thursa A. Lenard, Aug. 23, 1852.
(Aug. 26, 1852). Saml. H. Duncan, BM.
Silas M. Bobbett to Emma H. Mayfield, Aug. 23, 1852.
(Aug. 24, 1852). Jno. W. Croom, BM.
Bryant Caraway to Rachael Peel, Aug. 23, 1852. (Aug.
26, 1852). R. P. Caldwell, BM.
Charles E. Butler to Louisa Lee, Aug. 23, 1852. (Aug.
26, 1852). T. J. Carthel, BM.
Robert Sanford to Martha E. Conley, Aug. 30, 1852. (Sept.
2, 1852).
James S. Wood to Rhoda A. Robertson, Sept. 1, 1852.
(Sept. 1, 1852). J. M. Senter, BM.
William R. Haywood to Sarah A. Walker, Sept. 1, 1852.
J. H. Miller, BM.
William W. Lynch to Artena Northcut, Sept. 1, 1852.
(Sept. 1, 1852). G. S. Penn, BM.
Jacob Hicks to Sarah Reed, Sept. 2, 1852. Rodham
Maclin, BM.
Troy Frazier to Mary Jane Colburn, Sept. 2, 1852.
(Sept. 2, 1852). M. M. Seay, BM.
John M. Carroll to Elizabeth Wilson, Sept. 6, 1852.
(Sept. 7, 1852). Herrod Holt, BM.
John W. McKendrick to Martha Felts, Sept. 7, 1852.
(Sept. 9, 1852). Jno. T. Rice, BM.
J. B. Aslin to Nancy E. Patrick, Sept. 9, 1852. (Sept.
9, 1852). Elias Miller, BM.
Joel A. Light to Susan M. Yancey, Sept. 21, 1852. (Sept.
26, 1852). L. B. Gilchrist, BM.
Henry Hales to Mary F. Gallien, Sept. 22, 1852. Jas. A.
W. Hess, BM.
Benjamin F. James to Ellen Smith, Sept. 24, 1852. (Sept.
28, 1852). James Tatum, BM.
Wm. M. Harrison to America C. Wade, Sept. 27, 1852. Geo.
S. Penn, BM.
Daniel Evans to Elizabeth Andrews, Sept. 28, 1852. (Sept.
30, 1852). Jas. Anderson, BM.
James Ellis to Sarah L. A. Jennings, Sept. 30, 1852.
(Sept. 30, 1852). Saml. F. Dalton, BM.
William May to Frances Sain, Sept. 30, 1852. (Sept.
30, 1852). Jesse Greer, BM.
William J. Corbitt to Lucinda W. Crank, Oct. 1, 1852.
(Oct. 2, 1852). S. G. Crank, BM.
William Edward to Mary A. Wethington, Oct. 5, 1852.
(Oct. 6, 1852). John Edward, BM.

Benjamin F. Woods to Elizabeth N. Fletcher, Oct. 6,
 1852. (Oct. 12, 1852). Julias T. Thompson, BM.
John W. Arbuckle to Mary Ann Smith, Oct. 7, 1852.
 (Oct. 10, 1852). John Ogle, BM.
P. M. Dinwiddie to Catharine Bowers, Oct. 11, 1852.
 S. C. Lane, BM.
Clinton Brigance to Sarah H. Bledsoe, Oct. 12, 1852.
 (Oct. 13, 1852). Wiley S. Jones, BM.
John H. Lett to Elizabeth Wood, Oct. 12, 1852. (Oct.
 12, 1852). Solomon Collenes, BM.
Henry I. Ward to America C. Williams, Oct. 12, 1852.
 (Oct. 14, 1852). Jno. A. Wilkins, BM.
Lewis C. Crenshaw to Martha W. Wyatt, Oct. 13, 1852.
 (Oct. 14, 1852). H. Thompson, BM.
George C. Moore to Mahala Cathey, Oct. 21, 1852. (Oct.
 21, 1852). V. C. Wright, BM.
James M. Senter to Margaret E. Hess, Oct. 14, 1852.
 E. M. Witt, BM.
Cullen Cribbs to Sarah Hancock, Oct. 20, 1852. Jno. M.
 White, BM.
Andrew Bell to Parolle Yeates, Oct. 21, 1852. (Oct.
 21, 1852). Jno. Stubblefield, BM.
Samuel W. Hatchett to Susan M. Scrape, Oct. 21, 1852.
 (Oct. 21, 1852). Wm. T. Wilkins, BM.
John R. Fite to Mary E. Wallace, Oct. 23, 1852. (Oct.
 24, 1852). W. C. Penn, BM.
William T. Carroll to Martha R. Thedford, Oct. 23, 1852.
 (Oct. 28, 1852). Jno. M. Carroll, BM.
Levi Darr to Rosa Ann Herrington, Oct. 27, 1852. (Oct.
 27, 1852). Wm. Shaw, BM.
William A. Thomas to Sarah A. H. Davis, Oct. 27, 1852.
 (Oct. 28, 1852). Thomas King, BM.
James A. Thomas to Elizabeth Edmundson, Oct. 28, 1852.
 Wm. H. Holmes, BM.
Anthony M. Clement to Mary C. Patrick, Nov. 1, 1852.
 Caleb R. Clement, BM.
William M. Craddock to Catharine E. Jones, Nov. 1, 1852.
 (Nov. 3, 1852). Jas. M. Collingsworth, BM.
Marcus L. Grady to Sarah L. Hartsfield, Nov. 2, 1852.
 (Nov. 3, 1852). Jas. T. Smith, BM.
Henry A. McHenry to Cyntha A. McRee, Nov. 4, 1852.
 (Nov. 4, 1852). F. B. McRee, BM.
Thomas J. Williams to Martha R. Cole, Nov. 8, 1852.
 (Nov. 11, 1852). Wilson Williams, BM.
Andrew J. White to Sarah M. Thetford, Nov. 9, 1852.
 (Nov. 11, 1852). J. H. Waldrop, BM.
William M. Jack to Jane Cooper, Nov. 15, 1852. (Nov.
 15, 1852). Joel H. Harrison, BM.
James H. Grace to Lucy Ann Taylor, Nov. 17, 1852.
 (Nov. 18, 1852). Jas. F. Fowler, BM.
Hedge Peth to Sally Robinson, Nov. 18, 1852. John Dial, BM.
Frank L. Barkley to Mary M. McConnell, Nov. 19, 1852.
 (Nov. 22, 1852). A. G. Barkley, BM.
George W. Lovitt to Nancy Porter, Nov. 22, 1852. (Nov.
 23, 1852). M. L. Halford, BM.

Stephen F. Wetherford to Harrett Lottis, Nov. 22, 1852.
    Francis M. Allen, BM.
Thos. S. McAllester to Arreanna Pratt, Nov. 22, 1852.
    (Nov. 23, 1852). B. A. Yearar, BM.
Samuel M. Stone to Elizabeth Cribbs, Nov. 23, 1852. J.
    J. Wilborn, BM.
Allen Mobley to Mary E. W. Crawley, Nov. 29, 1852.
    (Dec. 7, 1852). Jno. L. Davis, BM.
Wiloly Gardner to Elizabeth McFarland, Dec. 1, 1852.
    (Dec. 2, 1852).
John Q. Marshall to Nancy McBride, Dec. 1, 1852. Joseph
    Barrett, BM.
Samuel M. Davidson to Allezarah A. Thomas, Dec. 2, 1852.
    (Dec. 2, 1852). R. D. Blair, BM.
Charles E. Fetherston to Jane Young, Dec. 4, 1852. F. L.
    Jones, BM.
William J. Cherry to Elizabeth C. Dement, Dec. 4, 1852.
    (Dec. 4, 1852). Wm. T. Dement, BM.
Robert S. Latta to Mary G. Guthrie, Dec. 6, 1852. (Dec.
    9, 1852). T. W. Retton, BM.
John Vanhog to Ann N. Brightwell, Dec. 6, 1852. (Dec.
    7, 1852). Gerigh Turner, BM.
W. F. Perry to Alminda N. J. Giles, Dec. 7, 1852.
    (Dec. 9, 1852). Henry Williamson, BM.
George W. Jones to Mary Jane Tyler, Dec. 7, 1852. (Dec.
    9, 1852). R. H. Alexander, BM.
William S. Crews to Elizabeth A. McWherter, Dec. 7, 1852.
    Jas. Edmundson, BM.
Henry C. Pittman to Sarah M. Yeargain, Dec. 8, 1852.
    (Dec. 9, 1852). Saml. L. Pittman, BM.
Elisha Rains to Emely V. Armstrong, Dec. 9, 1852. (Dec.
    9, 1852). Jas. M. Armstrong, BM.
Lorenza B. Boyd to Julian Dowell, Dec. 11, 1852. (Dec.
    15, 1852). James Dowell, BM.
Edmund F. Taylor to Nancy A. Hopper, Dec. 17, 1852.
    (Dec. 25, 1852). D. Halliburton, BM.
William D. Jones to Amanda J. Canaday, Dec. 20, 1852.
    (Dec. 20, 1852). Asa Robason, BM.
Henry Kelly to Martha A. F. Robb, Dec. 21, 1852. (Dec.
    21, 1852). E. W. Harvey, BM.
Samuel C. Lane to Martha Chrisp, Dec. 22, 1852. (Dec.
    23, 1852). N. M. Bowman, BM.
Alexander H. Mobley to Saloda Richardson, Dec. 23, 1852.
    (Dec. 23, 1852). Thos. W. Robertson, BM.
William E. Tilliman to Martha Sammons, Dec. 23, 1852.
    (Dec. 23, 1852). J. F. Patterson, BM.
John T. Browning to Eliza Balew, Dec. 29, 1852. (Dec.
    29, 1852). Stephen McPherson, BM.
Benj. F. Brock to Nancy A. Yeargain, Dec. 31, 1852.
    (Jan. 2, 1853). H. C. Pittman, BM.
John M. Jordan to Celea A. Woodard, Jan. 1, 1853.
    (Jan. 2, 1853). Alfred Flowers, BM.
Archelus Keathly to Margaret Linton, Jan. 1, 1853.
    J. A. W. Hess, BM.

GIBSON COUNTY MARRIAGES

Albert P. Phillips to Louisa Mullins, Jan. 3, 1853.
(Jan. 6, 1853). John C. Lacy, BM.
Lerry Collins to Eveline M. Murphy, Jan. 8, 1853. By
William Sugg, J.P. Robt. Bradford, BM.
William E. Crowder to Harrel Baker, Jan. 8, 1853.
Wesley Tiner, BM.
Edmund J. Glascock to Cassa A. Varner, Jan. 11, 1853.
(Jan. 11, 1853). Henry Meek, BM.
E. W. Moore to Martha E. Wherry, Jan. 13, 1853. (Jan.
18, 1853).
Albert Ross to Mary D. Bratton, Jan. 15, 1853. (Jan.
18, 1853). Alfred Ross, BM.
Alexander Norton to Cardine Canaday, Jan. 15, 1853.
(Jan. 16, 1853). Pinkney Tilghman, BM.
Pinkney Tilghman to Louiza Norton, Jan. 15, 1853. (Jan.
18, 1853). Alex Norton, BM.
George M. Taylor to Sophonia E. Gowan, Jan. 17, 1853.
(Jan. 17, 1853). Wm. J. Gowan, BM.
Drury Gowan to Fanny Hall, Jan. 17, 1853. (Jan. 19,
1853). H. W. Reed, BM.
William C. Ree to William J. Arnold, Jan. 19, 1853.
(Jan. 19, 1853).
John Baxter to Nancy J. McNail, Jan. 20, 1853. (Jan.
20, 1853). Wm. E. McNail, BM.
William R. Rooks to Mary J. Richardson, Jan. 21, 1853.
(Jan. 23, 1853). B. Gilchrist, BM.
Charles M. Johnson to Mary A. Pittman, Jan. 24, 1853.
(Jan. 27, 1853). J. A. W. Pittman, BM.
Henry Thompson to Virginia L. Moor, Jan. 26, 1853. (Jan.
26, 1853). W. E. Crenshaw, BM.
Henry Hale to Sarah Ann Sartor, Jan. 26, 1853. (Jan.
26, 1853). W. Sartor, BM.
Stephen Wallace to Lucretia Foren, Jan. 27, 1853. (Jan.
28, 1853). Bryant Pope, BM.
John Phelan to Emeline Hayes, Feb. 1, 1853. (Feb. 1,
1853). D. S. Dunaway, BM.
James Cook to Margaret Hicks, Feb. 8, 1853. (Feb. 8,
1853). Geo. P. Alilay, BM.
John P. Reager to Ellen M. Edmundson, Feb. 12, 1853.
(Feb. 17, 1853). B. J. Cooper, BM.
Nathan W. Ford to Malinda Lowry, Feb. 14, 1853. (Mar.
3, 1853). Wesley Tiner, BM.
William Barrett to Mexico Barton, Feb. 15, 1850. Smith
Parks, BM.
Eli W. Ing to Nancy E. Thomas, Mar. 18, 1853. (Feb.
20, 1853). J. M. McLaurine, BM.
Joshua Swindle to Drucella Holt, Feb. 18, 1853. (Feb.
19, 1853). Henry Williamson, BM.
Willes N. Campbell to Lewellen E. Cates, Feb. 21, 1853.
(Feb. 22, 1853). F. W. Bowin, BM.
James Organ to Emely F. James, Feb. 22, 1853. (Mar. 1,
1853). Wm. H. Woods, BM.
John H. Arnold to Sarah E. White, Feb. 23, 1853. (Feb.
1, 1853). Thos. W. Arnold, BM.

90

Thomas Carlton to Naomi Patterson, Feb. 23, 1853. (Feb.
24, 1853). Wm. Taylor, BM.
Samuel R. Fuqua to Milly Vick, Feb. 26, 1853. Drury
Pennington, BM.
Charles H. Ross to Celestia A. Henings, Feb. 28, 1853.
By Cullen G. Cribbs, M.G. F. H. Warren, BM.
John C. Thompson to Sarah E. McCaleb, Mar. 1, 1853.
(Mar. 10, 1853). J. A. Harwood, BM.
Robert H. Carr to Elenor J. McDaniel, Mar. 3, 1853.
(Mar. 3, 1853). R. D. Blair, BM.
Abner G. Lane to Mary R. Wade, Mar. 3, 1853. (Mar. 3,
1853). Audrea J. Lassiter, BM.
George M. Wilburn to Elizabeth Fite, Mar. 3, 1853. (Mar.
?, 1853). W. R. McDaniel, BM.
Abner W. Mason to Elizabeth Crosby, Mar. 7, 1853. (Mar.
8, 1853). John Umsted, BM.
Lazerus Fergarson to Sarah A. Grady, Mar. 9, 1853.
(Mar. 10, 1853). John S. Griffin, BM.
William C. Stephens to Julia Ann Ward, Mar. 9, 1853.
H. A. Crouse, BM.
James C. Blackshear to Elizabeth J. Blair, Mar. 10,
1853. By John M. Grier. Robert D. Blair, BM.
David R. Corkburn to Mary Ann H. Robertson, Mar. 12,
1853. Francis N. Allen, BM.
William P. Thompson to Margaret E. Wilson, Mar. 14, 1853.
(Mar. 15, 1853). M. J. Grey, BM.
Peter Wilson to Martha C. Fletcher, Mar. 15, 1853. (Mar.
19, 1853). Geo. M. Baisinger, BM.
Thadeous N. Terril to Lew A. W. Clay, Mar. 15, 1853.
(Mar. 16, 1853). M. J. Clay, BM.
Lorenzo D. Mathis to Martha A. E. Eathridge, Mar. 15,
1853. (Mar. 15, 1853). Jno. D. Mathis, BM.
Jasper N. Rentfro to Emily Bunn, Mar. 16, 1853. R. L.
Crafton, BM.
William Plyland to Malissa Crockett, Mar. 21, 1853. R.
N. Lett, BM.
Henry W. Pemberton to Mary M. Wallace, Mar. 21, 1853.
(Mar. 22, 1853). Jas. A. Rust, BM.
Alexander G. Little to Lucy Stone, Mar. 22, 1853. Wm.
P. Scott, BM.
Benjamin F. Arnold to Martha Ford, Mar. 28, 1853. (Mar.
29, 1853). Joel Arnold, BM.
Thos. W. Jernigan to Elizabeth J. Jones, Mar. 31, 1853.
Isaiah Holland, BM.
Miles H. Travis to Sarah R. Woodson, Apr. 2, 1853.
(Apr. 3, 1853). L. B. Gilchrist, BM.
W. A. Elam to Eliza E. Simmons, Apr. 7, 1853. G. S. Penn, BM.
Wilie L. Sexton to Mary E. Bledsoe, Apr. 19, 1853.
(Apr. 19, 1853). John A. Jackson, BM.
Samuel Martin to Margaret Oliver, Apr. 20, 1853. (Apr.
20, 1853). Thos. Higgins, BM.
Thomas Herndon to Louisa Thetford, Apr. 20, 1853. D. G.
Boyett, BM.
W. H. Wood to Martha H. Wood, Apr. 21, 1853. W. E.
Crowder, BM.

GIBSON COUNTY MARRIAGES

Robert B. Ozment to Fanny G. Hudson, Apr. 23, 1853.
(May 1, 1853). Chas W. Edward, BM.
Thomas M. Lemmond to Lucretia E. Kingcade, Apr. 23, 1853.
(Apr. 26, 1853). S. D. Hopper, BM.
John V. Morton to Sarah E. Scott, Apr. 27, 1853. (Apr.
27, 1853). Wm. F. Wilkins, BM.
William M. Campbell to Elizabeth V. Bass, May 2, 1853.
(May 2, 1853). Robt. Bradford, BM.
Terrish Turner to Peggy Brightwell, May 4, 1853. (May
5, 1853). T. E. Moore, BM.
Greenberry Cunningham to Nancy Martin, May 12, 1853.
(May 12, 1853). Henry Knott, BM.
James Ward to Mary F. Dement, May 12, 1853. (May 12,
1853). Ira J. Ward, BM.
John W. Morrow to Mary Ray, May 24, 1853. (June 1,
1853). L. H. Boyett, BM.
James Skiles to Mary Lowrance, May 26, 1853. (May 26,
1853). Daniel Hassell, BM.
Maj. W. Witherington to Mary Phelps, May 26, 1853.
(June 26, 1853). Thos. Shelton, BM.
William A. Harbor to Frances C. Cromes, June 4, 1853.
J. W. Maley, BM.
Ashley R. Wilson to Elizabeth A. Coleman, June 7, 1853.
(June 7, 1853). L. W. Blakemore, BM.
Josiah R. Carroll to Lavinia A. Thornton, June 11, 1853.
(June 26, 1853). Nathan Medows, BM.
John Reynolds to Malissa Cole, June 15, 1853. (June 16,
1853). Wm. England, BM.
John Oliver to Lacy Baily, June 16, 1853. (June 16,
1853). R. W. Davis, BM.
Isaac Cail to Martha H. Beavers. Jessee Greer, BM.
William W. Peeples to Mildred C. Nimmo, June 16, 1853.
(June 16, 1853). H. S. Bradford, BM.
William F. Jackson to Mary A. Walker, June 22, 1853.
(June 23, 1853). J. C. Haynes, BM.
James W. Allison to Martha P. Hamilton, July 2, 1853.
By R. G. Weddington, M.G. Jas. W. Cressap, BM.
William Williams to Sarah Arnold, July 2, 1853. (July
3, 1853). Wm. Williams, Jr., BM.
John A. Bailey to Nancy Porter, July 4, 1853. (July 4,
1853). S. W. Bailey, BM.
Asberry M. Webb to Nancy C. Ward, July 9, 1853. James
Ham, BM.
Griffin L. Roper to Mira E. Williams, July 11, 1853.
(Aug. 7, 1853). Jno. J. Clark, BM.
Jacob Mathis to Mrs. Caroline Drake, July 13, 1853.
(July 16, 1853). A. R. Love, BM.
William Baker to Mary Kelly, July 14, 1853. (July 31,
1853). J. F. Laurence, BM.
John McCullough to Edney Walls, July 14, 1853. (July
14, 1853). R. H. Walls, BM.
Stephen Pearce to Rebecca Cook, July 18, 1853. (July 18,
1853). Lafayette Faulkner, BM.
Solomon H. Hobgood to Elizabeth C. Carr, July 19, 1853.
(July 25, 1853). Andrew A. Carr, BM.

GIBSON COUNTY MARRIAGES

Newton W. Warren to Susan G. Mitchell, July 19, 1853.
(July 21, 1853). S. W. Sharp, BM.
Miles H. Follis to Mary Andrews, July 23, 1853. James
Kilzer, BM.
Elijah Morrow to Susan Ray, July 23, 1853. (July 24,
1853). J. A. Fleming, BM.
John Davidson to Susan C. Smith, July 26, 1853. (July
26, 1853). Jesse Sturdivant, BM.
David S. Phelan to Celea A. Cole, July 26, 1853. (July
26, 1853). Henry Meek, BM.
Major Howell to Sallie Woodard, July 28, 1853. (July 28,
1853). Erma Laper, BM.
John Hammons to Margaret E. Richardson, Aug. 8, 1853.
(Aug. 8, 1853). Frances M. Allen, BM.
David P. Barnett to Mary Jane Allison, Aug. 15, 1853.
(Aug. 16, 1853). Mathew H. Barnett, BM.
James E. Hays to Martha Ann Bell, Aug. 18, 1853. (Aug.
18, 1853). John F. Hays, BM.
Elisha Mathis to Mahulda Sanders, Aug. 22, 1853. (Aug.
22, 1853). James S. Haynes, BM.
William Gray to Ann Wilson, Aug. 22, 1853. (Aug. 23,
1853). A. N. Thompson, BM.
Daniel Reynold to Manerva B. E. Bledsoe, Aug. 23, 1853.
A. Bledsoe, BM.
James Y. Deshong to Lucenda C. Fielder, Aug. 30, 1853.
(Sept. 15, 1853). Allen G. Dodd, BM.
Thomas Mullens to Ferroby Demoss, Aug. 31, 1853. (Aug.
31, 1853). Jas. R. Goodman, BM.
Reese R. Long to Phebe Fletcher, Aug. 31, 1853. (Aug.
31, 1853). W. A. Fonville, BM.
Aron J. Gilliland to Narcissa C. Paris, Aug. 31, 1853.
(Sept. 2, 1853). E. H. Crocker, BM.
Joseph H. Fry to Nancy H. Wesson, Aug. 31, 1853. (Sept.
1, 1853). Hugh S. White, BM.
James C. McCraig to Mary C. Underwood, Sept. 6, 1853.
(Sept. ?, 1853). Saml. J. Bone, BM.
John Manley to Catherine Harber, Sept. 7, 1853. (Sept.
8, 1853). Jos. L. Strange, BM.
John W. Barron to Sarah Jane Noel, Sept. 8, 1853.
(Sept. 11, 1853). Jefferson Marcum, BM.
B. S. Boyett to Elizabeth Andrews, Sept. 10, 1853.
(Sept. 15, 1853). T. S. Turnham, BM.
Dolphin W. Cates to Susan A. Campbell, Sept. 12, 1853.
Willis N. Campbell, BM.
William J. R. Becton to Margaret S. Greer, Sept. 13,
1853. (Sept. 15, 1853). S. W. Armstrong, BM.
John H. Smith to Parthenia C. Henry, Sept. 13, 1853.
(Sept. 14, 1853). James A. McGee, BM.
Allen Green to Eveline Lee, Sept. 13, 1853. (Sept. 16,
1853). S. L. Jackson, BM.
John H. Robertson to Julia Ann Cooper, Sept. 15, 1853.
(Sept. 17, 1853). Wm. Jarrell, BM.
John D. Kersey to Martha P. Boucher, Sept. 15, 1853.
(Sept. 15, 1853). Bluford Terrell, BM.

GIBSON COUNTY MARRIAGES

Andrew J. Crawford to Evelina G. A. Heath, Sept. 17,
1853. (Sept. 19, 1853). W. T. Beard, BM.
James A. Morrison to Matilda A. Kimbro, Sept. 17, 1853.
D. M. Boon, BM.
Norman Norton to Elizabeth Innis, Sept. 19, 1853. (Sept.
21, 1853). Saml. Watts, BM.
Marion Armstrong to Elizabeth Parrish, Sept. 19, 1853.
(Sept. 19, 1853). J. M. Haynes, BM.
Henry Johnson to Martha Jane Stephens, Sept. 20, 1853.
(Sept. 21, 1853). H. Eckley, BM.
John S. Griffin to Susan E. Furgarson, Sept. 22, 1853.
(Sept. 23, 1853). Thos. W. Robertson, BM.
James H. Cunningham to Lackey Ann Askew, Sept. 26, 1853.
Wm. Warren, BM.
Allen A. Justice to Nancy A. M. Burney, Sept. 28, 1853.
(Sept. 28, 1853). Smith Parks, BM.
James N. Rust to Lucy A. Pemberton, Sept. 29, 1853.
(Sept. 29, 1853). Chas. W. Preddy, BM.
Jesse S. Blankinship to Elizabeth A. Blankinship, Sept.
30, 1853. (Oct. 2, 1853). Jas. H. Blankinship, BM.
John D. G. Wynn to Susan Vaughan, Oct. 2, 1853. Jno.
C. Foster, BM.
James White to Patience E. Flippin, Oct. 3, 1853. (Oct.
13, 1853). Jas. C. Martin, BM.
William H. Heath to Susan A. Campbell, Oct. 3, 1853.
(Nov. 17, 1853). James A. Shane, BM.
W. R. Etchison to Dovey Ennis, Oct. 3, 1853. (Oct. 6,
1853). N. B. Taylor, BM.
John C. Hartsfield to Catharine E. Truman, Oct. 3, 1853.
(Oct. 4, 1853). Jas. T. Smith, BM.
Benj. F. Elder to Margaret V. Hamilton, July 21, 1853.
(July 21, 1853). W. C. Penn, BM.
Jeremiah Smith to Margarett Cook, Oct. 4, 1853. (Oct.
4, 1853). Newton Yarbrough, BM.
Henry Hooker to Catharine Robinson, Oct. 5, 1853. (Oct.
5, 1853). T. S. Turnham, BM.
William M. Connell to Margaret Ann Holt, Oct. 5, 1853.
(Oct. 6, 1853).
Robert A. Porter to Mary M. Arnold, Oct. 5, 1853. (Oct.
6, 1853). V. B. Wright, BM.
Josiah L. Wade to Martha A. Underwood, Oct. 6, 1853.
(Oct. 7, 1853). George S. Penn, BM.
John Moore to Salina E. Allen, Oct. 7, 1853. (Oct. 13,
1853). John L. Fly, BM.
John Spencer to Tabitha Hopper, Oct. 8, 1853. (Oct. 9,
1853). Bradford Hopper, BM.
Aaron Springer to Cornelia Belew, Oct. 8, 1853. (Oct.
10, 1853). Thomas Little, BM.
William F. Gill to Olly Ann McDowell, Oct. 10, 1853.
(Oct. 12, 1853). J. L. Flippin, BM.
Dennis Thompson to Nancy Edmondson, Oct. 10, 1853.
(Oct. 13, 1853). J. A. W. Hess, BM.
John Thompson to Nancy Ann Wright, Oct. 11, 1853. (Oct.
13, 1853). R. H. McNail, BM.

GIBSON COUNTY MARRIAGES

Edmund Keely to Louise A. Battle, Oct. 12, 1853. (Oct. 12, 1853). H. A. Crouse, BM.
Thos. W. Robinson to Mary Louisa Woodard, Oct. 20, 1853. (Oct, 20, 1853). Jas. R. Dossett, BM.
Alexander Fox to Sarah A. Mitts, Oct. 20, 1853. (Oct. 24, 1853). A. J. Fox, BM.
Robert Bradford to Mary Baker, Oct. 22, 1853. (Oct. 23, 1853). H. W. Bradford, BM.
Benj. A. Yeargain to Elizabeth Pittman, Oct. 25, 1853. (Oct. 26, 1853). John M. Pratt, BM.
James H. Davis to Clarrasy Ann Connell, Oct. 26, 1853. (Oct. 27, 1853). W. M. Connell, BM.
Isaac L. Jetton to Lucreatia R. Sinclair, Oct. 27, 1853. G. Wright, BM.
Dennis Newter to Celemanda Mahon, Oct. 31, 1853. (Nov. 1, 1853). A. G. Black, BM.
Thomas P. Able to Nancy Oliver, Nov. 2, 1853. (Nov. 3, 1853). A. R. Middleton, BM.
Samuel Reed to Margaret H. Cox, Nov. 3, 1853. (Nov. 3, 1853). S. N. Lourance, BM.
Samuel S. Greer to Harrett Carl, Nov. 3, 1853. (Nov. 3, 1853). Wm. F. Ramsey, M.G.
William Lewis Cash to Jarucia Ann Phallis, Nov. 3, 1853. (Nov. 3, 1853). Willis P. Grissum, BM.
James A. Morrison to Matilda M. Kimbro, Nov. 3, 1853. (Nov. 3, 1853). Jas. W. Cresap, BM.
Thos. P. Wade to Martha W. Freeman, Nov. 4, 1853. (Oct. 4, 1853). W. H. Harvey, BM.
Samuel A. Jones to Mary Jane Vaden, Nov. 5, 1853. N. Pybass, BM.
Barnabas Edward to Mary J. Tigret, Nov. 9, 1853. John Dawson, BM.
John H. Wallace to Phebe A. Featherston, Nov. 10, 1853. (Nov. 10, 1853). Coleman H. Witt, BM.
Thomas H. Ward to Mary A. Gurganus, Nov. 12, 1853. Wm. H. Haggird, BM.
Weston Kealthley to Elizabeth Pate, Nov. 14, 1853. Marshall B. Keathley, BM.
John Glass to Mary Branson, Nov. 15, 1853. (Nov. 16, 1853). L. B. Gilchrist, BM.
Martin Belew to Patsey Bryant, Nov. 15, 1853. (Nov. 17, 1853). Geo. W. Brant, BM.
Zachariah Freeman to Agnes A. Bowers, Nov. 15, 1853. Willis Grady, BM.
Silas Edwards to Mary Freeman, Nov. 18, 1853. (Nov. 24, 1853). Seth T. Moon, BM.
Paul T. Barner to Elizabeth J. Glisson, Nov. 21, 1853. (Nov. 22, 1853). Stephen O'Daniel, BM.
Coleman H. Witt to Susan F. Hoskins, Nov. 21, 1853. (Nov. 23, 1853). Jno. L. Fly, BM.
Allen Flowers to Elizabeth J. Sims, Nov. 23, 1853. (Nov. 24, 1853). Wm. Flowers, BM.
James M. Burnett to Jane Parris, Nov. 26, 1853. (Nov. 27, 1853). Oliver T. Morris, BM.

William Crank to Mary Thompson, Nov. 28, 1853. (Dec. 1, 1853). Jas. M. Terrill, BM.

J. A. W. Pittman to Tericy Gilliland, Nov. 29, 1853. (Dec. 1, 1853). G. W. Robinson, BM.

D. J. Hawks to Eveline Keath, Dec. 5, 1853. R. M. Gowan, BM.

James Pugh to Elizabeth Ryster, Dec. 5, 1853. (Dec. 8, 1853). W. H. Ryster, BM.

Francis E. Woodide to Martha E. Day, Dec. 6, 1853. E. G. Stallings and Moses P. Cox, BM.

Richard Best to Mary Moss, Dec. 7, 1853. (Dec. 11, 1853). Jno. McFarland, BM.

William Covington to Nancy L. Lyon, Dec. 7, 1853. (Dec. 8, 1853). T. M. Covington, BM.

William S. Cody to Sarah Swan, Dec. 8, 1853. (Dec. 13, 1853). Jas. R. Cody, BM.

John Lyon to Louisa N. Massy, Dec. 14, 1853. (Dec. 14, 1853). N. G. Adkins, BM.

Rufus Blackburn to Jane C. Skiles, Dec. 15, 1853. (Dec. 15, 1853). Daniel D. Hassell, BM.

Benjamin S. Cowan to Margaret E. Skiles, Dec. 15, 1853. (Dec. 15, 1853). W. T. Woods, BM.

S. R. D. Brown to A. E. Alexander, Dec. 15, 1853. (Dec. 15, 1853). J. M. McLaurine, BM.

Rufus E. King to Ketsey Flowers, Dec. 17, 1853. (Dec. 24, 1853). John W. Brickhouse, BM.

Isaac C. Haynes to Ann E. Cunningham, Dec. 17, 1853. (Dec. 20, 1853). W. C. Robertson, BM.

William C. Robertson to Elizabeth Danner, Dec. 17, 1853. (Dec. 22, 1853). C. Martin, BM.

Thos. A. Tucker to Ester C. Etchison, Dec. 19, 1853. (Dec. 22, 1853). Wilson R. Etchison, BM.

B. L. Partee to M. C. Wade, Dec. 21, 1853. M. J. Clay, BM.

Charles A. Brown to Martha Needham, Dec. 21, 1853. (Dec. 22, 1853). Smith Parks, BM.

William W. Gallion to Elizabeth Baker, Dec. 22, 1853. Pleasant Dyer, BM.

John S. Dement to Rachael C. Smith, Dec. 22, 1853. (Dec. 23, 1853). S. A. Roliends, BM.

James Aslin to Mary Ann Smith, Dec. 24, 1853. Jas. Barham, BM.

Larkin H. Irwin to Martha J. Fargurson, Dec. 29, 1853. (Dec. 29, 1853). J. M. McLaurine, BM.

Levi S. Woods to Mary Jarman, Dec. 31, 1853. (Jan. 5, 1854.

James F. Gordan to Julia E. Barksdale, Dec. 31, 1853. (Jan. 1, 1854). John Gleason, BM.

George Reed to Elizabeth Taylor, Dec. 31, 1853. G. W. Reed, BM.

Governor Belew to Sarah Ann Bryant, Jan. 2, 1854. (Jan. 4, 1854). Geo. W. Bryant, BM.

A. G. Dodd to Sarah F. Fielder, Jan. 2, 1854. (Jan. 3, 1854). Peter L. Donaldson, BM.

William D. Ingram to Ann E. Woodruff, Jan. 3, 1854. (Jan. 3, 1854). W. G. Hartsfield, BM.

Jasper N. Hardy to Elizabeth M. Kelton, Jan. 4, 1854.
(Jan. 5, 1854). Jas. N. Hill, BM.
N. M. Travis to Ann Witherington, Jan. 4, 1854. A. O.
Daniel, BM.
David Bird to Elizabeth Legate, Jan- 5, 1854. (Jan. 12,
1854). J. W. Burress, BM.
William A. Walls to Rachel Hicks, Jan. 5, 1854. (Jan.
8, 1854). Jasper Lock, BM.
T. A. Tanner to Eoma Smith, Jan. 7, 1854. (Jan. 7, 1854).
R. C. Thomas, BM.
Thomas L. Jones to Emeline Thomas, Jan. 10, 1854. Jos.
R. Taylor, BM.
Benj. F. Kelton to Sarah A. Hardy, Jan. 11, 1854. (Jan.
12, 1854). Jas. N. Hill, BM.
Marian F. Parker to Vanleer S. Walker, Jan. 11, 1854.
(Jan. 12, 1854). W. Hazlewood, BM.
William Benthill to Frances A. Durley, Jan. 12, 1854.
(Jan. 12, 1854). W. P. Wallis, BM.
John W. Crockett to Dicy Jane Wilson, Jan. 12, 1854.
(Jan. 12, 1854). David W. Foster, BM.
Thomas C. Dickins to Margaret Jane Roberts, Jan. 14,
1854. (Jan. 17, 1854). R. Simpson, BM.
William F. Floyd to Mary E. Tyson, Jan. 16, 1854. (Jan.
16, 1854). Jno. Wilson, BM.
James N. McDaniel to Sarah J. Reed, Jan. 16, 1854. (Jan.
17, 1854). Robert H. Carr, BM.
John M. Dunlap to Mary L. Moore, Jan. 17, 1854. (Jan.
19, 1854). Needham H. Moore, BM.
John Knott to Arie F. Connell, Jan. 17, 1854. (Jan. 17,
1854). Martin Arnold, BM.
James A. Price to Martha E. West, Jan. 17, 1854. (Jan.
18, 1854). Jno. W. West, BM.
Henry Kennady to Mary Ann Biggs, Jan. 18, 1854. (Jan.
24, 1854). Needham Whitley, BM.
Henry Forristed to Mahaley Cantrell, Jan. 21, 1854.
(Jan. 22, 1854). Andrew J. Allen, BM.
Samuel C. Pierce to Rebecca C. Hunt, Jan. 23, 1854.
(Jan. 24, 1854). N. C. Pierce, BM.
Joseph Morris to Nancy Edward, Jan. 25, 1854. (Jan.
26, 1854). E. H. Crocker, BM.
George Day to Martha E. Lyons, Jan. 25, 1854. (Jan. 25,
1854). H. T. Heath, BM.
M. A. Dickey to M. W. Barnet, Jan. 30, 1854. (Jan. 31,
1854).
Joseph McKnight to T. E. McKnight, Jan. 31, 1854. (Jan.
31, 1854).
Davidson B. T. Bobbett to Eliza C. Lett, Feb. 2, 1854.
R. F. Bobbett, BM.
James N. Hill to Julia L. Kelton, Feb. 2, 1854. (Feb.
2, 1854). Thos. Price, BM.
John Kingston to Leathia P. Johnson, Feb. 4, 1854. (Feb.
5, 1854). W. P. Morgan, BM.
John D. Mathis to Mary J. Drake, Feb. 6, 1854. (Feb. 7,
1854).

David I. H. Templeton to Mary M. Knox, Feb. 7, 1854.
(Feb. 10, 1854).
James Bobbett to Lecia Wyatt, Feb. 7, 1854. (Feb. 7,
1854). L. B. Gilchtist, BM. (L. B. Gilchrist, BM. ?)
Allen Taylor to Fanny Jane Clay, Feb. 8, 1854. W. H.
Hyde, BM.
Simon Reynolds to Dolly Billips, Feb. 8, 1854. (Feb. 8,
8154). A. I. Allen, BM.
James H. Nowell to Frances J. Jackson, Feb. 8, 1854.
(Feb. 9, 1854). Jas. D. Jackson, BM.
John C. Bullington to Elizabeth Lee, Feb. 11, 1854.
(Feb. 16, 1854). Robt. Smith, BM.
Ashville B. Whiteherst to Elizabeth Breckhouse, Feb. 11,
1854. (Feb. 14, 1854). M. L. Holland, BM.
William W. Stanley to Eliza Jane Wilks, Feb. 14, 1854.
(Feb. 14, 1854). W. S. Halliburton, BM.
George S. Penn to Eliza Ellen Conner, Feb. 15, 1854.
Jno. A. Wilkins, BM.
Buford Terrill to Julia Bouchier, Feb. 15, 1854. (Feb.
15, 1854). Jno. Kinsey, BM.
A. G. Tilman to Isilla Waldrope, Feb. 16, 1854. James
Arnold, BM.
Travis F. Graddy to Mary Ann Keathley, Feb. 21, 1854.
(Feb. 23, 1854). Wm. Hines, BM.
Needham Whitley to Matilda C. Biggs, Feb. 22, 1854.
(Feb. 22, 1854). R. W. Biggs, BM.
Willis L. A. Grady to Delila Mobley, Feb. 23, 1854.
(Mar. 13, 1854). B. Ragan, J.P., BM.
Winfield S. Hicks to Nancy Jane English, Mar. 1, 1854.
(Mar. 28, 1854).
John H. Crawford to Narcissa Blankenship, Mar. 6, 1854.
(Mar. 10, 1854). Saml. S. Hill, BM.
D. D. Vaden to Polly Davis, Mar. 11, 1854. By G. M.
Sharp, J.P. L. B. Gilchrist, BM.
Hiram C. Trout to Sally N. Shelton, Mar. 13, 1854.
(Mar. 14, 1854). Caleb R. Clement, BM.
Turner Mobley to Sally G. Haynes, Feb. 15, 1854.
Harbert Mobley, BM.
Francis W. Shelton to Matilda Crank, Mar. 16, 1854.
(Mar. 16, 1854). Jno. J. Halloway, BM.
John Young to Martha Ann Little, Mar. 17, 1854. W. K.
Hall, BM.
Elijah Grier to Vina Hicks, Mar. 20, 1854. (Mar. 20,
1854). Thos. A. Flippin, BM.
Wilee Wallace to Sarah F. Bird, Mar. 25, 1854. (Mar. 26,
1854). L. D. Lawrance, BM.
James W. Crafton to Sarah J. Roe, Apr. 3, 1854. D. W.
Crafton, BM.
Jessee Needham to Semilda A. Barton, Apr. 3, 1854.
(Apr. 6, 1854). Benson Needham, BM.
Solomon A. Baily to Ellen Baily, Apr. 5, 1854. (Apr. 13,
1854). W. J. Barker, BM.
Jessee L. Tolen to Adalaid V. Cherry, Apr. 8, 1854. J.
M. Tucker, BM.

GIBSON COUNTY MARRIAGES

W. C. Penn to Eliza E. Bryant, Apr. 12, 1854. (Apr. 12, 1854). W. P. Wallis, BM.
Joel H. Blackshear to Tabitha C. Blair, Apr. 13, 1854. (Apr. 13, 1854). R. D. Blair, BM.
P. Jones to Sarah M. Tinkle, Apr. 13, 1854. T. W. Williams, BM.
D. W. Woodruff to E. C. Hill, Apr. 15, 1854. (Apr. 20, 1854). C. L. Hill, BM.
John Davis to Louisa Ragsdale, Apr. 15, 1854. (Apr. 18, 1854). T. J. Mound, BM.
Samuel Miller to Nancy E. Easterwood, Apr. 17, 1854. (Apr. 20, 1854). James M. Burress, BM.
Samuel A. Roberts to Ann I. Arnold, Apr. 22, 1854. Wm. J. Browning, BM.
Madison F. Herndon to R. E. C. Thomason, Apr. 22, 1854. Mat Bradberry, BM.
L. L. Williams to Virginia C. Carter, Apr. 27, 1854. J. A. W. Hess, BM.
James Hogan to Elizabeth Grishum, Apr. 28, 1854. (May 2, 1854). M. M. Seay, BM.
Oliver T. Morris to Jane Morris, May 2, 1854. (May 21, 1854). Jas. M. Burnett, BM.
L. W. Blakemore to C. F. H. McDowell, May 3, 1854. (May 3, 1854). J. A. Wilkins, BM.
Josiah Cooper to Nancy Jane Sane, May 3, 1854. (May 3, 1854). L. N. White, BM.
H. W. Bradford to Amanda Gillespie, May 10, 1854. (May 10, 1854). Thos. Bradford, BM.
Latima Brickhouse to Susan M. Tinkle, May 10, 1854. (May 11, 1854). C. L. Hutchason, BM.
Lafayett Varden to Rebecca Elender Gill, May 23, 1854. (May 23, 1854).
Elisha Keathly to Hepsy A. Grady, May 23, 1854. (May 25, 1854). B. S. Crawford, BM.
A. C. McGee to Margarette Jane Bogle, May 25, 1854. (May 26, 1854). Leander McGee, BM.
Jefferson Burton to Martha J. Wales, May 27, 1854. (May 28, 1854). J. T. Rust, BM.
John F. McCaslin to Susan Holt, May 29, 1854. (May 30, 1854). Jas. S. Sloan, BM.
William T. Grigsby to Emma Bright, May 31, 1854. (May 31, 1854). J. Hassell, BM.
Burrell M. Thompson to Mary Heard, June 3, 1854. (June 4, 1854). W. C. Patterson, BM.
James W. Webb to America Cunningham, June 5, 1854. George W. Webb, BM.
James Alexander to Percy Pope, June 8, 1854. (June 8, 1854). N. P. Vincent, BM.
Wm. G. Ward to Timitha E. Burrow, June 13, 1854. (June 13, 1854). John N. Ward, BM.
Isaac J. Rude to Isabellar Alexander, June 15, 1854. (June 15, 1854). John F. Comes, BM.
John T. Head to Mary A. Galard, June 22, 1854. (June 22, 1854). Mathew Bradberry, BM.

Paul C. Grafton to Margarett A. Davis, June 22, 1854.
(June 23, 1854). W. R. Phillips, BM.
Alexander Ray to Pemetea C. Weaver, June 22, 1854. C.
Bogas, BM.
W. C. Kerr to Ema C. Hall, June 29, 1854. A. A. Grigsby, BM.
William K. Bryant to Emily A. Blankenship, July 1, 1854.
E. L. Walker, BM.
D. A. McDaniel to Mary Ethridge, July 3, 1854. W. G.
Travis, BM.
James Bohannan to Tobithia Hundey, July 10, 1854. (July
10, 1854). Ira J. Ward, BM.
James Gurganus to Nancy M. Furgerson, July 12, 1854.
(July 12, 1854.) William Smith, BM.
Washington E. Jones to Sarah A. Ramsey, July 18, 1854.
(July 19, 1854). Eli Jones, BM.
Thos. W. Freeman to Frances Freeman, July 20, 1854.
(July 20, 1854). W. W. Freeman, BM.
Henry T. McFarland to Malissa C. Sloan, July 21, 1854.
(July 23, 1854). Jos. S. Sloan, BM.
Reding Hicks to Alvinia Hicks, July 25, 1854. (July 26,
1854). Andrew Ways, BM.
W. B. House to A. E. Wade, July 26, 1854. J. P. Wade, BM.
Richard A. Brown to Martha Williams, Aug. 2, 1854. (Aug.
2, 1854). Wm. H. Boyster, BM.
D. F. McFarland to Mary L. Jacobs, Aug. 3, 1854. (Aug.
3, 1854). T. D. Atchison, BM.
Jas. L. W. Brown to Susan S. Pearson, Aug. 9, 1854.
(Aug. 16, 1854). Wm. Smith, BM.
Albert G. Yancy to Elizabeth M. Sappington, Aug. 10,
1854. (Aug. 10, 1854). Jno. W. Wade, BM.
Thomas Bryant to Alvira Hersey, Aug. 10, 1854. (Aug.
10, 1854). S. J. Grimes, BM.
Ashley Hicks to Elsa Hicks, Aug. 12, 1854. (Aug. ?, 1854).
Redin Hicks, BM.
Roland Childs to Margarette M. Blair, Aug. 16, 1854.
(Aug. 17, 1854). G. W. Blair, BM.
Ransom Thompson to S. Willis, Aug. 19, 1854. R. A. Hall, BM.
David R. Burch to Martha J. Love, Aug. 21, 1854. James
Adair, BM.
Thos. G. Harbor to Malinda Lemons, Aug. 23, 1854. (Aug.
24, 1854). John Brown, BM.
James Copeland to L. A. Boaz, Aug. 24, 1854. (Aug. 25,
1854). S. Bell, BM.
William G. Baker to Mary A. D. Witherford, Aug. 30, 1854.
(Aug. 30, 1854). Wm. Walston, BM.
Richard Walls to Susan Hicks, Aug. 31, 1854. (Aug. 31,
1854). J. C. Patterson, BM.
James N. Reese to A. E. Berry, Aug. 31, 1854. (Aug. 31,
1854). Jno. Y. Armstrong, BM.
John D. Lacy to Sarah McAllister, Sept. 1, 1854. (Sept.
3, 1854). John Edwards, BM.
Albert L. Bobbett to M. I. S. S. Dickens, Sept. 1, 1854.
Sept. 5, 1854). B. F. Dickens, BM.
S. B. Farthing to Rebecca McGran, Sept. 1, 1854. (Sept.
2, 1854). J. S. Holder, BM.

J. A. Pyland to Mary E. J. McEwen, Sept. 6, 1854. (Sept.
6, 1854). Thos. H. Lanier, BM.
John C. W. Nunn to Mary A. E. Porter, Sept. 4, 1854.
(Sept. 5, 1854). A. G. Nunn, BM.
Richard Harper to Louisa E. Green, Sept. 4, 1854. (Sept.
4, 1854). W. H. Campbell, BM.
Dewitt A. Reese to Elizabeth J. Blakemore, Sept. 5, 1854.
(Sept. 5, 1854).
James Featherston to Laney George, Sept. 7, 1854. Robt.
Billingsly, BM.
W. B. Burns to Eliza Wisenor, Sept. 8, 1854. (Sept. 8,
1854). Jno. L. Dickson, BM.
John C. McCollum to Maniza P. Joyce, Sept. 9, 1854.
(Sept. 14, 1854). Allen McCollum, BM.
A. J. White to Martha M. Jacobs, Sept. 18, 1854. (Sept.
20, 1854). G. W. White, BM.
R. D. Jones to John P. Wade, Sept. 20, 1854. J. P. Wade, BM.
William J. Burrow to Mary New, Sept. 20, 1854. (Sept.
28, ?). J. B. Agee, BM.
Thos. D. Warmath to Harrett M. Green, Sept. 20, 1854.
Ben Sandeford, BM.
William J. Bryant to Lilly A. Barton, Sept. 24, 1854.
(Sept. 24, 1854). Wm. G. Penn, BM.
Samuel Mount to Frances Flippin, Sept. 27, 1854. R. J.
Nevil, BM.
Charles E. McWhirter to Sarah J. Kennedy, Sept. 27, 1854.
(Sept. 28, 1854). Jno. W. James, BM.
Moses Oliver to Sarah Linton, Sept. 27, 1854. (Sept.
28, 1854). Thos. D. Atchison, BM.
Cannon H. Lain to F. W. Chrisp, Oct. 3, 1854. Noah M.
Bowman, BM.
Willis B. Grissom to Margrette E. Cash, Oct. 3, 1854.
(Oct. 3, 1854). B. W. Cash, BM.
William H. Tuggle to Martha P. Alvis, Oct. 4, 1854.
A. H. Rust, BM.
A. R. Landrum to Nancy Biggs, Oct. 5, 1854. James W.
Landrum, BM.
J. J. Gardner to Margarette Hopkins, Oct. 9, 1854. (Oct.
9, 1854). Wm. Rogers, BM.
Robert S. Gordon to Mary J. E. Allbright, Oct. 9, 1854.
(Oct. 9, 1854). Wm. Shaw, BM.
Elias Jackson to Marion W. Hess, Oct. 9, 1854. (Oct.
11, 1854). Wm. Cullom, BM.
Samuel A. McDaniel to Mary A. Carr, Oct. 10, 1854. (Oct.
10, 1854). R. H. Carr, BM.
Samuel P. Linton to Eliza Ann Little, Oct. 10, 1854.
(Oct. 12, 1854). G. T. Richardson, BM.
William G. Knott to Artilla Holt, Oct. 10, 1854. (Oct.
11, 1854). H. Williamson, BM.
Isaac R. Thetford to Mary Jane Hill, Oct. 10, 1854.
Andrew M. Smith, BM.
Charles Tinsley to Jane Summers, Oct. 10, 1854. Jas. S.
Lovley, BM.
Saml. H. Wheeler to Sarah A. Taylor, Oct. 13, 1854.
(Oct. 14, 1854). J. Q. Reeves, BM.

A. F. Betts to Elizabeth J. Woods, Oct. 14, 1854. (Oct.
19, 1854). J. P. Taylor, BM.

William C. Patterson to Annis Taylor, Oct. 17, 1854.
(Oct. 17, 1854). Wm. Taylor, BM.

James R. Dossett to (?) Lowry, Oct. 17, 1854. P. K. Dossett, BM

R. C. Bass to M. E. Dyson, Oct. 17, 1854. W. C. Penn, BM.

Henry A. King to Susan Goodloe, Oct. 23, 1854. (Oct. 29,
1854). John H. King, BM.

Benjamin Rutledge to Angeline L. Burnett, Oct. 23, 1854.
(Oct. 29, 1854). A. G. Blanton, BM.

Hiram Partee to Lilly Mays, Oct. 24, 1854. (Oct. 25,
1854). R. H. Oldham, BM.

John M. Pratt to Sarah V. Smith, Oct. 24, 1854. (Oct.
26, 1854). W. R. Smith, BM.

Lafayett Green to Nancy Bradford, Oct. 25, 1854. J. W.
Crafton, BM.

W. R. D. Howarton to Sarah L. Lea, Oct. 26, 1854. (Oct.
29, 1854). C. C. Baber, BM.

R. G. Moore to Mary J. Hutson, Oct. 26, 1854. (Oct. 26,
1854). E. H. Harvey, BM.

Jonas Hoeser to Sirena Hart, Oct. 28, 1854. (Nov. 2,
1854). W. A. Hancock, BM.

W. R. Michael to Stacy Mullins, Oct. 30, 1854. (Oct.
31, 1854). A. P. Phillips, BM.

John C. Buchannan to Luiza J. Goodwin, Oct. 31, 1854.
Jas. G. Strong, BM.

William Felts to Laura V. Strong, Oct. 31, 1854. (Nov.
2, 1854). W. G. Roulhae, BM.

Lewis J. Salyton to Louisa H. Featherston, Nov. 1, 1854.
(Nov. 6, 1854). Henry Parker, BM.

William Bone to Camilla T. Moore, Nov. 2, 1854. (Nov.
24, 1854). T. W. Alford, BM.

John Rushing to Mary Bohannan, Nov. 3, 1854. Thomas King, BM.

B. H. Holland to Nancy E. Bottoms, Nov. 5, 1854. (Nov.
6, 1854). Jno. L. Conner, BM.

W. W. Moore to Elizabeth Watt, Nov. 6, 1854. (Nov. ?,
1854). Thos. E. Hale, BM.

John F. Ford to Martha J. McAlister, Nov. 6, 1854.
(Nov. 13, 1854). Berry Pittman, BM.

James A. McGee to Elizabeth H. Gillespie, Nov. 8, 1854.
(Nov. 9, 1854). Henry M. Jones, BM.

M. L. Hays to Julia A. Harrison, Nov. 11, 1854. (Nov.
12, 1854). John A. Hays, BM.

William Cole to Sarah Fowler, Nov. 13, 1854. (Nov. 16,
1854). W. P. Haley, BM.

D. C. Harris to Susan Umsted, Nov. 20, 1854. (Nov. 21,
1854). Adolphus Harris, BM.

Henry McGee to Martha Fleming, Nov. 21, 1854. (Nov.
21, 1854). D. M. McKnight, BM.

William Williams to Caroline Dawson, Nov. 28, 1854.
(Nov. 28, 1854). E. Wren, BM.

R. M. Gowan to Mary Jane McFarlen, Nov. 24, 1854. (Nov.
27, 1854). G. F. Richardson, BM.

James Baxter to Mary Heriod, Nov. 28, 1854. (Nov. 28,
1854). H. A. Welch, BM.

GIBSON COUNTY MARRIAGES

J. R. A. Blackburn to Martha B. Gibbs, Nov. 30, 1854.
(Nov. 30, 1854). C. W. Harrison, BM.
Marshall B. Keathly to Mary F. Wilson, Nov. 25, 1854.
B. A. Bowden, BM.
Thos. R. Crosbey to Elizabeth M. West, Nov. 28, 1854.
(Nov. 29, 1854). G. A. West, BM.
Jas. F. A. M. Avery to Nancy C. Gunner, Dec. 5, 1854.
(Dec. 7, 1854). A. H. Tatum, BM.
David Hassell to Susanah A. Butler, Dec. 6, 1854. (Dec.
6, 1854). Jno. Hassell, BM.
R. G. Aycock to Mary M. Woods, Dec. 12, 1854. Ed Cooper, BM.
James Claybrook to Lucinda A. Elam, Dec. 12, 1854. (Dec.
15, 1854).
George W. Carroll to Lucy M. Carrol, Dec. 13, 1854. M.
T. Halford, BM.
Thos. G. Taylor to Ann T. Reeves, Dec. 14, 1854. (Dec.
14, 1854). Wm. G. Taylor, BM.
Isham Bailey to Sarah A. Betts, Dec. 17, 1854. John C.
Porter, BM.
Erasmus B. Raines to Mary Ann Dunlap, Dec. 19, 1854.
(Dec. 20, 1854).
Granville M. Bottom to Easter O'Daniel, Dec. 21, 1854.
(Dec. 21, 1854). Martin L. Sloan, BM.
Martin L. Sloan to Rachael O'Daniel, Dec. 21, 1854.
(Dec. 21, 1854). Granville L. Bolton, BM.
Jas. A. McFarlen to Jane Moore, Dec. 21, 1854. (Dec.
21, 1854). J. M. J. McLaurine, BM.
Washington Riley to Emiline J. Roberts, Dec. 23, 1854.
(Dec. 24, 1854).
Henderson Sparkman to Elizabeth Roberts, Dec. 25, 1854.
(Dec. 27, 1854). G. H. Kelton, BM.
Thos. Woods to Silvian Harbor, Dec. 26, 1854. (Dec. 28,
1854). John Raney, BM.
B. F. Bobbett to Mary E. Berry, Dec. 27, 1854. (Dec. 28,
1854). B. F. Young, BM.
Jacob H. Hay to Sophia J. Lainer, Dec. 27, 1854. James
Tatum, BM.
J. J. McFarlen to Narcissa T. Coleman, Dec. 27, 1854.
(Dec. 27, 1854). Wm. McFarlen, BM.
Patrick Fanner to Ann Oliver, Dec. 29, 1854. (Dec. 29,
1854).
Gaih Holland to Mary L. Bledsoe, Dec. 4, 1854. (Dec.
4, 1854).
William Garrett to Electy C. Pyland, Dec. 30, 1854.
(Dec. 31, 1854).
William Cawthon to Isabella F. Baldridge, Dec. 30,
1854. (Jan. 1, 1855).
J. W. Coleman to Salina Keeth, Nov. 23, 1854. (Dec. 1,
1854). G. T. Richardson, BM.
William Poindexter to Eveline McFoslin, Jan. 1, 1855.
(Jan. 2, 1855).
William N. Adair to Eliza C. Senter, Jan. 1, 1855. (Jan.
4, 1855).
I. M. C. Goodloe to A. (?) Thomas, Jan. 1, 1855. (Jan.
1, 1855).

Samuel N. White to Nancy E. Hale, Jan. 1, 1855. (Jan. 4, 1855).

Elijah Jones to Nancy Mathews, Jan. 1, 1855. (Jan. 10, 1855).

A. S. Hart to Mary E. Corley, Jan. 3, 1855. (Mar. 30, 1855).

John A. Harpole to Sarah H. Harpole, Jan. 3, 1855. (Jan. 9, 1855).

Murry W. Foster to Mary P. Caples, Jan. 6, 1855. (Jan. 7, 1855).

John Williams to Martha Arnold, Jan. 9, 1855. (Jan. 9, 1855).

W. J. Becton to Elizabeth McGill, Jan. 10, 1855. (Jan. 11, 1855).

A. I. J. Mathis to Martha J. Rust, Jan. 10, 1855. (Jan. 10, 1855).

G. W. Long to Nancy Fletcher, Jan. 10, 1855. (Jan. 10, 1855).

James M. Bottoms to Ann F. Davis, Jan. 10, 1855. (Jan. 10, 1855).

Franklin S. Harvey to Sarah A. Gallion, Jan. 11, 1855. (Jan. 11, 1855).

J. W. Cannon to Sarah G. Simmons, Jan. 11, 1855. (Jan. 16, 1855).

Crawford Jones to Sarah A. Jones, Jan. 16, 1855. (Jan. 17, 1855).

Jacob Chapman to Margarett E. McLaine, Jan. 16, 1855. (Jan. 18, 1855).

R. C. Wade to E. J. Felts, Jan. 22, 1855. (Jan. 23, 1855).

John H. Parker to Mahala Phelan, Jan. 22, 1855. (Jan. 22, 1855).

Absolom F. Hays to Jane E. Agee, Jan. 24, 1855. (Jan. 24, 1855).

W. F. Carr to Nancy Briant, Jan. 24, 1855. (Jan. 25, 1855).

James T. Cock to Mary A. Kelton, Jan. 29, 1855. (Jan. 30, 1855).

Joseph Cooper to Jane Dunigan, Jan. 30, 1855. (Jan. 30, 1855).

Samuel Graddy to Martha A. Briant, Jan. 31, 1855. (Feb. 1, 1855).

W. R. Lanhann to Elizabeth L. Baird, Jan. 31, 1855. (Feb. 1, 1855).

James B. Kilzer to Sarah J. Adcock, Feb. 1, 1855. (Feb. 1, 1855).

Charles A. Bowls to Sarah A. Jackson, Feb. 1, 1855. (Feb. 3, 1855).

Jas. S. Holder to Emeline Farr, Feb. 1, 1855. (Feb. 1, 1855).

John L. Bivins to Virginia A. Roberson, Feb. 6, 1855. (Feb. 6, 1855).

A. J. Nale to Emily C. Hagard, Feb. 12, 1855. (Feb. 14, 1855).

GIBSON COUNTY MARRIAGES

Thomas J. Blair to Panthaer W. Williams, Feb. 12, 1855.
(Feb. 13, 1855).
Leander Wafer to R. Ritter Clementine Lee, Feb. 13, 1855.
(Feb. 13, 1855).
Samuel Doughtry to S. A. Ennis, Feb. 27, 1855. (Feb. 28,
1855).
W. A. McLain to Ronanah C. D. Thomas, Mar. 1, 1855.
(Mar. 1, 1855).
A. H. Chesap to Louisa J. Rust, Mar. 1, 1855. (Mar. 1,
1855).
William A. Wiles to Mary V. Dunlap, Mar. 6, 1855. (Mar.
6, 1855).
Absolum H. Tatum to Emly A. M. Avery, Mar. 7, 1855.
(Mar. 9, 1855).
Daniel T. Agee to Luemma S. Conlee, Mar. 13, 1855. (Mar.
13, 1855).
J. H. Ragan to Mary W. Hartsfield, Mar. 14, 1855. (Mar.
15, 1855).
James R. Davis to Manda H. Smith, Mar. 22, 1855. (Mar.
22, 1855).
John B. Weaver to Susan M. Mathis, Apr. 7, 1855. (Apr.
8, 1855).
Levi J. Turner to Margarett Patterson, Apr. 9, 1855.
(Apr. 10, 1855).
Ripley Brady to Mary J. Robb, Apr. 11, 1855. (Apr. 12,
1855).
Licurgas W. Williams to Amanda C. Walker, Apr. 19, 1855.
(Apr. 22, 1855).
Nonod Hicks to Amanda J. Walls, Apr. 24, 1855. (Apr.
26, 1855).
Benjamin Cooper to Casa Ames, Apr. 26, 1855. (Apr. 26,
1855).
John W. Brown to Henrietta L. Hauger, Apr. 30, 1855.
(May 3, 1855).
John Hassell to Elizabeth Jones, May 1, 1855. (May 1,
1855).
Caswell E. George to Elizabeth Gay, May 2, 1855. (May
2, 1855).
Hugh B. Robinson to Caroline R. Miller, May 3, 1855.
(May 3, 1855).
Samuel J. Bone to Emily Pettus, May 11, 1855. (May 13,
1855).
W. D. Baldridge to Elizabeth Routen, May 14, 1855. (May
15, 1855).
Calvin Clever to Margarette Swindle, May 15, 1855.
(May 16, 1855).
Patrick E. Singleton to Frances E. Lawrence, May 17,
1855. (May 20, 1855).
Robert Smith to Martha Browning, May 18, 1855. (May
20, 1855).
William H. McGee to Mary M. Wiles, May 21, 1855. (May
21, 1855).
William M. Lourance to Sardinia E. Arnold, May 26, 1855.
(May 27, 1855).

Robert R. Grady to Margarett A. Ragan, May 31, 1855. (June 9, 1855).

S. A. Jennings to E. O. Cherry, June 7, 1855. (June 7, 1855).

John Foutch to Emily Braden, June 9, 1855. (June 10, 1855).

William Massey to Ruth George, June 14, 1855. (June 14, 1855).

William G. Skiles to Melissa Glasgow, June 18, 1855. (June 19, 1855).

Jas. A. G. McEwen to L. S. Crawford, June 19, 1855. (June 20, 1855).

William H. Cail to Letty M. Slayton, June 21, 1855. (June 21, 1855).

Nelson Nusston to Sina Adeline Mathis, June 22, 1854. (June 22, 1855).

John W. Dickerson to L. M. Wright, June 25, 1855. (July 4, 1855).

E. N. Pierce to Catharine Strother, June 26, 1855. (June 27, 1855).

Andrew J. Pounds to Hannah Pruitt, July 2, 1855. (July 5, 1855).

Clinton Gaily to Mary Howard, July 9, 1855. (July 12, 1855).

Isham Thomas to Elizabeth Holt, July 10, 1855. (July 11, 1855).

James M. Dickson to Martha E. Flowers, July 12, 1855. (July 12, 1855).

Warren B. Seward to Martha E. Burrow, July 12, 1855. (July 13, 1855).

Bradford Edwards to Martha H. Waddy, July 14, 1855. (July 15, 1855).

H. M. Hamilton to M. C. Hamilton, July 16, 1855. (July 17, 1855).

Elmore C. Hopper to Mary E. Wilson, July 18, 1855. (July 19, 1855).

Ute S. Halliburtoh to Ann Travis, July 23, 1855. (July 23, 1855).

B. J. Cooper to Susan Ann House, July 24, 1855. (July 24, 1855).

Granville S. Sharp to Sarah A. Caps, May 21, 1855. (May 22, 1855).

John B. Butler to Martha M. Cassell, Aug. 1, 1855. (Aug. 1, 1855).

James M. Arnold to Elizabeth West, Aug. 3, 1855. (Aug. 5, 1855).

N. S. Pierce to Mary E. Arnold, Aug. 4, 1855. (Aug. 7, 1855).

Augustin Wood to Sarah Gouger, Aug. 11, 1855. (Aug. 12, 1855).

F. W. Hall to Elizabeth C. Duncan, Aug. 14, 1855. (Aug. 15, 1855).

Giles O'Daniel to Polly Eliza Sims, Aug. 15, 1855. By M. Flowers, M.G.

Robert B. James to Mary C. James, Aug. 19, 1855. (Aug. 19, 1855).

Harris J. Furgerson to Sarah P. Crafton, Aug. 18, 1855.
(Aug. 19, 1855).
R. M. Pierce to Nancy Barlow, Aug. 22, 1855. (Aug. 23,
1855).
William S. Martin to Lucretia A. Holland, Aug. 23, 1855.
(Aug. 23, 1855).
John Y. Cribbs to Mary Jane Andrews, Aug. 27, 1855.
(Sept. 4, 1855).
William S. Crocker to Melinda Nicholds, Aug. 28, 1855.
(Aug. 28, 1855).
R. G. Thomas to Parale F. Sinclair, Aug. 29, 1855.
(Aug. 29, 1855).
William Thomas to Margrette S. J. Coffman, Aug. 30, 1855.
(Sept. 9, 1855).
Levi Bodkin to Elizabeth C. Hillard, Aug. 30, 1855.
(Aug. 31, 1855).
John Pitts to Sarah Patterson, Sept. 3, 1855. (Sept. 4,
1855).
Ebenezer D. Tucker to Caroline T. Dickey, Sept. 4, 1855.
(Sept. 5, 1855).
James M. Kenady to Letta C. Tinkle, Sept. 5, 1855. (Sept.
5, 1855).
N. P. Richardson to Susan O. Cole, Sept. 8, 1855. (Sept.
9, 1855).
Yancy D. Glisson to Sarah C. Bryant, Sept. 10, 1855.
(Sept. 12, 1855).
A. H. Rust to Sarah J. Roe, Sept. 11, 1855. (Sept. 12,
1855).
Adam Davis to Frances Baker, Sept. 13, 1855. (Sept. 13,
1855).
G. M. Bradford to Mary E. Stults, Sept. 17, 1855.
(Sept. 17, 1855).
Alexander Hughs to Elizabeth Stamps, Sept. 18, 1855.
(Sept. 20, 1855).
Madison Hale to Martha Cribbs, Sept. 25, 1855. (Sept.
27, 1855).
James D. Ray to Melissa A. Morris, Sept. 29, 1855.
(Sept. 30, 1855).
W. J. Mays to E. B. Patterson, Oct. 1, 1855. (Oct. 2,
1855).
James H. Rogers to Mary A. E. Slaton, Oct. 1, 1855.
(Oct. 4, 1855).
James M. Rogers to Emmaline Marcum, Oct. 1, 1855. (Oct.
4, 1855).
Enos Norvell to Mary Williams, Oct. 3, 1855. (Oct. 4, 1855).
William A. Wyatt to Margarett A. Reed, Oct. 3, 1855.
(Oct. 4, 1855).
Henry Lowry to Jane Bodkin, Oct. 3, 1855. (Oct. 4,
1855).
Marion J. Philips to Mary J. Smith, Oct. 4, 1855. (Oct.
5, 1855).
George E. Hassell to Narcissa E. Butler, Oct. 6, 1855.
(Oct. 7, 1855).
Robert M. Barnett to Ann E. Drake, Oct. 15, 1855. (Oct.
18, 1855).

GIBSON COUNTY MARRIAGES

Samuel J. S. Berry to Julia A. E. Dickson, Oct. 20, 1855. (Oct. 24, 1855).

Walter N. Thedford to Mary M. Herndon, Oct. 22, 1855. (Oct. 24, 1855).

John A. Greer to Jane F. Bryant, Oct. 24, 1855. (Nov. 4, 1855).

Robert H. Brown to Elizabeth Stephens, Oct. 29, 1855. (Nov. 1, 1855).

Thomas A. Akin to Nancy M. Reed, Oct. 25, 1855. By George H. Wright.

Joshua Baker to Jennett West, Nov. 3, 1855. (Nov. 6, 1855).

Thomas J. Ingraham to Nancy J. Powell, Nov. 5, 1855. (Nov. 14, 1855).

William A. Via to Mary M. Key, Nov. 5, 1855. (Nov. 7, 1855).

C. S. Hutchens to Mary Tinkle, Nov. 6, 1855. (Nov. 6, 1855).

Samuel Brightwell to Manda Stanley, Nov. 10, 1855. (Nov. 11, 1855).

Thomas C. Bogle to Manarca F. S. J. W. Blankenship, Nov. 13, 1855. (Nov. 14, 1855).

J. J. Clark to Amanda W. Yancey, Nov. 19, 1855. (Nov. 22, 1855).

Marion J. Stephens to Martha P. White, Nov. 19, 1855. (Nov. 21, 1855).

Alford M. Witt to Louisa Hammonds, Nov. 21, 1855. (Nov. 22, 1855).

Newton S. Revel to Mary B. Hammonds, Nov. 23, 1855. (Nov. 25, 1855).

Pleasant W. Hopper to Lucinda A. Berry, Nov. 26, 1855. (Nov. 28, 1855).

Marshall B. Glisson to Martha M. Flowers, Nov. 26, 1855. (Nov. 29, 1855).

Thos. Y. Blacknall to Nancy H. Campbell, Nov. 28, 1855. (Nov. 29, 1855).

Johnathan J. Haeslip to Suta A. Middleton, Dec. 3, 1855. (Dec. 4, 1855).

Needham H. Cook to Mary A. Bolin, Dec. 4, 1855. (Dec. 9, 1855). M. L. Holland, BM.

Samuel Baker to Mary J. Baker, Dec. 6, 1855. (Dec. 6, 1855).

John W. Featherston to Tabitha C. Conlee, Dec. 6, 1855. (Dec. 6, 1855).

Henry C. Hicks to Kitty Ann Asburn, Dec. 10, 1855. (Dec. 11, 1855).

William H. Holmes to Ellenor Dozier, Dec. 10, 1855. (Dec. 11, 1855).

Francis P. Drinkard to Penelope J. Berry, Dec. 11, 1855. (Dec. 13, 1855).

Augustus C. Seavers to Elizabeth McLemore, Dec. 12, 1855. (Dec. 13, 1855).

William H. Ferrell to Ann Grissom, Dec. 15, 1855. (Dec. 16, 1855).

Alexander M. House to Sarah J. Shane, Dec. 17, 1855.
(Dec. 20, 1855).
William Shaw to Margaret E. Roe, Dec. 18, 1855. (Dec.
19, 1855).
John W. West to Nancy Kelly, Dec. 17, 1855. (Dec. 20,
1855).
William A. G. Toombs to Sarah M. Ward, Dec. 19, 1855.
(Dec. 19, 1855).
George N. Bell to Delizar Woods, Dec. 20, 1855. (Dec.
20, 1855).
Jas. R. Brown to Caroline Mobley, Dec. 22, 1855. (Dec.
22, 1855).
N. G. Jackson to Frances Wallis, Dec. 24, 1855. (Dec.
24, 1855).
Jasper Bullington to Jane Jones, Dec. 24, 1855. (Dec.
24, 1855).
David Sanford to Mary E. McGeehe, Dec. 24, 1855. (Dec.
28, 1855).
D. G. Hines to Nancy E. Warren, Dec. 24, 1855. (Jan.
2, 1856).
William H. Jackson to Louisa Foster, Dec. 26, 1855.
(Dec. 27, 1855).
N. W. Pigue to Lexanah Patterson, Dec. 27, 1855. (Dec.
27, 1855).
David Gage to Susanah Dowland, Dec. 31, 1855. (Dec. 31,
1855).
John N. Porter to Nelly B. Taylor, Dec. 31, 1855. (Jan.
1, 1855).
King G. W. Davis to Louisa Hutson, Jan. 1, 1856. (Jan.
25, 1856).
Samuel Hicks to Margarette Shain, Jan. 5, 1856. (Jan.
8, 1856).
J. D. King to Amanda Taylor, Jan. 5, 1856. (Jan. 6, 1856).
John Fanon to Louisa Martin, Jan. 5, 1856. (Jan. 10,
1856).
William C. Easterwood to Sylvina Jones, Jan. 10, 1856.
(Jan. 10, 1856).
John Bryant to Rody Flippin, Jan. 10, 1856. (Jan. 10,
1856).
Samuel C. Henderson to Martha McCraey, Jan. 12, 1856.
(Jan. 17, 1856). Jas. R. Maddrey, BM.
James Mobley to Eveline F. Brown, Jan. 15, 1856.
(Jan. 15, 1856). Willis Grady, BM.
Rufus A. Via to Mary J. Blankenship, Jan. 16, 1856.
(Jan. 16, 1856). Jas. F. Knox, BM.
M. S. Wallice to Sarah E. Conley, Jan. 16, 1856. (Jan.
16, 1856).
G. W. Sims to E. P. Wilson, Jan. 16, 1856. (Jan. 17,
1856). W. M. Senter, BM.
P. M. Replogle to Mary L. House, Jan. 17, 1856. (Jan.
20, 1856). Daniel Replogle, BM.
Harrison J. Conley to Nancy J. Ferless, Jan. 17, 1856.
(Jan. 17, 1856). Josiah A. Penn, BM.
Thos. Scott to Nancy Mullins, Jan. 21, 1856. (Jan. 22,
1856). Jos. Hampton, BM.

Houston Fitzgerald to Sallie Mitchell, Jan. 22, 1856.
(Jan. 22, 1856). D. H. Thomas, BM.
John G. William to Lydia L. Holt, Jan. 22, 1856. (Jan.
24, 1856). C. H. Williams, BM.
Daniel Hassell to Monah Thomas, Jan. 23, 1856. (July
24, 1856). David McKee, BM.
Richard H. Page to Sarah Hutcherson, Jan. 23, 1856.
(Jan. 23, 1856). J. A. Morrison, BM.
Presley Waldrop to Charity Aslin, Jan. 23, 1856. (Jan.
23, 1856). John Hague, BM.
Thos. G. Richee to Mary J. Kinsey, Jan. 26, 1856. (Jan.
29, 1856). W. W. Lynch, BM.
Lewis Penny to Margarette L. Tucker, Feb. 11, 1856.
(Feb. 13, 1856). Julias M. Tucker, BM.
James C. Holmes to Martha W. Miller, Feb. 11, 1856.
(Feb. 13, 1856). J. A. Wilkins, BM.
Rufus W. Webb to Sarah R. Webb, Feb. 13, 1856. (Feb.
13, 1856). J. M. Stone, BM.
Samuel W. Armstrong to A. E. McBroom, Feb. 13, 1856.
(Feb. 14, 1856). J. T. Thompson, BM.
Willis Grady to Armantha A. Bledsoe, Feb. 14, 1856.
(Feb. 14, 1856). Jas. G. Ray, BM.
James C. Smith to Julia A. J. E. Williams, Feb. 14,
1856. (Feb. 18, 1856). Andrew M. Smith, GM.
Thompson Hunt to Penelope Whichard, Feb. 18, 1856.
(Feb. 21, 1856). Jas. L. Trimble, BM.
Jacob M. Pate to Julia A. Bryant, Feb. 19, 1856. (Feb.
20, 1856). Stephen B. Jones, BM.
James W. Crafton to C. C. Moody, Feb. 20, 1856. (Feb.
20, 1856). H. J. Tuggle, BM.
D. W. Harrison to Elizabeth Rogers, Feb. 23, 1856.
(Feb. 24, 1856). Jas. Thomas, BM.
J. N. Peebles to E. J. Miller, Feb. 23, 1856. (Feb.
26, 1856). H. B. Robinson, BM.
Fordham Blackmon to Margarett C. Climer, Feb. 26, 1856.
(Feb. 26, 1856). J. M. Gunter, BM.
A. A. McKnight to J. A. Wilson, Feb. 25, 1856. (Feb.
28, 1856). J. C. A. Grier, BM.
Willis Witherington to Rachael E. Ridgeway, Feb. 26,
1856. (Feb. 27, 1856). Wm. M. Ridgeway, BM.
Smith K. Cocke to Mary E. Hutchans, Feb. 27, 1856.
(Feb. 27, 1856). S. T. Brightwell, BM.
Stephen Duncan to Amy E. Dickey, Mar. 3, 1856. (Mar.
4, 1856). W. C. Dickey, BM.
James M. Edmundson to Sarah M. Graddy, Mar. 4, 1856.
(Mar. 5, 1856). J. E. Wood, BM.
James Jones to Elizabeth Walker, Mar. 8, 1856. (Mar.
9, 1856). Eli Jones, BM.
M. R. Head to Catherine Cops, Mar. 12, 1856. (Mar. 13,
1856). W. H. Boyett, BM.
Eli Jones to Minerva Walker, Mar. 14, 1856. (Mar. 18,
1856). Samuel N. Miller, BM.
Archibal Pope to Darcus Porter, Mar. 19, 1856. (Mar.
20, 1856). Wm. A. Porter, BM.

John Weaver to Rebecca Marvan, Mar. 22, 1856. (Mar. 23, 1856). L. Weaver, BM.

William C. Shanklin to M. T. Mathis, Mar. 26, 1856. W. M. Mathews, BM.

Isaac L. Fletcher to Sarah J. Johnson, Apr. 1, 1856. (Apr. 2, 1856). W. A. Fletcher, BM.

J. C. Cooper to Emily Young, Apr. 1, 1856. William Dunegan, BM.

Nathaniel Williams to Sarah J. Wallice, Apr. 5, 1856. (Apr. 6, 1856).

Thos. E. Buchannan to Susan V. Goodin, Apr. 8, 1856. (Apr. 8, 1856). J. H. Buchanan, BM.

George Stafford to Melinda Craddac, Apr. 12, 1856. (Apr. 13, 1856).

Thomas E. Scales to Carrie L. Givens, Apr. 28, 1856. (Apr. 30, 1856). Wm. C. January, BM.

Noah Skipper to Sarah J. Davis, May 1, 1856. (May 1, 1856). Samuel Ferrell, BM.

Joseph Hutson to Julia A. Hoskins, May 3, 1856. (May 4, 1856).

James Redford to Louisa Cannon, May 9, 1856. (May 10, 1856). G. W. James, BM.

James M. Roberts to Elizabeth Fleming, May 21, 1856. (May 24, 1856). Robert Cherry, BM.

Cyrus Sharp to E. C. Johnson, May 27, 1856. (May 27, 1856). S. M. Sharp, BM.

Lewis J. Cherry to Sarah J. Morris, May 28, 1856. (May 28, 1856). Jesse Tolen, BM.

Wm. W. Slaydon to Martha E. Jackson, June 12, 1856. (June 12, 1856). Wm. Foster, BM.

R. C. Allen to Mary McBride, June 18, 1856. (June 18, 1856). H. W. Reed, BM.

Daniel H. Staton to Martha E. Dickson, June 27, 1856. (June 28, 1856).

Wm. W. Freeman to Elizabeth J. Fitzgerald, July 4, 1856. (July 4, 1856).

William Bathshears to Mary M. Langham, July 5, 1856. (July 12, 1856). Tom W. Neal, BM.

Mark Crocker to Mourning Hammons, July 7, 1856. (July 10, 1856).

Jessee Reed to Frances Kelly, July 7, 1856. (July 21, 1856).

John A. Steel to Nancy E. Sloan, July 10, 1856. (July 21, 1856).

John Dewberry to Louisa R. Draper, July 12, 1856. (July 13, 1856).

Caleb R. Clements to Barbia R. Patrick, July 15, 1856. (July 15, 1856).

James J. Baker to Eliza J. Pennington, July 21, 1856. (Aug. 4, 1856).

L. H. Jackson to Emeline Walker, July 21, 1856. (July 21, 1856).

A. J. McCorkle to Martha G. Pitts, July 21, 1856. (July 24, 1856). D. P. McCorkle, BM.

111

GIBSON COUNTY MARRIAGES

William F. Williams to Malessa Eudaly, July 22, 1856.
(July 29, 1856). W. M. Warmath, BM.
Dodson Hoskins to Julia Davis, July 24, 1856. (July
24, 1856). W. H. Davis, BM.
C. Carrol to Emily O. Daniel, July 25, 1856. (Sept. 10,
1856). M. Flowers, BM.
Robert Hale to Amandy C. Goodloe, July 29, 1856. (July
29, 1856). R. H. McNail, BM.
D. D. Vaden to Martha Parr, July 29, 1856. (July 29,
1856). H. Barker, BM.
J. Coleman Tharp to M. Precilla Shaw, July 30, 1856.
(July 30, 1856). L. L. Moore, BM.
H. W. Greer to Susan J. Wilson, July 30, 1856. (July
31, 1856). W. J. R. Becton, BM.
Francis M. Shaw to Elizabeth H. Willis, July 31, 1856.
(July 31, 1856). M. D. Holder, BM.
Giles Beluew to Tennessee Flippin, July 31, 1856. (Aug.
3, 1856). Tony Cribbs, BM.
Alex Williams to Priscilla Hammons, Aug. 4, 1856. (Aug.
10, 1856). L. H. Jones, BM.
James F. Bennett to Sarah F. Taylor, Aug. 4, 1856. (Aug.
4, 1856).
John Burrus to Eliza Smith, Aug. 5, 1856. (Aug. 6, 1856).
Robert H. Kelton to Elizabeth Norrod, Aug. 6, 1856.
(Aug. 13, 1856). F. M. Rutledge, BM.
Mathew M. Taylor to Martha W. Patton, Aug. 6, 1856.
(Aug. 7, 1856).
James R. Fletcher to Delia J. Copeland, Aug. 9, 1856.
(Aug. 14, 1856).
William J. Davis to Elizabeth Fletcher, Aug. 9, 1856.
(Aug. 13, 1856). J. H. Davis, BM.
Mark Ethridge to Mary J. E. Beny, Aug. 9, 1856. (Aug.
14, 1856).
P. M. Reeves to J. A. Ford, Aug. 13, 1856. (Aug. 13,
1856).
Eli Ray to Sarah Vickers, Aug. 13, 1856. (Aug. 13,
1856). T. C. Nevil, BM.
J. M. C. Q. Wright to C. J. Nelson, Aug. 15, 1856.
(Aug. 21, 1856). Isiah N. Reed, BM.
Jonathan S. Wiggs to Zelphia J. Lea, Aug. 21, 1856.
(Aug. 21, 1856). M. C. Wiggs, BM.
Jessee Blackburn to Sarah Bivens, Aug. 21, 1856. W. T.
Caneer, BM.
N. S. Hancock to Catharine McCrary, Aug. 23, 1856.
(Aug. 28, 1856). Joseph Ashlen, BM.
Francis M. Allen to Mary A. Horton, Aug. 28, 1856. (Aug.
28, 1856).
Stephen W. Lowry to Mary J. Ward, Aug. 25, 1856. (Aug.
26, 1856). S. M. Abbott, BM.
Thomas Dunlap to Mary Whitchard, Aug. 28, 1856. (Aug.
28, 1856).
Benj. Blankenship to Martha R. Bobbett, Aug. 29, 1856.
(Sept. 1, 1856).
Henry H. Skiles to Mary J. Wootten, Aug. 30, 1856.
(Aug. 30, 1856).

GIBSON COUNTY MARRIAGES

Terrell Branch to Rebecca Hundley, Sept. 3, 1856.
By S. M. Abbott, J.P.
George G. Dunn to Minerva A. Walton, Sept. 3, 1856.
(Sept. 3, 1856). H. B. Baker, BM.
William Thompson to Julia A. L. Holmes, Sept. 9, 1856.
(Sept. 9, 1856)
A. R. Love to Elizabeth L. Gant, Sept. 9, 1856. (Sept.
9, 1856).
Jacob Blessing to Susan G. Walls, Sept. 8, 1856. (Sept.
11, 1856).
J. H. Hudson to V. V. Williams, Sept. 9, 1856. (Sept.
9, 1856).
Elija Coker to Emer J. Criswell, Sept. 10, 1856.
(Sept. 11, 1856).
Whitson Cooper to Elizabeth Cook, Sept. 13, 1856. (Sept.
14, 1856).
Willis S. Barton to Elphady C. Wilson, Sept. 19, 1856.
(Sept. 23, 1856).
S. M. Carrington to Manassa Dickins, Sept. 19, 1856.
(Sept. 20, 1856). C. N. Roberts, BM.
John Edwards to M. J. Bratton, Sept. 22, 1856. Daniel
West, BM.
Orville Williams to Rebecca Elam, Sept. 23, 1856. By
J. L. Jordan, J.P. John Williams, BM.
Isaac N. Dozier to S. J. Roberson, Sept. 23, 1856. R.
M. Gilliam, BM.
W. J. W. Wilson to Alvirn H. Eckles, Sept. 25, 1856.
(Sept. 27, 1856). P. W. Lemons, BM.
Cullen Andrews to Mahaly C. Pollard, Sept. 25, 1856.
(Sept. 25, 1856).
W. T. Estes to M. E. Mathis, Sept. 29, 1856. W. H.
Campbell, BM.
John Wilson to Lena E. Graddy, Sept. 29, 1856. (Oct. 2,
1856). Robert Graddy, BM.
Isom Shoate to Elizabeth Young, Sept. 29, 1856. J. S.
Gullick, BM.
T. J. Ramsey to Martha A. Nettles, Sept. 30, 1856.
(Sept. 30, 1856). W. M. Kimbro, BM.
Elijah Wren to T. E. Greer, Oct. 6, 1856. (Oct. 16,
1856).
W. P. Mayfield to Metilda J. Clark, Oct. 6, 1856. (Oct.
9, 1856). Alexander Clark, BM.
Richard McAlilly to Ann L. McLean, Oct. 7, 1856. (Oct.
9, 1856). Benjamine Yarbrough, BM.
James M. Terrell to Sarah Dickson, Oct. 8, 1856. (Oct.
8, 1856). P. J. Carlton, BM.
Robert Caldwell to Susan Bolin, Oct. 8, 1856. By H. B.
Warren, M.G. W. T. Ownsby, BM.
James R. Reeble to Mary E. Banks, Oct. 8, 1856. (Oct.
8, 1856). C. D. C. Wallis, BM.
J. P. Woodson to Mary L. McMullen, Oct. 13, 1856. (Oct.
15, 1856). P. P. Woodson, BM.
William M. Davidson to Mary J. Mosley, Oct. 13, 1856.
Lee (?), BM.

Robert H. Thomas to Elizabeth P. Morris, Oct. 14, 1856.
H. Wilson, BM.

H. A. McHenry to Nancy C. Richer, Oct. 15, 1856. R. D.
Harwood, BM.

A. M. Davidson to Elizabeth Waldrop, Oct. 17, 1856.
(Oct. 18, 1856). H. Battle, BM.

William J. Hale to Frances A. McKelvey, Oct. 18, 1856.
(Oct. 21, 1856). J. H. Hale, BM.

A. R. Thomas to Mary J. Hale, Oct. 18, 1856. John Blackmon, BM

R. J. Carlton to Tobitha L. Slaton, Oct. 20, 1856.
(Oct. 21, 1856). Carson Patterson, BM.

William A. Blair to Jane E. Barker, Oct. 20, 1856.
(Oct. 20, 1856). R. D. Blair, BM.

John L. McDonald to E. A. Reeves, Oct. 20, 1856. (Oct.
22, 1856). William Gay, BM.

C. W. Edwards to Charlott D. Smith, Oct. 21, 1856.
(Oct. 21, 1856). Z. Biggs, Jr.

A. Smith to Perlina J. Kelly, Oct. 22, 1856. (Oct. 22,
1856). Jas. E. Rigsbee, BM.

Wiley P. Russell to C. A. Barron, Oct. 22, 1856. (Oct.
22, 1856). W. T. Barron, BM.

William R. Smith to Elvira Bryant, Oct. 22, 1856. J.
H. Smith, BM.

William E. Biggs to Elvina Hix, Oct. 22, 1856. B.
Crawford, BM.

Lafayett Grissom to N. V. White, Oct. 29, 1856. Wm. W.
McNeil, BM.

W. M. Thetford to Sarah Flowers, Oct. 29, 1856. W. R.
Harrison, BM.

John F. Patterson to Minerva Davis, Nov. 11, 1856. By
S. D. Shipman, M.G.

Isaac C. Mathis to Lucy C. Smith, Nov. 4, 1856. (Nov.
5, 1856). W. M. Mathis, BM.

Rufus D. Mathis to Nancy C. Edwards, Nov. 8, 1856. (Nov.
17, 1856). George Nevil, BM.

Joel T. Evans to Ann L. Robinson, Nov. 6, 1856. James
Tatum, BM.

A. M. Vaught to Nancy Daughty, Nov. 10, 1856. (Nov. 10,
1856). S. C. Vaught, BM.

James Y. Hix to Martha H. P. Sanders, Nov. 10, 1856.
(Nov. 11, 1856). C. C. Williford, BM.

Eli A. Summers to Martha Jane Daw, Nov. 12, 1856. W. H.
Campbell, BM.

Thomas Fisher to Mary Barker, Nov. 12, 1856. (Nov. 13,
1856). J. W. Glasgow, BM.

William A. Tinner to Cassa L. Carlton, Nov. 12, 1856.
(Nov. 12, 1856).

James E. Rigsbee to H. L. Cole, Nov. 13, 1856. (Nov.
13, 1856).

William J. Barron to Margarett F. Mathis, Nov. 17, 1756.
(Nov. 17, 1856). E. B. Russell, BM.

William M. Kerns to Martha S. Webb, Nov. 17, 1856.
(Dec. 18, 1856).

William Halliburton to Mary F. Allen, Nov. 19, 1856.
(Nov. 19, 1856). N. S. Halliburton, BM.

GIBSON COUNTY MARRIAGES

A. L. Lett to M. A. Baker, Nov. 22, 1856. M. A. Baker, BM.
William R. Sellers to Elizabeth A. Hunt, Nov. 24, 1856.
  (Nov. 24, 1856). J. L. Fletcher, BM.
B. Arnold to Rebecca Finch, Nov. 4, 1856. Wm. M. Halford, BM.
E. G. Rahkins to Elizabeth Roberson, Nov. 11, 1856.
  (Nov. 26, 1856).
Benj. F. Cooper to M. A. Belch, Nov. 25, 1856. (Nov. 25,
  1856). Jas. B. Cooper, BM.
J. N. Wright to Mary Flowers, Nov. 27, 1856. (Nov. 27,
  1856).
Samuel A. Goodman to Martha A. Ingraham, Dec. 1, 1856.
  (Dec. 4, 1856).
Lander L. Wood to Nancy D. Lee, Dec. 2, 1856. (Dec. 3,
  1856). John Lee, BM.
M. T. Parish to Mary D. Clements, Dec. 2. 1856. (Dec.
  2, 1856). P. H. Brooks, BM.
Seith Harrison to Mary C. Wade, Dec. 4, 1856. W. N. Wade, BM.
John W. Hill to Martha F. Jones, Dec. 6, 1856. (Dec.
  7, 1856).
John Flowers to Matilda Porter, Dec. 6, 1856. (Dec. 7,
  1856). Wm. A. Porter, BM.
James Keys to Mary E. Gordon, Dec. 10, 1856. N. P.
  Umant, BM.
Harris Bradford to Elen J. Briant, Dec. 11, 1856. (Dec.
  12, 1856). Thos. D. Newhouse, BM.
Henry Williamson to Clarissa C. Butler, Dec. 13, 1856.
  (Dec. 14, 1856).
John A. Wilson to M. M. Lane, Dec. 13, 1856. (Dec. 18,
  1856).
James S. Loveless to Martha J. Roberson, Dec. 15, 1856.
  (Dec. 16, 1856).
Zachy G. Jackson to Sarah J. Fite, Dec. 16, 1856. (Dec.
  18, 1856). John A. Rogers, BM.
D. M. Crockett to Elizabeth Bottoms, Dec. 17, 1856.
  (Dec. 18, 1856).
Nathan Evans to Rebecca Johnson, Dec. 23, 1856. (Dec.
  23, 1856). Wm. J. Ward, BM.
John H. McCutchan to Gilly Ray, Dec. 24, 1856. (Dec.
  24, 1856). D. D. McCutchan, BM.
William S. Eldridg to Rebecca E. Witt, Dec. 24, 1856.
  (Dec. 25, 1856). Jas. E. Rigsbee, BM.
James B. Hughes to Sophronia Blan, Dec. 27, 1856. (Jan.
  1, 1857). C. Blan, BM.
William D. Black to Sarah E. Hamilton, Jan. 1, 1857.
  (Jan. 1, 1857).
Thos. D. Newhouse to Frances L. Bryant, Jan. 1, 1857.
  (Jan. 2, 1857).
Henry C. Smith to Catharine Hunley, Jan. 1, 1857. (Jan.
  1, 1857).
Jas. A. Childress to Asa A. Coleman, Jan. 3, 1856.
  Arch C. C. Levy, BM.
Green M. Howell to Sarah Porter, Jan. 5, 1856. (Jan. 5,
  1857).
William S. Hartsfield to Caroline S. Lane, Jan. 5, 1857.
  (Jan. 6, 1857).

J. M. Davis to Parolle Cole, Jan. 10, 1856. (Jan. 10, 1857).

James Dowell to Eliza McWhirter, Jan. 8, 1857. J. J. Howard, BM.

John H. Dean to Rebecca Miller, Jan. 12, 1857. (Jan. 14, 1857). James R. Dean, BM.

James Hill to Delitha Thedford, Jan. 13, 1857. George Vaughn, BM.

Jonathan Wallice to S. A. Wallice, Jan. 13, 1856. L. D. Lawrence, BM.

Henry V. Replogle to Margarette E. Sharp, Jan. 13, 1857. (Jan. 14, 1857). D. B. Replogle, BM.

Thomas Amos to Eliza Miller, Jan. 14, 1857. (Jan. 14, 1857). W. W. Lynch, BM.

William Crews to P. Pope, Jan. 19, 1857. Bryant H. Pope, BM.

Jas. S. Wood to M. F. Hazlewood, Jan. 20, 1857. (Jan. 20, 1857). J. A. W. Hess, BM.

J. W. Lemons to Nancy A. Howell, Jan. 20, 1857. (Jan. 21, 1857). G. W. Lemons, BM.

Green B. Cooke to Eliz. Booth, Jan. 22, 1857. R. A. Cooke, BM.

J. D. Rentfro to Sarah McKeown, Jan. 22, 1857. (Jan. 22, 1857). B. McCaslin, BM.

Chapman Kinton to Susan F. Graddy, Jan. 24, 1857. (Jan. 24, 1857). Samuel A. Graddy, BM.

O. L. Chandler to Mary McAlister, Jan. 28, 1857. (Jan. 28, 1857).

William W. Smith to Emoline Canady, Jan. 30, 1857. (Feb. 3, 1857).

John W. Reach to Catharine D. Strong, Feb. 2, 1857. (Feb. 3, 1857).

Jas. A. Jack to Nancy Wallice, Feb. 10, 1857. (Feb. 10, 1857).

John S. Jack to Ann A. Gage, Feb. 10, 1857. (Feb. 11, 1857).

B. R. Fouster to Eliza Holt, Feb. 11, 1857. W. L. Agee and H. T. Heath, BM.

E. F. Taylor to Jane A. Flowers, Feb. 11, 1857. (Feb. 12, 1857). G. W. King, BM.

Wm. T. Agee to Martha A. Kelly, Feb. 12, 1857. (Feb. 12, 1857). Thos. G. Davis, BM.

W. A. Jones to Elizabeth W. Hess, Feb. 16, 1857. (Feb. 16, 1857).

Presley T. Beard to Narcissa Pope, Mar. 2, 1857. Bryant H. Pope, BM.

Jerry Bailey to L. A. Holder, Mar. 2, 1857. J. H. Battle, BM.

D. C. Caldwell to M. M. Cunningham, Mar. 2, 1857. George Shane, BM.

B. W. Ragan to Sarah C. McDonald, Mar. 3, 1857. (Mar. 3, 1857). Jas. A. Hartsfield, BM.

David C. Simons to M. J. Sexton, Mar. 5, 1857. Mar. 5, 1857). B. Crawford, BM.

John C. Smith to Mary E. Mitchel, Mar. 9, 1857. W. H. Boyett, BM.

William Butler to Ruthy B. Skiles, Mar. 10, 1857. (Mar. 11, 1857). Henry Parker, BM.

Thos. J. Wood to Lamanios Joslin, Mar. 12, 1857. (Mar. 12, 1857).

William H. Hunt to Flora White, Mar. 17, 1857. (Mar. 17, 1857).

Elisha Moore to Charlotta J. Waldrop, Mar. 25, 1857. (Mar. 25, 1857).

Matthew Wiggs to Rebecca Lee, Apr. 9, 1857. (Apr. 9, 1857).

James L. Benthel to Louisa C. Adkins, Apr. 22, 1857. (Apr. 22, 1857).

Joseph D. Smith to Mary F. McKelvey, May 30, 1857. (May 31, 1857).

John L. Connell to Cenith F. Mayfield, June 1, 1857. (June 2, 1857).

John Thomas to Eliza A. Carey, June 10, 1857. (June 28, 1857).

William R. Smith to Eveline Reed, June 19, 1857. (June 23, 1857).

Stephen C. Barker to Susan A. Goodman, June 20, 1857. (June 21, 1857).

J. W. Harrison to Pelina N. Ford, June 26, 1857. (June 28, 1857).

William Still to Mary Church, July 3, 1857. (July 5, 1857).

William Taylor to Lucinda Sanford, July 7, 1857. (July 7, 1857).

James T. Boyett to Margarett J. Baker, July 7, 1857. (July 8, 1857).

William Laymon to Emily E. Kelton, July 9, 1857. (July 9, 1857).

Cornelias Woolard to Mary Foren, July 21, 1857. (July 21, 1857).

Presley L. Bottoms to Arvazena Keathley, July 25, 1857. (July 26, 1857).

John M. Bolls to Perney E. Tyler, July 28, 1857. (July 30, 1857).

Wm. W. Jones to Susan E. Chitman, Aug. 7, 1857. (Aug. 16, 1857).

A. K. Hopper to Mary E. Combs, Aug. 27, 1857. (Aug. 27, 1857). J. N. Simes, BM.

L. H. Canady to Mahaly C. Cassells, Sept. 3, 1857. (Sept. 3, 1857).

William Watson to Frances Coleman, Sept. 12, 1857. (Sept. 18, 1857). Thos. J. Haley, BM.

Robert Gill to Eliza M. Goodman, Sept. 16, 1857. (Sept. 21, 1857).

Thos. Watt to Avolina G. Bledsoe, Sept. 29, 1857. (Sept. 28, 1858).

Horace Wilson to Elmira J. Thomas, Sept. 29, 1857. (Oct. 1, 1857).

C. N. Roberts to Flora Oliver, Aug. 29, 1857. N. H. Roberts, BM.

Thomas N. Sims to Jane Reasons, Aug. 31, 1857. W. D. Williams, BM.

J. T. Cannon to Mary E. Jackson, Sept. 11, 1857.
N. C. Patton, BM.
Thompson Edmundson to Mary A. Trosper, Sept. 14, 1857.
R. P. Edmundson, BM.
Robert Gill to Eliza M. Goodman, Sept. 16, 1857. Boyd
White, BM.
Robert S. Adams to E. H. Fielder, Sept. 22, 1857. J. S.
Fielder, BM.
L. L. Watson to A. L. Johnston, Sept. 24, 1857. U. A.
Fletcher, BM.
John R. Price to Edy Brogdon, Oct. 5, 1857. R. C. Dickens, BM
G. L. Short to Martha A. Pope, Oct. 8, 1857. Jno. P.
Reagor, BM.
C. M. Wheeler to Lucy J. Jones, Oct. 9, 1857. H. Y.
Jones, BM.
John Allen, Jr. to Louisa Harwood, Oct. 13, 1857.
Saml. D. Wilkins, BM.
William P. Dickson to Sarah J. Brightwell, Oct. 22, 1857.
Wm. T. Slayton, BM.
Lazarus Sires to Elizabeth E. Fouch, Oct. 13, 1857.
(Oct. 14, 1857).
Jessee Tucker to Kate M. Smith, Oct. 24, 1857. (Oct.
25, 1857). Washington Hobbs, BM.
E. A. Sharp to Sarah M. V. Baker, Oct. 26, 1857. (Oct.
27, 1857). J. M. McLaurine, BM.
R. J. Corley to Mary Cassa A. Hunt, Oct. 27, 1857.
(Oct. 28, 1857). S. M. Pierce, BM.
J. J. Knott to Elizabeth Ford, Oct. 29, 1857. Thomas
Aslin, BM.
Thos. R. Pickens to Mary J. Jones, Nov. 5, 1857. (Nov.
5, 1857). T. J. Wood, BM.
Daniel B. Fields to Isabella Watts, Nov. 3, 1857. J. H.
Fields, BM.
J. R. Carrol to S. Needham, Nov. 18, 1857. H. L. Miller, BM.
J. P. Taylor to M. J. Wheeler, Nov. 21, 1857. J. C.
Haynes, BM.
Geo. W. Bennett to L. F. Regenn, Dec. 1, 1857. R. N. Davis, BM
W. M. McDowell to M. A. Flowers, Dec. 1, 1857. B. W.
Battle, BM.
W. R. Hall to M. A. Bradley, Dec. 1, 1857. J. D.
Buford, BM.
William Stults to S. A. Wilson, Dec. 1, 1857. Spencer
Hall, BM.
J. J. Parker to M. Barker, Dec. 2, 1857. Lewis Wren, BM.
C. W. Cosley, Sr. to Jane Gullett, Dec. 2, 1857. W.
Cosley, Jr., BM.
N. A. Dickey to Sarah C. Kelton, Dec. 5, 1857. E. Tucker, BM.
W. S. Crocker to E. W. Barker, Dec. 3, 1857. (Dec. 3,
1857).
William M. Senter to Nancy J. Pemberton, Dec. 5, 1857.
(Dec. 6, 1857).
Rufus F. Reed to Mary E. Barker, Dec. 9, 1857. (Dec.
10, 1857).
William R. Fulghum to Susan V. Blakemore, Dec. 14, 1857.
(Dec. 16, 1857).

GIBSON COUNTY MARRIAGES

James W. Connell to Nancy Mullens, Dec. 21, 1857.
(Dec. 22, 1857).
Juleus A. Skiles to Menurva F. Davidson, Dec. 24, 1857.
(Dec. 24, 1857).
John Perry to Sarah Reed, Dec. 9, 1857. (Dec. 9, 1857).
James B. Tatum to Martha A. P. Avery, Dec. 29, 1857.
(Dec. 31, 1857).
G. H. Keaton to Jane Arnold, Nov. 2, 1857. H. Battle, BM.
Thomas B. Davis to Lucy A. P. Agee, Dec. 29, 1857. (Dec.
29, 1857).
B. M. Rutledge to Ann Shumate, Dec. 29, 1857. (Dec. 29,
1857).
T. H. B. Roberson to Nancy G. Stiggall, Dec. 30, 1857.
(Dec. 31, 1857).
Stephen B. Maner to Cynthia A. Patrick, Jan. 1, 1858.
(Jan. 10, 1858). D. C. Goodman, BM.
Harrison Conlee to Mary P. Penn, Jan. 2, 1858. B.
Landis, BM.
John F. Aslin to Eliza Jones, Jan. 4, 1858. (Jan. 7,
1858). J. W. Waldon, BM.
W. L. Sanders to Louiza M. Pounds, Jan. 4, 1858. (Jan.
5, ?). Benj. Yarbrough, BM.
R. G. Wedington to Jane T. Whitaker, Jan. 4, 1858. (Jan.
5, 1858). A. P. Foster, BM.
D. Connell to Louiza Philips, Jan. 4, 1858. (Jan. 7,
1858). W. H. Baldridge, BM.
Jarrett Perry to Elizabeth Gamer, Jan. 5, 1858. S. E.
Gardiner, BM.
William M. Busick to Sarah E. Pace, Jan. 6, 1858. (Jan.
6, 1858). F. M. Brownlow, BM.
David C. Goodman to Lucy F. Johnson, Jan. 9, 1858. (Jan.
12, 1858). G. W. Robinson, BM.
David C. Glimp to Annitta Brogdon, Jan. 11, 1858. (Jan.
12, 1858). Jno. M. Boswell, BM.
Francis M. Newhouse to Martha F. M. Roe, Jan. 13, 1858.
(Jan. 14, 1858). W. H. Logan, BM.
John N. Reed to D. E. Middleton, Jan. 13, 1858. (Jan.
17, 1858). Saml. D. Wilkins, BM.
Rolan T. Cook to Allis Hinson, Jan. 18, 1858. (Jan. 21,
1858). Mrs. J. Williams, BM.
L. J. Cook to Sarah C. Barksdale, Jan. 18, 1858. G. T.
Richardson, BM.
Abraham Glisson to Martha M. Ellington, Jan. 18, 1858.
T. W. Edwards, BM.
M. E. Mosley to Sarah J. Short, Jan. 18, 1858. T. W.
Edwards, BM.
William R. Harrison to Sarah J. Short, Jan. 19, 1858.
J. H. Harrison, BM.
John A. Nowell to C. P. Green, Jan. 20, 1858. Wm. M.
Senter, BM.
V. C. Wright to Nancy O. Ellington, Jan. 20, 1858. (Jan.
21, 1858). H. L. Miller, BM.
Elisha Farrow to Caroline Benson, Jan. 23, 1858. (Jan.
24, 1858). Jno. Bodkins, BM.

B. F. Jones to Sarah C. Foster, Jan. 25, 1858. By A.
R. Love, M.G. David C. Foster, BM.

M. C. Lane to E. W. Harri, Jan. 25, 1858. (Jan. 27,
1858). Spencer Hall, BM.

Franklin Williams to Tibitha Connell, Jan. 27, 1858.
J. W. Waldern, BM.

Robert Rutledge to T. J. Thetford, Jan. 27, 1858. (Jan.
28, 1858). J. W. Waldern, BM.

Andrew J. McCaslin to Sarah F. Holt, Jan. 27, 1858.
(Jan. 28, 1858). John W. Oliver, BM.

S. H. Couch to Elvira J. Baird, Jan. 27, 1858. T. J.
Stone, BM.

J. Lewis Janell to M. M. Booker, Feb. 1, 1858. (Feb. 1,
1858). L. C. Crenshaw, BM.

Albert H. Leigon to Elizabeth Bell, Feb. 1, 1858. (Feb.
1, 1858). Wm. Bell, BM.

George M. Fisher to Mary E. Jones, Feb. 4, 1858. (Feb.
4, 1858). John J. Dickson, BM.

D. S. Phelan to Eliz. P. Cail, Feb. 4, 1858. Parker Cail, BM.

Thos. B. Beavers to Angeline Jones, Feb. 4, 1858.
(Feb. 4, 1858). Parker Cail, BM.

Ambros House to A. L. Bolin, Feb. 9, 1858. J. R. Simmons, BM.

John L. Williams to Martha Zachry, Feb. 9, 1858. (Feb.
9, 1858). A. G. Blaton, BM.

Joel B. Vaughn to Susan Jane Spencer, Feb. 11, 1858.
(Feb. 11, 1858). John H. Parker, BM.

William J. Poindexter to Martha L. McFarlen, Feb. 15,
1858. (Feb. 17, 1858). J. W. McFarlen, BM.

T. J. Ford to Susan A. Vaughn, Feb. 17, 1858. (Feb.
17, 1858). R. G. Aycock, BM.

John P. Henry to Caroline S. Sharp, Feb. 18, 1858.
(Feb. 18, 1858). J. P. Sharp, BM.

J. B. Cassels to Arta M. Ford, Feb. 18, 1858. (Feb.
18, 1858). D. B. Bolin, BM.

Moses E. Mosley to Martha C. Bryant, Feb. 22, 1858.
(Feb. 22, 1858). John W. Bryant, BM.

Bryant Pope to R. J. Martin, Feb. 23, 1858. (Feb. 23,
1858). S. M. Becton, BM.

Wiley Bivens to Jane McFarlen, Feb. 24, 1858. (Feb. 25,
1858). J. W. Jones, BM.

F. P. Lowerence to R. C. Raines, Mar. 8, 1858. H. B.
Blakemore, BM.

James S. Pratt to Sarah J. McCartney, Mar. 8, 1858.
(Mar. 9, 1858). W. S. Pratt, BM.

D. B. Bayn to Ruth A. Hall, Mar. 9, 1858. (Mar. 10,
1858). M. Oppenheimer, BM.

Abraham Hancock to Rebecca Butram, Mar. 10, 1858. (Mar.
10, 1858). A. L. Dunlap, BM.

A. C. Penn to Gilly A. Rigsbee, Mar. 10, 1858. (Mar.
11, 1858). G. S. Penn, BM.

William Bradley to Aminda James, Mar. 13, 1858. (Mar.
14, 1858). Timothy Gleeson, BM.

Geo. W. Legion to E. D. Hall, Mar. 15, 1858. (Mar. 31,
1858).

GIBSON COUNTY MARRIAGES

R. B. Shepard to Eliza F. Patton, Mar. 16, 1857. Lemuel
F. Martin, BM.
Jas. D. Cousins to Mary Stephens, Mar. 26, 1858. (Apr.
3, 1858). Alexander Avery, BM.
Jas. N. Keys to Eliza J. Gordon, Mar. 27, 1858. (Mar.
28, 1858). G. H. Ramsey, BM.
W. B. Williams to Mary A. Wade, Mar. 30, 1858. (Mar.
30, 1858). J. E. Parker, BM.
Jas. Marcum to Elizabeth F. Sherell, Mar. 30, 1858.
Wm. B. Halliburton, BM.
F. J. Conley to Mahala Bryant, Apr. 1, 1858. (Apr. 1,
1858). J. R. Jordan, BM.
C. Conner to Louiza Nevils, Apr. 5, 1858. (Apr. 6,
1858). V. A. Cresap, BM.
William L. Paris to Elizabeth Chandler, Apr. 5, 1858.
(Apr. 8, 1858).
James H. Mangrum to Mahaley McCoy, Apr. 6, 1858. (Apr.
8, 1858).
Wilson S. Easterwood to Mary P. Reeves, Apr. 14, 1858.
(Apr. 14, 1858). James Thomason, BM.
J. W. S. Sappington to M. C. Wade, Apr. 14, 1858.
(Apr. 14, 1858). R. W. Davis, BM.
Daniel Tinkle to Nancy H. Vernon, Apr. 14, 1858. (Apr.
15, 1858). Richard Turner, BM.
David D. McCutchen to Mary M. McDongal, Apr. 15, 1858.
(Apr. 15, 1858). I. M. Bledsoe, BM.
John A. Rodgers to Sarah L. Scott, Apr. 21, 1858. (Apr.
22, 1858). R. E. Holmes, BM.
John M. Wilkes to Mary Thomas, Apr. 21, 1858. Stephen
King, BM.
Daniel McGran to Elizabeth Ingram, Apr. 26, 1858. (Apr.
27, 1858). John McGran, BM.
John W. Cail to Celia F. Fairless, Apr. 29, 1858. (Apr.
29, 1858). R. I. Combs, BM.
James M. Ray to D. A. Burnwat, May 4, 1858. (May 6,
1858). J. J. Beckham, BM.
John W. Marr to Permelia Mathis, May 4, 1858. John Ray, BM.
John H. Hensley to Susan L. Parten, May 12, 1858. (May
12, 1858). E. T. Butler, BM.
McFarlen Oakley to Jane S. White, May 19, 1858. (May
20, 1858). Wm. D. Baldridge, BM.
Elijah Stigall to Martha A. Raines, May 25, 1858. (May
27, 1858). Wm. H. Powell, BM.
Jas. Pearce to Martha M. Connell, May 31, 1858. Samuel
Hicks, BM.
William R. Stublefield to Mary Belch, June 1, 1858.
(June 3, 1858). John Stublefield, BM.
Everett Glisson to Metilda Long, June 1, 1858. Pleasant
H. Hunter, BM.
Jno. C. A. Greer to Margarett C. Oliphant, June 5, 1858.
(June 8, 1858). W. J. R. Becton, BM.
Jas. M. Baird to Julia F. Martin, June 7, 1858. (June
8, 1858). H. Holt, BM.
Joseph W. Furgarson to Sophia L. Blanton, June 9, 1858.
M. E. Pybass, BM.

GIBSON COUNTY MARRIAGES

S. Williams to N. J. Lewis, June 18, 1858. R. G.
Aycock, BM.

P. Ford to Margarett A. Kensey, June 18, 1858. (June
20, 1858). M. J. Roberts, BM.

Asberry M. Freeman to Susan C. Howard, June 26, 1858.
(June 30, 1858).

Isaac James to Affey A. Slaydon, June 29, 1858. (June
29, 1858). J. M. McLaurine, BM.

Jefferson Marcum to Lucretia A. E. Brent, July 1, 1858.
(July 1, 1858). Henderson Marcum, BM.

F. M. James to H. A. O. Daniel, July 2, 1858.

R. E. Holmes to S. E. Baldridge, July 3, 1858. (July
8, 1858). W. M. Holmes, BM.

Jas. H. Smith to Ann H. Patterson, July 5, 1858.

Thomas J. Alford to Martha R. Brightwell, July 5, 1858.
James Alford, BM.

Levi Evans to Martha A. Williams, July 14, 1858. R. W.
Davis, BM.

E. A. Levy to C. L. Crawford, July 17, 1858. (July 19,
1858). W. C. Crawford, BM.

Allen Bowers to Jane O. K. Allen, July 20, 1858. (July
21, 1858). M. B. Elder, BM.

John Nash to Mary Jane Anderson, July 23, 1858. (July
23, 1858). W. B. Nash, BM.

A. J. Fletcher to Martha Janes, July 28, 1858. (July 28,
1858). Hinton Y. Jones, BM.

Lewis L. Reynolds to Aminisa M. Brogdon, July 28, 1858.
(July 29, 1858). John O. Fox, BM.

James Ames to M. M. Keys, Aug. 9, 1858. David G. Keys, BM.

J. F. Graddy to L. E. C. Folks, Aug. 9, 1858. (Aug. 12,
1858). William Bell, BM.

T. M. Bryan to Mary A. Mosley, Aug. 18, 1858. (Aug. 20,
1858).

William Vaughn to Elizabeth Davis, Aug. 19, 1858. (Aug.
19, 1858). William Foren, BM.

William J. Brightwell to Mary M. Key, Aug. 23, 1858.
(Aug. 23, 1858). T. J. Alford, BM.

David G. Keys to Mary A. Farr, Aug. 24, 1858. (Aug.
26, 1858). Lafayette McHaney, BM.

James Coneway to Lydia Farthing, Sept. 2, 1858. (Sept.
2, 1858). B. Pearce, BM.

Richard Berry to Martha Berry, Sept. 6, 1858. D. T. Lewis, BM

William R. Nunn to Sarah Davidson, Sept. 6, 1858. (Sept.
9, 1858). A. J. Nunn, BM.

Martin V. Nance to Mary Davidson, Sept. 6, 1858. (Sept.
9, 1858). A. J. Nunn, BM.

William Pugh to Melvina C. Wilson, Sept. 6, 1858. (Sept.
8, 1858). John P. Fewell, BM.

W. L. Cunningham to Elen Cunningham, Sept. 6, 1858.
J. M. Brewer, BM.

Zachriah Richard Berry to Martha Rodgers, Sept. 6, 1858.
(Sept. 16, 1858).

Silas Mullens to Mary Fox, Sept. 7, 1858. (Sept. 8,
1858). W. L. Young, BM.

GIBSON COUNTY MARRIAGES

James F. Knox to Martha F. Blankenship, Sept. 8, 1858.
(Sept. 9, 1858). Thos. C. Bogle, BM.
D. B. Hall to Sarah E. Avery, Sept. 11, 1858. By C.
J. Maulam. J. L. Bethshares, BM.
William Hethcock to Eudora E. Sanford, Sept. 14, 1858.
(Sept. 16, 1858). James Sanford, BM.
Samuel Hicks to Maranda S. Mayfield, Sept. 15, 1858.
(Sept. 16, 1858). J. T. Thompson, BM.
Watson Gordon to Delia Barker, Sept. 15, 1858. (Sept.
16, 1858). John E. Glason, BM.
John W. Ballentine to Martha S. Acklin, Sept. 17, 1858.
(Sept. 18, 1858). William Bell, BM.
James M. Butler to Susan J. McKelvey, Sept. 20, 1858.
(Sept. 22, 1858). M. F. Martin, BM.
Robert T. Dickson to Emily A. Berry, Sept. 22, 1858.
W. H. McCaslin, BM.
Francis M. Barron to Canvass B. Russell, Sept. 28, 1858.
(Sept. 28, 1858). J. E. Coker, BM.
Henry S. Paris to Alsey Edwards, Oct. 14, 1858. J. C.
Martin, BM.
James S. Cannon to Angevona C. Jones, Oct. 5, 1858.
(Oct. 6, 1858). A. F. Dickson, BM.
J. L. Harder to B. J. Umsted, Oct. 5, 1858. (Oct. 5,
1858). C. M. Senter, Jr., BM.
G. W. Moore to Jane F. Nicholdson, Oct. 6, 1858. (Oct.
7, 1858). A. S. Baldridge, BM.
Julius Hale to Winie C. Harland, Oct. 7, 1858. (Oct. 7,
1858). W. N. Tatum, BM.
Thos. W. Williams to Sarah Barrett, Oct. 7, 1858. J. M.
McLaurine, BM.
William B. Boyett to Elizabeth A. Woddy, Oct. 8, 1858.
(Oct. 14, 1858). E. J. Garrison, BM.
Tobbert F. Conley to Cordelia J. Green, Oct. 9, 1858.
William R. Hall, BM.
W. V. Hill to Martha A. Oliphant, Oct. 11, 1858. (Oct.
13, 1858). J. N. Vaughan, BM.
Jas. T. Cannon to Elizabeth A. Doherty, Oct. 12, 1858.
(Oct. 13, 1858). D. M. Pearce, BM.
William T. Byers to Emily L. Carthel, Oct. 12, 1858.
(Oct. 13, 1858). J. T. McDowell, BM.
R. P. Sanders to M. A. Vaughn, Oct. 13, 1858. (Oct. 13,
1858). R. G. Aycock, BM.
T. S. Webb to Milly Moore, Oct. 16, 1858. (Oct. 17,
1858). Alfred Flowers, BM.
Alvis Baker to J. H. Cresap, Oct. 16, 1858. (Oct. 21,
1858). C. G. Barker, BM.
John M. Glasgow to Martha C. Fields, Oct. 19, 1858.
(Oct. 19, 1858). W. B. Rodgers, BM.
Blakers Flowers to Malinda Carey, Oct. 19, 1858. (Oct.
19, 1858). N. P. Davis, BM.
Jas. R. Taylor to Emily J. Spencer, Oct. 19, 1858. (Oct.
19, 1858). E. G. Robinson, BM.
P. K. Dossett to D. J. Mathis, Oct. 20, 1858. J. S.
McCulloch, BM.

Andy Hall to Rebecca Patterson, Oct. 20, 1858. James M. Hall, BM. (Free man and woman of color.)

Anderson Herndon to Mary Grissom, Oct. 21, 1858. (Oct. 21, 1858). Wm. A. Varner, BM.

Daniel H. Scates to Emma J. Biggs, Oct. 20, 1858. (Oct. 21, 1858). Zach Biggs, BM.

William Ballentine to Frances J. Holderfield, Oct. 23, 1858. (Oct. 28, 1858). F. M. Griffin, BM.

Carroll Jackson to Sarah E. Roseman, Oct. 27, 1858. (Oct. 28, 1858). C. W. Jackson, BM.

Henry H. Skiles to Sarah E. Phelan, Oct. 27, 1858. (Oct. 28, 1858). Moses Butler, BM.

Richard C. Tyler to Martha Bell, Oct. 28, 1858. (Oct. 28, 1858). A. G. Blanton, BM.

William B. Rogers to Sarah E. Keys, Oct. 28, 1858. (Oct. 28, 1858). Jas. H. Slayton, BM.

Thomas J. Hailey to Hannah W. Vaden, Oct. 28, 1858. (Oct. 28, 1858). A. H. Cruse, BM.

V. M. L. Taylor to Sarah F. Dodd, Oct. 29, 1858. P. A. G. McEwen, BM.

John C. Ferrell to Mary J. Shelby, Nov. 8, 1858. (Nov. 11, 1858). John W. Tiner, BM.

Thomas A. Ray to Elizabeth F. Biggs, Nov. 10, 1858. (Nov. 10, 1858). Zach Biggs, BM.

Francis Lamoine to Mary A. Humbles, Nov. 12, 1858. (Nov. 17, 1858). E. Pielzer, BM.

Robert J. Dodson to E. F. Cole, Nov. 8, 1858. (Nov. 18, 1858). Wm. Lourin, BM.

A. H. Johnson to Mary J. Abbott, Nov. 15, 1858. W. C. Barton, BM.

J. J. A. Roach to Saluda A. Wilson, Nov. 15, 1858. (Nov. 24, 1858). W. C. Barton, BM.

Jos. J. Brown to Sutilia C. Roberts, Nov. 16, 1858. (Nov. 17, 1858). F. G. Cates, BM.

Jacob S. Skiles to Mary J. Little, Nov. 18, 1858. (Nov. 18, 1858). Moses Butler, BM.

T. S. McKelvy to Rebecca E. Howard, Nov. 22, 1858. (Nov. 25, 1858). T. P. Akin, BM.

James E. Talley to Nancy P. Durley, Nov. 24, 1858. (Nov. 24, 1858).

William H. Swindle to Sarah E. Nevil, Nov. 24, 1858. (Nov. 25, 1858). J. H. Williamson, BM.

M. R. Considine to M. A. E. Quinn, Dec. 2, 1858. (Dec. 3, 1858). B. F. Harris, BM.

William Reynolds to Rebecca Farmer, Dec. 4, 1858. (Dec. 5, 1858). G. W. Davis, BM.

John Umsted to Nancy A. Shane, Dec. 6, 1858. (Dec. 7, 1858). Geo. Shane, BM.

Jas. N. Watt to Mary P. Austin, Dec. 6, 1858. (Dec. 12, 1858). S. B. Hix, BM.

Jas. A. McKnight to Rachael E. McDaniel, Dec. 9, 1858. (Dec. 9, 1858). Thos. S. Freeman, BM.

John W. Haley to Susan E. Haley, Dec. 15, 1858. (Dec. 16, 1858).

Hartwell Mosley to Nancy C. Ward, Dec. 15, 1858. (Dec. 15, 1858). A. C. Rutledge, BM.

John W. Oliver to Susan E. Haley, Dec. 15, 1858. B. R. Foster, BM.

Henry Arnold to Clementine S. Petty, Dec. 20, 1858. (Dec. 22, 1858).

Joseph H. Sharp to Mary E. C. Taylor, Dec. 22, 1858. (Dec. 26, 1858). Jesse B. Wheeler, BM.

A. P. Mays to Mary McFarland, Dec. 22, 1858. (Dec. 23, 1858). G. A. Massey, BM.

Robert T. O'Daniel to Frances E. Davis, Dec. 22, 1858. (Dec. 28, 1858). Wm. M. Ridgeway, BM.

George W. Blackwell to Margarette C. Harden, Dec. 22, 1858. (Dec. 28, 1858). (Free man and woman of color.)

Jas. D. Hight to Mary E. Watson, Dec. 23, 1858. (Dec. 23, 1858). R. R. Watson, BM.

J. T. Thompson to Margarett J. Crafton, Dec. 23, 1858. (Dec. 23, 1858). A. C. Nolen, BM.

Jeremiah Keathley to Sarah A. O'Daniel, Dec. 25, 1858. (Dec. 26, 1858). A. Withrington, BM.

E. G. Roberson to Nancy E. Blackburn, Dec. 25, 1858. (Dec. 28, 1858). J. H. Spencer, BM.

W. A. Turner to Patsy A. Corley, Dec. 27, 1858. (Jan. 22, 1859). L. C. Thompson, BM.

William H. Thompson to Sarah J. Corley, Dec. 27, 1858. L. C. Thompson, BM.

Lycurgus Boyett to Louiza E. Clark, Dec. 27, 1858. (Dec. 29, 1858). W. H. Boyett, BM.

Jesse H. Spencer to Jermima Blackburn, Dec. 28, 1858. (Dec. 28, 1858). J. D. King, BM.

A. H. Crews to Mary E. Hopkins, Dec. 28, 1858. (Dec. 28, 1858). A. C. Hess, BM.

John C. Jones to Martha J. Crawford, Dec. 28, 1858. (Dec. 29, 1858). John K. Pearce, BM.

F. M. Glover to Louiza McKelvy, Dec. 28, 1858. (Dec. 30, 1858). W. P. Boaz, BM.

John Balew to Amanda E. Bryant, Dec. 29, 1858. (Jan. 6, 1859). G. W. Robinson, BM.

Elijah B. Trosper to Martha E. Needham, Dec. 30, 1858. (Dec. 30, 1858). J. Y. Rutledge, BM.

P. H. Jackson to Eliza W. Shane, Jan. 3, 1859. (Jan. 4, 1859). W. M. Senter, BM.

Richard R. Watson to Sarah J. Cunningham, Jan. 4, 1859. (Jan. 4, 1859). R. W. Boyd, BM.

William A. Johnston to Amanda R. Seat, Jan. 5, 1859. R. N. Burns, BM.

John Blankenship to Lucinda Rooks, Jan. 5, 1859. (Jan. 6, 1859). R. T. Blankenship, BM.

William B. Terrell to Sarah E. Dodson, Jan. 7, 1859. (Dec. 10, 1859). J. T. Rutledge, BM.

H. T. Needham to E. A. Tyson, Jan. 8, 1859. (Jan. 9, 1859). E. B. Trosper, BM.

William Sinclair to Mary E. Reach, Jan. 10, 1859. (Jan. 22, 1859). G. M. Abbott, BM.

GIBSON COUNTY MARRIAGES

J. B. Ashley to C. L. Carlton, Jan. 13, 1859. (Jan. 13,
1859). E. W. Ferriss, BM.
William R. Bryant to M. A. E. Roe, Jan. 13, 1859. (Jan.
13, 1859). T. B. Roe, BM.
Joseph Nee to Matilda J. Hosea, Jan. 12, 1859. Jan. 12,
1859). W. H. McCaslin, BM.
Patrick Stewart to Ann L. Witherington, Jan. 13, 1859.
(Jan. 13, 1859). J. G. Rank, BM.
James H. Biggs to Mary A. McCombs, Jan. 13, 1859. W.
Biggs, BM.
W. W. Fonville to Martha J. Jarvis, Jan. 14, 1859. (Jan.
14, 1859). P. B. Rose, BM.
R. W. Davis to Susan R. Alexander, Jan. 15, 1859. (Mar.
20, 1859). J. H. Patterson, BM.
William Dover to Clary Richardson, Jan. 17, 1859. (Jan.
19, 1859). J. Z. Richardson, BM.
Arch B. Barron to Casey L. Fletcher, Jan. 17, 1859.
(Jan. 20, 1859). L. H. Russell, BM.
Marcus Clay to Margarett E. Turner, Jan. 18, 1859. (Jan.
20, 1859). John A. Jackson, BM.
B. F. Harris to Martha J. Penn, Jan. 24, 1859. R. N. Davis, B
Joseph H. McKnight to Nancy C. Fisher, Jan. 24, 1859.
(Feb. 1, 18--). J. A. Duncan, BM.
William Shane to Matilda A. Delph, Jan. 24, 1859. (Jan.
27, 1859).
Albert A. McAlexander to Mary A. Kennon, Jan. 26, 1859.
(Jan. 27, 1859). Jas. W. Robertson, BM.
John M. Davis to Fanny J. Zerico, Jan. 26, 1859. (Jan.
26, 1859). Wm. D. Baldridge, BM.
Samuel D. Alexander to Colista E. Boon, Jan. 27, 1859.
(Jan. 27, 1859). M. Butler, BM.
James H. Banks to Melissa L. Hopkins, Jan. 30, 1859.
(Jan. 30, 1859). R. N. Davis, BM.
Abram Gurganes to Mary Burrow, Jan. 31, 1859. (Feb. 2,
1859).
William M. Pipkin to Harriett Wilhington, Feb. 1, 1859.
(Feb. 3, 1859).
John McAfee to Frances A. Powell, Feb. 1, 1859. (Feb.
1, 1859). G. W. Webb, BM.
Lewis E. Mills to Emily L. White, Feb. 2, 1859. (Feb.
3, 1859). John M. Alexander, BM.
John W. Wingo to Elizabeth A. Campbell, Feb. 7, 1859.
(Feb. 7, 1859). David Carey, BM.
Mathew S. Hawkins to Sarah A. L. Kennedy, Feb. 7, 1859.
By A. R. Love, M.G. A. R. Love, BM.
F. M. Griffin to Susan C. Patterson, Feb. 12, 1859.
(Feb. 15, 1859). Thomas T. Taylor, BM.
Sidney F. Campbell to Sarah M. Allen, Feb. 16, 1859.
(Feb. 17, 1858).
Wm. H. Claxton to Martha C. Stone, Feb. 21, 1859. (Feb.
23, 1859). J. T. Tucker, BM.
Jas. C. Canady to Mary J. Spencer, Feb. 24, 1859.
J. T. Whitley, BM.
Reason Rutledge to Lucy Jane Davidson, Feb. 24, 1859.
(Feb. 24, 1859). Jno. H. Davidson, BM.

Thos. W. Noel to Nancy C. Sexton, Feb. 26, 1859. (Feb. 27, 1859).

W. H. Reeves to P. G. Danner, Mar. 1, 1859. R. H. Robertson, BM.

William Johnson to Lucinda E. Mathis, Mar. 2, 1859. (Mar. 3, 1859). J. M. McLaurine, BM.

John W. Wyatt to Mary C. Overall, Mar. 2, 1859. (Mar. 3, 1859). Jos. H. Wyatt, BM.

Charles H. Brown to Priscella P. Holcomb, Mar. 4, 1859. (Mar. 6, 1859). Charles L. Yancey, BM.

James B. Thompson to Sarah A. Dickinson, Mar. 5, 1859. (Mar. 7, 1859). H. C. Hopper, BM.

William H. Nelson to Martha A. Ray, Mar. 5, 1859. (Mar. 9, 1859). C. Cunningham, BM.

John H. Pounds to Mary Johnston, Mar. 7, 1859. (Mar. 15, 1859). G. P. Jamison, BM.

Jessee Tiner to Mary J. Taylor, Mar. 8, 1859. (Mar. 8, 1859). Charles Ferrell, BM.

William L. Lawrence to Symantha C. Word, Mar. 9, 1859. (Mar. 9, 1859). I. G. Davis, BM.

J. L. Burrow to Elizabeth R. Burrow, Mar. 12, 1859. (Mar. 13, 1859). Richard Howard, BM.

A. Hunt to Emeline Legett, Mar. 14, 1859. (Mar. 15, 1859).

James H. Smith to Lucinda C. Mathis, Mar. 15, 1859. (Mar. 16, 1859).

Samuel J. Cook to Nancy E. McCoy, Mar. 14, 1859. (Mar. 18, 1859). W. R. Wetherford, BM.

Thomas J. Akin to Louiza Bryant, Mar. 17, 1859. (Mar. 18, 1859). J. H. Flippin, BM.

Calvin Flowers to Martha Wollard, Mar. 21, 1859. (Mar. 22, 1859).

Jeremiah Desmond to Jane Day, Mar. 24, 1859. (Mar. 24, 1859). C. Cunningham, BM.

James Williams to Elizabeth Flowers, Mar. 24, 1859. (Mar. 27, 1859). Alfred Flowers, BM.

C. C. Stockard to Mary E. Green, Mar. 26, 1859. (Mar. 27, 1859). Elijah Lasiter, BM.

Isaac M. Bledsoe to Elizabeth Ray, Apr. 7, 1859. (Apr. 7, 1859).

Jonathan Davis to Caroline Pearce, Apr. 18, 1859. J. M. Anderson, BM.

William Patton to Reen Allice Hale, May 2, 1859. (May 3, 1859). Joseph Nanon, BM.

Thomas Baird to Irena Stewart, May 11, 1859. (May 12, 1859). Wm. A. Verner, BM.

W. D. Sanders to Melissa C. Lane, May 12, 1859. (May 12, 1859). S. D. Wilkins, BM.

Franklin Singly to Rozanah Smith, May 12, 1859. By A. R. Love, M.G.

William Buchanan to Ruthy M. McKelvy, May 17, 1859. (May 17, 1859). J. W. Weatherspoon, BM.

James R. West to Lucy Gill, May 23, 1859. (May 24, 1859).

GIBSON COUNTY MARRIAGES

William R. Pearce to Amanda E. Woodson, June 1, 1859.
(June 2, 1859).
William S. Kelton to Hester Ann Rucker, June 1, 1859.
Jas. J. Hill, BM.
W. F. Blakemore to Martha D. Parker, June 7, 1859.
(June 7, 1859).
John H. Betts to Martha E. Ford, June 9, 1859. (June 9,
1859).
William Thornton to Dorthula Greer, June 30, 1859. (June
30, 1859).
Nathaniel Moore to Hellen M. Spurier, July 4, 1859. (July
5, 1859). A. H. Harpole, BM.
William J. Anderson to Martha A. Holmes, July 5, 1859.
(July 5, 1859).
Harry S. Heath to Eliza J. Campbell, July 12, 1859.
(July 12, 1859). Thomas D. Lanier, BM.
John E. Gleason to Henritta A. Vaden, July 14, 1859.
(July 14, 1859).
John M. Crockett to Emily Patterson, July 15, 1859.
(July 17, 1859). James S. Holder, BM.
F. E. Becton to Susan Thomas, July 16, 1859. (July 17,
1859). S. M. Becton, BM.
V. H. Bell to Narcissa Bradford, July 25, 1859. (July
25, 1859). R. F. King, BM.
Richard Turner to Martha M. Flowers, July 25, 1859.
(July 31, 1859).
John M. Dunlap to Louisa Kee, July 29, 1859. (Aug. 2,
1859). William Dunlap, BM.
Henry Wells to Mary S. Bassinger, Aug. 1, 1859. (Aug.
1, 1859). John M. Jones, BM.
B. F. Bean to P. M. Gay, Aug. 1, 1859. By A. R. Love, M.G.
Nathaniel H. Graves to Sarah A. Porter, Aug. 1, 1859.
(Aug. 1, 1859). F. M. Nobles, BM.
F. G. Rich to A. E. M. Coleman, Aug. 4, 1859. J. B. W.
Ridley, BM.
G. W. Talley to Sarah Jones, Aug. 9, 1859. (Aug. 10,
1859).
W. B. Weddington to S. M. Gallian, Aug. 11, 1859. (Aug.
14, 1859). Zach Biggs, BM.
A. A. Senter to Emily F. Elam, Aug. 17, 1859. (Aug.
18, 1859).
S. A. Elam to F. O. Reeves, Aug. 18, 1859. James
Claybrook, BM.
Harris Bradford to Annitha Wallice, Aug. 20, 1859.
(Aug. 20, 1859).
John N. Bell to Ruth A. Raines, Aug. 25, 1859. (Aug.
25, 1859). Ben F. Collingsworth, Jr., BM.
B. S. Flowers to Mary F. Ferress, Aug. 25, 1859. (Aug.
25, 1859). G. C. Ferress, BM.
William M. Davis to N. A. Rentfro, Aug. 25, 1859. (Aug.
25, 1859). E. S. Tilghman, BM.
John J. McFarland to Sarah A. Burch, Aug. 29, 1859.
(Aug. 30, 1859). Jones W. McFarlen, BM.
C. B. Heard to Mary E. Jones, Aug. 29, 1859. (Aug. 30,
1859). S. J. Peoples, BM.

128

GIBSON COUNTY MARRIAGES

James H. Holt to E. J. Blankinship, Sept. 1, 1859.
(Sept. 2, 1859).
Stephen Duncan to T. E. Dickey, Sept. 6, 1859. (Sept.
6, 1859).
Granville Amos to Tibitha C. Furgerson, Sept. 6, 1859.
(Sept. 6, 1859). C. Brownlee, BM.
John C. Carlton to Sarah J. Ashley, Sept. 8, 1859.
(Sept. 8, 1859). J. M. Davis, BM.
Joseph Howard to Mary J. Harland, Sept. 9, 1859. (Sept.
11, 1859). Giles Bryant, BM.
Alfred P. Yancy to Emiline J. Ragan, Sept. 10, 1859.
(Sept. 15, 1859). E. W. Ragan, BM.
Jas. H. Slaydon to Kizzy Barker, Sept. 12, 1859. (Sept.
13, 1859). J. H. Rodgers, BM.
Paul Mullins to Ferdy A. Young, Sept. 12, 1859. (Sept.
14, 1859). G. W. Akin, BM.
A. D. R. Swindle to Nancy J. Leggett, Sept. 13, 1859.
(Sept. 14, 1859). John W. Swindle, BM.
Levi Evans to Martha Loller, Sept. 15, 1859. F. M. Allen, BM.
John E. Coker to Sarah E. Boen, Sept. 16, 1859. (Sept.
20, 1859). E. J. Coker, BM.
James M. White to Elizabeth McCartney, Sept. 17, 1859.
(Sept. 22, 1859). William White, BM.
I. N. Dozier to Luvisa P. Baker, Sept. 20, 1859. (Sept.
22, 1859). P. H. Mathis, BM.
N. M. Hopper to Mary I. Forsythe, Sept. 22, 1859. (Sept.
23, 1859). H. C. Hopper, BM.
Miles Welch to Lucretia Forsythe, Sept. 24, 1859. (Sept.
25, 1859). W. G. Clement, BM.
James H. Orr to Amanda C. Greer, Sept. 26, 1859. (Sept.
26, 1859). J. W. Elder, BM.
W. G. Sappington to Alice C. Wade, Sept. 28, 1859.
(Sept. 28, 1859). J. M. McLaurine, BM.
John W. James to Mary N. Bradford, Sept. 28, 1859. (Sept.
28, 1859). William Bell, BM.
W. W. Freeman to Mary F. Fitzgerald, Sept. 29, 1859.
(Sept. 29, 1859). Thos. J. Freeman, BM.
J. H. Hedgecock to Mary F. Mount, Sept. 29, 1859. (Sept.
29, 1859). W. W. Johns, BM.
William G. Bryant to Lucy A. D. Andrews, Oct. 4, 1859.
(Oct. 6, 1859). Boyd White, BM.
Henry Roberson to Sarah L. Blackmon, Oct. 5, 1859. (Nov.
6, 1859). Peter Ragsdale, BM.
James M. Jones to M. E. Browning, Oct. 7, 1859. G. W.
Robinson, BM.
William H. Smith to Saphronia H. Pace, Oct. 8, 1859.
(Oct. 9, 1859). F. M. Brownlow, BM.
Nathan Patrick to Lucinda McCaslin, Oct. 10, 1859.
(Oct. 11, 1859). W. D. Johnson, BM.
Josephus S. Perry to Mary Reynolds, Oct. 11, 1859.
(Oct. 12, 1859). W. G. Knott, BM.
Stephen H. Russell to Dolla Ann Dunigan, Oct. 11, 1859.
(Oct. 12, 1859). W. H. Callis, BM.
George Cook to Margarette E. Comes, Oct. 12, 1859.
(Oct. 13, 1859). Richard McKelvy, BM.

GIBSON COUNTY MARRIAGES

E. D. Screws to Ann E. Ballentine, Oct. 15, 1859. (Oct. 16, 1859). J. H. Ballentine, BM.

W. A. Lee to Lucy E. Taylor, Oct. 15, 1859. (Oct. 16, 1859). J. J. Richardson, BM.

J. M. Porter to M. P. Thompson, Oct. 17, 1859. (Oct. 18, 1859). S. D. Wilkins, BM.

Joseph D. Leach to Amanda C. Cribbs, Oct. 19, 1859. (Oct. 20, 1859). E. Cribbs, BM.

Geo. H. West to Martha A. Gardner, Oct. 22, 1859. (Oct. 27, 1859). J. H. Edwards, BM.

James M. Banister to Roda A. Hague, Oct. 25, 1859. (Oct. 26, 1859). J. A. Peel, BM.

Benj. P. Tyson to Mary V. Bledsoe, Oct. 27, 1859. (Oct. 26, 1859). J. G. Phelan, BM.

Thos. A. Field to Matilda H. Harrison, Oct. 31, 1859. (Nov. 1, 1859). E. E. Hamilton, BM.

John J. Goodman to Sarah A. Jones, Nov. 3, 1859. (Nov. 3, 1859).

J. P. King to M. J. Peoples, Nov. 8, 1859. (Nov. 9, 1859). W. L. Horner, BM.

Joseph A. Foster to Malissa H. Canada, Nov. 8, 1859. (Nov. 8, 1859). C. D. C. Wallis, BM.

A. E. McAdoo to S. F. Stone, Nov. 17, 1859. (Nov. 20, 1859). David McGee, BM.

M. C. Oakley to Mary A. L. Sanders, Nov. 21, 1859. (Nov. 23, 1859).

N. W. Wrenn to Sarah A. Williams, Nov. 23, 1859. (Nov. 24, 1859).

Geo. W. Benson to Allice Bevel, Nov. 25, 1859. (Nov. 27, 1859).

A. R. Wilson to Susan C. Coleman, Nov. 29, 1859. (Nov. 29, 1859).

W. C. Nowell to H. M. Johnson, Nov. 30, 1859. Joseph W. Pierce, BM.

Robert W. Cozzart to Catharine F. Powell, Dec. 2, 1859. (Dec. 8, 1859). Benj. Emison, BM.

John Reynolds to Jane Wallice, Dec. 2, 1859. (Dec. 3, 1859). Josias Thetford, BM.

A. G. Stalens to Mary C. Ragan, Dec. 5, 1859. (Dec. 5, 1859). W. R. Nunn, BM.

F. L. Hudson to Mary S. S. Gay, Dec. 7, 1859. (Dec. 7, 1859). J. H. Hudson, BM.

William H. Harris to Amanda McFarland, Dec. 7, 1859. (Dec. 8, 1859).

W. A. Archer to Selina C. Sanders, Dec. 7, 1859. (Dec. 7, 1859). Alvin Talbott, BM.

John O. Johnson to Amanda Branch, Dec. 8, 1859. (Dec. 8, 1859). B. H. Battle, BM.

Richard F. Butler to Mary A. E. English, Dec. 14, 1859. (Dec. 14, 1859). Daniel Williams, BM.

R. N. Davis to Belle J. McClellan, Dec. 15, 1859. (Dec. 15, 1859). S. W. Caldwell, BM.

E. W. Boyett to S. A. Mitchell, Dec. 22, 1859. (Dec. 25, 1859). W. H. Boyett, BM.

GIBSON COUNTY MARRIAGES

William M. Roberson to Barshebn E. Blackwell, Dec. 22, 1859. (Dec. 22, 1859). Geo. Blackwell, BM. (A free man and woman of color.)

Franklin Exum to Parthena J. Mayfield, Dec. 26, 1859. (Dec. 26, 1859). J. M. Blankenship, BM.

Aaron Sanders to Mary M. Coop, Dec. 27, 1859. T. J. McCulloch, BM.

David C. Blankinship to Mary E. Carter, Dec. 27, 1859. (Dec. 28, 1859). David F. Bird, BM.

Josias Thedford to Hannah Thedford, Dec. 27, 1859. (Dec. 27, 1859). R. B. Flowers, BM.

Charles T. Latta to Martha J. Coleman, Dec. 28, 1859. (Dec. 28, 1859). M. D. L. Abbott, BM.

Mathew Marcum to Mary S. Huckaby, Dec. 28, 1859. (Dec. 28, 1859). James M. Rogers, BM.

John A. Bolen to Martha Jordan, Dec. 30, 1859. (Jan. 3, 1860). W. B. Conner, BM.

L. B. Crowder to Susan G. Baker, Dec. 30, 1859. (Dec. 30, 1859). A. W. Moody, BM.

Marion Holder to Louiza V. Goodman, Jan. 2, 1860. (Jan. 5, 1860). Governor Belew, BM.

N. S. Burrow to Nancy J. London, Jan. 2, 1860. (Jan. 4, 1860). T. H. Agee, BM.

J. S. McWhorter to Mary S. Caraway, Jan. 2, 1860. J. F. Allen, BM.

H. C. Booth to F. D. Avery, Jan. 2, 1860. (Jan. 4, 1860). W. R. Nunn, BM.

W. C. Jones to Pruda A. Barn, Jan. 3, 1860. (Jan. 4, 1860).

James W. Hinson to Sarah Horton, Jan. 4, 1860. (Jan. 4, 1860). W. J. R. Becton, BM.

J. Thomas Boswell to E. Jane Avery, Jan. 7, 1860. (Jan. 8, 1860). Alex Avery, BM.

J. M. Beluw to Martha Hall, Jan. 9, 1860. (Jan. 10, 1860). John I. Holloway, BM.

William E. Bledsoe to Mary A. Clark, Jan. 10, 1860. (Jan. 10, 1860).

Henry C. Vaden to Louiza J. Hailey, Jan. 11, 1860. (Jan. 11, 1860). J. C. Akins, BM.

Christopher Cooper to Mary E. Webb, Jan. 12, 1860. (Jan. 13, 1860). T. J. Callis, BM.

James D. Jackson to Susan F. Williams, Jan. 19, 1860. (Jan. 19, 1860).

W. T. Anington to Emma C. Levy, Jan. 18, 1860. (Jan. 18, 1860). H. B. Blakemore, BM.

J. S. Thomas to Martha L. Ing, Jan. 18, 1860. (Jan. 19, 1860). T. J. Claxton, BM.

J. M. Bradshaw to Sarah David, Jan. 21, 1860. (Jan. 22, 1860). J. G. Lemons, BM.

Burnell Flowers to Mary A. Flowers, Jan. 21, 1860. (Jan. 22, 1860). T. M. Cartwright, BM.

Wm. H. Dodson to Mary A. Ashley, Jan. 23, 1860. (Jan. 23, 1860). William Ashley, BM.

William Pearce to Jacsabena Moss, Jan. 24, 1860. (Jan. 24, 1860). Thos. J. Hailey, BM.

131

GIBSON COUNTY MARRIAGES

D. H. Woldridge to Martha J. Senter, Jan. 24, 1860.
(Jan. 25, 1860).

Pascal A. Ellington to Sidney S. Hall, Jan. 29, 1860.
(Jan. 29, 1860). W. J. Carol, BM.

Thos. F. Warden to Eliza Owens, Jan. 30, 1860. (Feb.
7, 1860). Wm. Ashley, BM.

John W. Sexton to Mary W. Good, Feb. 1, 1860. (Feb. 1,
1860).

Willis H. Mathis to Caledonia J. Norton, Feb. 2, 1860.
(Feb. 2, 1860). Jas. H. Smith, BM.

S. W. Redmon to Emeline F. Brassfield, Feb. 2, 1860.
(Feb. 2, 1860). Elam Godwin, BM.

William H. Wilkes to Amandy J. C. P. Howell, Feb. 4, 1860.
(Feb. 4, 1860). W. H. Standly, BM.

A. G. Crocker to Irmandy S. Baker, Feb. 6, 1860. (Feb.
7, 1860). W. H. Baker, BM.

Lycurgus Thompson to Sarah J. Corley, Feb. 9, 1860. (Feb.
9, 1860). W. H. Turner, BM.

W. C. Davidson to Mary S. Mosley, Feb. 14, 1860. (Feb.
14, 1860). J. H. Davidson, BM.

B. F. Watkins to Sarah Emarson, Feb. 18, 1860. T. H.
Norvell, BM.

W. C. Childress to Frances Herington, Feb. 20, 1860.
(Feb. 20, 1860).

W. G. Black to Tobitha A. Thomas, Feb. 20, 1860. (Feb.
20, 1860).

Thos. Flowers to Carroline Warren, Feb. 24, 1860. (Feb.
26, 1860). J. E. Wood, BM.

W. J. Overall to Clementine Hutcherson, Feb. 28, 1860.
(Feb. 28, 1860). Dale Barns, BM.

W. H. Wreen to Cemantha L. Tinkle, Feb. 28, 1860. (Mar.
1, 1860).

Henry G. Philips to Sarah J. Fitzgerald, Mar. 6, 1860.
(Mar. 7, 1860). Green Williams, BM.

R. D. Fitzgerald to O. Hartsfield, Mar. 7, 1860. J. W.
Buford, BM.

Jas. G. Blakemore to R. C. Wade, Mar. 8, 1860. H. B.
Blakemore, BM.

C. W. Hix to Louisa C. Hunt, Mar. 9, 1860. (Mar. 11,
1860). R. M. Martin, BM.

B. S. Vaneaton to Sarnisa Huie, Mar. 13, 1860. (Mar.
14, 1860).

D. C. Dickey to E. A. Allison, Mar. 16, 1860. John W.
Allison, BM.

Thos. Martin to Sarah A. Greenwell, Mar. 26, 1860. (Mar-
26, 1860). S. W. Holgood, BM.

M. V. Baird to Olly B. Hopper, Mar. 30, 1860. (Mar. 30,
1860). H. W. Sanders, BM.

H. A. Longworth to Julia A. Grier, Apr. 2, 1860. (Apr.
5, 1860).

A. F. Betts to Frances Grady, Apr. 5, 1860. (Apr. 5,
1860).

O. L. Morris to Letha A. Pearce, Apr. 6, 1860. (Apr.
8, 1860). R. C. Crocker, BM.

Jas. T. Holt to L. Butler, Apr. 10, 1860. (Apr. 10, 1860). W. G. Knott, BM.

E. B. Cayce to J. E. McCulloch, Apr. 23, 1860. J. W. Buford, BM.

N. F. Stallings to Mary Carr, Apr. 28, 1860. (Apr. 29, 1860). Z. T. Conner, BM.

S. B. Pope to Mary E. Martin, Apr. 28, 1860. (May 1, 1860). B. H. Pope, BM.

David Hall to Nancy Morris, May 7, 1860. (Apr. 8, 1860). Jonathan Hall, BM.

W. H. Eaton to A. C. Carey, May 10, 1860. C. M. Carey, BM.

J. W. Penn to Collie H. Stedwell, May 16, 1860. (May 17, 1860).

Benj. Phillips to S. C. Thomason, May 17, 1860. (May 17, 1860). James Phillips, BM.

Jabes H. Flippin to Patience A. Holt, May 19, 1860. (May 21, 1860). C. H. Ross, BM.

Isaac Mathis to Metilda S. Dowland, May 22, 1860. (May 22, 1860). Geo. W. Nevil, BM.

W. T. Nicholson to J. A. Mays, May 23, 1860. J. A. Nicholson, BM.

J. K. Lowrance to A. C. Cherry, May 28, 1860. (May 28, 1860).

Smith Hamilton to Adeline Parks, May 30, 1860. (May 31, 1860).

Jessee Dewberry to Frances S. Cotton, June 2, 1860. (June 3, 1860). J. H. Biggs, BM.

A. A. Davidson to Cornelia E. Overall, June 5, 1860. (June 6, 1860). W. L. Arrington, BM.

Wesley P. Mount to Melinda P. Williams, June 9, 1860. (June 17, 1860). James Mount, BM.

J. F. Fletcher to Metilda F. Butram, June 13, 1860. (June 13, 1860). W. A. Fletcher, BM.

Robert Thomas Parks to Mary Elizabeth Grissom, June 17, 1860.

Armstrong (cont.)
James M. 71
Jas. M. 49, 89
Jno. Y. 100
Julia A. 58
Marion 94
Martha 79
Permela 40
S. W. 93
Samuel W. 110
Tibitha 61
Arnol, Jane 75
Arnold, Ann I. 99
B. 115
B. F. 58, 66
Benj. F. 67
Benjamin F. 91
Booker 46
David 39
Ezra I. 14
Frances C. 60
Henry 125
Jacob W. 66
James 22, 39, 56, 98
James M. 106
James P. 84
Jane 119
Joel 62, 65, 67, 70,
91
John B. 73
John H. 90
Littleberry B. 85
Lucendia 78
Martha 104
Martha A. T. 40
Martin 97
Martin B. 54
Mary 79
Mary E. 106
Mary M. 94
Mary N. 54
Nancy 25
Nancy J. 85
Richardson 46
Sarah 92
Sardinia E. 105
T. G. 85
Thos. W. 90
William J. 90
Arrington, W. L. 133
Asburn, Kitty Ann 108
Asher, Mary E. C. 12
Ashlen, Joseph 112
Ashley, Calvin 83
J. B. 126
Mary A. 131
Sarah J. 129
William 131
Wm. 132
Ashlin, John 25
Askew, Lackey Ann 94
Asler, D. I. 74
J. B. 80
Aslin, Charity 110
J. B. 87
John F. 119
Saml. 23
Samuel 34
Thomas 118
Atchison, Jno. G. 35,
43
John G. 39
Robert 39
Surgener 49
Surgner 32
T. D. 85, 100
Thos. D. 101
William (Jr.) 69

Atchison (cont.)
Wm. 38, 56
Atkenson, Sarah 29
Atkins, Sarah B. 53
Attman, Martha 84
Atty, Ann Eveline Van 72
Austin, Mary P. 124
Avery, Alex 23, 131
Alexander 121
E. Jane 131
Eliza 9
Emly A. M. 105
F. D. 131
H. B. 4
Harriett A. T. 69
Henry D. 45
Henry P. C. 44
J. T. J. 69
Jas. F. A. M. 103
John W. 31
Martha A. P. 119
Mary N. W. 54
R. T. S. 23
Sarah A. E. 44
Sarah E. 53, 123
Silas 54
Unia 45
Wineford 6
Aycock, R. G. 103, 120,
122, 123
Babb, Green B. 53
Henry 44
John 31
Polly 23
Baber, Alex 29
C. C. 102
Lucy A. 27
Badget, George 52
Bady, Joyner W. 82
Bailey, Alston 52
Benjamin A. 51
Eliza N. 12
Henderson 55
Isham 103
Jeptha T. 45
Jerry 116
John A. 92
Joiner 58
Mortica 58
Peleg 12, 51, 55, 58
S. W. 92
William 32
William H. 48
Baily, Ellen 98
Jane 12
Lacy 92
Moddica 48
Solomon A. 98
Bain, Elizabeth 5
William 49
Baird, Charles G. 48
Elizabeth L. 104
Elvira J. 120
James M. 86
Jas. M. 121
M. V. 132
Mary 36
Sarah J. 86
Thomas 127
Thos. D. 79, 86
Wilson 25
Baisinger, Geo. M. 91
Sarah M. 64
T. J. 64
Baker, Alvis 123
Anney 50
B. 34, 43
Elizabeth 96

Baker (cont.)
Elizabeth F. 47
Emly A. 80
Frances 107
H. B. 113
Harrel 90
Henderson 37, 76
Irmandy S. 132
James 7
James J. 111
James S. 54
Jno. W. 79
John W. 75
Joshua 108
Josiah 18
Luvisa P. 129
M. A. 115
Mahala A. 53
Malissa 10
Margarett J. 117
Mary 95
Mary J. 64, 108
P. P. 52, 66
Pinkny 42
Samuel 4, 108
Sarah M. V. 118
Susan G. 131
Thomas 7
W. H. 132
William 22, 92
William G. 66, 100
Wm. D. 121, 126
Baldridge, A. S. 123
Isabella F. 103
Isabella N. 52
John S. 60
Mary N. 78
Nancy 18
S. E. 122
W. D. 105
W. H. 119
William H. 62, 77
Balentine, Mary K. 55
Baleu, James M. 25
Balew, Eliza 89
John 125
Baley, Betsey 5
Cary 12
Isabella 36
Jacksy 51
John W. 44
Johnathan 53
Jonathan 12
Martha 39
Martin L. 58
Obediance 14
Sally 4
William 4
Ball, Elizabeth 86
Ballance, Charlott 37
Emely 56
Ballard, Willis 44
Ballentine, Ann E. 130
D. 65
Davis 63
J. H. 130
Jessee 55
John W. 54, 123
Jos. 81
Peter 65
William 124
Ballintine, Mahetable
24
Bane, Elizabeth 1
Sarah Ann 86
Sary 1
Wine 7
Banister, James M. 130

Banister (cont.)
William 18
Banks, Hiram H. 24
James H. 126
Mary E. 113
Barham, Ann 74
Jas. 96
Mary A. 34
Barker, C. G. 123
Celey 39
Delila 123
E. W. 118
Gray 39
Gray B. 79
H. 58, 63, 112
Israel M. L. 85
Jane E. 114
Jno. A. 86
Kizzy 129
M. 118
Mary 114
Mary E. 118
Rebecca 54
Stephen C. 117
W. J. 98
Wesley G. 83
William E. 67
Barkley, A. G. 88
Frank L. 88
Barksdale, Horace R. 73
Julia E. 96
N. F. 83
Nathan 3, 12
Nathaniel F. 85
Sarah C. 119
Barlow, M. T. 59
Nancy 107
Barn, Pruda A. 131
Barner, Paul T. 95
Barnes, America 29
Gabriel 56
Sarah 21
Thomas 46
Barnet, M. W. 97
Barnett, David P. 93
Mathew H. 93
Robert M. 107
Barns, Arthur 31
D. H. 48
Dale 132
Daniel 49
Daniel H. 30
Eliza J. 39
Barret, Wilson 28
Barrett, Joseph 89
Sarah 123
William 90
Wilson 35, 61
Barron, Arch B. 126
Arthur 49
C. A. 114
Francis M. 123
John W. 93
Mary M. 85
Nathan 21
W. T. 114
William J. 114
Barrot, Franklin 23
Barrott, Franklin 33
Joseph 47
Marcus 50
Sarah J. 62
Barten, Sarah A. 47
Bartlett, Sarah 31
Barton, H. L. M. 30
H. M. L. 29, 62
John M. 62
Lilly A. 101

Barton (cont.)
Mexico 90
Nancy 26
R. W. 51
Rebecca E. 58
Robert W. 34
Semilda A. 98
Spencer G. 35, 40
Thos. G. 75
W. C. 124
William C. 51
Willis S. 113
Basinger, John 50
Margaret 21
William A. 41
Bass, Alexander 67
Edward 64
Eliza 23
Elizabeth V. 92
Isaac W. 76
James H. 53
Joseph J. 46
Martha E. 67
Mary T. 60
Matilda W. 79
R. C. 102
Wyatt 40
Bassinger, Mary S. 128
Bates, John C. 20
Judia 14
Mary 25
Roseana M. 26
Bathshears, William 111
Battle, B. H. 130
B. W. 118
Deborah J. 85
Elizabeth 27
H. 114, 119
Harmon 42, 79, 85,
87
Henry 27, 42
J. H. 116
Louisa A. 95
Baxter, James 102
John 54, 90
William 11
Bayn, Ann 59
D. B. 120
M. F. 59
Mastin F. 59
Bayne, Mary 4
Bays, George W. 15
Baysinger, Elizabeth 10
James M. 51
Jno. 23
Thos. J. 30
Wm. A. 30
Beacham, Abner C. 17
Beadles, Alex M. 63
Bean, B. F. 128
Benjamin 23
Martha Ann 24
McKelva 42
Nancy 35
Beantrell, Jobe 48
Beard, Jamima 40
Presley T. 116
Thomas 61
W. T. 94
Beaty, Jasper N. 74
Beaver, Anna 19
Beavers, Martha H. 92
Thos. B. 120
Beazley, Elizabeth S.
27
Beazly, Virlinda C. 17
Beck, Alsey M. 76

Beckham, J. J. 121
Sarah 20
Becton, Delitha 15
F. E. 28, 128
Frances E. 84
Fred E. 15
Frederick 63
S. M. 120, 128
W. J. 104
W. J. R. 112, 121, 131
William J. R. 93
Wm. J. 24
Belch, Elisha 46, 49
M. A. 115
Mary 121
Belew, Aaron 38
Cornelia 94
Frances C. 71
Governor 78, 96, 131
Hanah 36
Harvy 33
James M. 38
Jane 38
John 79
Martha 41
Martin 95
Bell, Andrew 88
Ann 33
Barbary Ann 86
Eliza 69
Elizabeth 120
Ellen 34
Ellen C. 67
Emeline R. 46
George N. 109
James 12, 77
James G. 84
John N. 35, 128
John W. 72
Joshua 15
Leroy H. 30
Martha 9, 124
Martha Ann 93
Mary 18
Mary M. 54
Michel 12
Nancy P. 38
Narcissa 15
R. G. 84
Robert 80
S. 100
Sarah 72
Thos. 23
V. H. 31, 128
Valentine 78
Volentine 31
Vollentine 38
Wesley 35, 38
William 46, 122, 123,
129
William H. 12
Wm. 38, 120
Belleu, Jas. M. 33
Bellew, Elizabeth 26
Sarah P. 26
Bells, Eliza J. 84
William 84
William H. 70
Bellue, Joseph 25
Beluew, Jiles 112
Beluw, J. M. 131
Benett, J. H. 40
Bennett, Geo. W. 118
James F. 112
Benson, Caroline 119
Beo. W. 130
Martha 44
Martin 74

Benson (cont.)
  Milly 63
  Richard I. 73
Benthall, Wm. 79
Benthel, James L. 67,
  117
  Laban 58
  Sarah A. 53
Benthill, William 97
Beny, Mary J. E. 112
Berge, Richard H. 18
Berry, A. E. 100
  Amanda 59
  Andrew 24
  Cassandra 85
  Elizabeth 69
  Emely A. 123
  Harriet M. 86
  John 80
  Lucinda A. 108
  Martha 122
  Mary E. 103
  Matilda C. 59
  Penelope J. 108
  Pennlope June 24
  Purnetta A. 85
  Reddiee 48
  Richard 122
  Samuel J. S. 108
  Sarah 11
  Zachriah Richard 122
Best, Richard 96
Bethell, W. D. 24
  Wm. D. 26
Bethshares, J. L. 123
  Jas. L. 79
Betts, A. F. 102, 132
  Abrm 6
  Alen 6
  John H. 128
  Margrett 55
  Sarah A. 103
Bevel, Allice 130
Bhass, Sarah 13
Biard, Rosannah L. 29
Biggs, Elizabeth F. 124
  Emma J. 124
  Isaac J. 85
  J. H. 133
  James 65
  James H. 126
  Martha 65
  Martha A. 48
  Mary Ann 97
  Mary E. 65
  Matilda C. 98
  Nancy 86, 101
  Nehemiah 42
  R. W. 98
  Reuben 8
  Ruben 6
  Ruben (Sr.) 7
  Ruben W. 7
  Rubin 27
  W. 126
  William E. 114
  Z. 82
  Z. (Jr.) 114
  Zach 124, 128
  Zachariah 27, 36
  Zacheriah 6
Bigham, Hugh M. 2, 9
Bilch, Elisha 37
Billingsley, Adaline 69
  Adaline E. 76
  Artina 56
  B. 63
  E. 3, 51

Billingsley (cont.)
  Elijah 3
  Mary 27
  Mary L. 62
  T. 49
  W. 56
Billingsly, Elijah 2
  Elisha 7
  Mahaly 16
  Robt. 101
  Sonya 70
  Wm. B. 76, 81
Billips, Dolly 98
  William J. 73
Bills, W. H. 83, 84
  Wallace 84
Binyon, William B. 45
Bird, David 97
  David F. 131
  Elizabeth A. 78
  James B. 81
  Levina 66
  Sarah F. 98
Bishop, Wiley 24
  William 53
Bittney, Jane 78
Bivens, S. C. 73
  Sarah 112
  Wiley 120
Bivins, John L. 104
Black, A. G. 95
  Alexander 15
  Duncan H. 72
  W. G. 132
  William D. 115
Blackburn, J. R. A. 103
  James 54
  Jermima 125
  Jessee 67, 112
  Nancy E. 125
  Rufus 96
  William 52
Blackley, Samuel 24, 75
Blackmon, Fordham 110
  John 114
  Sarah L. 129
Blacknall, Thos. Y. 108
Blackshear, James C.
  91
  Joel H. 99
Blackwell, Barshebn E. 1
  131
  Geo. 131
  George 5
  George W. 125
Blain, Mary C. 75
Blair, A. B. 77
  Andrew 5, 11, 20
  David D. 20, 29
  Elizabeth J. 91
  Ephraim 2, 4
  G. W. 100
  John D. 6
  Margarette M. 100
  Martha J. 49
  Mary E. 74
  R. D. 89, 91, 99, 114
  Richard 26
  Robert D. 91
  Tabitha C. 99
  Thomas B. 6
  Thomas J. 105
  William A. 114
Blakemore, Elizabeth J.
  101
  H. B. 120, 131, 132
  James B. 32
  James S. 71

Blakemore (cont.)
  Jarusa A. 63
  Jas. B. 4, 9
  Jas. G. 132
  L. W. 92, 99
  Nancy S. 2
  Sarah J. 1
  Susan V. 118
  W. F. 128
  William T. 18
Blaloch, Sampson 83
Blalock, Allen 13
Blan, C. 115
  Sophronia 115
Blancett, (?) 75
  Jessee 47
Blanchet, John 50
Blankenship, Benj. 112
  Eliza Jane 36
  Emily A. 100
  Geo. W. 63
  J. M. 131
  Jas. 36
  Jas. M. 80
  John 125
  Manarca F. S. J. W.
  108
  Martha F. 123
  Mary 35
  Mary J. 109
  Mary P. A. 53
  Narcissa 98
  Pemilia A. 54
  R. T. 125
  Thos. R. 84
Blankinship, David C.
  131
  E. J. 129
  Elizabeth A. 94
  Jas. M. 94
  Jesse S. 94
  John C. 55
  John W. 79
Blann, William 11
Blanton, A. G. 102, 124
  Sophia L. 121
Blaton, A. G. 120
Bledsoe, A. 93
  A. W. 40
  Albert W. 47
  Armantha A. 110
  Avolina G. 117
  Centhy 28
  Dizey 58
  Elizabeth 33
  Elizabeth B. 55
  Ellenor 6
  Emaline 28
  Francis 21
  Francis A. 25
  George W. 19
  H. H. 47
  H. N. 45
  Harrett 70
  Harriat Jane 12
  Hawkins 36
  Hearvy 14
  I. M. 121
  Isaac M. 127
  James L. 26
  John H. 52
  John R. 46
  Joshua 37
  Louisa 15
  Madison 12, 52
  Major 27, 64
  Manerva B. E. 93
  Martha Ann 25

Bledsoe (cont.)
  Mary L. 14, 103
  Mary N. 52
  Mary V. 130
  Sarah H. 88
  Susan Y. 75
  Wellington H. 28, 45
  William E. 131
  Wm. G. 33
  Wm. N. 55
  Zachariah 73
Blessing, Jacob 113
Bloys, Elizabeth 8
Blunt, Louisa 55
Boals, James 6, 7
Boaz, L. A. 100
  W. P. 125
Bobbett, Albert L. 100
  B. F. 103
  D. J. 53
  Davidson B. T. 97
  Elizabeth 16
  Francis M. 36
  Henry 36
  Isaac 61
  J. (Dr.) 57
  James 41, 43, 98
  M. G. 80
  M. J. 68
  Martha C. 80
  Martha R. 112
  R. F. 97
  Silas M. 87
  Stephen J. 52
  Susan 30
Bobbitt, Dorraty 29
  Henry 26
  Z. L. 47
Bodkin, Jane 107
  Levi 107
  Steel 20
  William L. 62
Bodkins, James 14
  Jno. 119
Boen, Sarah E. 129
Bogas, C. 100
Bogle, Margarette Jane
  99
  Robert 50
  Robt. E. 49
  Thomas C. 108
  Thos. C. 123
Bohanan, M. 52
Bohannan, James 100
  Mary 102
Boland, Green 8
Bolen, John A. 131
Boles, Robert 7, 9
Bolin, A. L. 120
  D. B. 120
  Mary A. 108
  Susan 113
Boling, G. B. 37
  Green 8
  Thomas 3
  William 1, 3
Bolls, John M. 117
Bolton, Granville L. 103
Bone, Hugh Y. 29, 32
  Margaret E. 36
  Martha 22
  Saml. J. 93
  Samuel J. 105
  William 102
Bonfels, L. F. 42
Booker, M. M. 120
Boon, Ann E. 58
  Benjamin 28, 75

Boon (cont.)
  Colista E. 126
  Cynthia I. 56
  D. M. 94
  Elizabeth 12
  Gilbert 32
  James E. 53
  James H. 79
  Martha 20, 83
  Ratliff 50
  Sion 36, 51, 57
  William 60
Booth, Eliz. 116
  Eudora M. 55
  Greenwood 72
  H. C. 131
  Ratliff 60
  Saml. 25
  Samuel 50
Boreing, Susana 2
Borran, Nancy 34
  Sarah A. 42
Borrin, Parzada 28
Boswell, J. Thomas 131
  Jno. M. 119
  Thos. L. 26
Bottom, Granville M. 103
Bottoms, Elizabeth 115
  James M. 104
  Nancy E. 102
  Presley L. 117
Boucher, Martha P. 93
Bouchier, Julia 98
Boun, Pricilla 22
Bourman, Elenor E. 52
Bowden, B. A. 103
Bowder, Elizabeth 80
Bowen, William 14
  Zachariah 26
Bower, E. R. 74
  Elijah R. 54
Bowers, Agnes A. 95
  Allen 122
  Catharine 88
  David 49
  Elizabeth N. 56
  Mary 20
  Philemon Y. 6
  Thomas 14
  Thos. N. 32, 55
Bowin, F. W. 90
Bowlen, Mary 33
Bowling, Andrew J. 82
  Burges 19
  Nancy 19
Bowls, Charles A. 104
Bowman, Abagal A. 51
  Cassandra 36
  N. M. 89
  Narcissa 61
  Noah M. 101
  Rebecca M. 78
  Wm. 27
Boyce, Isham 58
Boyd, Elijah 16
  James M. 22
  Lorenza B. 89
  R. W. 125
  Robert 84
  Susan 16
  Zuby 47
Boyett, B. 45
  B. S. 93
  Cullen J. 57
  D. G. 29, 49, 91
  Derham 28
  E. W. 130
  James T. 117

Boyett (cont.)
  Joseph P. 72
  L. H. 92
  Lucenda 80
  Lycurgus 125
  Martha 83
  Thomas 57
  W. H. 110, 116, 125,
    130
  William B. 123
Boyle, R. E. 66
Boyles, Nancy 21
  Wm. 8
Boyls, Nancy 15
Boyster, Wm. H. 100
Boyt, Baptist 19
  Elijah 7, 9
  Exaline 9
  Nancy 23
  Rebecca J. 42
Boytt, Clorence 7
  Eli 12
  Martha 42
Bradberry, Almira 7
  Ann 17
  Jacob 14
  James J. 7
  Jas. J. 20
  John 58
  Mat 99
  Mathew 99
  Piercy 3
  Polly T. 15
  Sarah 81
Bradbury, John 57
Braden, Emily 106
Bradford, Fanny 7
  G. M. 107
  H. S. 92
  H. W. 95, 99
  Harris 54, 115, 128
  James C. 51, 52
  Levi R. 41, 51, 52,
    53, 54, 55
  Mary 2, 30
  Mary N. 129
  Nancy 102
  Narcissa 128
  Robert 95
  Robt. 90, 92
  Spincer 41
  Thomas 76
  Thos. 99
  William 73
Bradley, Ana 12
  M. A. 118
  Margaret W. 41
  Sarah 36
  William 120
Bradlow, J. A. 57
Bradshaw, J. A. 48
  J. M. 131
Brady, Ripley 105
Brahan, James 8
Brambalow, William S. 73
Bran, Mary 23
Branch, Aaron 31
  Amanda 130
  Archelus B. 76
  Benjamin C. 53
  Bryant M. 22
  Hepsey Ann 83
  Jesse L. 39
  Jessee L. 49
  Mary 70
  Sarrah 35
  Terrell 113
Brand, Barnet 43

Branson, Mary 95
  Tandy M. 84
Brant, Geo. W. 95
Brassfield, (?) (Mrs.) 7
  Emeline F. 132
  George S. 57
Bratton, George S. 17
  James H. 58
  John W. 17
  M. J. 113
  Malinda 14
  Margarett 11
  Margarett Ann 73
  Mary 36
  Mary D. 90
  Mary J. 51
  William M. 67
Breat, Wm. 9
Breckhouse, Elizabeth 98
Brent, Eliza J. 65
  Lucretia A. E. 122
Brewer, George W. 78
  J. M. 122
  James M. 20
  Wm. C. 83
Briant, Boyd F. 7
  Elen J. 115
  John 7
  Martha A. 104
  Martin 21
  Nancy 104
Brickhouse, A. R. 51
  Harrett 58
  Jno. W. 86
  John W. 96
  Latima 99
Bridgemon, William A. 18
Bridges, Cintha W. 31
  R. 86
  William H. 11
Brigance, Clinton 88
Bright, Emma 99
Brightwell, Ann N. 89
  L. L. 56, 59
  Martha R. 122
  Mary L. 56
  Nancy 84
  Peggy 92
  S. T. 110
  Samuel 108
  Sarah J. 118
  William J. 122
Britenham, Hannah M. 32
Britingham, John 6
Britt, Edmund 5
Brock, Benj. F. 89
Brogden, Polley Ann 39
Brogdon, Allen 64
  Aminisa M. 122
  Annitta 119
  Edy 118
Brooks, J. H. 50
  P. H. 115
  William S. 73
Brooten, Mary 39
Brooton, Charlott 35
Brown, Ann 45, 85
  Candis 59
  Charles A. 96
  Charles H. 127
  Elizabeth 31
  Eveline F. 109
  Gabriel 47
  Henry 4
  Henry C. 81
  Jackson 32
  James 18, 19
  Jane W. 74

Brown (cont.)
  Jas. L. W. 100
  Jas. R. 109
  John 100
  John W. 105
  Jonas 26
  Jos. J. 124
  Levi 68
  Martha A. 77
  Mary W. 69
  Milton 5, 6, 15
  Rebecca 3
  Richard A. 100
  Robert H. 108
  S. R. D. 96
  Sarah 47
  Wilson 5
Browne, James 19
Browning, John T. 89
  Lucy 64
  M. E. 129
  Martha 105
  Nancy 26
  Wm. J. 99
Brownlee, C. 129
Brownlow, F. M. 119, 129
Bruce, John H. 44
  Martha 53
  Sarah 70
  Susan M. 44
Bruff, Lethia 20
  Matilda 7
  Thompson 21
Brummet, Leah 4
Brunson, Anny 29
  Martha Jane 69
  Sarah Ann 69
Bryan, T. M. 122
Bryant, Amanda E. 125
  Avira L. 84
  Boyd F. 5, 24
  Carroline 27
  Cornelia 49
  Eliza E. 99
  Elizabeth 60
  Elvira 114
  Frances L. 115
  Frederick 10
  Geo. W. 96
  Giles 129
  Jane 5, 7
  Jane F. 108
  John 109
  John W. 120
  Julia A. 110
  Laurel 24
  Louiza 127
  Mahala 121
  Martha C. 120
  Martha E. 50
  Martin 21
  Mary A. 53
  Nancy A. M. 79
  Patsey 95
  Sandal 57
  Sarah A. 28
  Sarah Ann 96
  Sarah C. 107
  Thomas 100
  William M. 129
  William J. 101
  William K. 100
  William R. 126
  Zachariah 34
Bryett, T. H. 52
Bryson, John 12
Buchanan, H. R. 17, 19, 85

Buchanan (cont.)
  J. H. 111
  William 127
  Wm. S. 79
Buchannan, John C. 102
  Thos. E. 111
Bueff, T. C. 60
Buford, J. D. 118
  J. W. 132, 133
  Semion E. 35
Bulington, Wm. 42
Bullard, James 47
  Susan 75
Bulleton, Rachal 53
Bullington, Jasper 109
  John C. 98
  Julia 42
  Mark 26
  Soniza 70
Bunn, Emily 91
Bunnell, Elizabeth C. 65
  Lyda Ann 32
  Marcila A. 55
Bunting, Sarah G. 20
Burch, David R. 100
  Sarah A. 128
Burgan, B. F. 40
  Benjamin F. 40
  Canzey 79
  Elizabeth J. 43
Burgess, Robert E. 79
Burkhart, Nancy A. 29
Burnam, H. T. 33
  Henry T. 38
Burnes, Manirva 76
Burnett, Angeline L. 102
  James M. 95
  Jas. M. 99
Burney, John F. 81
  Nancy A. M. 94
Burns, Isaac 58
  R. N. 125
  W. B. 101
Burnwant, Chesley L. 78
Burnwat, D. A. 121
Burr, Sidy 73
Burress, George W. 82
  J. W. 97
  James M. 99
Burris, James 76
Burrow, A. L. 27
  Banks M. 13
  Elizabeth R. 127
  Ephraim 16
  J. L. 127
  James R. 66
  Martha 57
  Martha E. 106
  Mary 126
  N. S. 131
  Sarah E. 79
  Timitha E. 99
  William J. 101
Burrus, John 112
Burton, Eliza A. H. 26
  J. H. 47
  Jefferson 99
  Wm. H. 24
Busby, John 47
Bush, Ann Jane 11
  John N. 65
Busick, William M. 119
Butler, Carroline 41
  Charles E. 87
  Christopher C. 80
  Clarissa C. 115
  Deby D. 66
  E. A. 67, 68, 78

Butler (cont.)
  E. C. 66, 68
  E. N. 68
  E. T. 121
  Epsey M. 55
  James M. 123
  John B. 106
  Julian 13
  L. 133
  M. 126
  Martha 75
  Mary E. 36
  Moses 124
  Narcissa E. 107
  Richard F. 130
  Susanah A. 103
  William 5, 12, 17, 19,
    117
  William G. 69
  Wm. 36
  Wm. Y. 86
Butram, A. 37
  Andrew P. B. R. 73
  John H. 60
  Metilda F. 133
  Nancy 68
  Rebecca 120
  Simeon 28
Byers, William T. 123
Byrne, Ransom H. 5
Bysinger, Susana A. 19
  William A. 19
Cabb, W. F. 43
Cabler, John D. 19
  Nicholas W. 29
Cail, Eliz. P. 120
  Isaac 92
  John W. 121
  Parker 120
  William H. 106
Caldwell, D. C. 116
  Luther M. 63, 66
  M. R. 81
  O. B. 78
  R. P. 87
  Robert 113
  Robert P. 81
  S. W. 130
Caleb, Columbus W. 84
Calhoun, Jane 27
Callis, T. J. 131
  W. H. 129
Cameron, John T. 8
Campbell, Alexander 14
  Eliza J. 128
  Elizabeth A. 126
  John 26
  Letha 32
  Mary P. 15
  Mary S. 69
  Nancy 68
  Nancy H. 108
  Polly 4
  Sidney F. 126
  Susan A. 93, 94
  Unity 10
  W. H. 101, 113, 114
  Willes N. 90
  William 8
  William M. 92
  Willis N. 93
Camy, A. S. 54
Canada, George 52, 62
  James 70
  Malissa H. 130
  Sarah 60
Canaday, Amanda J. 89
  Cardine 90

Canaday (cont.)
  Charlotta 81
  Isaac 65
  Mary C. A. 81
  Rutha 29
Canadey, Elizabeth 24
Canady, Archabald 41
  Emoline 116
  George 41
  Hardy 8
  Isaac 16
  Jas. C. 126
  L. H. 117
  Thos. 24
Caneer, W. T. 112
Cannon, Bevely 49
  Beverly 35
  Elizabeth 54
  H. L. 77
  J. T. 118
  J. W. 104
  James 36, 61, 77
  James S. 123
  Jas. T. 123
  Jno. 77
  John N. 69
  Louisa 111
  Margaret 55
  William 53, 54, 69
Cantrel, Berry 38
Cantrell, Duke 2
  Geo. W. 18
  Mahalay 97
  Malinda 9
  William 18
Cantrol, Charlott 43
Caple, Benjamin D. 85
  Mary E. 86
Caples, Mary P. 104
Caps, Sarah A. 106
Caraway, Bryant 87
  Jesse 83
  Jessee 35
  Mary S. 131
Care, Andrew A. 26
  E. J. (Miss) 26
  Mary 24
Carey, A. C. 133
  C. M. 133
  David 126
  Eliza A. 117
  John 46
  Malinda 123
  William 46
Carl, Marrett 95
Carlton, C. L. 126
  Cassa L. 114
  John C. 129
  John D. 8
  P. J. 113
  R. J. 114
  Thomas 91
  Thos. 51
Carnahan, James B. 9
Carnes, Adam 47, 49
Carney, Ann M. 84
Carnigay, Bryant 45
Carns, Absolum 43
  Martha 49
Carol, W. J. 132
Carr, Andrew A. 30, 56,
    92
  Eliza Ann M. 73
  Elizabeth C. 92
  James 73
  John A. 83
  Mary 133
  Mary A. 101

Carr (cont.)
  R. H. 101
  Robert H. 56, 91, 97
  Violet L. 23
  W. F. 104
  William 86
  William F. 43
Carradine, John 12
  William 12
Carrahan, James P. 18
  Martha 18
Carraway, Bryant 80
  Bryant C. 47
  James 28
Carray, Jesse 28
Carrington, S. M. 113
Carrol, C. 112
  J. R. 118
  Lucy M. 103
Carroll, D. 119
  Elizabeth 39
  Euvilinah M. 59
  George W. 103
  Harriett H. 12
  J. H. 43
  J. R. 84
  James 16
  James A. 38
  Jno. M. 27, 88
  John 40
  John C. 44
  John H. 44, 53
  John M. 87
  Josiah R. 92
  Lucy 68
  Mary 26
  Moladeous B. 67
  Sarah 32
  W. R. 61
  William R. 60
  William T. 88
  Wm. J. 84
Carry, Ann 20
  Nathan 20
Carten, James W. 25
Carter, Catharine 65
  Fanny 31
  J. W. 64
  James 22
  James G. 31
  Mary E. 131
  Philip B. 25
  Virginia C. 99
  Wiley S. 55
Carthal, Sarah C. 40
Carthel, Almira 83
  Emily L. 123
  T. J. 80, 83, 87
Cartwright, Elizabeth J.
    52
  T. M. 131
Caruthers, Thomas J. 5
  Thos. I. 10
  Thos. J. 1, 3
Casey, Anney (Mrs.) 49
Cash, Arthur 68, 75
  B. W. 101
  James 77
  Jno. E. 58, 82
  Margrette E. 101
  William Lewis 95
Cashar, Martin F. 73
  Sarah J. 80
Cashion, E. M. 76
Cassell, Jesse 42
  Lucenda J. 82
  Martha M. 106
Cassells, Carline 65

Connell (cont.)
James A. 13, 80
James W. 119
Jas 62
John 25
John L. 117
Jonathan 16
Martha M. 121
Mary 25
P. M. 65
Tibitha 120
W. M. 95
William 17
William M. 94
William W. 49
Wm. B. 23
Conner, C. 121
Eliza Ellen 98
Francis L. 34
Jno. L. 102
W. B. 131
Z. T. 133
Connley, Alfred 39
Considine, M. R. 124
Convill, William B. 14
Conway, Priscilla (Mrs.)
53
Conwell, Matilda 2
William B. 50
Conwill, Wm. B. 29
Cook, Alexander 36
Avy 35
E. G. B. 35
Elizabeth 8, 29, 113
Elsey 38
George 129
Henry 73
James 90
L. J. 119
Mack R. 11
Margaret E. 75
Margarett 94
Needham H. 108
Rebecca 92
Rolan T. 119
Sally 10
Samuel J. 127
Sarah 77
W. 53
Cooke, Green B. 116
R. A. 116
Coop, Jane 9
Margaret E. 57
Mary M. 131
Sarah R. 79
Coope, Rachael 20
Cooper, A. 4, 52
Alexander 3
B. J. 86, 90, 106
Benj. A. 77
Benj. F. 115
Benjamin 105
Charrity 62
Christopher 131
Christopher S. 76
Ed 103
Ephraim 72
Henry 57
Hugh 46, 47
J. C. 111
Jane 88
Jas. B. 115
John 54
John N. 67
Joseph 104
Joseph W. 44
Josiah 99
Julia Ann 93

Cooper (cont.)
Margarett 48
Martha 41, 69
Martha A. 36, 50
Mary 46, 69
Mary E. 55
Nancy S. 61
Rebecca 47
Sabra 35
Solomon 86
T. 39
Whitson 113
Wilson 46
Copeland, Delia J. 112
James 100
Racal (Mrs.) 58
Cops, Catherine 110
Corbitt, William J. 87
Corkburn, David R. 91
Corley, Mary E. 104
Nathaniel H. 61
Patsy A. 125
R. J. 118
Robt. J. 62
Sarah J. 125, 132
Thomas 41
Willy 52
Corrington, Addison 10
Cosley, C. W. (Sr.)
118
W. (Jr.) 118
Costler, William 48
Cotton, Frances S. 133
Couch, S. H. 120
Counsal, Alta 59
Counts, Robert 84
William 22
Cousins, Jas. D. 121
Thos. B. 47
Covington, Caleb H. 79
Henry G. 16
Larcus 84
T. M. 96
William 96
Cowan, B. S. 70
Benjamin S. 96
Isaac F. 70
Margaret J. 75
Margarett A. 74
Cowen, Benjamin F. 63
Henry F. 64
Cox, Alexander 10
Jas. A. 79
Margaret H. 71, 95
Moses P. 96
Nancy 66
Sapponia 47
Thena Jane 77
W. R. 86
William T. 71
Wm. T. 66
Cozzart, Robert W. 130
Craddac, Melinda 111
Craddock, Mary 72
Sarah J. 15
Thos. J. 84
William M. 88
Wm. M. 79, 84
Crafford, Nancy S. 40
Crafton, D. W. 98
Daniel W. 2, 21
J. W. 102
James W. 98, 110
John B. 32
Lucy 76
Margarett J. 125
Martha M. 19
Mary 82

Crafton (cont.)
Paul C. 19
Paul S. 2
R. L. 91
Richard L. 14
S. S. 15
Samuel S. 7
Sarah 18
Sarah P. 107
Sarah W. 42
Saul L. 2
Silas M. 14
William 7
Wm. W. 16
Crage, John 65
Craig, Easter D. 14
Elizabeth 9
Elvira 44
Jasper W. 77
Margaret W. 4
Sally M. 2
William 9
Wm. 29
Wm. H. 41, 44, 50, 51
Wm. W. 13
Craige, Eliza 37
Jane 59
Juliana 31
Samuel 31
William B. 59
Crain, Nancy 32
Crane, Susan 7, 9
Crank, James A. 80
John D. 49
Lucinda W. 87
Matilda 98
S. G. 87
William 96
William G. 62
Craven, S. 51
Crawford, Andrew J. 94
B. 29, 61, 114, 116
B. S. 99
Benoni 6
C. L. 122
Elizabeth 68
John H. 98
L. S. 106
Martha J. 125
W. C. 49, 122
Wm. C. 52, 53
Crawley, Mary E. W. 89
Creel, Nathaniel 77
Crenshaw, Elizabeth A.
44
L. C. 120
Lewis C. 88
W. E. 90
Wm. E. 70
Cresap, J. H. 123
Jas. W. 95
V. A. 121
Cress, G. W. 65
Cressap, Jas. W. 92
Crews, A. H. 125
Chrrinda 29
James 43, 49, 73
John 29, 54
Susan C. 54
William 116
William S. 89
Wm. S. 80
Cribbs, (?) (Dr.) 10
Amanda C. 130
Cullen 88
Doctor 9
E. 130
Elizabeth 89

Cribbs (cont.)
Gilbert 8
Jno. R. 28
John 3
John Y. 107
Johnston 1
Margaret Jane 75
Martha 107
Nancy 3
Sarah J. 61
Tony 112
William 1, 3, 8, 10
Wm. T. C. 61
Cribs, John R. 3
Crider, Daniel B. 28
David 19
Frances M. 33
Rosonna 17
Samuel J. 19
T. B. 28, 39, 40
Thos. B. 45
Crisp, Eliza G. 27
Mary J. 50
Crissman, James H. 83
Criswell, Emer J. 113
Crocker, A. G. 132
E. H. 23, 29, 44, 93,
97
Edwin H. 44
Elias H. 51
Frances M. 26
Irene M. 59
Mark 111
R. C. 59, 132
Rufus 67
W. S. 118
William L. 68
William S. 107
Crockett, D. M. 115
Elizabeth 6
Elizabeth J. 52
Elizabeth S. 74
Elvira 77
George W. 32
Hester 21
Jane 37
John 14, 15
John M. 128
John W. 9, 10, 15, 17,
20, 97
Malissa 91
Margaret 7
Martha Jane 64
Mary 17, 42
Nancy 14, 19
Rebecka 2
Rebecka E. 31
Robert 26
Robert P. 40
Robt. P. 22
William 7
Cromes, Frances C. 92
William 8
Croom, Jno. W. 87
Crosbey, Thos. R. 103
Crosby, Elizabeth 91
Cross, Angeline 8
E. W. 32
Freeman 25, 39
Jane 26
Crossby, Mary R. 68
Crossland, Edwin 63
Crouse, H. A. 91, 95
Crowder, L. B. 131
W. E. 91
William E. 90
Crue, Charles 29
Cruse, A. H. 124

Cudd, Simeon 70
Cullom, Wm. 101
Culp, Drucilla 12
Cummings, John 14, 16,
29
Cunningham, Allen F. 66
America 99
Ann E. 96
C. 127
Elen 122
Greenberry 92
James 27, 31
James H. 94
James M. 76
John A. 56
Lucinda 44
M. M. 116
Mary J. 85
Samul. 52
Sarah 82
Sarah J. 125
Thos. 76
W. L. 122
William C. 51
Currey, A. S. 48
Algermon S. 42
Algernon S. 60
Curry, John S. 28
Curtice, Joseph 1
Curtis, Calvin J. 43
Edward 7, 28, 36
Humphrey 31
James 7, 11
John 36
Noah 23
Peletha 28
Sampson 10
Thomas 86
Cutler, J. J. G. 65
Cyrus, David 83
Dabb, James 9
Dair, David 54
Dale, Marilda M. 68
Daley, Nathan 60
Dalton, Catharine 58
Saml. F. 87
Daly, Nathan 57
Daniel, A. O. 97
Emily O. 112
H. A. O. 122
Walter E. 29
Danner, Elizabeth 96
Levi G. 54, 64
P. G. 127
Darnald, Hannah H. 64
John 46
Darnell, Susan A. 82
Darnold, William M. 67
Darr, Levi 88
Daugherty, Clary 8
Daughtry, Mary 43
Daughty, Nancy 114
Dausson, Johnathan 13
David, Sarah 131
Davidson, A. A. 133
A. L. 27
A. M. 114
A. S. 5, 28
Alfred 48
Alfred F. 34, 51
Elizabeth Ann 22
Harratt E. 34
J. H. 132
James C. 66
Jno. H. 126
John D. 20, 21
John W. 30

Davidson (cont.)
Judith J. 20
Julia L. 19
Lucy Jane 126
M. L. 39, 61
Mariah E. 45
Martha M. 61
Mary 122
Mary E. 87
Menurva F. 119
Miles L. 34
Robert B. 31
Sally 8
Samuel M. 89
Sarah 122
Thomas B. 68
W. C. 132
W. H. 19
William 56
William M. 113
William O. 48
Wilson L. 21, 26
Wm. J. 29
Wm. O. 40
Davidsson, Harriett 13
Sabry 5
Davis, A. 27, 36
Abigal 23
Adam 107
Alderson 46
Anderson 12
Angaline E. 34
Ann F. 104
Elijah 1
Eliza 67, 72
Elizabeth 122
Elizabeth C. 12
Emanuel 69
Frances E. 125
G. W. 124
H. H. 47
Hazekiah J. 42
Hiram 4
I. G. 127
Isham F. 69
J. H. 112
J. M. 116, 129
James 84
James H. 95
James R. 105
Jno. L. 89
John 3, 99
John C. 56, 59, 62
John D. 81
John L. 7, 18, 31,
40, 44, 45, 49, 52
John M. 126
Jonathan 127
Julia 112
King G. W. 109
Louiza C. 82
Margarett A. 100
Maria 57
Mary J. 33
Minerva 114
N. P. 123
Polly 98
R. N. 118, 126, 130
R. W. 92, 121, 122,
126
Robert N. 85
Sally 10
Sarah A. H. 88
Sarah J. 111
Sarah S. 3
Thomas B. 119
Thos. G. 116
W. H. 112

144

Davis (cont.)
 Wesley B. 35
 William J. 112
 William M. 128
 Wm. B. 40
Daw, Martha Jane 114
Dawson, Hiram 6
 John 95
 Johnathan 25, 28
 Johnithan 63
Dawtry, Bryant T. 50
 Sean 74
 Susan C. 80
Day, George 97
 Jane 127
 Martha E. 96
Dean, Eliza 81
 James R. 116
 John H. 116
 Martha E. 37
 Rebecca 62
Delph, Daniel 11
 Matilda A. 126
Dement, Elizabeth 52
 Elizabeth C. 89
 James T. 85
 John S. 96
 Martha E. 81
 Marting S. 59
 Mary F. 92
 Wm. T. 89
Demoss, Ferroby 93
Dennis, Haskey 25
Denwiddie, Alex M. 63
 Rebecca J. 43
Deshong, James Y. 93
Desmond, Jeremiah 127
Dewberry, Jessee 133
 John 111
Dial, Abraham S. 19
 David 4
 Hester Ann 7
 James M. 62
 John 88
 Milly 4
 Sarah 19
 William K. 62
Dibrell, J. B. 81
 Joseph B. 7
Dibrill, Lean G. 17
Dickason, Eli 21
Dickens, B. F. 100
 Emely K. 71
 Hasty 61
 Juda 56
 M. I. S. S. 100
 R. C. 118
 Richard 42
 Wm. T. 46
Dickerson, John W. 106
 Lewis 55
 Martha 51
Dickey, Amy E. 110
 Anderson 43
 Caroline T. 107
 D. C. 70, 132
 David 5
 George W. 8
 M. A. 97
 Mary 60
 Mary Ann 72
 N. A. 118
 Polly 46
 Rebecca Jane 70
 Sary 9
 T. E. 129
 W. C. 110
Dickins, Louisa 82

Dickins (cont.)
 Manassa 113
 Reuben C. 85
 Richard 36
 Robert 60
 Teressa H. 70
 Thomas C. 97
 W. 33
 William T. 53
Dickinson, Sarah A. 127
Dickson, A. F. 123
 D. B. 51
 David B. 55
 George W. 78
 James M. 106
 Jno. L. 101
 John J. 120
 Julia A. E. 108
 Letha 12
 Levina I. 10
 Martha E. 111
 Mary Eliza 69
 Mary R. 12
 Nathanial 26
 Pegy 2
 Robert T. 123
 Sarah 113
 Sarah J. 67
 William P. 118
 Wm. T. 44, 55
Dicky, Ann 50
Didrell, J. B. 13
 Sarah E. 75
Diel, J. N. 66
Diggins, Nancy 18
 Sally 11
Dill, J. N. 47
 Jerrimiah H. 37
 John 22, 41
 Larry 41
 Leroy R. 47
 Nancy 18
 S. P. 39
 Z. N. 37, 47
 Zebelum N. 42
 Zebolum 18
 Zebulm 2
 Zebuln 4
Dillard, William N. 26
Dinny, Solomon 59
Dinwiddie, P. M. 88
Dinwiddy, Jno. H. 36
Diskill, Joseph Y. 26
Dixon, David B. 1
 John H. 1
 Lydia 3
Dockings, Sarah 32
Dockins, Susan C. 78
Dodd, A. G. 96
 Allen G. 93
 James M. 61
 Sarah F. 124
Dodson, Jonah Y. 59
 R. J. 59
 Robert J. 59, 124
 Sarah E. 125
 Wadkins D. 63
 Watkins H. 49
 Wm. H. 131
Doherty, Elizabeth A. 123
Dolan, Elizabeth 85
 Jane 64
 Lyda 67
Doland, Elizabeth 46
Donaldson, Ann E. 34
 Ebenezer 2
 Elizabeth A. 24

Donaldson (cont.)
 H. 16
 Humphrey 12, 14, 19, 20
 James 58
 Jane C. 59
 Jas. 69
 John 49
 Joshua 20, 22, 24, 28, 31
 Julia 26
 Margarett J. 58
 Mary A. 49
 Peter L. 96
 Sarah J. 53
 Susan G. 71
 William 43
 Wm. J. 37
Donel, Harriet 18
Doolin, P. A. 39
Doonel, Wm. 18
Dorset, Mary 30
 Mary A. 61
Dorsett, Person K. 66
Dossett, James R. 102
 Jas. R. 95
 P. K. 102, 123
Doud, Melinda 67
Dougherty, E. C. 37
 Jas. F. 10
 William S. 8
 Wm. S. 8
Doughtry, Samuel 105
Dover, William 126
Dowell, Charlotte 11
 James 83, 89, 116
 Julia Ann 28
 Julian 89
 W. B. 64
 Wiley B. 43
 William 18
Dowland, David 11
 Henry 11
 Jno. T. 85
 Metilda S. 133
 Susanah 109
Dowlen, Timothy 57
Downey, William 16
Doxey, James 27
 Lener 38
 Simon 78
 Wilson 65
Dozer, Nany 29
 Philip 38
 William 29
Dozier, Ellenor 108
 I. N. 129
 Isaac N. 113
 Peter L. 61
Drake, Ann E. 107
 Caroline (Mrs.) 92
 Mary J. 97
Draper, Louisa R. 111
Drinkard, Francis P. 108
Driskell, Ferney G. 37
 J. S. 52
 Julia A. 52
 Nancy L. 46
Driskill, William R. 43
Dryden, Jonathan B. 22
Duberry, Nancy 60
Duet, Rosa Ann 63
Duffee, Nancy 36
 P. M. 36
Duffy, Henry 33
Dugan, John 79
Duggan, James B. 48

Etchison (cont.)
W. R. 94
Wilson R. 96
Etherage, Ellenander 27
Etheredge, Jerred 15
Rachael 15
Sarah 15
Etheridge, John 38, 70
Joseph J. 26
Ethridge, Jerrod J. 64
Mark 112
Mary 100
Rhoda 71
Thos. H. 46
Eudaley, Martha 77
Eudaly, Clement 50
Harrit 50
Malessa 112
Evans, Catharine 16
Daniel 87
David C. 78
Ely 15
Jno. W. 2,3
Joel T. 114
John 38
John W. 5, 11, 14
Levi 122, 129
Martha M. 59
Morning P. 64
Nathan 115
Thomas 10
Everett, Benjamin F. 85
Evins, Abner 50
Abner A. 66
John 51
Ewing, Abner 37
Z. C. 81
Exum, Franklin 131
Ezell, Calvin S. 81
Fair, Edward 71
Mary Jane 71
Fairless, Celia F. 121
Fanner, Patrick 103
Fanon, John 109
Fargurson, Martha J. 96
Farmer, Mildred E. 66
Rebecca 124
Farr, Emeline 104
Mary A. 122
Farris, Martha A. 84
Robert 7
Sarah 24
Thos. H. 84
William 68
Farrow, Elisha 119
Farthing, Lydia 122
S. B. 100
Solsly 47
Fasthing, Salesbury 8
Faulkner, Lafayette 92
Fawbess, Soniza C. 72
Featherston, James 101
John W. 108
Louisa H. 102
Phebe A. 95
William J. 52
Feeley, Daniel 76
Feeman, T. S. 75
Felts, E. J. 104
Martha 87
William 102
Fergarson, Allen 56
Lazerus 91
Ferguson, Allen 11, 14
Mary 14
William 6
William J. 14
Wm. 5, 11

Ferless, Nancy J. 109
Ferrel, Thomas 75
Ferrell, Alfred 43, 45
Charles 127
John C. 124
Major 45
Maranda 47
Samuel 82, 111
William H. 108
Ferress, G. C. 128
Mary F. 128
Ferril, Martha H. 68
Nancy 70
Ferrill, Thomas 59
Ferris, Geo. C. 51
George C. 51
Ferriss, E. W. 126
Fetherston, Charles E.
89
Fewel, Benj. 45
Benjamin 14
Fewell, Benj. C. 38
John P. 122
Field, Delila S. 72
Thos. A. 130
Fielder, E. H. 118
J. J. 30
J. S. 118
John J. 19
Lucenda C. 93
Sarah F. 96
Wm. P. S. 30
Fielding, Matilda J. 16
Fields, Andrew T. 43
Daniel B. 118
Elizabeth G. 16
Elizabeth J. 35
Francis 20
Hansford A. 70
J. H. 118
J. T. 49
James H. 43
John T. 43
Julia A. 21
Luzuna M. 74
Martha C. 123
Mary Ann 35
Mary M. 71, 73
Nancy J. 41
Peter G. 55
Sarah 32
Thos. F. 57
W. D. 33
William B. 71
Wm. D. 44
Fifer, Mary P. 58
Pernemus 50
William 67
Finch, Boldin 5
Rebecca 115
Finey, Mary Ann 24
Finley, John 29
Robert F. 18, 20
Fisher, George M. 27,
120
John H. 37
Mary Jane 27
Nancy 8
Nancy C. 126
Nancy M. 8
Pleasant 15
Thomas 114
Thos. H. 37, 40, 48
William O. 83
Wm. O. 69
Fite, Elizabeth 91
John R. 88
Martha 7

Fite (cont.)
Mary 63
Phebe 19
Sarah J. 115
Thos. J. 34, 35, 81
W. C. 20, 27
William C. 39
Wm. 36
Wm. C. 11, 34
Fitzgerald, Elizabeth J.
111
Houston 110
Mary F. 129
R. D. 132
Sarah J. 132
Fleming, Elizabeth 111
Erasmus A. 86
J. A. 93
Martha 102
Fletcher, A. J. 122
Abner J. 74
Barbary 66
Casey L. 126
Elizabeth 28, 112
Elizabeth N. 88
Elvy 37
Henry 17, 21, 47
Isaac L. 111
J. F. 133
J. L. 115
James R. 112
Jonah 37
Joseph 6
Josiah 16, 17, 19
Lucy 81
Malinda 45
Martha 15
Martha C. 91
Mary Ann 87
Matilda 40
Nancy 21, 104
Paul 51
Phebe 93
Reuben 10, 23
Thomas 6, 8, 19, 20
U. A. 118
W. A. 111, 133
William 8, 9
Flinn, Philip 36
Flinter, Charity 15
Stewart 12
Flippin, A. R. 61
Frances 101
J. H. 127
J. L. 94
J. T. 36
Jabes H. 133
James A. 52, 61
Jas. A. 70
Jesse 22
Jno. L. 28
Joseph T. 41
Patience E. 94
Rody 109
Tennessee 112
Thos. A. 36, 98
William J. 70
Flowers, Alfred 55, 56,
89, 123, 127
Allen 82, 95
Asher 20, 37
B. S. 128
Barnabas 54, 56, 57
Barnabus 66
Blakers 123
Briant 22
Bryant 22
Burnell 131

147

Flowers (cont.)
Calvin 54, 80, 127
David 46, 57, 64
Edmund 43
Edmund K. 66
Edney 40
Eliza 33
Elizabeth 20, 44, 127
Harrett 49, 84
Henry 13, 23
Hillorry 19
Jacob 22, 57, 75
Jacob C. 84
Jane A. 116
Jesse 7, 22
Jessee 34, 55
John 13, 28, 43, 115
John W. 20, 23
Ketsey 96
Leoma 43, 74
Leoma (Jr.) 41
M. 106, 112
M. A. 118
Martha 57, 70
Martha E. 106
Martha M. 108, 128
Mary 41, 54, 77, 115
Mary A. 131
Matt W. 42
Michael 36, 40, 41
Nancy 86
R. B. 131
Sarah 114
Sarah A. 65
Sarah J. 38
Susan (Mrs.) 39
Tempy 38
Thomas 40
Thos. 132
Wile 7
Wm. 95
Floyd, Elizabeth A. 34
William F. 97
Fly, Fanny P. 2
Jno. L. 95
John 11
John L. 64, 94
Martha T. 17
Mary 16
Micajah 60
Winiford 26
Wm. D. 18, 30
Folks, L. E. C. 122
Follis, Miles H. 93
Fonville, Edwin 11
John 11
Julian 4
W. W. 126
William A. 15
Ford, Arta M. 120
Edmond 21
Elizabeth 118
J. A. 112
John 1, 6, 32
John F. 102
Josiah S. 62
Martha 91
Martha E. 128
Mary Ann 74
Nathan W. 90
P. 76, 122
Pelina N. 117
Rebecca 5, 7
Sterling B. 66, 71
T. J. 120
Foren, Alex 17
George W. 75
Lucretia 90

Foren (cont.)
Mary 117
William 22, 122
Forest, Mark 5
Watson 18
Forester, Charles 20
Dillard 9
James 8, 20
John B. 51
Mary 18
William 8, 9
Forran, Harriet 22
Forren, Alex 47
William 47
Forrester, Anne 4
Charles 10, 33
Rebecka 6
Forristed, Henry 97
Forsythe, Lucretia 129
Mary I. 129
Fortune, William 41
Forville, W. A. 93
Foster, A. P. 119
Andrew P. 28
B. R. 125
David C. 120
David W. 97
Hamilton 66
J. C. 58
James P. 73
Jno. C. 94
John C. 42, 47
John W. 40
Joseph A. 130
Louisa 109
Mary A. 42
Murry W. 104
Nancy 80
Robt. B. 65
Sarah C. 120
Thos. H. 40
William B. 71
Wm. 111
Fouch, Elizabeth E. 118
Fouster, B. R. 116
Foutch, John 106
Sarah Jane 81
William V. 84
Fowler, Ellender 38
Hannah 80
Hardy 32
Isaac 35, 47, 48, 86
Jas. F. 88
Martha 18
Mary 44
Milly B. 75
Nancy 15
Sarah 102
William S. 76
Winney 12
Fox, A. J. 95
Alen 4, 10, 14
Alexander 95
Allen 25, 30, 69
Daniel 69
Darcus 54
Edward 25
Elizabeth 10
Enoch 54
Jackson 30
John O. 76, 122
Johnston 46
Mary 122
Nany 40
Paton 7
Polly 2
William 7, 57, 62
Wm. 69

Fox (cont.)
Wm. T. 76
Franklin, Robert 4
Frayer, Helana S. 57
Frazer, Rachel 11
Frazier, Troy 87
Freeman, Asberry M. 122
Claiborn A. 53
Cynthia W. 83
Edmund A. 65
Eliza Jans 15
Elizabeth 77
Frances 100
Kinchen 20
Kinchin 17
Martha W. 95
Mary 95
Precilla H. 22
R. F. 81
Rachael 23
Richard 22
Thomas J. 86
Thomas W. 83
Thos. J. 129
Thos. S. 124
Thos. W. 100
W. W. 100, 129
William 8, 9, 35
Wm. W. 111
Zachariah 95
Frierson, Margaret E. 42
Frost, Isaac N. 55
Louisa 35
Fry, Joseph H. 93
Fuel, Ben 2
Benjamin 5
Rubin 40
Fuell, Benjamin 51
John P. B. 45
Fulerton, Margarett 8
Fulghum, William 4
William R. 118
Fuller, Arthur 24
Leathen 23
Spivy 12
Fullerton, Hugh A. 24
John S. 29
S. C. 69
Saml. C. 67
Fuqua, Clement F. 37
Elizabeth 50
Lucinda E. 68
Samuel R. 91
Stephen 16
William 37
Fuquea, Samuel R. 40
Furgarson, Barnet 39
Emaly 58
Joel 52
Joel F. 44
Joseph W. 121
Mary E. 81
Pheby 32
Susan E. 94
Teletha (Mrs.) 52
Thomas 56
Thos. 52
Wm. 36
Furgenson, Martha J. 74
Furgerson, Harris J. 107
Nancy M. 100
Tibitha C. 129
Gage, Alfred 46
Ann A. 116
David 52, 109
Milford 41, 67
Gague, William 73
Gailard, Narcissa 21

Gaily, Clinton 106
Galard, David C. 77
  Mary A. 99
Galey, Clinton 44
Gallian, S. M. 128
Gallien, Mary F. 87
Gallion, Sarah A. 104
  William W. 96
Gambell, John 6
Gamer, Elizabeth 119
Gammon, Marmaduke 34
  William R. 57
Gant, Elizabeth L. 113
  Martha J. 47
  William 48
  William H. 42
Gantry, G. W. 13
Gardiner, S. E. 119
Gardner, Ann Louiza J.
  71
  David 35
  J. J. 101
  James W. 37, 60
  Jane Ann 63
  Jemmina A. 83
  Martha 58
  Martha A. 130
  William 50, 60
  Wiloly 89
Garrett, William 103
Garrison, E. J. 123
  M. F. 25
  Matthew M. 72
Garrott, Vinson 54
Garwood, Joseph 28
Gaskins, Amos 13
  Thomas 15
  Thos. 13
Gateley, J. M. 85
Gately, Henry 21
  J. M. 59
  John W. 59
Gather, Elizabeth 54
Gatley, Jno. W. 62
Gauger, Daniel 46
Gault, Henry M. 49, 50
Gay, Alfred 17
  Elizabeth 105
  Mary S. S. 130
  P. M. 128
  William 114
Gaynin, Wm. S. C. 58
Gaza, Joshua 42
Gee, Rebecca 51
  Smith H. 20
  Wm. 29
Genest, Louisa 28
Gentry, Caroline 16
  Frederick B. 16
  George W. 20
  Mary C. 11
  William 21
George, C. E. 53, 58
  Caswell E. 50, 60, 105
  James T. 53
  Laney 101
  Ruth 106
Geylard, Thomas 4
Gibbs, J. L. 85
  Judy F. 56
  Martha B. 103
  Turner R. 34, 50
Gibson, Anderson 39
  Irvin 35
  James 27, 66
  James H. 50, 76
  Lucenda 25
  Mary 34

Gibson (cont.)
  Mary O. 1
  Sarah H. 22
  Sarah J. 76
  William 22, 30, 64
Gilbrath, Jas. 83
Gilchrist, Amanda G. 19
  B. 90
  I. B. 37
  Juliana 10
  L. B. 41, 42, 44, 45,
    47, 50, 69, 84, 86,
    87, 91, 95, 98
  Lucion B. 66
  Martha E. 9
  Robert J. 12
  L. B. 98
Giles, Alminda N. J. 89
  James J. 79
  Jas. J. 87
  Pernu 55
Gill, Elizabeth A. F. 41
  George W. 50
  John P. 68
  Lucy 127
  Rebecca Elender 99
  Robert 117, 118
  William F. 94
Gilland, Sarah 16
Gillespie, Amanda 99
  Elizabeth H. 102
  Jno. C. 3
  John C. 31
  Lucy A. 79
  Mariah W. 76
  Mary Ann 79
  Sarah J. 49
Gilliam, R. M. 113
Gilliland, Aron J. 93
  Elizabeth 28
  Francis 18
  J. W. 67
  Jno. W. 82, 84
  Liddy 26
  Malinda 52
  Manerva 45
  Tericy 96
Gillum, William P. 3
Givens, Carrie L. 111
  S. D. 30
  Saml. D. 35
  Samuel D. 42
Glaason, Mary Ann E. 73
Glascock, Edmund J. 90
  Jones 49, 51
  Martha 30
  Nany 51
  Peter 41
  S. M. 30
  Scarlet M. 30, 41
  Spenson 51
Glasgow, J. W. 47, 114
  Jas. W. 27
  John M. 123
  Melissa 106
Glason, Cenith C. 73
  John E. 123
  Sarey 7
Glass, John 95
  John H. 79
  Mathew A. 11
Glasscock, Lucenda 19
  Malinda 10
  Nancy 22
  Polly 5
  Rachael 17
  Sarah 23
Gleason, John 96

Gleason (cont.)
  John E. 128
  Nancy 22, 29
  Timothy 71
Gledsoe, Mary E. 91
Gleeson, Timothy 120
Glesson, Patrick 47
Glidewell, Nany 42
Glidwell, Samuel 18
Glimp, David C. 119
Glisson, Abraham 119
  Abram 45
  Barbery 84
  Clarissa 77
  Daniel 80
  Elizabeth J. 95
  Everett 121
  George W. 84
  Harrett 83
  Marshall B. 108
  Rachal 65
  Saml. 77
  Stephen H. 86
  W. H. 84, 86
  Yancy D. 107
Glover, F. M. 125
Godwin, Elam 132
Goff, Carline M. 37
  Join 33
  Thomas W. 24
Gooch, Bennet 39
  Bennett 39
  Winney 45
Good, Mary W. 132
Gooden, Bartlett 64
  William W. 24
Goodin, Susan V. 111
Goodloe, Amandy C. 112
  Aqula J. 49
  I. M. C. 103
  Susan 102
Goodlow, Robert H. 18
Goodman, D. C. 119
  David C. 119
  Eliza M. 117, 118
  Elizabeth 23, 35
  F. G. 10, 16, 23, 34
  Frances 85
  Jas. R. 93
  John J. 130
  Louiza V. 131
  Mary Ann 68
  Mercilla 12
  Samuel 31
  Samuel A. 115
  Susan A. 117
  William 10, 15
  William (Jr.) 18
  William B. 68
  William L. 9
Goodrich, Catharine 61
  Edmond W. 33
  Gedion 57
  Phebi Jane 56
Goodwin, Elam 77
  Green B. 72
  Luiza J. 102
  Meedy 86
Gordan, James F. 96
Gordon, David 2, 3
  Eliza J. 121
  Mary E. 115
  Robert S. 101
  Sarah Jane 69
  Watson 123
Gosey, Mark 18
Gossett, Burrell 23, 34
  Wesley R. 59

Gouger, Daniel 31
  Sarah 106
Gowan, Drury 90
  R. M. 96
  Richard M. 82
  Sophonia E. 90
  William J. 82
  Wm. J. 90
Grace, James H. 88
Graddy, Catherine 40
  J. F. 122
  Jessee 58
  Lena E. 113
  Robert 113
  Samuel 104
  Samuel A. 116
  Sarah M. 110
  Susan F. 116
  Travis F. 98
Grady, Frances 132
  Hepsy A. 99
  Hester 45
  Jane C. 58
  Jesse 4
  Marcus L. 69, 88
  Rigdon 22
  Robert R. 106
  Sarah A. 91
  William 54, 110
  Willis 95, 109
  Willis L. A. 98
Grafton, Paul C. 100
Grant, Matilda W. 17
Grave, Andrew 36
Graves, J. L. 84
  Joseph S. 85
  Nathaniel H. 128
Gray, Hester H. 6
  Nicholas 6
  William 93
Grayer, Sarah M. 57
Grayor, Charlotte 10
Green, Allen 93
  C. P. 119
  Cordelia J. 123
  Edmund 55
  Fanny 50
  Harrett M. 101
  John 52, 60
  Lafayett 102
  Louisa E. 101
  Martha T. 70
  Mary E. 127
Greenwell, Sarah A. 132
Greer, Amanda C. 129
  Dorthula 128
  H. W. 112
  James 84
  Jason 82
  Jesse 87
  Jessee 92
  Jno. C. A. 121
  John A. 108
  Julia Ann 85
  Margaret S. 93
  Nancy O. 82
  Rowland 70
  Samuel S. 95
  Susan C. 84
  T. E. 113
  Thos. 74, 85
  Zachariah 83
Greggory, Mary 34
Gregory, Catharina 82
  Jane 41
  Margaret 13
  Thomas 45
Grey, Archer T. 84

Grey (cont.)
  M. J. 91
Grice, Elizabeth 31
  William 48
Grier, A. M. 84
  Elijah 98
  J. C. A. 110
  Jacob T. 41
  James P. 30, 36, 37,
    44, 50
  Julia A. 132
  Martha Ann 67
  Nancy Jane 39
  Quincy M. 68
  S. A. 50
Griffee, John H. 9, 12
  Margaret 9
  Penelope 11
Griffey, Charles 61, 73
Griffin, Allen 26
  Andrew J. 81
  Arreana 22
  F. M. 124, 126
  Jas. M. 68
  Jerome 20
  John S. 91, 94
  Joshua J. 83
  Margrat G. 23
  Martha 86
  Sarah 30
  Stanley 16
Griffy, Elizabeth 13
  Margaret E. 60
  Sarah A. 73
Grigory, May 37
Grigsby, A. A. 100
  A. A. P. 33, 41
  Sarah 65
  William T. 99
Grimes, S. J. 100
Grisham, George W. 52
Grishum, Elizabeth 99
Grissom, Ann 108
  James 61
  Lafayett 114
  Mary 124
  Mary Elizabeth 133
  Willis B. 101
Grissum, Willis P. 95
Grist, Jas. H. 85
  Sarah 69
Groom, C. R. 69
Grundy, James P. H. 4
Guess, Elizabeth 31
Guinn, William C. 59
Gullett, Jane 118
Gullick, J. S. 113
Gunner, Nancy C. 103
Gunter, Elizabeth 43
  Flora 67
  J. M. 110
  Mary 49
Gurganes, Abram 126
Gurganus, James 100
  Mary A. 95
Guthrie, Mary G. 89
Gwinn, Nancy 64
Hadin, George W. 51
Haeslip, Johnathan J.
  108
Hagard, Emily C. 104
Haggird, Wm. H. 95
Hague, John 110
  Mary C. 68
  Roda A. 130
  Selina A. 62
Haguewood, Elizabeth 32
Hail, Elizabeth 44

Hail (cont.)
  Emeline J. 37
  John 37
  Joseph 69
  Lydia A. 72
  Mary 63
  Mary A. 27
  Mary E. 82
  Thomas 13
Hailey, Elizabeth 31
  Louiza J. 131
  Margaret A. 73
  Mary 63
  Pheby 42
  Thomas J. 124
  Thos. J. 131
  W. H. 39
Haily, William 39
Hains, James T. 11
  Milly 3
Haislip, Johnathan J. 65
  William 65
Haist, David 47
Hale, E. W. 33
  Henry 90
  J. H. 114
  Joana 43
  Jos. J. J. 70
  Joseph J. J. 72
  Joseph P. 76
  Julius 123
  Lucy 40
  Madison 107
  Mary 79
  Mary J. 114
  Nancy E. 104
  Reen Allice 127
  Robert 112
  Thos. E. 102
  William J. 114
  Wm. H. 70
Hales, Henry 87
Haley, David L. 7
  Edward 15
  George 85
  John A. 9
  John W. 124
  Martha 8
  Sterling 80
  Sterling B. 7, 13
  Susan E. 124, 125
  Thos. J. 117
  W. P. 102
Halford, J. M. 46
  James M. 62
  Jas. M. 26
  John E. 37
  John R. 29
  Joseph W. 36
  M. L. 88
  M. T. 103
  Sarah 55
  Sarah L. 42
  William M. 43
  Wm. M. 62, 115
Haliburton, Susan 54
Hall, Andy 124
  Ann Row 10
  Bennett G. 53
  Burton 52
  Caswell P. 71
  D. B. 123
  David 133
  David B. 83
  E. D. 120
  Elizabeth Ann 35
  Ema C. 100
  Emely 12

Hart (cont.)
 Selay A. 36
 Sirena 102
Harte, J. 36
Harts, Jane 25
Hartsfield, Jas. A. 116
 John C. 94
 Mary W. 105
 O. 132
 Sarah L. 88
 W. G. 96
 William S. 115
Harvey, E. H. 102
 E. W. 89
 Franklin S. 104
 W. H. 95
 William H. 74
Harvy, R. H. 39
 Willie S. 30
Harwood, J. A. 91
 James A. 17, 49
 Louisa 118
 R. D. 114
Haskins, Edward 8
 Spill C. 20
Hassell, Daniel 92, 110
 Daniel D. 69, 96
 David 103
 George E. 107
 J. 99
 Jno. 103
 John 86, 105
 John P. 3, 22
 Jordon 10
 Margaret 41
 Mary H. 85
Hast, Judy 49
Hatcher, Henry 81
Hatchett, Hardinia J. 70
 Mary A. 57
 Nancy L. 32
 Rufus K. 76
 S. W. 46, 68, 75, 78
 Saml. W. 45
 Samuel W. 88
Hauger, Henrietta L. 105
Hawkins, Ann M. 25
 Jane 34
 Lucinda 25
 M. B. 25
 Mathew S. 126
 Merica 10
 Moses B. 19, 51
 R. W. 59
 W. H. 51
Hawks, D. J. 96
Hay, Jacob H. 103
 Jeremiah 67
 Jerimiah 57
 John B. 57
Hayes, Emeline 90
 J. A. 41
 John 38
Haynes, Granville 40
 Isaac C. 86, 96
 J. C. 79, 92, 118
 J. M. 94
 James S. 93
 Numan 30
 Sally G. 98
Hayns, America 34
 Franklin 60
 James S. 43
 Nancy 48
Hays, Absolom F. 104
 Ann M. 40
 Hugh D. 25
 J. M. 55

Hays (cont.)
 James 23, 24
 James E. 93
 James H. 50
 Jane 65
 Jessee J. 55
 Jno. F. 65
 John 2
 John A. 42, 102
 John B. 2
 John F. 66, 93
 M. L. 102
Haywood, William R. 87
Hazelwood, Joseph F. 72
 Martha 45
Hazlewood, M. F. 116
 W. 97
 William R. 68
Head, Henry 27
 John T. 99
 M. R. 110
Heard, C. B. 128
 Mary 99
Heath, Evelina G. A. 94
 H. T. 97, 116
 Harett J. 43
 Harry S. 128
 Mary Ann 74
 Richard 18
 William H. 94
Heathcock, John 18
Hector, Martha 9
Hedgecock, J. H. 129
Hefley, Henry W. 62
Hellard, George C. 78
Henderson, John O. 76
 Samuel C. 109
 Vilott Amanda 24
 William 53, 85
Hendrick, Daniel R. 32
 Elizabeth 9
 William 20
 Wm. R. 32
Hendricks, Mary 31
Hening, Mary J. E. 61
Henings, Celestia A. 91
Henry, Cornelia F. 67
 John P. 42, 120
 Johnathan 22
 Parthenia C. 93
 Samuel 8
Hensley, John H. 121
Herington, Frances 132
Heriod, Mary 102
Herndon, Anderson 124
 J. W. 22
 Madison F. 99
 Mary M. 108
 Thomas 91
Herod, John H. 16
Herrington, Rosa Ann 88
Herron, William 32
Hersey, Alvira 100
Hess, A. C. 125
 Elizabeth W. 116
 J. A. W. 61, 89, 94,
  99, 116
 James A. W. 10, 11
 Jas. A. W. 10, 87
 Louisana 10
 Margaret E. 88
 Maria 31
 Marion W. 101
 Mary Adaline 63
 N. J. 27, 31, 34
 Neilson J. 35
 Nelmen I. 3
 Nelson I. 3, 7, 11, 14

Hethcock, William 123
Hickey, Sally 1, 3
Hickman, Jabez 25
 Martha Ann 26
 William 76
Hicks, Alvinia 100
 Ashley 100
 Elsa 100
 Henry C. 108
 Jacob 87
 James 12
 Jane 7
 Jobe 15
 Margaret 31, 90
 Michael H. 35
 Ninod 105
 Rachael 97
 Redin 100
 Reding 100
 Samuel 109, 121, 123
 Susan 100
 Vina 98
 William C. 57
 Winfield S. 98
 Wm. C. 28, 35, 37,
  44, 48
Higgins, Ann E. 19
 James N. 33
 M. M. 33
 Michael 8
 Moley J. 39
 Sarah Ann 14
 Thos. 91
Hight, Elizabeth M. 84
 Jas. D. 125
 R. A. 84
Hignight, Mary 21
Hill, Allen 34
 Alvadas 33
 Awella D. 34
 Baird 4
 Betheny 80
 C. L. 99
 Catharine H. 35
 E. C. 99
 Green 36
 James 116
 James N. 97
 Jas. J. 128
 Jas. N. 97
 John H. 80
 John S. 45
 John W. 115
 Mary 85
 Mary Jane 101
 Pleasant 14
 Saml. S. 98
 W. V. 123
 Wm. L. 83, 85
Hillard, Cloa 36
 Elizabeth C. 107
 Pherraby 63
Himbrough, George 31
Hines, D. G. 109
 Solomon 21, 22
 Thomas J. 21
 Wm. 98
Hinsen, J. B. 36
Hinson, Allis 119
 James W. 131
 Jas. S. 82
Hintom, Edwin H. 48
Hisaw, David 51
 June 52
Hite, Christopher 24
Hix, C. W. 132
 Elvina 114
 James Y. 114

Keathley (cont.)
Sina 33
Sophonia E. 82
Keathly, Archalus 35
Archelus 89
Branch 76
Charrity 57
Elisha 57, 99
Elizabeth 28
Marshall B. 103
Murtial B. 76
Nancy 46
Keating, Jane N. 54
Keaton, G. H. 119
Kee, Louisa 128
Keely, Edmund 95
Keenan, Michel 54
Keeth, Salina 103
Keith, John 27
Kell, Pennell 6
Kelley, Joseph 14
Kellough, Samuel 35
Kelly, Alee 13
Frances 111
Henry 89
James 15
Jane 80
Martha 41
Martha A. 116
Mary 92
Nancy 109
Perlina J. 114
Sophia 34
Kelton, Benj. F. 97
Elizabeth M. 97
Emily E. 117
G. H. 103
Julia L. 97
Lavina 39
Mary A. 104
Robert H. 112
Sarah C. 118
Thos. W. 62
William S. 128
Wm. P. 33
Kelzoe, Nany 55
Kenaday, Thos 26
Kenady, Abron 26
James M. 107
Mary 35
Rachell 16
Kenday, Eliza 38
Kennady, Henry 97
Jas. M. 84
Kenneday, Henry 20
Kennedy, Hardy 19
James 2
Polly 4
Sarah A. L. 126
Sarah J. 101
Thos. J. 80
Kennon, Mary A. 126
Kensey, Margarett A. 122
Nancy 38
Kerns, William M. 114
Kerr, John N. 30
W. C. 100
Kersey, John D. 93
Kevit, Louisa 22
Key, Mary E. 108, 122
Keys, David G. 122
James 115
Jas. N. 121
M. M. 122
Sarah E. 124
Killingsworth, Rebecca 41
Kilzar, Elijah 51

Kilzer, Elijah 50
James 93
James B. 104
Kilzoe, Elijah 53
Kimbro, John 26, 27
Matilda A. 94
Matilda M. 95
Rebecca E. 62
W. M. 113
Kincey, Samuel 69
King, Abraham 8
Alen 14
Augustus W. 2
Austin A. 4
Benassa 65
Biddy 60
Francis H. 6
G. W. 116
Henry 41, 42
Henry A. 102
Isabella 80
J. D. 109, 125
J. P. 130
James H. 72
John A. 79
John H. 102
John R. 3
M. B. 54, 57
Margaret 53
Mary A. 66
Mary Ann 15
Phillip 58
R. F. 69, 128
Rufus E. 96
Rufus F. 84
Sarah 71
Stephen 69, 121
Thomas 88, 102
Thomas W. 9
Thos. 79
Thos. Jas. Nicholas 54
William A. 63
Kingcade, Lucretia E. 92
Kinley, John 9
Kinsey, Elizabeth 43
Felix G. 75
Henry 31
Jno. 98
Joseph J. 81
Mary J. 110
Peter H. 75
Samuel 70
Kinton, Chapman 116
Kirby, Henderson 70
Kirkman, Robert S. 52
Kirkpatrick, John 43
Kirksey, Abraham 12
Martha A. 26
Young 12
Kirsey, Elizabeth 9
Klyce, Andrew J. 38
Duke 50
Knight, Sally H. 19
Knott, Elizabeth 54
Henry 71, 92
J. J. 118
John 97
Polly 49
Sarah 63
W. G. 129, 133
William G. 101
Know, Absolom 14
Knox, Absolom 14, 34
James F. 123
Jas. F. 109
John 34

Know (cont.)
Jordan 69
Mary M. 98
Sarah B. 69
Lacey, Mary 14
Lacy, John C. 90
John D. 100
Polly A. 24
Lain, Abner G. 79
Cannon H. 101
Lainer, Sophia J. 103
Lammons, James 4
Lamoine, Francis 124
Lamons, Nancy 7
Landers, Mary 29
Landin, Meriah E. 28
Landis, B. 119
Benj. 68
Benjamin 75
J. B. 46
Landran, Robert 9
Landrum, A. R. 101
Adam 87
James W. 101
Jas. W. 85
Robert 17
Lane, Abner G. 91
Caroline S. 115
Eva J. 60
Joel 60
M. C. 120
M. M. 115
Melissa C. 127
Polly 23
S. C. 88
Saml. C. 86
Samuel C. 89
William 36, 39
Willis H. 38
Langford, James E. 69
John W. 74
N. S. 69
Langham, Mary M. 111
Langley, William W. B. 10
Wm. W. B. 10
Lanhann, W. R. 104
Lanier, Thomas D. 128
Thos. H. 101
Lankford, Nicholas L. 11
Laper, Erma 93
Lasiter, Elijah 127
Lasly, John H. 52
Lassiter, Andrew 51
Audrea J. 91
Jas. M. 22
Jesse 33
Lathain, Frances 29
Latham, Leander 85
Latta, Charles T. 131
Harvey M. 17
James 61
Robert S. 89
Lattie, Elizabeth 5
Nancy 19
Latty, Margaret 33
Laughter, Martha 22
Sopha W. 43
Laurance, Adaline 81
Laurence, J. F. 92
Lavis, Elizabeth J. 37
Lawrance, Charles J. 43
George M. D. 49
H. C. 23
L. D. 98
Lawrence, Frances E. 105
George W. 86

Lawrence (cont.)
  Isaac 15
  L. D. 116
  Leander D. 56
  William L. 127
Laymon, Absolum B. 68
  Franklin 68
  Isaac 44
  James 23
  John 23
  William 75, 117
Lea, Eliza J. 58
  George W. 58
  J. J. J. A. 67
  Jerman W. 46
  Martha A. 50
  Mary E. 67
  Robert F. 79
  Sarah L. 102
  Zelphia J. 112
Leach, Joseph D. 130
Leamons, Nancy 9
Lee, Elizabeth 98
  Eveline 93
  George W. 59
  J. J. A. 81
  John 115
  John C. 79
  John J. J. 59
  Louisa 87
  Nancy D. 115
  R. Ritter Clementine
    105
  Rebecca 117
  W. A. 130
Leeton, Wiliam 13
Legat, Tabitha A. 27
Legate, Elizabeth 97
  Maniza 13
Legett, Emeline 127
Leggatte, Samuel C. 16
Leggatt, Nancy J. 129
Legion, Geo. W. 120
Leigon, Albert H. 120
Lemmond, Thomas M. 92
Lemmons, Isaac 40
  Joel G. 29, 41
  Mary 40
  Wm. A. 31
Lemons, G. W. 116
  J. G. 131
  J. W. 116
  Malinda 100
  P. W. 113
Lenard, Thursa A. 87
Lenord, S. P. 77
Leonard, William 8, 9
Lepperd, Samuel 43
Lester, William 44
Lett, A. L. 75, 115
  Eliza C. 97
  John H. 88
  R. N. 91
  Robert M. 63
Levey, Archibald C. 34
Levy, Arch C. C. 115
  Archd. C. 27, 33, 50,
    55
  E. A. 122
  Emma C. 131
  Henry C. 32, 39
  Lewis 15, 17, 18,
    19, 50
Lewis, D. T. 122
  Darthul 7
  James 39
  Joel B. 61
  Martha 35

Lewis (cont.)
  Mary 10
  N. J. 122
  Obadiah 4
  Sarah 8
  Sarah A. 85
  Susan M. 61
Lidrow, Reuben 73
Liggett, Joseph 54
  Samuel C. 66
Light, Joel A. 87
Lightfoot, Ed 12
Lile, John W. 54
  Mary F. 11
Lindsly, Mary Ann 37
Linton, John F. 16
  Margaret 89
  Samuel P. 101
  Sarah 69, 101
Lions, Mary 86
Lite, John 44
  Sarah L. 30
Little, Alexander G. 91
  David 21
  David H. 10
  Eliza Ann 101
  Elizabeth 60
  Elizabeth A. 84
  Fair M. 6
  Howell 36
  Ira T. 82
  John D. 5
  Joshua 17
  Margrett D. 35
  Martha Ann 98
  Mary E. 75
  Mary J. 124
  Sally 5
  Thomas 94
Littlefield, Andrew 26
  Ben 22
  Harriet 4
  Perry H. L. 22
Livingston, Francis M. 67
  Jas. M. 67
  William C. 67
Lock, Elizabeth W. 46
  Jasper 97
Locke, George 24
Locks, Martha J. 63
Logan, James J. 38
  W. H. 119
Loller, Martha 129
London, Nancy J. 131
Long, G. W. 104
  Henry 30, 56
  Metilda 121
  Nancy 41
  Reese R. 93
  William 29
Longworth, H. A. 132
Lorance, Samuel L. 34
Lottis, Harrett 89
Lourance, S. N. 95
  William M. 105
Lourence, Thomas B. 18
Lourin, Wm. 124
Love, A. R. 92, 113,
    126, 127
  Albert G. 32
  Edward 1
  Lemuel 35
  Martha J. 100
  R. B. 41, 49
  Sarah 66
  William K. 22
  Wm. C. 29
Loveless, James S. 115

Lovell, John M. 85
Lovett, Chana 76
  G. M. 85
  Jane 82
  Nancy 47
Lovewell, Jane 1
Loving, William 44
Lovitt, George W. 88
Lovley, Jas. S. 101
Lowary, Henry 28
Lowerence, F. P. 120
Lowery, Sally 4
  William 16
Lowrance, J. K. 133
  Mary 92
Lowry, (?) 102
  Henry 107
  John B. 16, 18
  Mahaly 16
  Malinda 18, 90
  Nancy 64
  Nancy J. 66
  Samuel 66
  Stephen W. 112
  Wm. W. 68
Lucas, F. (Dr.) 74
Luster, Elizabeth 13
  Stephen 18
Lynch, James H. 59
  John 25, 28, 30, 31,
    52
  Missouri F. 82
  Sarah 19
  W. W. 110, 116
  William W. 87
Lyon, Eliza 9
  Elizabeth 38, 45
  James 40
  John 96
  John W. 58
  Luize E. 9
  Nancy L. 96
  Richard B. 73
  Sarah E. 46
  W. C. 59
Lyons, A. 32
  Alexander 30
  Mariah 62
  Martha E. 97
  Nancy 48
  Susan 66
Lytaker, Elizabeth 2
  Finas 16
Mackleroy, Micajah 17
Maclin, Landon C. 16,
    17
  Rodham 87
  William P. 59
Madaras, Eno Real 35
Maddrey, Jas. R. 109
Madison, Baily 18
  Elizabeth M. 82
  Richard 39
  Robert 40
  Sabra 38
Mahon, Bentley 79
  Celemanda 95
  Howel H. 79
  Lucinda 7
Mainard, Gideon W. 26
Mainor, Patiance C. 47
  Susannah 20
  William 65
  Zella 20
Maley, J. W. 92
Malone, Carroline 41
  Malinda 4
  Mary A. 65

Malone (cont.)
  Samuel 21
Mandenall, Elisha 49
Maner, Stephen B. 119
Mangrum, James H. 121
Manley, Green R. 40
  John 93
Mann, William H. 81
Manring, David 63
Many, John H. 1
Marchbanks, Giles 10
  Williams 10
Marcum, Emmaline 107
  Henderson 122
  Jas. 121
  Jefferson 77, 93, 122
  Mathew 131
  Nancy 78
Markham, Wilie 73
Marlin, Granville H. 61
Marr, John W. 121
Marshall, John Q. 89
Martin, Barbary R. 64
  C. 96
  Camilla 71
  Drury 6
  Frances 72
  Hannah M. 34
  J. C. 123
  James 69
  James H. 23
  James N. 64
  Jas. C. 94
  John 54, 62, 65
  Julia F. 121
  Lemuel F. 121
  Louisa 109
  M. F. 123
  Margaret M. C. 61
  Mary A. 23, 62
  Mary E. 133
  Nancy 1, 92
  R. J. 120
  R. M. 132
  Rhodham 36
  Samuel 91
  Thos. 132
  Tibitha 84
  William 8
  William S. 107
Marvan, Rebecca 111
Mason, Abner W. 91
  David B. 26
  J. R. 61
  Mary 4
Massay, Joseph 31
Massee, Cary H. 25
  Sarah 33
Massey, Duncan 28
  Elizabeth 13
  G. A. 125
  Katharine J. 60
  Wiley B. 62
  William 106
Massy, Louisa N. 96
Mastisa, Mary 15
Mathews, Calaway 78
  Colbert 1
  L. D. 34
  Nancy 104
  Rebecca J. 5
  Sarah 33
  Tennessee 30
  Thomas 28
  W. M. 111
Mathis, A. I. J. 104
  Cyrus E. 55
  D. 38

Mathis (cont.)
  D. J. 123
  Edwin 8
  Elisha 93
  Isaac 133
  Isaac C. 114
  Jackson 17
  Jacob 25, 92
  Jacob T. 86
  James 17, 80
  James C. 65
  Jno. D. 91
  John D. 97
  Joseph 38
  Joseph A. W. 66
  Lebanon D. 38
  Lorenzo D. 91
  Lucinda C. 127
  Lucinda E. 127
  M. E. 113
  M. T. 111
  Margarett F. 114
  Mariah J. 36
  Martha Ann 73
  Mary Ann 75
  Mary E. 82
  P. H. 129
  Permelia 121
  Rebecca 42
  Rufus D. 114
  Sina Adeline 106
  Susan M. 105
  Susana E. 25
  Thos. P. 82
  Valentine 75
  W. M. 114
  William 23
  William T. 68
  Willis H. 132
Matthews, David F. 19
  Joseph E. 19
Maxley, William 19
Maxwell, Jesse 2
  Jessee 4
May, Benjamin 15
  Clayrindy 67
  Francis 46
  James H. 60
  James S. 57
  William 54, 59, 67,
    87
Mayfield, A. B. 22, 37,
    54
  A. B. P. 22, 43
  Amey P. 23
  Ann E. 37
  Cenith F. 117
  Emma H. 87
  Hulda E. 31
  Isaac N. 21
  Jane T. 77
  John S. 22
  Joseph G. 78
  Maranda S. 123
  Mary 13
  Mary R. 21
  Nancy 49
  Newton 84
  Parthena J. 131
  Polly 49
  Sopha 63
  W. P. 113
Maynor, Jas. 29
Mayo, Andrew 85
  Joel 49
  Manie 1
Mays, A. P. 125
  D. R. 30

Mays (cont.)
  David R. 30
  Drury 33
  J. A. 133
  J. W. D. 20
  J. W. N. 40
  John 20
  John W. H. 21
  Julia A. 75
  Lilly 102
  Rebecca J. 19
  Susan 59
  W. J. 107
  Watson P. 21
McAdoo, A. E. 130
McAfee, John 126
McAlelly, Elizabeth 15
  Margarett 57
McAlester, Daniel E. 65
McAlexander, Albert A.
    126
  James 46, 47
  Jno. J. 55
McAliley, George P. 56
McAlilly, Geo. P. 49
  Richard 113
McAlister, Martha J.
    102
  Mary 116
McAllelly, Richard 14
McAllester, Thos. S.
    89
McAllila, Mary J. 53
McAllilly, John 14
McAllister, Daniel E.
    65
  Sarah 100
McAnelly, Alexander 57
McAttiby, Z. P. 79
McAvery, Thomas H. 10
McBride, David 8
  Elizabeth 5
  Hester R. 44
  Hugh M. 55
  J. F. 55
  James 8, 33
  Mary 6, 111
  Nancy 89
  Sarah J. 47
  William 5, 6
McBroom, A. E. 110
McBryde, William M. 65
McCain, William N. 61
McCalab, Amanda 61
  John F. 67
McCaleb, Hugh S. 60
  S. E. 68
  Sarah E. 91
McCalister, Isabella E.
    44

  Jno. R. 44
McCall, Matilda T. 38
McCallester, Sarah S.
    40
McCallister, Margaret R.
    70
McCalop, Matilda 48
McCalvy, Roenna 27
McCarey, Ellender 52
McCartney, Elizabeth 129
  Sarah J. 120
  William 85
McCaslin, Andrew J. 120
  B. 116
  Green 17, 19, 20
  John F. 99
  Lucinda 129

157

McCaslin (cont.)
Martha Ann 76
Nancy 19
Susan E. 80
W. H. 123, 126
William 19
McCasling, William 78
Willis F. 69
McClary, James 28
Margarett 8
Mary L. 22
Matilda 3
McClay, Abegail 2
McClellan, Belle J. 130
McCleur, Mary 25
Nancy 59
McCloud, Jessee J. 23
McClour, Wm. C. 33
McClur, Jane 39
McClure, Catharine Ann
68
Joseph 5
Mary 25
McCollam, Thomas W. 83
McCollister, Elizabeth
Jane 72
McCollum, Allen 101
David 22
James 35
Jno. C. 56
John C. 101
McCombs, Mary A. 126
McConnell, Mary M. 88
McCorkle, A. J. 111
D. P. 111
Hiram R. A. 74
Robt. A. H. 4, 5
McCormack, Haden 9
McCortney, Middleton 15
McCoy, Mahaley 121
Martha 73
Nancy E. 127
McCracken, Sarah A. 64
McCraey, Martha 109
McCraig, James J. 93
McCraken, Robert P. 82
McCrary, Catharine 112
McCulloch, J. E. 133
J. S. 123
John S. 65
M. T. 34, 35, 39, 40
Miles T. 34
T. J. 131
McCullock, Francis O. L.
10
McCullough, John 92
M. T. 39
McCutchan, D. D. 115
David C. 24
John H. 115
Martha 72
McCutchen, David D. 121
McCutcheon, D. C. 26
Nancy E. 52
McDaniel D. A. 49, 100
Elenor J. 91
Eliza J. 65
James N. 97
Luny 7
Lura A. 81
Martha A. 53
Mary J. 64
Rachael E. 124
Sally 7
Samuel A. 101
W. R. 91
McDermet, William D. 12
McDermitt, James 59

McDermitt (cont.)
Jas. 59
Rila 13
McDonald, George D. 82
John L. 114
Sarah E. 116
McDongal, Mary M. 121
McDougald, Alexander 17
Archibald C. 53
Daniel 17, 19
Sarah 46
McDougle, Margaret 6
McDougold, Ann 33
Rebecca 48
McDowell, C. F. H. 99
J. D. 68
J. M. 25
J. T. 123
James H. 16
Margaret L. B. 25
Olly Ann 94
W. M. 118
McDummet, James 21
McDurmitt, Elizabeth 58
Nancy 42
McElvy, Jas. 56
McEwen, F. L. W. 6
Green B. Y. 56
Jas. A. G. 106
Mary E. J. 101
P. A. G. 124
McFall, Alexander R. 7
McFarland, Amanda 130
D. F. 100
Dicey 82
Elizabeth 89
Henry T. 100
Jno. 96
John 85
John J. 128
Mary 125
Radford 16
Thornton 30
William 30
McFarlen, Emeline M. 62
J. J. 103
J. W. 120
Jane 120
Jas. A. 103
John 47
Jones W. 128
Martha L. 120
Mary Jane 102
Wm. 29, 103
McFoslin, Eveline 103
McGarett, Sarah 21
McGarrity, B. M. (Miss)
22
Elizabeth 24
McGee, A. C. 99
David 130
Henry 61, 102
James A. 93, 102
Jas. A. 83
Jerry 5
Leander 99
Richard 57
William H. 105
McGeehe, Mary E. 109
Unica 20
McGehe, William 71
McGehee, James E. 41
McGhee, Martha N. 54
McGill, Elizabeth 104
McGran, Daniel 121
John 121
Rebecca 100
McGregory, Wm. 13

McGriegor, William 16
McHaney, Lafayette 122
McHenry, H. A. 114
Henry A. 88
McIlwain, G. G. 64
McIntosh, John 2
McIver, Donald 3
McKay, Silas H. 30
McKee, David 110
James 4
Mary Ann 30
R. D. 50
McKelva, Nancy K. 83
McKelvey, Frances A.
114
John W. 83
Mary F. 117
Susan J. 123
McKelvy, J. W. 80
Jas. 30
Louiza 125
Martha 45
Richard 129
Ruthy M. 127
T. S. 124
McKendrick, Emily 3
John W. 87
McKenny, W. J. 63
McKentosh, John A. 43
Nancy A. 43
McKeown, Nancy 14
Sarah 116
McKezick, Mahaly 24
McKiley, Richard 13
McKilvy, William C. 44
McKinly, Wm. L. 8
McKinney, Mary A. 20
McKirby, Abraham 7
McKneely, Thos. 23
McKnight, A. A. 110
D. M. 102
David 55
David M. 76
James A. 10
Jane Isabella 18
Jas. A. 124
John J. 24
Joseph 97
Joseph H. 126
Margarett W. (Mrs.)
51
Mary E. 76
Nancy E. 24
Silas M. 4
T. E. 97
William F. 5
Zaby 11
McLain, Chas. S. 34
W. A. 105
McLaine, Margarett E.
104
McLamore, Rebecca J. 61
McLand, William 23
McLane, Daniel 54
McLary, John B. 6
Samuel 18
McLaurine, J. M. 90, 96,
118, 122, 123, 127,
129
J. M. J. 103
Madison 15
Mary E. 67
McLean, Ann L. 113
Charles P. 36
McLeary, Docia 3
McLemore, Abraham 2
Elizabeth 108
Young A. 6

McLeod, John 33
McLinn, William 48
McLour, Mary 83
McMahan, Rebecca 14
McMahon, Elizabeth 24, 27
  Rachel 5
McMillin, Eland 8
  Jane 8
McMin, John 81
McMinn, Elizabeth 64
  Jno. W. 84
  Martha A. 18
  Mary S. 77
  Samuel 45
  Sarah 34
  William 50
McMullen, C. D. 66
  Lucy 66
  Margaret 84
  Mary L. 113
  Nathan 2, 5
McMullin, Eli 13
McNail, Nancy J. 90
  R. H. 94, 112
  Wm. E. 90
McNeely, A. H. 26, 84
McNeil, Wm. W. 114
McNutty, Michal 34
McPherson, Stephen 71, 89
McRee, Cyntha A. 88
  F. B. 88
  F. R. 67
  P. D. 47
McSharp, John 57
McWherter, Elizabeth A. 89
  Elizabeth J. 52
  Jas. S. 56
  Lucenda D. 27
  Margaret A. 86
McWhirter, Charles E. 101
  Eliza 116
  Elizabeth A. L. 45
  Myranda 45
  Sentha L. N. 53
  William M. 51
McWhite, Joseph 33
McWhorter, J. S. 131
  Jeremiah 20
  Rebecka 9
  Rhoda Ann 9
Meadows, Nathan 68
Meddleton, B. F. 34
Medeoris, Sarah H. 18
Medlin, George C. 53
  Malvinia 79
Medows, Nathan 92
Meek, Henry 28, 48, 90, 93
  Jno. W. 31
  Thomas H. 87
Melton, Centha Ann 31
  Robert 35
  Tillman 66
  Wiley 27, 33
Meritt, Minerva 76
Merrick, J. E. 83
Merrit, Thvizah 38
Merritt, Elizabeth 57
  Emeline 33
  Mahala 51
Messick, Lydia A. F. 80
Meurhead, Nancy 20
Michael, W. R. 102
Middleton, A. R. 95
  D. E. 119

Middleton (cont.)
  Suta A. 108
Mifflin, A. 52
  Armstrong 55
Miflin, Caswell 62
Miles, Hinton 40
Miller, C. 12
  Caroline R. 105
  Caswell 9, 10, 11
  David 13
  E. J. 110
  Elias 57, 74, 87
  Eliza 116
  Eliza Jane 82
  Elizabeth 20
  G. W. 33
  H. L. 118, 119
  Harrett A. 85
  J. A. 40
  J. H. 87
  Jno. A. 40
  Joel 4, 5
  John H. 41
  Julian 42
  Juliza F. A. 40
  Margarett 12
  Martha W. 110
  Mary 29
  Mary Ann E. M. 40
  Polly C. 2, 4
  Rebecca 116
  S. B. 71
  Samuel 99
  Samuel N. 110
Millone, Martha 54
Mills, Lewis E. 126
Milton, Elizabeth N. 44
  Monan 50
  Tilghman 52
Minton, Theodrick 70
Mirack, Louisa 16
Mitchel, Mary E. 116
  Sarah A. 4
  Zady M. 41
Mitchell, Adaline T. 15
  Elizabeth 10
  Elizabeth E. 68
  Garret G. 86
  George W. 18
  Isaac C. 62
  J. D. 67
  J. W. C. 29
  Julian 7
  M. A. E. 22
  R. W. 39, 67
  S. A. 130
  Sallie 110
  Sarah 62
  Susan G. 93
  Thomas C. 41
  Wm. N. 27
Mitts, Hester Ann 10
  Polly 7
  Sarah 57
  Sarah A. 95
Mixon, John 4
  Samuel B. 13
Mobley, Alexander 71
  Alexander H. 89
  Allen 89
  Caroline 109
  Delila 98
  Francis 2
  Harbert 98
  James 109
  Johnathan 61
  Rachal 62

Mobley (cont.)
  Turner 98
  Wiley O. 65, 84
  William 36, 83
  Wm. 61
  Zachariah 32
Mobly, Elizabeth 2
  Wm. 30
Mojles, Jas. 68
Monan, Joshua 10
Money, John H. 4
Montgomery, Eliza J. 30
  Frances 30
  Henderson 31
  Isabella R. 62
  James 24
  Jas. 8
  Martha A. 52
  Matilda 37
  Sally 8
Moody, A. W. 131
  C. C. 110
  Mary D. 87
  Milly 3
Moon, James M. 27
  Seth T. 95
Moor, Virginia L. 90
Moore, Ann D. 26
  Arthur 66
  Camilla T. 102
  Caswell J. 58
  Catharine 57
  E. W. 90
  Elisha 117
  Elizabeth J. 44
  G. W. 123
  George C. 88
  George W. 45, 66, 71
  Harrett 52
  Harriet E. 73
  Ichabud 55
  Iehabud 80
  Isral 25
  Isral C. 29
  James A. 31
  James M. 14, 35
  James W. 22
  Jane 103
  John 94
  John M. 19
  John W. 20
  Joseph W. 44
  Josiah 9
  L. L. 112
  Larkin L. 36
  Levina 24
  Marian 84
  Martha 60
  Mary 25, 74, 86
  Mary J. 51
  Mary L. 97
  Milly 123
  Nathaniel 128
  Needham 47
  Needham H. 97
  Parmelia A. 50
  R. G. 102
  Sarah E. 61
  Seth T. 77
  Sirena 52
  Stephen 47
  Susan 11
  T. E. 92
  W. W. 102
  Watkins 45
  William B. 3, 12
  William G. 13
Morgan, Catherine 50

Morgan (cont.)
    Jessee B. 75
    John 6, 19
    John B. 4
    Martha F. 81
    Mary 63
    Mary Ann 23
    Milton R. 65
    Nancy 3
    Polly 6
    Thomas C. 42
    W. P. 97
Morphus, Martha 31
Morris, Charles 73
    Dilly 30
    Elizabeth P. 114
    James 5, 7
    Jane 99
    Joel 32, 38
    Joseph 97
    Lafayett 66
    Mary 25, 35
    Melissa A. 107
    Nancy 133
    O. L. 132
    Oliver T. 95, 99
    Sarah J. 111
    Susan Ann 62
    William H. 36
Morrison, J. A. 110
    James A. 94, 95
Morrow, Elijah 93
    John W. 92
    Sintha 87
Morten, Sarah T. 49
Morton, J. V. 68, 78
    James 27, 45
    Jno. V. 59
    John V. 57, 92
    Josiah T. 32
    Martha H. 33
    Susan A. 42
    Susan N. 19
    Thomas 11
Moseley, Hillory W. 70
    William T. 86
Mosely, Elizabeth E. 23
    G. B. 23, 38
    Geo. R. 22
    J. E. 38
Mosley, Hartwell 125
    M. E. 119
    Mary A. 122
    Mary J. 113
    Mary S. 132
    Moses E. 120
    William 55
Moss, Desdimony 6
    Elizabeth 1
    Hudson W. 25
    Jacsabena 131
    Mary 96
    Sarah 2, 25
Motley, Emeline 41
    James 59
    William 82
Motly, Elizabeth 55
    Martha 52
Moudy, Frances C. 56
    Rebecca C. 60
Mound, T. J. 99
Mount, James 133
    Mary F. 129
    Samuel 101
    Wesley P. 133
Muirhead, Mary 8
Muirheid, Enoch 9
Mullens, Nancy 119

Mullens (cont.)
    Silas 122
    Thomas 93
Mullins, Louisa 90
    Nancy 109
    Paul 129
    Sinah M. 82
    Stacy 102
Murchean, Rutha 17
Murdock, A. J. 74
Murphey, Catharine 7
Murphrey, Thos. B. 12
Murphy, Benjamin W. 19
    Charles W. 39
    Elizabeth 11
    Eveline M. 90
    Malinda 3
    Manervia S. 39
    Thos. B. 19, 52
    William 29
Murray, F. W. 85
Muyrhead, George P. 25
Mydyett, Jesse 15
Myers, Benj. 32
Mynor, Rurey 47
Myrick, Dorcas 17
    Elvira 17
    Weasly 17
    Wesley 17
Nail, William R. 79
Nale, A. J. 104
Nance, Lemuel 43
    Lucinda J. 83
    Martin V. 122
    S. B. 77
Nanon, Joseph 127
Nash, John 122
    W. B. 122
    William F. 45
Neal, Tom W. 111
Neavill, N. T. 38
Neding, Alfred 6
Nedry, William 23
Nee, Joseph 126
Needham, Benson 98
    Elizabeth 36
    Franklin 60, 62
    H. T. 125
    Jessee 98
    Lewis 6, 9
    Martha 96
    Martha E. 125
    S. 118
    W. 83
    Washington 62
Neely, Samuel 37
Neilson, H. D. 9
    Hugh D. 7, 14
    Wm. L. 25
Nelson, Anna 5
    C. J. 112
    William H. 127
Nesbitt, Jane E. 49
Nettles, Heavry 17
    Martha A. 113
Nevil, Geo. W. 133
    George 114
    R. J. 101
    Sarah E. 124
    T. C. 112
Nevils, Louiza 121
    Margaret 22
    Mary 82
New, Mary 101
    Ruth A. 80
Newbern, William J. 50
Newell, Elum 26, 45
    Elum F. 49

Newell (cont.)
    Jane 45
    Joseph 57
    Margrett 26
    Uriah 57
Newhouse, Anna H. 21
    Francis M. 119
    Nancy 57
    Prudance 61
    Thos. D. 61, 115
    Wm. W. 42
Newter, Dennis 95
Nicholasson, Obed 24
Nichold, Henry 81
    Lucy E. H. 77
Nicholds, Melinda 107
Nicholdson, Jane F. 123
Nicholls, Nathan 58
Nichols, Frances 44
    John W. 75
Nicholson, J. A. 133
    Joseph 19
    W. T. 133
Nimmo, A. C. 28, 33,
        43, 46, 51
    Jane N. 75
    Martha A. 42
    Mildred C. 92
Nisbitt, Martha A. 85
Noble, Lucrecca 21
Nobles, Absolum W. 61
    Benjamin 23
    Eliza 46
    Emely J. 59
    F. M. 128
    Hinna 12
    James 10
    Jamima 37
    John 11
    Joshua 67
    Margaret A. 73
    Margarett S. 73
    Mary A. 27
    Mary Ann 64
    Nancy 9
    Nathaniel 60, 67
    Prier W. 72
    Sarah 18
Noel, Sarah Jane 93
    Thos. W. 127
Nolen, A. C. 125
Nonan, Wm. J. 86
Norman, Daniel W. 59,
        61
    Nathan J. 66
    Nathaniel P. 83
    Robert 82
    Robert J. 74
Norrid, Abraham E. 60
Norrod, Elizabeth 112
Northcott, Emeline 3
Northcut, Artena 87
Northcutt, Adeline 7
    Bitha Lavina 17
    William C. 16
Northern, J. W. 34
    Jno. M. 24
    Jno. W. 85
Norton, Alex 90
    Alexander 90
    Caledonia J. 132
    Louiza 90
    Norman 94
Norvell, Enos 107
    T. H. 132
Nowell, James H. 98
    John A. 119
    W. C. 130

Nuckles, Elizabeth 62
  Mary Ann 34
  Sarah J. 48
Nuckolds, Jas. W. 55
Nunn, A. G. 101
  A. J. 122
  Jas. H. 59
  Jno. C. W. 86
  Joel 76
  John C. W. 101
  Mary 45
  Sarah 57
  W. R. 130, 131
  William R. 122
Nusston, Nelson 106
O'Daniel, Easter 103
  Giles 106
  Rachael 103
  Robert T. 125
  Sarah A. 125
  Stephen 53, 95
O.Neal, Absolum H. 70
Oakes, John 12
Oakford, William S. 67
Oakley, M. C. 130
  McFarlen 121
Odel, James 22
Odell, Terry 10
Odle, Margrett 28
Ogle, John 88
Ogles, John L. 86
Oglesby, Elisha 6
  Matty 6, 9
  Susannah 12
Olaver, Lucy J. 65
  Rebecca 43
Oldham, R. H. 102
Oliphant, Margarett C.
  121
  Martha A. 123
Oliver, Ann 103
  Flora 117
  Isaac S. 69
  John 92
  John W. 120, 125
  Margaret 91
  Moses 101
  Nancy 95
  Robert L. P. 69
  Sarah C. 86
Olsabrooks, Mary 28
Oneal, Dionico M. 66
  Lavina 28
  Love 42
  S. 29
  Samuel 34
Oppenheimer, M. 120
Organ, James 90
Ormes, Sally 6
  Thomas 11
Orms, Mariah 39
  Mary 39
Orr, A. B. 47
  Eleazer P. 82
  James H. 129
  Jas. H. 82
Ousler, George L. 77
Overall, Christina Jane
  34
  Cornelia E. 133
  John 5, 31
  John B. 68
  Mary C. 127
  W. J. 132
Overman, Utha 41
Owen, Lucy Ann 59
Owens, Eliza 132
  Lucinda 3

Ownsby, W. T. 86, 113
Ozment, Robert B. 92
Pace, Saphronia H. 129
  Sarah E. 119
Page, Elizabeth 4, 67
  Mary C. 28
  Nancy E. 75
  Pleasant R. 24
  Rebecca A. 33
  Richard H. 110
  Wm. C. 13
Paine, Rachal 44
  Thomas N. 45
Palmer, Rutha 49
Palmore, Charlott 36
  Elizabeth 70
  Thomas 80
Parhan, C. R. 66
Paris, Henry S. 123
  Narcissa C. 93
  Sarah 70
  William L. 121
Parish, Charles 10
  M. T. 115
Park, Smith 40
Parker, A. 50
  Carroll S. 45
  Catharine 49
  Deborah 3, 11
  Elizabeth 14
  Felix 1, 61
  Frunler 69
  H. 50, 62, 63
  Henry 36, 43, 48, 102,
    117
  Hosa 32, 61, 62
  Hosia 64
  Irwin 62
  Isaac 11
  Isham I. 74
  Isham J. 58
  J. E. 121
  J. J. 118
  John 2, 21
  John H. 104, 120
  Joseph 9
  L. E. A. (Mrs.) 78
  Marian F. 97
  Martha A. V. 51
  Martha D. 128
  Martha W. 71
  Nathan 2, 11, 15
  Sally 6
  Susan 86
  Thomas H. 58
Parkin, H. 23
Parks, Adeline 133
  Elizabeth 10
  Nancy Ann M. 81
  Robert Thomas 133
  Smith 55, 56, 58, 64,
    65, 67, 69, 81, 83,
    90, 94, 96
  William 43
Parr, Allen 36
  Martha 112
Parris, Jane 95
Parrish, Elizabeth 94
  Mary Ann 81
  Susan 77
Partee, B. L. 96
  Hiram 32, 102
  Jesse D. 19
  L. B. 5
  Squire B. 4
Parten, Susan L. 121
Partiel, William H. 86
Pate, B. A. 30

Pate (cont.)
  Dicy 34
  Elizabeth 95
  J. R. 83
  Jacob M. 110
  James 45
  John R. 76, 77
  Joseph 22
  Martha 30
  Martha E. 76
  Mary 61
  Penelope 35
Patison, Henry 28
Patrick, Andrew 61
  Barbia R. 111
  Cynthia A. 119
  Eliza Jane 82
  Hollan 32
  Jessee A. 84
  Mary C. 88
  Nancy E. 87
  Nathan 129
Patterson, Andrew A. 14
  Ann H. 122
  Berry 25
  Burrel 15
  Burrell 22, 28
  Carson 39, 53, 114
  E. B. 107
  Elizabeth A. 84
  Emily 128
  Hester A. 66
  J. C. 100
  J. F. 89
  J. H. 126
  J. M. 70
  James 5, 56
  James M. 66
  Jane 5
  John F. 114
  John R. 26
  Lexanah 109
  Margaret 51, 84
  Margaret C. 14
  Margarett 105
  Martha 56
  Mary 15, 44, 56, 58
  Nancy 25
  Naomi 91
  P. P. 32
  Rebecca 124
  Robert I. 14
  Sarah 9, 55, 107
  Susan C. 126
  Susan M. 79
  W. C. 99
  William 32, 56
  William C. 102
Patton, Abraham 2
  David 8
  Eliza F. 121
  Emaly V. 66
  George 9
  James 41
  John B. 41
  Martha W. 112
  N. C. 118
  Newton C. 68
  Thos. A. 25
  William 127
Paul, S. S. 28, 34, 35,
    36, 37, 45, 48, 55
  Sherod S. 29
Payne, Jonnah 81
Peace, William B. 72
Peacock, R. W. 86
Peal, Martha 55
  Sarah 52

Peal (cont.)
  Winaford 56
Pearce. B. 122
  Caroline 127
  D. M. 123
  Elizabeth 76
  James H. 82
  Jas. 121
  Jo-n K. 49, 125
  Leander 60
  Letha A. 132
  Ruben 2
  Stephen 92
  William 131
  William R. 128
Pearson, Susan S. 100
Peary, F. K. 24
Pebbles, J. N. 110
Pecks, Joseph 13
Peel, J. A. 130
  Louiza 78
  Mary E. 75
  Rachael 87
Peeples, William W. 92
Pemberter, Joshua L. 78
Pemberton, Henry W. 91
  Lucy A. 94
  Nancy J. 118
Pendergrass, Nancy 35
Penn, A. C. 39, 120
  Amanda E. 50
  G. S. 87, 91, 120
  Geo. S. 87
  George S. 94, 98
  J. W. 133
  Jacob F. 28
  Josiah A. 109
  Josiah F. 78
  Martha J. 126
  Mary P. 119
  Mary R. 74
  Pinkney R. 82
  Richard C. 56
  Sarah E. 50
  W. C. 94, 99, 102
  Wm. C. 78, 88
  Wm. E. 83
  Wm. G. 101
Penney, James 42
  Martha A. 27
Penning, Eliza J. 111
Pennington, D. 16
  Drury 91
  J. 45
  Mary E. 53
Penny, Caleb 42
  Jas. 36
  Lewis 110
Pentegrass, Lucinda 54
Penyman, J. L. 64
Peoples, M. J. 130
  S. J. 128
Pepkins, John D. 82
Permenter, Braton 71
Perminter, James 58
Perry, Asa 45
  Benj. W. 2
  Frances 42
  Francis 3, 66
  George 70
  Jarrett 119
  John 119
  Josephus S. 129
  Lewis 45, 49
  W. F. 89
Perteat, Elizabeth 36
Peth, Hedge 88
Petis, Mary Ann 16

Petit, Nasibet 35
Pettit, James 51
  N. 51
Pettus, Carroline 37
  Elizabeth 83
  Emily 105
  Rebecca W. 20
  Sam K. 37
  William 53
Petty, Clementine S. 125
Pettyjohn, Sarah 53
Phaland, Eliza 71
Phalen, James G. 43
Phaling, John 23
Phallis, Jarucia Ann 95
Phelan, D. S. 120
  David S. 36, 93
  Elendar A. 42
  J. G. 130
  John 78, 90
  Mahala 104
  Sarah 49
  Sarah A. 78
  Sarah E. 124
  Wm. H. 78
Phelps, Mary 92
Philips, Elizabeth 21
  Henry G. 132
  Louiza 119
  Marion J. 107
  Nancy A. 31
  Robert 57
Phillips, A. P. 102
  Albert P. 90
  Benj. 133
  Caroline 69
  Celina 37
  Charles C. 21
  Harrison 3
  James 133
  James O. 40
  Jane 41
  John F. 55
  Martha T. 67
  Mary 53
  Sidney 64
  Virginia F. 73
  W. R. 100
Phipps, James B. 56
Pickens, Thos. R. 118
Pielzer, E. 124
Pierce, E. N. 106
  Henry M. 83
  John W. 70
  Joseph W. 130
  N. C. 97
  N. S. 106
  R. M. 107
  S. M. 118
  Samuel C. 97
Pigue, N. W. 109
Pinington, Martha A. 57
Pinion, Martha A. 52
  Solomon 29
Piolate, Caroline 47
Pipkin, Jonas S. 78
  William M. 126
Pipkins, Rebecca 3
Pirce, Rubin 32
Pircey, James 24
Pistole, Watt 1
Pitchford, Lively 5
Pittman, Berry 102
  Elizabeth 95
  H. C. 89
  Henry C. 89
  J. A. W. 90, 96
  L. G. H. 65

Pittman (cont.)
  Leuvenia M. 65
  Mary A. 90
  Saml. L. 89
  Saml. S. 79
  Samuel L. 65
Pitts, John 107
  Martha G. 111
Plyland, William 91
Poindexter, William 103
  William J. 120
Pole, John H. 38
Polk, John 52
Poll, John H. 41
Pollard, Elizabeth 3
  Isaac 13
  Mahaly C. 113
  Milton 64
  Otha C. 56
  Rebecca 5
  Sarah Ann 70
  Stephen 3, 17
  Susan 83
Pool, Whitson 69
Pope, Archibal 110
  B. 29
  B. H. 133
  Bryant 90, 120
  Bryant H. 116
  Eliza 41
  Jane B. 54
  John W. 25
  Martha 32
  Martha A. 118
  Mary 73
  Narcissa 116
  P. 116
  Peney 33
  Percy 99
  Robert 16
  S. B. 133
  Sentha J. 51
Porter, Andrew 24
  Charles 12, 15
  Darcus 110
  J. M. 130
  James 15, 27, 54
  James R. 82
  John C. 27, 62, 103
  John N. 109
  Malinda 40
  Mary A. E. 101
  Matilda 40, 115
  Nancy 88, 92
  Nancy P. 15
  Robert A. 94
  S. J. 39
  Sarah 115
  Sarah A. 128
  Sidney J. 32, 38, 45
  Susan M. 76
  Wm. A. 110, 115
Portis, Clinton D. 73
  Sarah A. 73
Poston, John L. 65
Pound, Martha 24
Pounds, Andrew J. 106
  Elizabeth R. 42
  J. M. 57
  James M. 57
  John H. 127
  Julia 57
  Louisa M. 119
  Nancy J. 84
  Sarah 80
  Thomas L. 67
Powden, Hooper J. 80
Powell, Catharine F. 130

Ross (cont.)
  Alfred 73, 90
  Andrew J. 26
  C. H. 133
  Charles H. 33, 91
  Elizabeth 47
  James 60
  Mary Ann 21
  Melvan 20
  Melvin 17
  Roda 8
  Thomas 21
  Thos. 20
  William A. 50, 51, 68
Roulhae, W. G. 102
Roundtree, Elvira L. 18
  Evalina M. 34
  Wm. T. 34
Rountree, W. T. 54
  Wm. T. 53
  Woodson 29
Routen, Elizabeth 105
Rowntree, Nancy 56
Roycroft, A. J. 39
Rucker, Catharine 32
  Hester Ann 128
Rude, Isaac J. 99
Runaldo, Mary 8
  William S. 11
Runalds, Elenor M. 49
  Elizabeth 56
  John R. 62
  Mahaly 38
  Mary 43
  William 63
Runolds, James 27
  Thomas 2
Rushin, Mahaley 39
Rushing, John 102
Russ, Emaline 11
Russell, Canvass B. 123
  E. B. 114
  Elijah B. 85
  John 10
  L. H. 126
  Stephen H. 129
  Wiley P. 114
Rust, A. H. 101, 107
  Ellender 45
  Geo. C. 11
  J. T. 99
  James N. 94
  Jas. A. 91
  Jestin 3
  Louisa J. 105
  Martha J. 104
  Mary Elizabeth 69
  Samuel P. 6
  Samuel S. 1
  Sarah B. 11
  William H. 72
Rutherford, Wright H. 56
Rutledge, A. C. 125
  Ann E. 56
  B. M. 119
  Benjamin 102
  David N. 83
  Emely J. 73
  F. M. 112
  J. T. 125
  J. Y. 125
  James 82
  Mary A. 81
  Reason 126
  Robert 120
Rutlidge, Angeline 47
Ryster, Elizabeth 96
  W. H. 96

Sadberry, Jordian W. 67
Sain, Frances 87
  Henry 55
  Mary 51
  William 29
Sainford, Cynthia 81
  Samuel 62
Sale, Dorithey 67
  Ezekiel 44
  John 71
  John C. 44
Salemon, Mary S. 55
Sales, Cyntha P. 39
  William 48
Salph, Willoughby 46
Salyton, Lewis J. 102
Sammons, Betsey 5
  Martha 89
  Mris Milley 46
  Wiley F. 86
  William 12
  Wm. 11
Samons, Jas. J. 7
Sandeford, Ben 101
  N. D. 28
  N. S. 43
Sanderford, Martha 85
  Pricella J. 64
  Sarah Ann 72
  Virginia F. 65
Sanders, Amanda 81
  Edmond 48
  Elijah 55, 59
  Geo. C. 7
  H. W. 132
  Joshua 62
  Mahulda 93
  Mariah P. 55
  Martha B. 71
  Martha H. P. 114
  Martha J. (Mrs.) 63
  Mary A. L. 130
  Pleasant 59
  R. P. 123
  Selina C. 130
  W. D. 127
  W. L. 119
  William P. 58
  Wm. 58
  Woodson J. 57
Sanderson, Overall 9
Sandford, Jessee 58
  Polly 17
  Sarah P. 76
Sane, Nancy Jane 99
Sanford, David 109
  Eudora E. 123
  James 123
  Lucinda 117
  Robert 87
  Susanah C. 12
Sappington, Elizabeth
    M. 100
  J. W. S. 121
  W. G. 129
Sartor, Mary B. 57
  Sarah Ann 90
  W. 90
Saunders, Aaron 131
  John M. 16
  Wm. R. 34
Sawyer, M. H. 34
Sawyers, Peter 44
  Wm. R. 22
Scales, Thomas E. 111
Scallarn, Elizabeth 6
  John 6
Scallion, Benj. F. 59

Scallion (cont.)
  Lavina 21
  Washington 23
Scalldrn, John 8
Scates, Daniel H. 124
Schrborough, Jno. 79
Scipper, Martha 44
Scott, Elisha 86
  Elizabeth 78
  Elizabeth A. 68
  Elizabeth G. J. 86
  James 13, 26, 29
  James W. 70
  John D. 4
  Lemuel 5, 8
  Levina 51
  Lions C. 28
  Lirzah 5
  Margarette 38
  Sarah E. 92
  Sarah L. 121
  Sterling B. 65
  Thos. 109
  Thos. S. 27
  William 60
  William D. 19, 72
  William P. 84
  Wm. P. 91
Scrape, Eliza E. 57
  Susan M. 88
  William C. 51
Screws, E. D. 130
Seals, Solomon 7
Seat, Amanda R. 125
  Angeline J. L. 17
  Elizabeth 4
  Idortha S. A. 38
  Mary Jane 36
  Robert 6, 9, 12
  W. B. 65
Seavers, Augustus C. 108
Seay, L. P. 33, 34, 41,
    45, 58
  Luke P. 9, 10, 42, 45
  M. M. 87, 99
Sedwick, Salmon 2
See, Abraham B. 6
  Louis 11
  Luke P. 6
Self, Mark 14
  Mary 14
  Mary Elizabeth 74
  Milly A. 73
  Willoughby 14
Sellars, Elizabeth 7
  John 10, 12
  Kisiah 19
  Matilda Cela Ann 68
  Nancy 11, 20
  Richard C. 59
  Robert 12
Sellers, John 4, 33
  Kizza 33
  Nancy 27
  Nancy E. 81
  Robert 2
  William R. 115
Selph, Ann M. 64
  Mary 13, 40
  Willoughby 13
Semons, Nancy Ann 69
Senter, A. A. 128
  Alvin 37, 58, 80
  C. M. (Jr.) 123
  Eliza C. 103
  Frances 60
  J. M. 87
  James M. 60, 61, 69, 88

Senter (cont.)
Martha J. 132
Martha Jane 72
Moses E. 35
W. M. 109, 125
William M. 118
Wm. M. 119
Sepune, Daniel 40
Serape, W. H. 31, 38, 43
Wm 27
Seratt, Jos. 4
Joseph 9
Polly 4
Serratt, Elizabeth 25,
32
Elizabeth M. 35
Washington 32
Seward, Warren B. 106
Sewell, Samuel 8
Sexton, Andrew 75
Eliza Jane 80
James 30
John W. 132
Linsfield 30, 47
M. J. 116
Martha E. 68, 78
Mary 32
Nancy C. 127
Peter 33, 46
Sarah Ann 68
Sarah J. 70
Tennessee 63
Wilie L. 91
William 47
Shain, Margarette 109
Sham, William 9
Shane, A. M. 56
Eliza W. 125
Elizabeth 14
Geo. 124
George 15, 36, 40, 116
James A. 94
James S. 68
John 11
Julia Ann Jane 72
Martha 11
Mary E. 84
Nancy 58
Nancy A. 124
Nancy E. 79
Samuel 11, 62
Sarah J. 109
William 126
Shanklin, William C. 111
Sharp, Caroline S. 120
Cyrus 28, 111
E. A. 118
Elizabeth 68
G. M. 54, 86
Granville S. 106
J. P. 120
J. W. 78
James M. 20, 24
Joseph 32
Joseph H. 125
Margarette E. 116
Mary 42
S. M. 111
S. W. 93
T. A. 57, 78
Sharrod, Richard 3, 4,
11
Shavour, John C. 38
Shaw, Centha 27
Francis M. 112
Hannah 63
Hugh 86
John D. 10

Shaw (cont.)
Lemiza 52
M. Precilla 112
Maranda J. 60
S. 25
Simpson 25
Solomon 7
Solomon H. 3
William 109
Wm. 86, 88, 101
Zachariah 36
Shearer, Henry 24
Shelby, Mary J. 124
Shelton, Francis W. 98
Hardy W. 70
Martha W. 62
Sally N. 98
Thos. 92
Shenill, Alfred 14
Shepard, R. B. 121
Saml. 31
Shephard, Richard L. 70
Sherell, Elizabeth F.
121
Sherman, Parson M. 31
Wm. J. 59
Shern, Frances 31
Sheron, Jas. H. 31
Sherrod, Nathaniel 4
Richard 17
Sherron, Aaron 31
Elizabeth 21
H. 24
Jas. H. 52
Lucretia 47
Nancy 57
Nathaniel K. 49
Shipman, Elizabeth C.
67
Jacob S. 44, 82
Marinda 61
Nancy P. 44
Shoate, Ison 113
Short, C. A. 64
Delila 31
Elizabeth 39
G. L. 118
Sarah J. 119
Shumate, Ann 119
Sigman, Amedia A. 84
Sigmon, Joel B. 64
Sigmor, Nancy A. 83
Sile, John W. 47
Simes, J. N. 117
Simmons, A. J. 43
C. D. 25
David 37
Edney Ann 29
Eliza E. 91
J. R. 120
P. H. 70
Penelope 19
Pleasant H. 71
Sarah G. 104
Simms, John C. 37
William H. 64
Simons, David 36, 42
David C. 116
Henry J. 41
John B. 71
Martha 9
Simpson, George W. 63
Harmon 14
Louisa 51
Mahala 75
Martha (Mrs.) 46
R. 97
Sims, Docia M. 80

Sims (cont.)
Elizabeth C. 77
Elizabeth J. 95
G. W. 109
Polly Eliza 106
Thomas N. 117
Sinclair, Lucreatia R.
95
Parale F. 107
Peter 19
William 125
Sinclear, Elizabeth 55
John F. 37, 47
Singleton, Elizabeth 13
Mary 16
Patrick E. 105
Singly, Franklin 127
Sires, Lazarus 118
Skiles, Henry H. 112,
124
Jacob S. 124
James 92
Jane C. 96
Juleus A. 119
Margaret E. 96
Ruthy B. 117
William G. 69, 106
Skipper, Harrett 59
Noah 111
Thomas 58
Skyles, Ann S. 69
Slaton, Mary A. E. 107
Tobitha L. 114
Slaydon, Affey A. 122
Jas. H. 129
Wm. W. 111
Slayton, Jas. H. 124
Letty M. 106
Wm. T. 118
Slemon, R. S. 12
Sloan, Elizabeth H. 18
Frances 21
Jas. S. 99
Jos. S. 100
Kissiah C. 37
Malissa C. 100
Martin L. 103
Nancy E. 111
Robert R. 21
Samuel H. 76
Thomas 21
Smally, Elizabeth M. 36
Smiley, A. H. 50
A. N. 57
Smith, A. 114
Absolom 18
Alexander 48
Andrew M. 101, 110
Arthur 28, 30
B. G. 79
Barnett 18
Benj. 20
C. W. 49
Caroline 21
Catharine 29
Charles W. 28, 35
Charlott D. 114
Dicy 21
Dovey 26
Eda 22
Edward 9
Eliza 82, 112
Elizabeth 3, 5, 16
Ellen 87
Eoma 97
Erwin 12
Everett 26
Everitt 26

167

Stuart, Alfred 50
  Elizabeth 23
  John B. 24
  William C. 50
Stubblefield, Jno. 88
Stublefield, John 121
  William R. 121
Stults, Mary E. 107
  William 118
Sturdivant, Jesse 93
Summers, Eathea M. B. 72
  Eli A. 114
  Jane 101
Summons, Eliza 41
Suratt, Joseph 10
Swan, Sarah 96
Swindle, A. D. R. 129
  D. W. 60
  Elizabeth 60
  James T. 44
  John 53
  John W. 129
  Joshua 56, 90
  Margarette 105
  William H. 124
Talbott, Alvin 130
Taliafero, E. L. 51
Taliaferro, E. T. 46
  Edwin T. 54
  Elizabeth W. 19
  John A. 8
  Virginia C. 79
  Walker 46
Taliferro, Jno. A. 11
Talkington, Samuel G. 85
Talley, G. W. 128
  James E. 124
  William 24
Tally, Benj. F. 56
  Kentiance G. 44
  Mary 51
  Nancy (Mrs.) 51
Taner, Nancy 17
Tanner, David 29
  T. A. 97
Tarvin, Garrat 22
  Milton T. 22
Tate, John 25
  Louiza C. 76
  Manerva 44
  Rachal A. 60
  Sarah R. 74
  William P. 34
Tatom, Levina 29
Tatum, A. H. 103
  Absolum H. 105
  Elizabeth 81
  G. W. 77
  James 87, 103, 114
  James B. 119
  John P. 81
  Lucanda E. 78
  Lucretia C. 77
  W. N. 123
Taylor, Abram 58
  Allen 65, 98
  Amanda 109
  Annis 102
  Benjamin F. 42
  Clementine 56
  E. F. 116
  Edmund F. 89
  Elizabeth 96
  Frances M. 81
  George M. 90
  J. P. 102, 118
  Jas. R. 123
  John D. 80

Taylor (cont.)
  Jos. R. 97
  Joseph R. 45
  Jurasha 32
  Lamb 55
  Lemuel 48
  Leonard 42, 48, 50,
    70
  Lucy Ann 88
  Lucy E. 130
  Margaret (Mrs.) 55
  Martha Jane 83
  Martin Y. 71
  Mary 36
  Mary Ann 82
  Mary E. C. 125
  Mary J. 127
  Mary Jane 77
  Mathew M. 112
  N. B. 94
  Nancy 79
  Nathaniel 48
  Nelly B. 109
  Rebeckha 9
  Robert 84
  Robert H. 64
  Samuel 71
  Sarah A. 101
  Sarah F. 112
  Sarah L. 78
  Thomas 10
  Thomas T. 126
  Thos. C. 37
  Thos. G. 57, 103
  V. M. L. 124
  V. N. S. 84
  Vinson M. L. 51
  W. 83
  W. (Dr.) 62
  Wiley 29, 74
  William 58, 117
  William J. 61
  Wm. 91, 102
  Wm. G. 103
Temple, Martha A. 63
Templeton, David I. H.
    98
Terrall, Washington 29
Terrell, Benjamin F. 33
  Bluford 93
  F. J. 24
  Harry 14
  James M. 45, 113
  Mary 9
  Robert 9, 35
  William B. 125
  William H. 71
Terril, Mary Cedona 51
  Thadeous N. 91
  Buford 98
  Frances S. 85
  Franklin J. 76
  George W. 15, 33
  J. M. 37
  James M. 33
  Jas. M. 96
Terry, Alexander 46
  James M. 40
  John H. 25
  Phillip G. 82
Thadwick, John R. 74
Tharp, Isaac 63
  J. Coleman 112
  Jessee 58
  Thos. 63
Thedford, Constant 47
  Delitha 116
  Denis 6

Thedford (cont.)
  Edward 78
  Elizabeth R. 49
  Elvira 57
  Hannah 131
  Honey 13
  Jno. R. 4
  John 18
  John L. 75
  John R. 4, 80
  Josiah L. 4
  Josias 131
  Margaret 22
  Martha R. 88
  Mary 22
  Nancy 48
  Sally 3
  Sandford 45
  Sarah M. 41
  Susan 58
  Thomas J. 51
  Thos. J. 53
  Thos. J. N. K. H. 57
  W. 26
  Walter 1, 56
  Walter M. 29
  Walter N. 108
  William 4, 6, 26
  Wm. 40
Thetford, Edwards 67
  Elizabeth 16
  Hiram 54
  Honey 15
  Isaac R. 101
  J. T. 55
  Josias 130
  Louisa 91
  Nancy 19
  Sampson 7
  Sanford 47
  Sarah M. 88
  T. J. 120
  W. M. 114
  Walter 18
  William 19
  William N. 16
Thomas, A. (?) 103
  A. R. 114
  Abner D. 17, 35
  Abner S. 76
  Alfred A. 39
  Alfred James 56
  Allezarah A. 89
  America J. 17
  Caroline 20
  Caroline C. 79
  D. H. 110
  David 3
  David E. 49
  Ellendor L. 24
  Elmira J. 117
  Emeline 97
  H. J. 10, 12, 14
  Henry 54
  Hiram 14
  Hiram J. 13, 20
  I. 31
  Isham 106
  J. S. 131
  James A. 40, 88
  James S. 50
  Jas. 110
  John 117
  John F. 47
  Kesia 46
  Martha A. 50
  Martha E. 27
  Mary 121

Thomas (cont.)
Mary A. 35
Mary Jane 39
Milton 67
Monah 110
Nancy E. 90
R. C. 97
R. G. 107
Rachael M. 71
Rachal L. 29
Redden C. 57
Robert H. 114
Ronanah C. D. 105
S. Y. 17, 63
Samuel Y. 26
Sarah 6
Susan 38, 75, 128
Thomas D. 63
Tobitha A. 132
William 107
William A. 88
Thomason, James 65, 121
Martha A. 35
R. E. C. 99
S. C. 133
Thomasson, Elizabeth C. 65
Thompson, A. N. 93
Archells 20
Archuelas 53
Burrell M. 99
Charity T. 12
Charles L. 49
Dennis 94
Elizabeth 23
Elizabeth J. 12
Ephram 31
H. 88
Henry 90
Hezekiah C. 86
J. T. 110, 123, 125
James 32, 53
James B. 127
James P. 84
James W. 79
Jno. C. 84
John 94
John C. 91
John M. 21
Julias T. 88
Julias T. 69
L. C. 125
Lavina 14
Levinia E. 41
Lycurgus 132
M. P. 130
Martha A. T. 42
Mary 53, 96
Ransom 100
Richard 62
Susannah M. 63
Tennessee 71
William 44, 113
William H. 125
William P. 91
Wm. 43
Thorn, Thomas 49
Thornton, Lavinia A. 92
William 128
Thweatt, William K. 43
Tidrow, Charles H. 81
Tidwell, Mary 18
Richard 62
Tigret, Chesterfield 57
Mary J. 95
Tilghman, A. J. 56
E. S. 128
Eli 32

Tilghman (cont.)
Elizabeth E. 62
Mirna 60
Pinkney 90
Robert C. 83
Tilliman, William E. 89
Tilman, A. G. 98
Jeremiah A. 81
Tincle, Catherine 24
Salley 1
Tiner, Jessee 127
John W. 124
Wesley 90
Tinkle, Cemantha L. 132
Daniel 5, 121
George W. 35
Letta C. 107
Lindsey K. 9
Mary 108
Sarah M. 99
Susan M. 99
Wm. E. 30
Tinner, William A. 114
Tinsley, Charles 101
G. B. 68
Geo. B. 78
James G. 86
Wm. 39
Tipton, James 12
Todd, David 23
Tolen, Jesse 111
Jessee L. 98
Toler, John S. 72
Toller, Winneford 12
Tombs, Owen 19
Tomlin, John L. H. 59
Tomlinson, Sidney H. 67
Toombs, William A. G. 109
Toten, Margarett 23
Totten, A. W. 34
A. W. O. 22
James S. 5, 7, 15
Jas. L. 3, 4, 5, 8
Matilda 8
Trafton, Benjamin 44
Traftor, Elizabeth 74
Trainer, Thomas 13
Travis, Ann 106
Miles H. 67, 72, 91
N. M. 97
W. G. 100
Trayner, Margarett 14
Traynor, Jerry 22
Lucinda 29
Thos. 31
Treumen, Mulinda 24
Trimble, Jas. L. 110
Robert B. 83
Trosper, E. B. 125
Elijah B. 125
James 17
Jane 30
Mary A. 118
Mulindy 29
Peter 29
Robert 39
Trout, Adam 18
Elizabeth 37, 57
H. C. 42
Hiram C. 54, 98
John 76
Nancy J. 43
Sarah A. 62
Truman, Catharine E. 94
Trusty, Benj. F. 52
Henderson 7

Trusty (cont.)
Herrington 7
Tucker, Alfred 81
E. 118
Ebenezer D. 107
Edmund V. 29
Gideon 12, 17
J. M. 98
J. T. 126
James 81
James W. 40
Jerman 66
Jessee 118
John P. 42
Jos. 66
Julias M. 83, 110
Margarette L. 110
Mary F. 50
S. R. 35, 85
Saml. R. 62
Samuel R. 48, 68
Thos. A. 96
Tuggle, H. J. 110
W. H. 64, 79
William H. 101
Turner, Admira 75
Alexander 44
Ann H. 38
Arthur 70
Berlinda 32
Dority 61
Elenor M. 77
Gerigh 89
James 4, 16, 18, 44, 52, 66, 77
Jeremiah 16
Jessee 19
Levi J. 105
Lydia J. 45
Margarett E. 126
Martha 76
Mary J. 45
Richard 121, 128
T. R. 29
Terrish 92
Thomas G. 19
Thos. T. 47
W. A. 125
W. H. 132
William C. 85
Turnham, T. S. 93, 94
Turpin, Caron Ann 30
Tuter, John F. 43
Twigg, Jacob M. 76
Rebecca 63
Tyler, Ann E. 81
Gabriel S. 14
Geo. S. 11
Martha 74
Mary Jane 89
Perney E. 117
Richard C. 124
Tyner, Jessee 40
Tyson, Benj. P. 130
E. A. 125
Lydia 83
Mahala 56
Margarett 27
Mary A. 3
Mary E. 97
Matilda 80
Reuben 9
T. D. 56
William R. 56
Udaley, Andrew 40
John 25
Umant, N. P. 115
Umstard, Mary A. 60

169

Ward, Mary 17, 69
  Mary J. 112
  Mildred 40
  Nancy C. 92, 125
  Nancy M. 52
  Sarah M. 109
  Surmanthilus E. 77
  Thomas H. 95
  William 80
  William G. 74
  Willis C. 79
  Wm. G. 99
  Wm. J. 115
Wardbanks, William 4
Warden, Thos. F. 132
Warmack, Benjamin 60
  Burwell 35
Warmath, Micajah W. 77
  Thomas D. 101
  W. M. 112
Warran, Robt. 32
Warren, Carroline 132
  Catharine J. 80
  Edwin 35
  F. H. 91
  James H. 9
  John G. 9
  Margratt 28
  Nancy E. 109
  Newton W. 93
  Robt. 32
  Sarah Ann 77
  William 7, 32
  Wm. 94
Warrin, Allfred 32
  Edwin 9
  Henry 9
  Martha 28
  Robert 33
  William 33
  William C. 46
Watkins, B. F. 132
Watson, Beverly B. 75
  David 17
  Elizabeth 16
  Frances 40
  Geo. W. 29
  George 16
  George W. 28
  James M. 24
  John 45
  L. L. 118
  Mary E. 125
  R. R. 125
  Richard R. 125
  Ruthy 21
  Sarah 19
  Thomas M. 19
  William 117
Watt, Elizabeth 102
  J. Emly 77
  James N. 38
  Jas. N. 124
  John M. 68, 82
  Miriah S. 74
  Rebecca 85
  Thomas 44
  Thos. 117
Watts, Clemsa 44
  Delilah 57
  Fanny M. 71
  Isabella 118
  Malichi 21
  Milichi 8
  Saml. 94
Ways, Andrew 100
Weaks, James H. 81
Weatherford, Elizabeth
  65

Weatherford (cont.)
  Nancy J. 66
Weathers, James E. 50
Weatherspoon, J. W. 127
  Jas 60
  Jas. R. 22
  Jos. 45
  Joseph 48
  Susan 6
  Thomas 13
Weaver, John 111
  John B. 105
  L. 111
  Pemetea C. 100
Webb, Albert J. 65
  Asberry M. 15, 92
  Calvin 35
  Charity 21
  Elizabeth 75
  Emely 31
  G. W. 126
  George W. 99
  Hugh 58
  I. H. D. 69
  Isah 25
  Isiah 58
  James W. 99
  Jeremiah 30
  John W. 24
  L. D. 69
  Lee Ann 38
  Leroy D. 59
  Levi 52
  Louiza 11
  Lucretia A. 36
  Mahalia 44
  Martha J. 58
  Martha S. 114
  Mary E. 131
  Miranda 47
  Robert M. 69
  Rufus W. 110
  Sam'l. C. 8
  Samuel 2, 4
  Sarah R. 110
  Sutelda E. 72
  T. S. 123
  Wilban 19
  William C. 21
  William H. 64
  Wm. H. 69
  Wm. T. 51
Webber, Andrew J. 79
Weddington, W. B. 128
Weddle, Jeremiah G. 63
Wedington, R. G. 119
Welch, Aley A. H. 26
  Elizabeth 13
  H. A. 4, 102
  Harriet H. 4
  Harrod P. 6
  Henry 20, 21
  Henry A. 26
  James 20
  Jane F. 50
  Mary 64
  Marzell 45
  Miles 129
  Nancy 17
  Polly 47
  Richard 46
  Wm. R. 6
Wellingsford, Isaac
  17
Wells, Henry 128
  John M. 55
Wert, John 24, 27
Weseney, Sarah Ann 82

Wesson, Nancy H. 93
West, Daniel 50, 113
  Elizabeth 53, 106
  Elizabeth M. 103
  G. A. 103
  Geo. H. 130
  Gilbert A. 68
  James R. 127
  Jennett 108
  Jno. W. 97
  John W. 109
  Julia A. 77
  Manerva M. 72
  Martha E. 97
  Mary 38
  Mary Ann 60
  Noel E. 32
  Ollin 39
  Owen 39
  Phillip 66
  Richard L. 74
  Sarah J. 51
  Thomas J. 58
  Wiley W. 64
  William H. 81
Wetherford, Stephen F.
  89
  W. R. 127
Wetherington, Henry T.
  82
Wetherspoon, Thos. M.
  20
Wethington, Mary A. 87
Wheeler, C. M. 118
  Jesse B. 125
  M. J. 118
  Saml. H. 101
Wherry, Martha E. 90
Whetty, Felise G. 37
Whichard, Penelope 110
  Reuben 21
Whitaker, David 10
  Jane T. 119
Whitchard, Mary 112
  Rubin 27
White, A. H. 23
  A. J. 101
  Absolum A. 24
  Allen 3
  Allen S. 28
  Andrew J. 88
  Benj. 3, 5, 9
  Boyd 118, 129
  Edw. H. 37
  Elgin C. 28
  Emily L. 126
  Erastus 37
  Flora 117
  Frances A. 25
  G. T. 81
  G. W. 101
  George T. 65
  Hugh S. 93
  J. M. 27
  James 94
  James M. 129
  Jane Mariah 73
  Jane S. 121
  Jno. M. 88
  Jno. W. 41
  John M. 22
  L. N. 99
  Levy 58
  Malinda 22
  Manirva 61
  Margaret C. 78
  Martha P. 108
  Mary Ann 10

171

White (cont.)
Mary E. J. 37
N. V. 114
Patience 33
Pete M. 35
Richardson P. 52
Samuel N. 104
Sarah Ann 79
Sarah E. 83, 90
Sarah S. 22
William 74, 129
William R. 58
Wm. A. 63
Whiteherst, Ashville B.
  98
Whitehurst, Moses F. 52
Whitley, J. T. 126
Josiah 20
Judia 10
Lucratis 19
Needham 97, 98
Susan 71
Whitlocke, Mariah D. 42
Ro. E. 42
Whitlow, Geo. M. 33
Mary E. 46
Whitson, John D. 16
Whitten, Massalon 40
Wichard, Rubin 65
Wicks, Ann E. 85
Wiggins, Thos. 5
Wiggs, Jonathan S. 112
M. C. 112
Matthew 117
Wilborn, J. J. 89
Narcissa 10
Wilbourn, Elijah 48
William J. N. 61
Wilbourne, Narcissa 16
Wilburn, Cabb 5
George M. 91
Joshua 5. 7
Wildar, Susan 43
Wildur, Mary 43
Wiles, Mary M. 105
William A. 105
Wilhington, Harriett 126
Wilkerson, Harriott 48
Wilkes, John M. 121
Mary J. 74
William H. 132
Wilkins, Emeline 33
Harrett J. 81
J. A. 99, 110
Jno. A. 79, 88, 98
John A. 52, 60
L. J. 29, 30, 43
Mary 17
Mary A. 65
S. D. 127, 130
S. J. 15
Saml. D. 118, 119
Samuel J. 47
Sarah L. 65
Sarah S. 83
T. A. 61
Wm. F. 92
Wm. T. 62, 68, 88
Wilks, Eliza Jane 98
Elizabeth 32
Francis M. 43
Heneretta C. 73
Modnca 54
William, John G. 110
Williams, A. J. 33, 36,
  38
Alex 112
Allen C. 86

Williams (cont.)
Amanda Katharine 5
America C. 88
Arthur 6
Arthur A. 59
Benj. P. 64
Benjamin J. 63
C. H. 110
Charles 6, 21
Charles W. 20, 24
D. A. 62
Daniel 130
Daniel L. 67
Delphi 53
Emry 61
Franklin 120
Green 30, 31, 132
J. (Mrs.) 119
J. W. 61, 64
James 6, 127
James C. 13
John 40, 104, 113
John B. 80
John L. 120
John W. 79
Johnson 15
Johnston 67, 84
Joseph 14
Julia A. J. E. 110
L. B. (Miss) 30
L. L. 99
Licurgas W. 105
Martha 100
Martha A. 122
Martha Ann 33
Mary 52, 107
Matilda 11
Melinda P. 133
Mira E. 92
Nancy 27, 54
Nancy C. 12
Nathanial 41
Nathaniel 111
Orville 113
Panthaer W. 105
Polly 26
S. 66, 122
Sarah A. 130
Seth 16
Stephen 5
Susan F. 131
Susanah C. 4
T. W. 99
Thomas 5
Thomas J. 88
Thos. 21
Thos. W. 44, 123
V. V. 113
W. B. 121
W. D. 117
W. P. 31
William 7, 38, 56,
  58, 92, 102
William F. 112
William S. 21
Wilson 55, 63, 72,
  88
Wm. 70
Wm. (Jr.) 92
Williamson, Elizabeth
  26
H. 101
Henry 56, 89, 90,
  115
J. H. 124
James A. 87
Jas. M. 53
Jas. W. 13

Williamson (cont.)
John 35
Williford, C. C. 114
Willis, Elizabeth H. 112
Hinton 13
S. 100
Susan J. 77
Wills, Jesse I. 85
Jessie J. 57
Willson, Sarah 11
Wilson, A. R. 130
Ann 93
Ashley R. 92
Banna E. 45
Dicy Jane 97
Dolly 67
E. P. 109
Eliza P. 81
Elizabeth 49, 87
Elphady C. 113
H. 114
Horace 117
J. A. 110
James 31, 80
James M. 12, 13
Jane M. 48
Jas M. 6
Jefferson 13
Jno. 97
John 113
John A. 115
John C. 3
Lucresa 9
Malissa 81
Margaret E. 91
Mary A. 35
Mary E. 106
Mary F. 103
Melvina C. 122
Peter 91
S. A. 118
Saluda A. 124
Shadrack 86
Susan J. 112
W. J. W. 113
William 8
William P. 18
Winchester, L. 19
Wingo, John W. 126
Winn, Mary J. 59
Minor M. 58
Wisenor, Eliza 101
Wit, Mary Jane 47
Witherford, Mary A. D.
  100
Witherington, Absolum
  82, 83
Ann 97
Ann L. 126
W. (Maj.) 92
Willis 110
Witherspoon, James R.
  29
Jas. R. 27
Joseph 75
Thos. M. 27, 29
Withrington, A. 125
Witson, James 57
Witt, Alford M. 108
Coleman H. 95
E. M. 85, 88
Eliza Ann 36
James S. 56
John 4
Rebecca E. 115
W. H. 84
William H. 54
Wm. H. 41

www.ingramcontent.com/pod-product-compliance
Lightning Source LLC
Chambersburg PA
CBHW061740270326
41928CB00011B/2312